Winner of the 2016 CASEY Award for Best Baseball Book of the Year
Finalist for the 2017 PEN/ESPN Award for Literary Sports Writing

PRAISE FOR *The Last Innocents*

"*The Last Innocents* is a great American story. Baseball in the southern California sun, Maury Wills stealing, Vin Scully narrating, life spinning and sweeping like a Koufax curveball toward the future—the tableau could not be richer for a writer as evocative as Michael Leahy."   —David Maraniss, author of *Clemente: The Passion and Grace of Basball's Last Hero*

"In an excavation as deep and probing as his splendid book on Michael Jordan, the prodigiously talented Michael Leahy sheds a revealing light on what now seems like an ancient era in baseball."

—Mark Kram, author of the PEN Literary Award–winning *Like Any Other Day*

"To read Michael Leahy's well-crafted, resolutely human *The Last Innocents* is to feel the anger that welled up inside the Dodgers of the era. . . . Mr. Leahy thrives as he describes how the Dodgers navigated this strange new world."   —John Schulian, *Wall Street Journal*

"A book that seeks to place the team within a broader historical and cultural context. . . . This is the strength of *The Last Innocents*, the way it moves beyond the game to the issues underneath."

—*Washington Post*

"The must-read baseball book of this spring and summer so far."

—Mike Vaccaro, *New York Post*

"Brilliantly reported and undeniably powerful. . . . I can't count the times reading this book I stopped, looked up, and said 'Holy shit,' and long before reaching the halfway mark I was slowing down to savor every word. . . . *The Last Innocents* is an incredible read."   —Jeff Polman, CrookedScoreboard.com

The Last Innocents

The Last
Innocents

The Collision of the
Turbulent Sixties and the
Los Angeles Dodgers

MICHAEL LEAHY

HARPER

NEW YORK · LONDON · TORONTO · SYDNEY

A hardcover edition of this book was published in 2016 by Harper,
an imprint of HarperCollins Publishers.

HarperCollins books may be purchased for educational, business, or sales
promotional use. For information, please e-mail the Special Markets Department at SPsales@harpercollins.com.

FIRST HARPER PAPERBACKS EDITION PUBLISHED 2017.

Designed by William Ruoto

Library of Congress Cataloging-in-Publication Data has been applied for.

ISBN 978-0-06-236057-1 (pbk.)

HB 12.06.2022

For Jane and Cameron

So we shall let the reader answer this question for himself: who is the happier man, he who has braved the storm of life and lived or he who has stayed securely on shore and merely existed?

—Hunter S. Thompson, *The Proud Highway: Saga of a Desperate Southern Gentleman, 1955–1967*

I had one shot to make it in life—not in baseball—in life. I was fighting for my survival. . . . So if this didn't work out, I don't know. . . . My life would be over.

—Maurice Wesley Parker III, Los Angeles Dodgers, 1964–1972

Contents

Genesis

I t came to this one night in New York City, during the middle of the 1956 World Series between the Dodgers and Yankees. After arguing in a bar with a Yankees supporter about the merits of their two teams, a twenty-five-year-old Dodgers fan went home, returned with a rifle, and shot dead his antagonist, who happened to be a local police detective.

These things happened.

No other American sport at the midpoint of the twentieth century sparked such fervor, idolatry, rage, madness. No other game was as sectarian in the adoration and hatreds it instilled; in the way it divided cities and sometimes families; and in the speed with which its young, strapping idols, in some cases ambling into stardom straight out of cornfields and back alleys, became deities for one group of fans and demons for another. Ticker-tape parades lionized the game's winners. Merciless ridicule rained down on vilified losers. The emotional well-being of ordinarily sensible men and women rose and fell with their teams. The agonizing faithful of entire street blocks sat on stoops listening to radio broadcasts during a pennant race.

There was nothing else on the planet quite like it.

And luck had much to do with the game's good fortune.

The truth went unadmitted during its boom years, but baseball largely owed its supremacy over American professional team sports, and its hold on the American psyche, to having launched itself before its rivals. In the nineteenth century, the major leagues sprang from the starting gate alone. This propitious bit of timing counted for everything. The fledgling organization that in time would come to be known as the National Football League wouldn't be created until 1920; the enterprise eventually to be called the National Basketball Association wouldn't arrive until 1946. By then baseball had been America's chief sporting passion for decades, boosted early by a bit of marketing genius. The sport had captivated romantics with a dream event whose transcendent name—the World Series—would leave all competitors in its shadow for the first two-thirds of the twentieth century.

If anything, on the eve of the 1960s, that shadow seemed to be lengthening. The mania for the game presented the perfect breeding ground for new baseball gods to be born in the American West, the ideal moment for the arrival of the Los Angeles Dodgers. The 1950s had been baseball's most thrilling decade yet. The dynastic New York Yankees, as famous as any team in the world, stood as a symbol of American glamour and power. The National League's burgeoning racial diversity and new talent made its challenges to Yankee superiority more heart-stopping than ever. In 1955 Brooklyn finally bested the Yankees to win its first World Series. The following year the Series spawned magic, in the form of a no-hit perfect game, with Brooklyn as the victim. The feat came from an unlikely Everyman, the hard-throwing but erratic Don Larsen, who was king for a day while pitching for a Yankees squad that, in regularly making gods out of flawed mortals, reclaimed the Series championship and looked as though it might reign forever.

So hypnotic was the World Series that it had risen to be a somewhat illicit holiday. It took priority over many adults' jobs and children's schooling during the week or so that it lasted. Hordes of men and women sneaked away from workplaces all over the country to watch the nationally televised afternoon games. Taverns filled. Classrooms were suddenly missing a few children. Normally attentive students concealed transistor radios in notebooks, stealthily listening to the coast-to-coast broadcasts. Big-city pedestrians, away from their offices, paused for long stretches in front of appliance-store display cases, where brand-new televisions showed the games from start to finish.

The obsession led strategists of both major political parties during the presidential campaign of 1960 to realize the obvious: they wouldn't have the complete concentration of a significant bloc of voters until the great battle of early October—the one pitting the imperious Yankees against the National League pennant-winning Pittsburgh Pirates—finally ended. "There is a politicians' rule of thumb, particularly hallowed by Democratic politicians, that no election campaign starts until the World Series is over," wrote Theodore H. White in 1961, in his renowned book on the 1960 campaign. Many Americans couldn't focus on the contest between John Kennedy and Richard Nixon until after Pirates second baseman Bill Mazeroski hit the winning home run in the bottom of the ninth inning of the decisive seventh game of the Series, giving Pittsburgh its first World Championship in thirty-five years.

By then, just to win a league pennant and reach the Series had become a cherished prize, nearly as big as winning the Series itself. Nine years earlier, with the sport at the zenith of its popularity, baseball presented fans with the most electrifying finish to any game in its history. With the Dodgers facing the Giants in the climactic contest of a three-game playoff for the 1951 National League pennant, Brooklyn led in the bottom of the ninth inning at the Polo Grounds, only to lose on a three-run homer off the bat of Giants third baseman Bobby Thomson against Dodger reliever Ralph Branca. The Giants' euphoria was equaled in intensity only by Dodger despondency. Yet the game cloaked both the winner and loser with a glory and mystique that were portable when the two rivals bolted to the West to-gether, seven years later. As always, baseball was the biggest victor.

This had implications for Los Angeles. The Dodgers, winners of the 1959 World Series in only their second year in the city, dominated the Southern California sports market, relegating the NFL's Los Angeles Rams to secondary status, along with the NBA's Los Angeles Lakers, a franchise that arrived in 1960 from Minneapolis. The two junior sports were still several years away from the gripping theater that would accompany the introduction of the Super Bowl, Monday Night Football, and national telecasts of the NBA Finals. Other than a riveting championship game won in sudden-death overtime by the Baltimore Colts over the New York Giants in 1958, the NFL could point to nothing, in the broad public's view, that matched the drama of an average World Series. Nor had the attention the press paid to the accomplishments of professional football and basketball's stars come close to rivaling the adoration heaped on the milestone achievements of baseball's legends. The most famous record in American sports—Babe Ruth's sixty home runs in 1927—had been showered that year with a reverence equaled in the country only by the awe for Charles Lindbergh's Atlantic crossing.

Bereft of the glittering athletic stages necessary for supreme drama, neither professional football nor basketball had produced cultural divinities like Babe Ruth and Lou Gehrig, Joe DiMaggio and Ted Williams, Jackie Robinson and Roy Campanella, Henry Aaron and Stan Musial, Mickey Mantle and Willie Mays, or, in 1961, Roger Maris, who would break Ruth's single-season home run record that autumn, after surpassing Mantle during a summer duel that transfixed America.

Football's only romantic heroes, figures who included the Olympic track legend Jim Thorpe, the University of Illinois's Red Grange, and the Four Horsemen of Notre Dame, tended to spring from stirring collegiate contests. The NFL's inability to spawn stars of the magnitude of baseball's avatars or college football's golden boys evinced its lesser standing. At times during the 1940s and '50s, the Rams featured two glamorous quarterbacks, Bob Waterfield (who was married to film siren Jane Russell) and the immensely talented Norm Van Brocklin. Yet never did their fame rival that of baseball's kings, which neatly reflected the disparity in status between the two sports.

As the 1960s arrived, the most famous rivalries in professional athletics—notably those between the Dodgers and Giants and the Yankees and Boston Red Sox—as well as the largest corps of new sports stars, like the Dodgers' emerging pitching sensation Sandy Koufax, still belonged to baseball, leaving professional football as overshadowed as ever. The image of baseball's dominance in Los Angeles was on display nearly any weekend the two sports clashed head-to-head. The mediocre Rams, playing a 1962 regular season game on a sunny September afternoon in the Los Angeles Memorial Coliseum, drew fewer than 27,000 spectators. That was because more than 42,000 fans at that moment were in Dodger Stadium.

Baseball's primacy was evident in the habits of young Americans especially. Several generations of ambitious boys and men—budding leaders, eggheads, and ruffians alike—had gravitated to the proving grounds of baseball sandlots. A robust and aggressive prospect named Mario Cuomo, a New York City native later to be his state's governor, excelled as an outfielder during the early 1950s on the freshman baseball team at St. John's University before accepting a contract signing bonus to play in the Pirates organization. He became a minor leaguer, only to suffer a beaning to his head during his first season that abruptly ended his athletic career.

Decades earlier, a teenage Franklin Delano Roosevelt, short on athletic ability but desperate to win his peers' approval, took the position of lowly equipment manager for the Groton School baseball squad. In 1944, delivering one of the last campaign speeches of his life on a rainy day in Brooklyn's Ebbets Field, FDR shared a wish with the crowd: he hoped to see a game there someday. Grateful Brooklynites and fervent Dodger fans responded with a guttural roar, as if the president had expressed an intimate yearning to break bread with them. The moment served as a reminder of baseball's linchpin status in the nation's big cities. Simultaneously, it was a warning to any politician eager to bond with the urban electorate: failing to understand the tribal pull of baseball meant failing to understand America. Similarly, failing to possess a major-league team meant a city couldn't rightly call itself an elite metropolis. It was a truth not lost on Los Angeles, which received a major boost to its image when the major leagues finally arrived.

During the 1950s, it didn't matter where you lived: baseball, and the Dodgers, reached everywhere. In the middle of the decade the Dodgers organization had fifteen minor-league teams scattered around North America, guaranteeing that the franchise would leave an impression on sports lovers from Montreal to the Rockies, and from Montana down to the Lone Star State. One of those fans, a young Texan named Bob Oswald, had no major-league team to see anywhere close. But he occasionally attended the games of a Dodgers Double-A farm club, the Fort Worth Cats, whose roster back in 1955 included a speedy but struggling shortstop named Maury Wills. Oswald enjoyed the casual atmosphere of the Cats' little ballpark, which emboldened the zany and raucous among the small crowds to cheer and jeer when the mood struck.

The Cats were fun, a nice diversion for Oswald. For more scintillating baseball, he tuned to radio and TV broadcasts of distant major-league games, especially those of the Yankees, his favorite team.

As the years passed, his sporting interests grew. He liked the great collegiate football powerhouses, especially Notre Dame, a team nearly as admired as the Yankees, he thought. A side benefit of rooting for Notre Dame was that his younger brother, Lee, who'd never had much interest in baseball, enjoyed football. Bob spent considerable time looking after his kid brother. Their father had died before Lee was born. Their mother, Marguerite, was generally cold and indifferent. She told them they were burdens, placing them in a New Orleans orphanage for a while, along with their older half brother, John.

All three boys eventually found themselves back with their erratic mother. They took refuge in games and outdoor activities. The two younger brothers enjoyed tossing around a football. "Lee really threw a pretty good pass," Bob remembers. "He was right-handed and he had good coordination. It was something we could share."

In time Bob got away from his mother for good, enlisted in the Marines, and later married. His little brother, buffeted by their mother's frequent moves, began to drift as a teenager. In early adulthood, Bob and Lee lost track of each other for a while. After Lee did a stint in the Marines, Bob heard that he had renounced all ties to America and moved to the Soviet Union, where he began living as a Marxist.

In the summer of 1962, following three years in Russia, Lee came back to Texas, finished with Soviet life but as devoted a Marxist as ever. He brought with him a young Russian wife and a baby. Bob picked them up at the Dallas airport, Love Field. He couldn't have cared less about his political differences with Lee, so happy was he just to be with his kid brother again. They had a great Thanksgiving dinner together with their families, and Lee talked with him for a bit about football.

By then Bob had a new team to root for, an NFL franchise founded in 1960 called the Dallas Cowboys. The Cowboys were just part of a recent bounty of riches for Texas sports fans. The state now had a second professional football team, located in Houston, and its first major-league baseball team, a National League expansion club called the Houston Colt .45s, a name aptly suited for a big, rugged land proud of its frontier justice roots. Texas professional sports were on the map, Bob marveled.

Sometimes, television would show the Yankees or Dodgers on the Game of the Week. Halfway across the country, he could turn on a live game happening in New York or Los Angeles. He watched Mickey Mantle, whom Bob was on his way toward meeting someday, though he had no way of knowing it, no way of seeing what was ahead for his family, either the horrific days or the gentle mercies. Life for the moment was great. He was doing well as a sales coordinator for a brick company in a Dallas suburb, with plenty of time left over for his close-knit family, an occasional round of golf, and hunting and fishing outings. The 1960s, he mused, were incredible. Jobs were plentiful for those who wanted them. Something exciting always seemed to be happening in the country. Rockets blasting off from Cape Canaveral. Capsules with astronauts landing in the Atlantic Ocean right on your television. To turn on the TV meant seeing sporting events a couple of times a week. Cowboy games. Baseball games. Mickey Mantle in Yankee Stadium. Sandy Koufax in Dodger Stadium. It was just wonderful, he thought. Had there ever been a better time?

The Last Innocents

Chapter 1

Surviving the Sixties

Most men must wait for their chance in baseball, as in life. The wait ruins many. Some succumb in the minor leagues to despair, a few to drink or drugs, the rest usually to an erosion of talent and will. Even for the minor-league lifer doing everything right, it becomes increasingly difficult to believe that his dream will ever be realized. It is hard to keep holding on.

In defiance of time, the smallest of players in this locker room has clung to the dream. He waited nearly all of the 1950s in the minors. Everything in a baseball life that matters has come to him late. It makes what is happening to him at this moment in 1962 a tad surreal. This small, lithe, light-skinned black man, once nothing more than a journeyman minor-league shortstop, once so little regarded that his own organization sought to trade him away, sits in the locker room at Dodger Stadium, suddenly a national celebrity. He is closing in on the greatest season of his career, on the brink of breaking a hallowed major-league record held by a baseball immortal, Ty Cobb. Life has never been so exhilarating. Wherever he goes in Los Angeles, people clamor to be introduced to him. Entertainers want him on their television shows. Privately, he has become closely attached to a famous and beautiful white actress, in the process drawing the silent scrutiny of an alarmed Los Angeles Dodgers executive.

A measure of Maury Wills's new fame can be found in the pile of mail strewn in his locker. Alongside the pile sits a close friend, Sandy Koufax, on the brink of becoming baseball's greatest pitcher. It says something about the America of 1962 that Koufax is opening and reading Wills's mail, and that Wills pores over Koufax's. It says something about the country that each man knows it's smart not to run the emotional risk of reading his own mail.

A black and a Jew, the two men are united in wanting to protect each other. Some of the letters are just too hateful, too ugly, to be read aloud. Koufax thinks he can anticipate the ugliest by the crude pencil-scribbled addresses and big crazy-looking block printing on some envelopes. "Oh, here's one you don't want to read, Maury," he says, scanning a letter, ribbing his friend a little, laughing, trying to keep the mood light about a subject that has worried both in the past, especially as Wills gets closer to breaking Cobb's forty-seven-year-old single-season stolen base record. It will be another twelve years before Henry Aaron breaks Babe Ruth's lifetime home run record. Wills is the first black man in history poised to take a cherished baseball record away from a white legend. Some racists around the country can't take it, sending these anonymous missives that make no secret of their hope to see him fail, even be harmed. No danger is inconceivable during that volatile year. Civil rights workers have been beaten that summer during sit-in protests and marches in the South. The imminent court-ordered enrollment of a black student named James Meredith at the segregated University of Mississippi will spark a white riot on campus that leaves two dead. Wills tries staying focused on the game.

The two friends open more envelopes. Wills comes upon yet another anti-Semitic letter meant for his friend, returning Koufax's gentle teasing over notes to be avoided. "You don't want to read this one, Sandy," Wills chortles. "This guy is serious."

Throughout the season, they have spent hours talking after games as each man receives treatment—Wills for his bruised and hurting legs, and Koufax for chronic pain in his pitching arm. For months the twenty-nine-year-old Wills coped alone with his hate mail. Finally, it became too much. He took a chance and began showing the letters to Koufax, something he hasn't done with anyone else on the team.

What accounts for a bond between men? Wills wonders. They rarely hang out together away from stadiums. Each is a born compartmentalizer, their friendship largely confined to locker rooms and baseball diamonds. But their intense mutual admiration and shared zeal for winning has made them close, especially in these postgame hours when Wills benefits from Koufax's soft-spoken observations, less direct advice than subtle reassurance that things will be okay; that each has the other's back; that the strangeness of their lives is simply a function of the game, as is the craziness of some fans, media, and baseball management. "Here's another letter you don't want to read, Maury," Koufax adds.

He leaves it at that, falling quiet. He is often the shell that closes as quickly as it opens. Long accustomed to his friend's reserve, Wills laughs, and they're done for another night.

THE HOMECOMING

This is a story about the odyssey of seven players during the turbulent 1960s. It also points a lens at some of their closest teammates and worthiest foes, as well as those in Dodger management who dominated their professional lives. It is a story about what it was like to be a major leaguer when the country was turned upside down by tumult, when players struggled to understand their place both in America and in a game controlled by baseball owners whose wishes were fiat. It is a story about players who made tens of millions for their team on the field but enjoyed few rights off it. It is a story about confusion and, ultimately, the kind of piercing self-discovery gained by players—like most people—only after struggles outside the public eye. The players' private evolutions occurred while they performed in the most glamorous of settings, amid the Los Angeles Dodgers' pennant chases and the team's World Series appearances—three in a four-year span, which culminated in two World Championships.

They were ballplayers, not crusaders. Still, the sport had made some of them idols, and eyes were always on them, as if in fans' constant belief that what they did would prove inspiring. Yet even as they starred in games watched by millions, they coped with anxieties and indignities their fans knew nothing about—some of their wounds deeply personal, others more common to the times, though no less painful.

At moments, their anguish reflected historic divisions coursing through the country. Some of the players, like Wills, had experienced the humiliations of stark racism and segregation for years and never would entirely get over the scarring. Several were disturbed over time by the escalation of the Vietnam War—in which they knew people who had gone into battle—and by the strife in America's inner cities, where many had grown up.

Their tensions and dissatisfaction with the established order seeped into their baseball lives, with white and black Dodgers alike coming to believe they were being exploited. They fumed about their lack of real bargaining power, the front office's meddling in their private lives, and baseball executives' efforts to pressure them into accepting additional commitments, including overseas exhibition games, after a regular season ended.

Servility defined all aspects of their relationships with the Dodgers owner, Walter O'Malley, and the owner's general manager, Buzzie Bavasi. Players were barred from using agents in negotiations, denied contracts that lasted any longer than a single baseball season, and routinely subjected to salary cuts if their on-field productivity suffered in the wake of injuries. Dodger stars began asking questions once regarded as unthinkable. Privately, they talked about possible salary holdouts, where once they would have quietly accepted whatever management offered. They planted the first seeds of a rebellion.

But even at their most disgruntled, they chiefly remained ballplayers, with the mind-sets of ballplayers. The seven players—Maury Wills, Wes Parker, Sandy Koufax, Tommy Davis, Jeff Torborg, Dick Tracewski, and Lou Johnson—cared most about winning. Even when their salaries were absolutely shameful during their early seasons, they'd at least had the euphoria that sometimes accompanied winning. No story about them can begin without focusing on the one who needed to win most, the one who would go to virtually any maniacal length to do it. The one who would—and did—throw a ball between the eyes of an onrushing San Francisco Giants baserunner and knock him out cold. The one who sharpened the spikes of his running shoes with a file before intentionally sliding into a Milwaukee Braves foe, slicing up his knee. The one who, in a moment of intense frustration, actually burst into tears once on the field after an umpire's call had gone against him.

By 1962 his teammates viewed Wills as the Dodgers' fiercest competitor. He was their lineup's leadoff man, their offensive catalyst, their demanding on-field leader, and their hardworking, often tormented dynamo, capable of inspiring many of them even as he sometimes infuriated others.

The frenzy of his record-breaking 1962 season exposed the full range of his emotions, his ecstasy in moments of great victory and his fury when a teammate's mistake or a foe's rough play damaged the Dodgers' standing or his own pride. In his relentless drive, he felt his stresses mounting. In its intensity, so much about the season, both the good and bad, had added to his pressures. One of the year's high marks seemed to have come when the National League tapped him to play in the All-Star game, and he returned to his native Washington, DC, the site of the first of two All-Star games that year.

It was a triumphal and emotional homecoming. He saw members

of his family and signed autographs for local children in whose eyes he saw the same awe he had once reserved for his favorite players in the city.

For a while, the trip had the quality of a wonderful dream. How amazing, he thought, that the All-Star Game would be played just a short car ride from his old home, in District of Columbia Stadium, commonly called DC Stadium. He had spent many afternoons seeing the Senators of the past play in old Griffith Stadium, that palace where he had first thrilled as a child to the mingled grown-up smells of stale cigars and flat beers, where he had fantasized about donning a major-league uniform, though no black man had yet been given one. It was in Griffith Stadium, not long after Jackie Robinson had integrated the sport, where he participated in his first mass professional tryout alongside hundreds of other nobodies. He couldn't wait to step foot now on a Washington diamond as one of the game's elites. He basked in the pride of his family and friends, who marveled over his big blue equipment bag, the one festooned with the logo of the Los Angeles Dodgers.

On the day of the game, he didn't travel on the National League team bus to the stadium. Instead, spending part of the morning with his family, he rode to DC Stadium with a friend, who dropped him off at a gate in front of the players' entrance.

There, a security guard denied him entry, refusing to believe he was a player even after Wills gave his name and showed the guard his Dodgers gear bag.

"Get outta here, boy," the security guard said.

Wills said he couldn't leave. He was a player.

"Get outta here. I'm not gonna say it again. You don't belong here, boy."

"I'm a player."

"I told you to move, boy."

It had been a while since a white man called him "boy." Wills pleaded with the guard to summon a National League official or player. At last the guard saw Cincinnati outfielder Frank Robinson, a black star who knew Wills well.

Do you know this guy? the guard asked Robinson.

Robinson took one look at Wills. "Hell, never saw him in my life."

Baseball players have a "sick sense of humor—they pride themselves on it," Wills would observe later. Robinson kept walking. A desperate Wills looked around for someone else. The guard had again ordered him to leave when a stunned National League official recognized Wills and swiftly ushered him into the clubhouse.

The rest of the day went well. President Kennedy threw out the honorary first pitch from his box seat near the dugouts. In the locker room, Wills saw his teammate and fellow All-Star Don Drysdale, the National League's starting pitcher. Then he ran into Pittsburgh's Dick Groat, selected as the National League's starter at shortstop. Groat, whom he liked, surprised him with an apology that Wills hadn't sought. "You should be the starter at short, Maury," Groat said. "You're the one having a great season."

Wills didn't enter the game until the sixth inning, when he pinch-ran for the legendary Cardinal Stan Musial, promptly stole second base, and scored the first run of the game when Groat singled. Newsreel footage caught JFK applauding the play. Then Wills led off the eighth inning by singling against Cleveland's Dick Donovan. When Giants third baseman Jim Davenport followed by lining a sharp base hit on a couple of hops to Detroit's left fielder Rocky Colavito, Wills made an unusually wide turn at second base, trying to tempt Colavito to throw behind him to the Yankees' second baseman, Bobby Richardson.

It was a sucker play, a favorite Wills ploy. Colavito took the bait, gunning a throw to Richardson as Wills dashed toward third base in a bold baserunning move that American Leaguers, accustomed to a brand of ball that featured many sluggers but few speedsters, seldom saw. Richardson made a quick throw to third, but Wills beat it, diving past a protesting Brooks Robinson. The National League's next hitter, Giant Felipe Alou, hit a fly ball into foul territory down the right-field line. From the time the ball left Alou's bat, it looked like nothing more than a routine out and a squandered at-bat for the National Leaguers. But Wills saw an opportunity. As the American League right fielder Leon Wagner, a star for the Los Angeles Angels, glided into foul ground and made the catch, Wills tagged up and raced to the plate, narrowly beating Wagner's throw in what would be the game's final run, in a 3–1 National League victory. He won the game's Most Valuable Player laurels, taking home with him a large trophy that he made sure the loathsome security guard had a good look at as he exited the stadium. "I still don't think the guy believed I was who I said I was," he remembers.

Wills viewed the day as miraculous. But the image of the security guard would haunt him forever, a nagging reminder of too many incidents like it. Such pain was all the more reason now to have Koufax regularly read the sealed, anonymous letters addressed to him. When the two friends finished, Wills went out and stole more bases, getting ever closer to Cobb and the record. Better than anyone else, he realized the magnitude of his imminent achievement, and the improbability of his place here.

THE MIRACLE

During the 1950s, as he languished for eight full seasons in the minors, Wills thought at several points that his career would end there. His failure, in turn, would mean the end of his productive life. He viewed himself as a man with no marketable skills outside baseball. He had turned his back on college, rejecting a football scholarship offered by an all-black school, Virginia State University, whose coaches had watched him star as a single-wing running back at Cardozo High School in Washington, DC. At eighteen, as a skinny five-foot-ten, 160-pound pitcher and occasional shortstop who boasted he could hurl a ball through a wall, he invested all his hopes in baseball. Signed for a $500 bonus and a salary of $150 a month, he joined the Dodgers' minor-league organization in 1951, just four years after Jackie Robinson had become the major league's first black player. It was an era when minority ballplayers remained rarities and could expect to face a torrent of racial taunts at ballparks.

Euphoric at the opportunity awaiting him, Wills never pondered the looming harassment. During his first year in the Dodgers organization, he rode a train to get to the club's immense spring training facility, known as Dodgertown, formerly the site of an American naval installation. The grounds held a mythological appeal for young players who had never seen it. Depicted as a baseball utopia, Dodgertown had an enormous swimming pool, tennis courts, volleyball and badminton courts, an immense cafeteria and dining area, a billiards table, a theater in which to screen recently released films, and a putting green that at the time was merely the prelude to a real golf course. The facilities were available to major leaguers and minor leaguers alike, and if a player ever wanted a dip in the Atlantic Ocean during his off hours, the beach was just a stroll away.

Aboard the train, Wills envisioned the glorious accommodations in which he would soon be setting foot, a kind of heaven that would serve to confirm his shimmering future.

He arrived to find the vast complex sitting in the quiet, muggy, nearly all-white Florida town of Vero Beach. Segregation was the norm in Vero, blacks unwelcome in most establishments; nearly all restaurants there were off-limits to them. Like many young black players at the time, Wills rarely set foot out of Dodgertown. And, like all Dodgers, whether minor or major leaguers, he lived in the military-style barracks that had been used in the past to house US Navy personnel. But the minor leaguers lived in more crowded conditions, which seemed to scream what they would face over the next few weeks: a weeding-out process. Each of the rooms housed eight dreamers, with four sets of double-deck cots on which they could collapse at the end of long practice days, and a communal bathroom shared with everyone else on the floor. Heating and air-conditioning were nonexistent.

Immediately, the stifling minor-league barracks became the symbol of everything Wills wanted to escape. His goal was to reach the building across a small street, where the Dodgers' major leaguers lived and where the accommodations guaranteed more room, in what looked to Wills like an indicator of the occupants' exalted status. Looking for the swiftest route to success, he gave up his dream of pitching in favor of becoming an infielder.

Starting his career in Class D ball, the lowest rung of the minors, Wills hit a respectable .280 and stole 54 bases for the Dodgers farm club in Hornell, New York. Soon he was a full-time shortstop, beginning a slow, frustrating, ultimately depressing climb. Each season began for him at Dodgertown, where, during the lunch hour in the cafeteria, he and other minor leaguers had to wait until the major leaguers filled their trays before getting food for themselves. Watching Jackie Robinson and the rest of the famous faces filing past, Wills was filled with awe and envy, hardly able to stand another day in Vero Beach's minor-league gulag, which had become a daily reminder of his failure to break through.

His anxiety grew with his understanding of the steep odds facing him in the Dodgers organization, where a half dozen minor-league prospects stood ahead of him in the competition to eventually succeed the Dodgers' starting shortstop and future Hall of Famer Pee Wee Reese. The candidates included a young dynamo named Mike Korcheck, who played above Wills for the Dodgers' Double-A Fort Worth club. Even some of his shortstop competitors believed Korcheck possessed all the necessary tools to be a big-leaguer—speed, power, a reliable glove, and a great arm. Then, after yet another spring training, in a reminder of life's uncertainties and their own fragility, the Dodgers' minor leaguers woke up one morning to hear that Korcheck had died in an automobile accident.

Yet nothing happening anywhere altered the status of Wills, who had impressed few Dodger officials. Scouts thought he was neither an excellent defensive player nor a long-term offensive threat. One of his rivals, a future Dodger infielder named Dick Tracewski, who though a year younger played for a Dodger farm club a rung above Wills's, listened one day as a Dodger official said offhandedly that Wills was a subpar fielder. The word circulating through the organization was that Wills bobbled too many balls and hadn't displayed the necessary range for making plays on grounders hit deep into the hole between shortstop and third base. While his arm was strong, his throws were often off-target and in the dirt. And his offense didn't compensate for his perceived defensive deficiencies; he'd never demonstrated power or finished a year with an exceptionally high batting average. The most logical question about Wills seemed to be when the organization would trade or dump him.

By his eighth season in the minors, nothing about Wills had much changed, including his batting stance. He hit right-handed, and right-handed pitchers with sharp curveballs still gave him fits. Scouts and coaches estimated that Wills batted less than .150 against curveballs, an abysmal statistic that guaranteed he would never see the major leagues. His chief problem with the pitch, coaches believed, was that he flinched whenever a curve came anywhere near his body. It was a cutting observation; it implied that he regularly, if unconsciously, failed a test of nerves. There seemed no likely remedy, for the look of the pitch would never change. A curve thrown by a right-handed pitcher typically starts off near the shoulder of a right-handed hitter, before sharply breaking away from him and down over home plate. When a curve approached Wills, his shoulder and head subtly jerked. His backside often dipped and moved back. The flaw appeared fatal.

"Afraid" was the worst slur of all in baseball. It made Wills livid, ready to fight. No one doubted his effort or physical toughness. He fought teammates, foes, and anybody else when challenged; his pugnacity was fierce and well known. But the truth was undeniable: the curve frazzled him, even as he heatedly denied it.

By this time he'd thought of quitting. As his 1958 campaign began with the Dodgers' Triple-A club in Spokane, Washington, his prospects looked more dismal than ever. Prospective stars, it was argued, do not spend eight years in the minors. Prospective stars are not ignored by the vast majority of other major-league organizations, which had shown their disregard for Wills by making no effort to trade for him. His only unique ability seemed to be that he could run and steal bases, and though this skill was eye-popping at times, it made him at best a novelty show in his critics' eyes, a track sprinter in a baseball uniform. Wills, who had heard the whispered assessment, believed it was code for saying he played black; that he had adopted the style of the old Negro Leagues and sandlots of his roots.

Indeed, his past gave birth to his approach. He'd spent his youth in the tough, virtually all-black area of northeast Washington, DC, known as Anacostia. He lived in a housing project called Parkside, the seventh of thirteen children born to Guy O. and Mabel Wills. His dad was a hardscrabble Baptist minister, his mom an elevator operator. Wills found his way onto the Parkside's baseball sandlots. With no money in the family for sporting equipment, he would usually fashion a baseball glove out of a paper bag and brace himself for the pain that came with fielding hard ground balls. He occasionally received tips from Anacostia's semipro ballplayers, who on weekends at Parkside competed in organized games with caps fashionably askew and whiskey bottles sometimes jutting out of back pockets.

The semipros' weekend games were neighborhood attractions. None of these rakish players would ever have a chance to display their skills for the all-white professional leagues, but they became heroes to the young Wills. At once bold, talented athletes and self-styled entertainers, their speed and antics thrilled the little boy. They bunted for hits. They stole bases. They exuded bravado and boasted hilariously: *I'm gonna steal that bitch's jockstrap.* They dared to talk trash to an opposing pitcher, telling him what they were going to do before they did it. Always, in defiance of baseball's conventions, they ran with abandon. They turned what looked like ordinary singles into improbable doubles, and doubles into triples.

The major leagues had left prodigious talent to wilt on such sandlots. Young Wills could easily have been just one more youth who never got out of Parkside. The youngster dreamed of joining the semipros' ranks and playing with a whiskey bottle in his back pocket, too, until one summer day in 1943, when local officials ushered a white stranger in a sparkling baseball uniform to the sandlot to visit the children of the neighborhood. The white man's name was Jerry Priddy. He played second base for a team and a league the ten-year-old Wills had never of heard before: the Washington Senators of the American League. The team played somewhere far outside Parkside—somewhere the boy had never seen. Someone gave Wills a baseball glove to use, and Jerry Priddy played a game of catch with him. "He threw some ground balls to me and said I was good," said Wills; "that I should get my parents to buy me some shoes. It was the day I stopped wanting to be one of the guys on the sandlot. I wanted to a major leaguer like this man in that nice uniform. Sometime after that, I took some buses and went off to see my first Senators game at Griffith Stadium."

Griffith Stadium was only about thirty minutes and two bus rides away, but the ballpark might as well have been on Pluto, so vast was the chasm between Parkside and everywhere else in white Washington. As a small boy, Wills hardly ever glimpsed a neighborhood outside his own. Parkside's black residents couldn't swim in most public pools or eat in the nearby white-only restaurants of Washington, Virginia, and Maryland. The child took it for granted that white people lived somewhere else, ate somewhere else, went to school somewhere else, and that black people wouldn't ever play, swim, or live around white people.

Born into this arrangement, Wills seldom protested its indignities, even after nearly a full decade of enduring them in the minors. His fury, when he displayed it, was largely directed at himself and his own shortcomings as a player. He had crying jags when going through a bad slump. He suffered through bouts of depression. Resigned to absorbing racist barbs, he focused on his game to the exclusion of all else, the ranks of the ignored often including his young wife, Gertrude, and their children, with Wills desperate to show the Dodger brass he was deserving of attention. Nothing worked. Even as he climbed the rungs of the minors into the Pacific Coast League's Triple-A ball— just one step from the majors—those who speculated over the prime candidates to succeed an aging Pee Wee Reese never mentioned his name. He'd been reduced to fodder for a possible trade, though even this seemed unlikely, since no other team was expressing interest.

The 1958 season, the Dodgers' first in Los Angeles, would be Reese's last. For a year already, the team had been mostly playing the declining legend at third base, a quiet signal that his days as a player were nearing the end. Dodger brass had believed that a heralded young player in the organization, Bobby Lillis, could be Reese's successor. But Lillis's bat disappointed officials. As the season rolled along, it became increasingly apparent that the heir apparent was reliable veteran Don Zimmer, whose numerous advantages over all his rivals included the fact that he'd been an occasional relief for Reese over five seasons, including the Dodgers' 1955 championship year.

Known as "Popeye" for his resemblance to the cartoon character, Zimmer had likely lost his best years during Reese's reign at shortstop. Zimmer's bad breaks were more than figurative: no one else in the Dodgers organization had been so prone to horrific injuries. In 1953, while leading the Triple-A American Association in homers and RBIs, he had suffered a beaning that left him unconscious for more than a week and unable to speak for nearly two months, with doctors drilling holes in his skull to ease a life-threatening swelling.

Left with blurred vision for several more months, the twenty-two-year-old Zimmer had been told by doctors that his career was finished. It wasn't. Zimmer became a utility player for Brooklyn, able to play any position in the infield. Then, in a 1956 game against the Cincinnati Reds, disaster struck again: a fastball broke Zimmer's cheekbone and ended his season. Eventually doctors had to fill the holes drilled in his head with a special metal. Zimmer, complaining about nothing, quietly emerged from his rehabilitation to resume his role behind Reese and fill in wherever else the Dodgers needed him. By 1958 his stoic perseverance had made him beloved, the model of the selfless team player, the only deserving successor to Reese in his boosters' eyes.

At five-nine and a strongly built 175 pounds, Zimmer seemed a symbol of the Dodgers' robust future, a multifaceted talent who possessed something that Wills never would—home run power. Zimmer had hit 15 homers for Brooklyn in 1955 in only about a half season's worth of games—a star-in-waiting, believed many Dodger officials. Even Wills regarded him as a player with great gifts—a strong arm, a sure glove, and a competitive fire that matched Wills's own. By the midpoint of the 1958 season, Zimmer was the provisional starting shortstop, as the slowing and injured forty-year-old Reese faded into the shadows. The Dodger brass was prepared to take another look at the rookie Lillis if Zimmer faltered, but the new shortstop's play was quickly ending all talk of alternatives. The wisdom of Zimmer's elevation seemed beyond question, and Wills felt no bitterness, only envy and an escalating worry that his time was running out.

It was. The baseball world ignored Wills as much as ever. He was hitting less than .250 in Spokane. By mid-season he was in a funk, for the first time showing signs to worried coaches of giving up. The once obsessively driven practice player, who had thought nothing of badgering lazy teammates, was now occasionally horsing around and cutting corners during pregame warm-ups. One afternoon, the new Spokane Indians manager, Bobby Bragan, noticed him not even bothering to hit right-handed during his last batting practice cuts, just walking into the batter's box closest to him and desultorily stroking a few pitches as a lefty.

Bragan walked over and surprised him with a pair of questions. "You ever thought of hitting left-handed? Of trying to switch-hit?"

"No," Wills said.

Bragan put an arm around him. He'd never done that before. Something was up. Wills braced himself. "I think you should try to do it," Bragan said. "I think you're afraid of the curve."

It was the old criticism, and it infuriated Wills. Usually he told whoever said it that he wasn't afraid of a damn thing. But this time, worn down and desperate, he just listened. Bragan said it looked as though he possibly had the swing to hit as a left-hander. Maybe, Bragan suggested, Wills could be developed into a switch hitter. If they could make it happen together, Wills wouldn't ever again see a curveball that began as a pitch thrown at his body. He would hit left-handed against right-handed pitchers, and right-handed only against left-handed pitchers. Any curve thrown to him by any pitcher would start on the outer half of home plate, far away from his body. Bragan believed the change would eliminate Wills's flinching for good.

Hitting left-handed would also place Wills one step closer to first base, Bragan pointed out. It would undoubtedly mean more chances to beat out ground balls for infield singles. But the whole scenario would depend on Wills first learning to hit effectively as a left-hander against real pitching. What Bragan didn't say was that the chances of it working out were remote. Most switch-hitting experiments end terribly, with the typical hitter awful from both sides of the plate. To have any chance, Wills would need constant practice, and he didn't have time to waste.

Let's work on it, Bragan prodded.

A morose Wills agreed to try.

Within a couple of weeks, he was officially a switch-hitter. For the remainder of the year, his improvement at the plate was at best paltry. He ended the 1958 season with a measly .253 average, though Wills and Bragan saw reason for hope, even if no one else in the Dodgers organization did. The brass still wanted to unload him. Fresco

Thompson, who headed the Dodgers' minor-league organization, later admitted that the club looked to "give Wills away." Finally the front office found a possible suitor, the Detroit Tigers, who had their own problems at shortstop and were willing to consider any slightly promising minor leaguer. The Dodgers said the Tigers could have Wills for only $35,000—they wouldn't even need to send along a player in exchange. The Tigers vacillated, their interest shaky. What had Wills really done, after all? Tiger officials agreed to the deal only under the condition that, if they didn't want Wills after evaluating him, they could nullify the transaction.

The Tigers brought Wills to spring training, but soured on him quickly enough that he was back with Spokane in plenty of time for the start of the 1959 regular season. At twenty-six, he'd been cast off by two organizations now. It was a new low. Bragan resumed working with him on his switch-hitting. And then, as Wills later remembered, "It just kind of happened. Things clicked. I was meant to be a switch-hitter, I guess . . . I was a different player."

He was hitting a strong .300 and stealing bases at will. His defense had never been better. Bragan started telling any Dodger officials who'd listen that, with the glory days of Reese behind them, Wills was the best shortstop in the organization, that his speed on the bases regularly rattled opponents and altered games, that the front office would be crazy not to take a closer look at him.

But the Dodgers already had Zimmer, fresh off his first capable season as Reese's successor and apt to be the regular for years. Then, just as Wills seemed destined for oblivion, a calamity changed several lives at once. The Dodgers discovered that a slightly hobbled Zimmer had been concealing a fractured toe. With Zimmer suddenly out, the backup Lillis entered the starting lineup. Bragan ramped up his campaign on Wills's behalf. He spent some mornings barraging Dodgers general manager Buzzie Bavasi with phone calls about how Wills was tearing up the Pacific Coast League. Bragan would later recount the conversations for Wills.

You'll want him if you just take a look at him, Bragan told Bavasi, adding that Wills had become the team's on-field leader.

"No, he can't play," Bavasi replied. "He's been in the organization forever. He can't hit. He's not much of a fielder."

You're wrong—he can do it all, Bragan said. He will do anything to win. Anything. He's your guy.

Meanwhile, Wills's curiosity about Bragan was growing. Wills knew a little about the manager's Alabama boyhood, but he had heard much more about a part of Bragan's playing career that the older man wished could be forgotten. While a backup catcher for Brooklyn in 1947, Bragan was among several Dodger players who signed an inflammatory petition declaring they didn't want a black player as a teammate. A few weeks later, after watching Jackie Robinson on a road trip, a chastened Bragan said he had been altogether wrong, that it was an honor to play with Robinson. But the shame of his original stance still trailed him, even though by the time Bragan arrived at Spokane he had done managerial stints in Pittsburgh and Cleveland and most of baseball seemed to have forgiven him, if not forgotten.

Wills dared to ask why Bragan hadn't wanted to play with Robinson.

"I was just raised that way, Maury," Bragan said, his face sagging in sadness.

By then Wills revered Bragan, to whom he thought he owed his on-field improvement and whatever chance he might have of reaching the majors. A religious man, Wills would come to believe that Bragan was placed by God in Spokane to help him, and that he himself had been assigned to play in Spokane so that Bragan could teach him to switch-hit and make amends for the wrongs done to Robinson. He would never forget Bragan putting his arm around him on the day they confronted his fear of the curveball. Bragan was his miracle. Thank God for Bobby, he thought. Bragan's life had taught him about the possibility for change and redemption in his own. Standing there, he couldn't take the old manager's pained expression.

"Bobby, don't worry about it," he said.

WILLS'S CRUCIBLE

A couple of weeks later, in early June, Wills abruptly had to say good-bye to Bragan. The day had begun with a phone call from Bavasi to Bragan, who was with his team in Phoenix for a game that evening. The message was terse. Lillis was being sent to Spokane, effectively demoted. Wills was being called up to the majors. Bavasi wanted him to meet the Dodgers in Milwaukee for a game against the Braves.

Wills didn't even have an equipment bag. He packed his spiked shoes, glove, and some clothes into a cardboard box tied with a string and headed for the Phoenix airport. On the flight to Milwaukee, his hands trembled as he held a cup of coffee. When he entered the visitor's clubhouse at Milwaukee's County Stadium amid a few mumbled greetings from his new teammates, his cardboard box received the most attention. He heard a peel of cackles, followed by a faintly mocking question that revealed both some Dodger veterans' antipathy to newcomers and Wills's sensitivity.

You bring your lunch in there, kid?

More cackles.

He couldn't think of what to say.

Quickly inserted into the lowly eighth spot in the Dodgers' starting lineup, Wills got off to a horrific major-league start, with only one hit in his first twelve at-bats. His struggles grew worse. Teary-eyed and shaken, he pleaded with Dodgers manager Walter Alston to get rid of him—"Send me back to Spokane, Skip."

Alston was not one for pep talks. But his ease told Wills that there was no crisis; it was far too early to panic. "Don't worry about it, kid," the manager said, as Wills remembers. "Hang in there."

Still, for a month Wills seemed unlikely to last. His misery was compounded by being in Los Angeles, where he knew no one. His connections with teammates were few. His small apartment felt like a tomb. He rushed each day to get to the team's temporary home in the cavernous Los Angeles Memorial Coliseum, in a futile effort to find his batting stroke. Major-league pitchers confounded him. The stress threatened to push him over the edge.

Zimmer was soon back, having rehabbed his toe enough that he could make an occasional start at shortstop. The veteran and newcomer were effectively battling for the starting position. In mid-July, Wills's batting average began ticking upward, not dramatically, but enough to ease the anxiety of some club officials and coaches. By late July, Alston had installed Wills as the regular shortstop.

The decision was unpopular with a group of veterans once among the stars of the team in Brooklyn. Their anger opened a window onto the divide between the aging gods and an emerging band of younger players, all part of the Dodgers' Los Angeles rebirth. Wills sensed the tensions rising. During a road trip in late July, he found himself on a quiet Cincinnati hotel elevator alone with Zimmer, the team's center fielder and future Hall of Famer Duke Snider, pitcher Clem Labine, and two other veterans. He felt a menacing air. Heads down, Snider, Zimmer, Labine, and the others seemed to be mumbling in his direction, he thought. "You're not gonna make it; you don't belong here," he heard more than one of them whispering.

Not daring to answer, he stared at the elevator floor.

The players never overtly threatened him. But with nowhere to go as the elevator slowly rose and the muttering continued, Wills was scared. "I thought they were going to kick my ass," he recalls. "Then the elevator stopped. I got out as fast as I could. I ran to my room. Ran."

Shaken, he sat on his bed. He tried to replay who had said what. He couldn't make sense of it all, but felt convinced they had meant to intimidate him. It would be crazy to complain to anyone, he decided.

A young black player just didn't gripe without drawing unwanted attention. Might be dubbed a troublemaker. Besides, he wasn't certain of the motives of the players on the elevator. Did they merely dislike any newcomer who'd taken a starting position from one of their friends? None of the players involved had a reputation for racism. Snider and Labine had been close to Robinson and the team's next two black superstars, future Hall of Fame catcher Roy Campanella and Cy Young Award–winning pitcher Don Newcombe. And Zimmer had talked about benefiting from the tutelage of Robinson.

The Dodgers were famously intolerant of overt racists. A decade earlier, the front office had dispensed ultimatums and pointedly traded away white players who protested about playing with Robinson or any other African American. It had become part of the franchise's lore that the Dodgers had done more to advance the cause of racial opportunity than any other team in professional sports. In addition to Robinson, Campanella, and Newcombe, the Dodgers' prominent African American signings had included pitcher Joe Black, infielders Jim Gilliam and Charlie Neal, outfielder Sandy Amoros, and catcher John Roseboro. Some major-league clubs in the 1950s still had yet to sign a single black player.

In 1959 Wills was just another in an ever-expanding corps of black Dodger players who, within another year, would form the majority of the team's starting lineup, the rare time that the major leagues had seen more black than white faces on a ball field. As time passed, he thought that race had probably played at most a small part in what had occurred on the elevator, and perhaps none at all for most of his antagonists. Increasingly, he focused on their ages and backgrounds. All older, all Brooklynites, they were in their twilight as players. Once they had been indispensable to the team, but no longer. That had to be scary, he thought, realizing how much his own career's uncertainty unnerved him. And he knew how much the others on the elevator cared about Zimmer, who hadn't ever tasted stardom as a player and now never would.

There was not a damn thing fair about baseball, Wills thought. "I started thinking that, down deep, they probably mumbled at me not because I was black but because the shortstop position didn't belong to me—it belonged to Zimmer; that's what they felt. I learned eventually to love them. . . . But what happened to me on that road trip had an effect on me for the rest of my career. It inspired me to be more aggressive—more aggressive in games, more aggressive with the people I played with. I worked harder than the other people around me, and I'd always worked hard to begin with. But I kept it all inside for a while. It made it easier on me that we had a great end to the season."

The Dodgers won the National League pennant after defeating the Milwaukee Braves in a playoff. Wills had hit .260 for the season, not great but a decent average for a rookie whose opening days had been so dreadful. Amazingly, only seven months after being spurned by the Tigers and sent back to Spokane as rejected goods, he found himself playing shortstop in the 1959 World Series against the Chicago White Sox.

Wills's solid performance helped the Dodgers win the Series in six games. Over the next few weeks, he felt his life had changed forever. He received a check for $11,231 from Major League Baseball, the share for each player on the Series' winning team. It seemed like a fortune to him, more money than he had made from the Dodgers and the Spokane Indians for the entire 1959 regular season. But neither his delight over the extra cash nor the Series victory exceeded his thrill at imagining what it would be like at the next spring training in Dodgertown. Finally he could enter the major-league wing there, as a mark of his new status in the Dodgers organization.

He arrived in February 1960, excited, only to discover he didn't have a room in the major-league wing. The front office had assigned him again to the minor-league barracks, as if 1959 and the World Series had never happened. He sobbed convulsively. His worst fears had been realized: he would face a challenge for his job. The club still had doubts about him. It only made matters worse that the other starting Dodgers of the 1959 infield—first baseman Norm Larker, second baseman Neal, third baseman Gilliam, and catcher Roseboro—had casually settled into their major-league rooms, their status unquestioned. Wills was alone in his humiliation. Wet-eyed, fighting to regain his composure, he found Bavasi and bitterly protested.

Bavasi was unmoved. "Keep busting your ass," he said, ending the conversation.

A healthy Zimmer was back and intent on reclaiming his shortstop position, joined by another rival, a longtime Dodger prospect named Chico Fernandez. Yet Wills still had an admirer in Alston, who made certain he played in enough spring training games to show off his skills. In the end, Wills held on to his job. Quickly, Zimmer was traded to the Chicago Cubs. His battle with Wills lost, Zimmer would flourish in the coming decades as a coach and manager. But everything about the spring of 1960, even Zimmer's abrupt departure, taught Wills cold lessons about the game: "It wasn't like you ever completely made it with the club. You realized they might get rid of you at any time. . . . I was always looking over my shoulder after that."

His latest ordeal had ratcheted up his anxiety. Early during the 1960 season, he found himself in a terrible slump again and sought help from Dodger coach Pete Reiser. Choked up, he poured out his fears.

Reiser, not one for coddling a player, said brusquely: "Be here tomorrow two hours before anybody else."

The next morning, alone in the hot Coliseum, Reiser spent a half hour pitching batting practice to Wills and studying his hitting stroke.

Stop trying to pull pitches, Reiser demanded. Stop trying to hit everything so damn hard. Just stroke the ball. There's no need for a hard swing. When you're hitting left-handed, I don't want to see you hitting any more balls to right field. I want you to hit everything to center field or left field. If the pitch is on the outside part of the plate, hit it to left field and only left field. Make the game easier for yourself.

Reiser worked with Wills for weeks, along the way delivering homespun homilies intended to help Wills recognize the need for patience. "He had all these sayings," Wills remembers. "He'd say, 'The elevator to success is always out of order.' It meant, Keep working. It will come. He'd say, 'Successful people make it a habit to do things that failures don't like to do.' I just did what he said and hoped for the best. I hit every pitch up the middle or to the opposite field. He kept working with me until I got it. Reiser was like Bobby Bragan. He helped save me."

By then, Dodger officials had discovered that, if anything, Wills possessed fewer natural gifts than they'd imagined. He wasn't even as fleet as touted. Despite his skill at base stealing, several other prospects in the organization were faster. It had become well known among the officials that a young minor-league outfielder named Willie Davis, on his way to becoming a Dodger starter and perhaps a major star, had considerably more raw speed.

But no player worked longer hours than Wills. And he had a guile that matched his drive. During a spring training, when he faced off against Davis and two other prospects in a 60-yard dash across the outfield grass, Wills characteristically searched for an advantage. Away from the others, he quietly approached the man serving as the race's starter and asked how he would send the runners on their way.

I'll just say, Ready, set, go, the man responded.

Could you say that again? Wills prodded.

Ready, set, go.

No, I mean, could you say it *exactly* the way you're going to say it? Ready . . . set . . . go.

Thanks.

Wills perfectly timed the start of the race. He had replayed the cadence of the man's voice for so long in his head—"Ready . . . set . . ."—that he perfectly anticipated "go" and bolted in the same instant. Davis couldn't catch him. It became obvious that no one would ever be able to match his speed over a very short distance, say, the thirty yards between first and second base. But a larger point was made by the race's end: no one on the team would ever be able to match his preparation, tenacity, or savvy.

The moment reflected his approach to everything. While his teammates typically used the last half hour before a game to relax in the clubhouse, Wills sat in the dugout and watched the other team's starting pitcher warm up, in search of weaknesses to be exploited in pursuit of stolen bases. He looked for tics and subtle movements in a pitcher's delivery that would serve as tip-offs when the opponent was hurling a pitch or throwing to first base in a pickoff attempt.

Nineteen sixty was Wills's breakout year. With Reiser's continued help, his hitting improved to the point that Alston decided to try him as a leadoff hitter, in place of the longtime veteran Jim Gilliam. At about the same time, the manager told him that he no longer had to wait for a steal sign from a coach—he was on his own.

Wills's career would never be the same. He thrived in the leadoff spot, his .295 average by season's end quietly placing him in the top ten of all National League hitters. But it was his stealing that captured the most attention. He broke Jackie Robinson's Dodger record of thirty-seven steals before September, and finished the year with a National League–leading fifty thefts, the first time anyone in the league had stolen so many bases since 1923.

By then, teammates like Tommy Davis had taken notice of Wills's zeal, the desperation of it. "He could never be happy if we lost anything," remembers Davis, who had seen close-up just how miserable Wills could be when the team struggled. It set him apart, Davis believed, from some players for whom personal achievements went a long ways toward lessening defeat's sting. Wills could steal three bases in a game, but if the Dodgers were caught in a losing streak, he'd be in his own hell, just sitting in front of his locker, staring off at something no one else could see. Davis knew Wills would do anything to avoid losing, no matter how painful or ruthless: he'd play with a bad leg, dive for balls with a sore hip, spike an opponent, hit a baserunner with an elbow, or if need be fight a Dodger who challenged his methods. If everybody acted like Wills, their clubhouse might be a more volatile place, but they'd win more, too, Davis thought. Wills had come to insist on respect. And his zest for preparation meant that he was ready for any possible confrontation, on or off the field, with a foe or a teammate.

Which best explains Wills's decision to have a special face-to-face meeting in 1960 with teammate Norm Larker. Larker was the Dodgers' capable first baseman, a powerful six-footer who was contending that year for the National League batting crown. A few hours before a game, Larker began hitting low liners toward some outfielders. The missiles were just missing Wills, who, busily fielding grounders, asked Larker to knock it off. Larker, who outweighed Wills by thirty pounds, hit a couple of more shots in his direction.

"If I hit you and you don't come after me, you're gutless," Wills remembers Larker saying.

Wills responded by hurling a ball that struck Larker in the kneecap. Without another word, he quietly ran into the clubhouse for a fight that he knew would happen within the next couple of minutes. Long having considered the possibilities of a locker room altercation with somebody bigger, he removed his spiked shoes and put on his rubber-soled shoes, which would provide good traction on the concrete floor for the coming brawl. Livid and ready to fight, a slip-sliding Larker stumbled in his spikes, and Wills quickly took him down to the floor. He had Larker draped over a trunk and was punching the bigger man at will when teammates broke them apart. It was another case of attention to detail overcoming size and strength, Wills proudly believed. It was the triumph of a small but passionate man in love with preparation.

His relaxation was limited to playing a few musical instruments, though music was a hobby in name only. He didn't really have casual playtime, only passions. As with everything else in his life, he was driven to get better on his ukulele, guitar, and banjo, the last of which he practiced every day on the road, sometimes to the consternation of his roommate, John Roseboro.

Wills knew the costs of his drives, realized he often missed out on the pleasures of life, big and small. He was interested in the presidential candidacy of a young senator from Massachusetts, John Kennedy, whom the Democrats nominated in 1960 on a mid-July night, in the Los Angeles Sports Arena. The very next evening, with the Dodgers on a road trip, Kennedy delivered his acceptance speech in the Coliseum, looking directly out onto the field where Wills and his teammates played their home games, the grass bathed in a beautiful twilight, the speech nationally televised. A few of his curious teammates set aside time to watch parts of it. But Wills, preoccupied as always with preparation and privacy, somehow missed it, asking himself later how this could happen.

Characteristically, by spring training of 1961, he'd begun worrying anew about a challenge to his job. That season, with the Dodgers finishing as runner-ups in the pennant chase to Cincinnati, he led the National League in steals again and hit a solid .282. Bill White, the Cardinals' star first baseman, took Wills aside one day before a game and told him that he had been the one and only subject of a Cardinals' pregame defensive meeting, a reflection of his growing stature. "It was the worst thing somebody on another team could've said to me—it gave me so much confidence," he remembers. Wills made his first All-Star team that season, and won the first of his two Gold Glove awards, as the best defensive shortstop in the league. But all those years in the minors, and his treatment during the early stages of 1960, would forever leave him uncertain about his standing with Bavasi and the Dodgers. "Flash in the pan—I always thought they were going to see me as a flash in the pan," he says. "And then I'd have to find a way to do it all over again."

Yet by 1962 he was a star, having become the most confounding weapon in all of baseball. With his batting average hovering around .300, he successfully stole bases on about 90 percent of his attempts, despite the best efforts of opposing pitchers, and even a few teams' cheating grounds crews, to slow him down. During the late stages of the season, it became clear he had an opportunity to break Cobb's record of ninety-six stolen bases, set in 1915, or thirty-two years before a black man ever set foot in the major leagues.

Americans love the chase of an immortal's record. The pursuit evokes apparitions and gods; it sparks feelings of trespass on the gods' turf. Just a year earlier, Roger Maris had broken the single-season home run mark of the sport's Zeus. As Wills dashed toward history, baseball suddenly couldn't get enough of him or the ghost he was eclipsing. The specter of the late Cobb, commonly viewed during the era as baseball's most famous sociopath and unabashed racist, guaranteed that writers and fans would ceaselessly recount old tales of the bad boy's alleged depravities and hatreds, heightening the historical drama taking place on the field, making Wills's feat all the more riveting.

Newspapers counted off his steals as he drew closer to Cobb. Yet, if anything, the numbers overshadowed Wills's greatest impact: he was changing how baseball was played, and in the process altering how fans watched it. He was, to be sure, a player principally known for one great skill, and so arguably a specialty performer. But so too—in baseball and in life—are other performers specialists; so too is the archetypal home run slugger; so too is the great mezzosoprano. In bringing more attention than ever to base stealing as an art, Wills was doing nothing less than remaking the game's aesthetics. He was inspiring future Hall of Famers, Lou Brock among them, to stretch the limits of their own great running and stealing skills. Simultaneously, his talent was drawing fans' attention to how speed could change not only the outcome of a game but its look, infusing it with more thrills and athletic beauty while guaranteeing fewer dreary breaks in the action. His dashes sparked the kind of deafening roars in Dodger Stadium that fans of other teams—with their tepid station-to-station singles, and mammoth home runs followed by pudgy sluggers' gingerly jogs around the bases—seldom heard.

Watching Wills had become a participatory experience for normally blasé Dodger spectators, who typically stopped whatever else they were doing to fixate on him when he reached first base and began taking his lead off the bag. His coiled presence there abruptly changed the energy in a ballpark. There would be a rising swell of noise, like the anticipatory roar of a boxing arena before the opening bell. The pitcher, taking his stretch position, would glance over his shoulder, intent on holding him as close as possible to first base.

Thousands of screaming Dodger fans chanted, "Go, go, go, go . . ."

Vin Scully, the Dodgers' play-by-play announcer, faced the difficult task of telling a radio audience what was happening within about three seconds—for that's as long as it lasted: "*Wills goes . . . The pitch is a strike. . . . The throw down to second. . . . And Maury's beaten it again.*"

The Dodgers enjoyed a comfortable lead in the National League standings. Their seeming march toward the pennant, coupled with Wills's pursuit of Cobb, fueled attendance at Dodger Stadium in the inaugural year of the new ballpark. The team's home attendance was on pace to break the major-league record and exceed 2.5 million spectators, the crowds to grow even larger as pivotal games remained against the hated Giants.

Nothing in the local news rivaled the fascination over the pennant race and Wills. Richard Nixon, defeated for the presidency by Kennedy only two years earlier, had returned to his native California to run for governor, unsuccessfully, against Democratic incumbent Edmund "Pat" Brown. In Los Angeles, reaction to the political contest was tepid: major news about the Dodgers frequently pushed Nixon and Brown off the front pages. For a few days in August, the death of Marilyn Monroe from an overdose of pills dominated headlines. But over time, everything else gave way to the craze surrounding the Dodgers. Even the city's ordinarily reliable obsession with all things Hollywood—entertainment industry updates, award ceremonies, and fan-magazine gossip that included items such as *West Side Story* winning Best Picture at the Oscars, Doris Day teaming with Cary Grant in *That Touch of Mink*, and Elizabeth Taylor and Richard Burton wrapping up the shooting of *Cleopatra* en route to divorcing their mates and marrying each other—was eclipsed in 1962 by the latest news of the Dodgers' fortunes.

The media dominance of the Dodgers reflected the mood of a city still enraptured with a team that had arrived only four years earlier. Equally important was the cozy familiarity of the Dodgers' cast. With baseball free agency not yet in existence, most of the team's players stayed with the Dodgers, as part of the same long-running summer drama, for years at a time, as players did in all of major-league baseball's big cities. Even those who weren't sports fans in Los Angeles generally recognized names that were constants on TV news and in the city's newspapers: Wills, Gilliam, Roseboro, Koufax, Drysdale, Willie Davis, Tommy Davis, Ron Fairly, Frank Howard, Wally Moon, Larry Sherry, Ron Perranoski.

The first-place Dodgers were riding the outstanding performances of several players at roughly the midseason point of 1962. Koufax had already won fourteen games, seemingly on his way to winning twenty-five or more. Drysdale was en route to his own twenty-five-win season. The team's solid twenty-nine-year-old veteran Johnny Podres—who had shut out the Yankees to win the climactic game of the 1955 World Series—would deliver the team another fifteen games. On the brink of stardom, Tommy Davis was hitting at a torrid rate, triggering speculation that he was a candidate to win the Most Valuable Player Award.

But increasingly, opponents focused on Wills, against whom frustrated foes were becoming wickedly inventive. In San Francisco, the Giants' grounds crew took to soaking the infield dirt around first base, forcing Wills to begin his steal attempts in mud and leaving him so angry that he was fined by the National League for criticizing the umpires and the league's failure to punish the

Giants. In Pittsburgh, the Pirates' grounds crew deposited several wheelbarrows of sand around first base, forcing Wills to run on a surface akin to a beach. Opposing first basemen like Bill White, who were friendly to Wills off the field, became brutes on it, tagging him hard around the head and chest. "Why are you doing that, brother?" he groaned to the Giants' Willie McCovey, who shot back, "Stop calling me brother," before hitting him across his cheek and temple.

Nothing slowed him. He successfully stole at the same 90 percent clip, the image of his invincibility on the bases growing, with some infielders convinced that umpires had begun making calls in advance of Wills's arrival at a base, assuming that the master thief would always be safe. Chicago Cubs shortstop Andre Rodgers furiously protested a call of safe from umpire Jacko Conlin that seemingly had been made while the catcher's throw was still in the air and Wills several feet from second base. An amused Wills saw and heard the same thing as Rodgers, who was still screaming that Conlin hadn't even waited for Wills to reach the bag. *How can you call him safe when he's not there yet?*

Conlin chided Rodgers: "You guys haven't thrown him out all season. What makes you think you're going to get him now?"

Wills noticed he was suddenly getting the benefit of the doubt from umpires on close calls—it was one of the perks of being regarded as a special talent, he realized.

By then, his steals were usually coming in bunches—two, three, and four in a single game. One morning in September, he awakened to the certainty that he was going to break Cobb's record. "I just knew I was going to do it; it was going to happen," he said. It felt as though he was living a dream.

Then the dream was momentarily put on hold. He received word that Buzzie Bavasi wanted to speak with him. Wills had no idea about the subject matter of the meeting. But by the time it ended, Wills would be as shaken as ever.

THE RICH BOY

About six thousand miles away from Wills, during the late summer, a young American man sits alone in a small Paris hotel room, waiting on a Frenchwoman. A recent college graduate, the scion of a wealthy Los Angeles family, twenty-two-year-old Maurice Wesley Parker III—known to his family and friends as Wes—has spent the summer of 1962 drifting around Europe on his family's money. Long skilled at beating himself up, he worries over what his idleness portends. His despair and self-loathing are symptoms of his greatest fear: he has no clue what he will do with himself when this trip ends.

It would be impossible to discern his misery by glancing at him. He projects the kind of ease that comes with money, manners, and years of training. Blue-eyed, tall, and slim, with tousled blond hair and a firm jaw, he looks like he just walked off the cover of a fashion magazine, a cross between Gatsby and the All-American collegiate athlete he once was. His looks and affability have made much in his life effortless, like attracting women. He met this latest one on the southeast coast of France, in the city of Nice. Tan and blond, she emerged from the Mediterranean Sea in a bikini, nimbly stepped around prone bodies on the beach, and flashed a playful smile of apology so charming that Parker bolted up from his own blanket to introduce himself, only to discover that neither spoke the other's language. It didn't matter. Her cousin translated for them, and they spent the next two weeks together in Nice. Her name is Annick. He is waiting in this hotel room for Annick to arrive in Paris, her hometown, where he came ahead of her to see another friend.

A mistake, probably. Having seen the friend and said good-bye, he has been alone for days, knowing no one else in Paris, which, even with its splendors, couldn't depress him more at this moment. It has been raining for three straight days, and he is stuck in this grim room, no bigger in length he'd guess than about fifteen feet, bare of anything except a desk, a chair, a phone, and this small bed on which he has tossed his raincoat and stretched out in his jeans, feeling altogether lost. This has become my pitifully pointless little existence, he thinks. Hopping around Europe. Chasing women.

With nothing else to do, he is reading a newspaper, the *International Herald-Tribune*, in hopes of finding a job in Europe—any decent job really, maybe something in international relations or business, so that he doesn't have to go back to the States. It's hopeless. Another look at the job openings section now serves only as a reminder that he doesn't have what European employers are looking for. He isn't bilingual, for one thing. Downcast, he absently glances at the sports section and the baseball standings. Back in America, the Dodgers are in first place. It's depressing on some level to see any reference to baseball and the Dodgers. He spent much of his adolescence attending Dodgers games with his father. Obsessed with baseball as a kid, he played in high school and college as a standout left-handed first baseman and outfielder. Tabbed as a Little All-American during his junior year—the "Little" serving as a reference to the league of small private colleges in which he competed—he was good enough that a few professional scouts watched him play, though no one offered him a contract. Just the same, he continued to excel, poised to become the captain of the Claremont Men's College team. But shortly before his senior year, in a shock to his coach, he abruptly walked away from both the game and Claremont.

He hasn't touched a ball or bat in more than a year. It was *his* decision, he tells people, as was his move to leave Claremont, in favor of spending his senior year at the University of Southern California. He explains that Claremont is an all-men's college, and he simply wanted to be at a university that had some women. What he doesn't tell them is that he transferred to USC because he thought he might flunk out if he remained at Claremont, a private school, just outside Los Angeles. He couldn't have handled the humiliation; he's dealt with enough shame in his family life that he doesn't know if he could handle any more failure and pain. But by bolting from Claremont, he's forfeited his last year of collegiate athletic eligibility. *His* decision, he tells himself. He needed a college degree more than he needed baseball. So baseball is behind him for good. He feels worse about it on some days than others. This is one of the bad days. He can imagine his father in Dodger Stadium at this moment. He can picture him happily lounging in their family's season seats, great field boxes, located just outside first base. The image serves to remind him of just how adrift he feels.

It wasn't always this way. He had a purpose once. He can picture himself grabbing baseball mitts and a bat as a small boy and going outside to play and practice with his younger brother, Lyn, on their family's three-acre lot. It sat on Saltair Avenue, just above Sunset Boulevard, in Los Angeles's affluent Westside community of Brentwood. The neighborhood was prime California utopia, with manicured grounds, eucalyptus and palm trees, tall hedges to wall off curious outsiders, and vacant land nearby that called to mind wide-open country living—all of it just ten minutes from the Pacific Ocean. The brothers could play anywhere, though few lawns were as nice as their own. Their front yard was about ninety feet square—the exact dimensions of a baseball diamond, perfect for the two to hit balls hard at each other. Sometimes they moved their games from the lawn to their peaceful street, their play periodically interrupted by the passing cars of well-heeled neighbors. One day the actor Cesar Romero, annoyed at having to slow as the brothers moved aside, barked at them to get the hell out of the road: "Goddamn kids, why don't you do that on your lawn? You've got the biggest yard around."

Not quite the biggest. Retired five-star army general Omar Bradley, the Parkers' neighbor to the immediate south, in the direction of Sunset Boulevard, enjoyed a six-acre spread, on which the World War II field commander generally stayed out of sight. The neighborhood was a sanctuary for the reclusive and famous. Hollywood royalty lived all around the Parkers: Romero, Rita Hayworth, Tyrone Power, Ed Wynn, and Gary Cooper, whose daughter Maria attended the exclusive John Thomas Dye School with young Wes, in nearby Bel Air.

Fred Peters, a man who managed a store's furniture department but was best known around town as the brother of screen legend Carole Lombard, was the Parkers' next door neighbor to the north. The director Frank Capra lived right around the corner, as did the actor Fred MacMurray, whose son Fred Jr. would occasionally drive with Wes to their high school. When he dropped by the Brentwood Country Mart for a snack, it wasn't unusual for him to see luminaries like the actress Barbara Stanwyck and her husband, actor Robert Taylor. During the 1940s and '50s the Parker family had their own status, their membership at the Beach Club in Santa Monica and the Los Angeles Country Club denoting their specialness. Nothing was beyond their means. At night, though his parents didn't permit him or his two siblings to watch television, his father screened recent full-length motion pictures in their home. The boy had all the trappings of privilege.

His future seemed foreordained, full of exhilarating opportunities, much like Los Angeles itself. In the wake of World War II, anything seemed within reach for the city's inhabitants, the thriving suburbs yet another reminder of California's status as a boom state. The burgeoning aerospace and defense industries there guaranteed robust growth for decades to come. Suburban bedroom communities were sprouting up all over, with California's soaring indices mirroring those of the country. As the early 1950s ushered in the presidency of war hero Dwight Eisenhower, a walking symbol of America's post–World War II supremacy, America was at its zenith.

But the country was not devoid of tensions. The long Korean War had claimed 35,000 American lives. The United States and Soviet Union were engaged in a cold war that left millions in each country worried about a surprise nuclear attack. Julius and Ethel Rosenberg were convicted and executed for passing nuclear secrets to the Soviet Union, with the specter of what came to be called the Red Scare preoccupying Americans. Many California schoolteachers were forced to recite loyalty oaths, and rapt Los Angelenos watched as, beginning in the late 1940s, Congress hunted alleged Communists in the film and television industries, part of a widespread federal inquisition that resulted in the blackballing and imprisonment of Americans convicted of lying to congressional committees about suspected Communist ties. Shameful in their reckless destruction of reputations and frenzied trampling of fundamental rights, the investigations drove notable members of the West Los Angeles entertainment community to turn against their own, including a subpoenaed Robert Taylor, who came out of his Brentwood manse to appear before a congressional committee, describe a prominent screenwriter as a reputed Communist, and cast doubt on the trustworthiness of actor Howard Da Silva, who was ultimately blacklisted.

Yet none of the tumult touched either the Parker family or the Hollywood royals on Saltair Avenue. The Parkers were Republican conservatives, and their family fortune, which came in large part from old money and long-standing enterprises, insulated them. From the outside looking in, life could scarcely have been easier or better for young Wes.

If there was anything visibly missing in his early childhood for a boy who so loved baseball, it was that Los Angeles had no big-league presence: the Dodgers were still many years away from even pondering the possibility of leaving Brooklyn. The closest major-league team to the boy was halfway across the country in St. Louis. But he couldn't miss what he didn't know. He was fascinated by the only big-time baseball he had ever seen in person—a pair of exciting local minor-league teams, the Hollywood Stars and Los Angeles Angels, who played in the Pacific Coast League. In 1948 his busy father had taken him for the first time to see the Stars, who played at Gilmore Field in Hollywood, a tidy ballpark that seated about 13,000 and whose spectators regularly included Jack Benny and other stars.

Parker's father knew a lot about all the teams. He enthralled his son with stories about baseball, having grown up in the Boston area, where he had played the game as a talented high school infielder. His athletic skills, which had been good enough that the Red Sox offered him a tryout, seemed encoded in the family genes. His own father, the first Maurice Wesley Parker, had been an expert marksman and a champion billiards player in Massachusetts. On the other side of the family, young Wes's mother, growing up in a Chicago suburb, had been a champion amateur golfer at her country club. The boy's lineage had bestowed an abundance of physical gifts. He seemed destined to excel in a sport that rewarded precision timing in hitting and fielding a small ball.

The boy could see that, even in middle age, his father was agile, which made it all the more puzzling to him that his dad had never accepted that offer to try out for the Red Sox. He asked about it one day and his father explained that Wes's grandfather had forbidden it. The opportunity had come during the hangover from the raucous 1920s, an era when gifted but flawed giants, led by Babe Ruth, dominated baseball's headlines. The country had sunk into the Great Depression. It was no time for anyone to make a personal mistake that might consign him to destitution, believed the Parkers' patriarch, who explained that he wanted Wesley Jr. kept far away from a sport with so many carousers, drunks, and philanderers. The boy should find something better to do with his life than to hang around people of ill repute; he needed to find a secure profession and escape the cruelties of the Depression.

Although a talented athlete himself, the original Maurice Wesley Parker had little time for sports. His renowned skills with pool cues and guns were merely hobbies. He hungered for knowledge, attending Harvard Medical School for a stretch. The Parker family struggled to scrape by on what he earned as a classical violinist and music teacher. During high school Wesley Jr. walked around with cardboard in his shoes to cover up the holes. A banker's son took his girlfriend away from him.

He left Massachusetts in the early 1930s to sell insurance in New York, which was still reeling from the stock-market crash of 1929. Investors had been ruined, breadlines were long, and new jobs were virtually nonexistent. "You had to be alert walking around in New York," Wesley Jr. would wryly tell young Wes later. "Because bodies were always falling out of the sky."

The early '30s were dispiriting for Wesley Jr. Later he would tell his oldest son that by then all his dreams and goals had been reduced to one: not to be poor. Struggling to hawk insurance policies, he eventually went to Chicago, where, at a party in the mid-1930s, he met his future wife, the answer to his worries. Inestimably rich, Mary Joslyn had grown up pampered and sheltered in the wealthy Chicago suburb of Hinsdale, on an eight-acre estate ("I could've taken an eight-iron out of my golf bag and I wouldn't have been able to hit a ball from one end to the other," Wes observed of his mother's childhood grounds).

Mary Joslyn's father was the founder of an Illinois telephone company, part of a new class of American utility barons. No suitor could have been more unlike Mary Joslyn than Maurice Wesley Parker Jr. But their attraction was easy for their firstborn son to understand. "My dad was as handsome as a movie star," Parker said. "He was flat broke when he met my mom. The insurance business hadn't worked out for him. But he was a charmer. He would've been the kind of guy she had never seen before. He knew all the tricks. He overwhelmed her with his charm."

Soon they married, and in 1936 they had a daughter, Celia. Not long after the birth of Wesley III in November 1939, the young couple moved to the fashionable Los Angeles community of Bel Air, where Mary's father put them up in his winter home, to be sold decades later to the actress Mary Tyler Moore. By 1941, thanks to his new family, Wesley Jr. walked into a new life, a lucrative new job, a new world of opportunities and pleasures. With World War II under way, his father-in-law and some partners had opened an enormous factory in Santa Monica that made parts for American bombs to be dropped on Hitler's forces. Wesley Jr. was offered part ownership of the company and a chance to help run it. The once poor boy was rich. Soon, he and his young family moved into their dream house in Brentwood.

W es Jr.'s spacious home included a bar around which he could host guests and listen to his favorite music. His wife had hired a live-in housekeeper, who looked after their three children, leaving the couple with more time to throw lavish parties. Wes Jr. built his business and social connections while she exhibited her skills as an efficient hostess.

He settled into the comforts that had been his dream. But his marriage became a disaster, full of raging arguments aggravated by his wife's irascibility and his heavy drinking. Soon he began spending less time around the house, visiting friends and attending local athletic events. "My dad was absent so often," Parker recalls. "And when he was around at night, he drank so much."

So predictable were Wes Jr.'s routines that the boy knew what his father would likely be consuming once he arrived home: an Old Fashioned or two accompanied by a couple of vodka martinis. Typically during the weeknight imbibing, it would be calm in the house for a while. Wes and his little brother would lie on the carpet and sometimes shoot marbles. Their father would read his evening newspaper while having his drink or, if he had company, stand by the bar and make conversation. Classical music would frequently be playing over a radio, a reminder of the original Maurice Wesley Parker's career as a poor but accomplished violinist and teacher. Young Wes loved the music. And it would usually be a wonderful hour, until his parents' fights began, or until he ran into his own problems with them, especially with his mother.

She controlled who he could see, the friends he made, and when and where he could play—if he was permitted to play at all. She mocked him, told him he was worthless, and frequently beat him. One memory remained especially vivid: one morning, she dragged nine-year-old Wes into her bedroom and hit him over and over with a hard hairbrush. On other days, his father struck him. But most of the abuse would come from his mother, whose fury seemed to have no end. Saltair Avenue and the rest of Brentwood would never know.

It was an era when governmental agencies meant to look after the well-being of children were feckless, and parents enjoyed un-questioned sway over their sons and daughters. Wes's fear was com-pounded by his sickliness. He had chronic asthma as a child and regularly needed oxygen at night to sleep. His asthma, a bout of pneumonia, and severe allergies left him debilitated for long peri-ods and unable to take physical education classes. He had to repeat the fourth grade because he missed so much school. Later, he would calculate he missed about two months of school a year through the seventh grade, leaving him forever behind as a student and plagued by fears of academic failure.

But nothing and no one so preoccupied him as his mother. He spent his childhood trying to read her moods, terrified when he went to sleep that she might harm or even kill him before morning came. "I thought I could be gone anytime," he said. "Some nights I thought the asthma would get me. And my parents were dangerous. I didn't know what my mom might do. And my father, with all his drinking, was a mess. Until I was fifteen or so, I lived every day like it might be my last."

Meanwhile, his parents' domestic quarrels left little time to tend to their children's daily needs. By default, such responsibilities were assumed by the family's live-in housekeeper, a Jamaican immigrant named Judith Coy, who cared for the Parker children from the start of each morning. Her presence brought a semblance of normalcy to Wes's life, and he adored her.

Still, Coy's powers had terrible limits, the boy saw. She couldn't possibly raise questions with his parents about the abuse in the home without losing her job. She didn't dare acknowledge the wrong even around the children. "She did the best she could," Wes recalls. "She cared. She was like my real mother." It was as if, Wes thought, the housekeeper's primary mission was to provide love to ease the pain of his parents' abuse.

Once home from school, Wes felt the safest place was as far away as possible from his mother. He hurried to get outside. The outdoors offered nearly everything he loved: a chance to practice baseball with his brother, to hurl dirt clods in happy battles with other kids, and to find peace in Saltair's wide-open spaces. "The outdoors represented life," he remembers. "Inside the house was death. I tried to stay outside and play as long as possible."

In time, his play took him to the local Little League, about ten minutes away, on Sepulveda Boulevard, in the community of Westwood. The site was a social intersection. It brought the well-to-do children of Brentwood and Pacific Palisades together with middle- and working-class kids from the public schools of West Los Angeles.

Public school kids: that's how a nervous skinny Wes, always to be taught in elite private schools, regarded them. They seemed tougher, sassier, funnier, and more skilled in verbal combat. He knew he was alien to them, a rich boy who went to some fancy-pants school on Chalon Road in Bel Air, with other skinny rich kids just like himself. Already reeling from his treatment at home, he had no idea how to deal with the mocking he received from them. His lack of self-esteem made him an easy target. At youth baseball fields, he was regularly picked on for his genteel ways and appearance.

The kids teased him for wearing a cowboy belt instead of a baseball belt. He didn't keep his baseball socks up the right way, they said. The bill of his baseball cap wasn't shaped like a half-moon, the way all the cool kids' were—his cap was flat and dumb, so he looked like a stupid baby. The public school kids would say anything to him, and he took it, intimidated into silence.

He was a decent little ballplayer, not great but good enough as a pint-size pitcher that his proud father, often so stern when he wasn't drinking, talked about Wes's Little League play to friends in the baseball world he'd met during his travels. One was Chuck Dressen, the manager of the Brooklyn Dodgers, who in 1951, long before the Dodgers ever dreamed of coming to the West Coast, inscribed a photo of himself for the eleven-year-old child: "To Wes Parker, A grand little pitcher with a brilliant future. May be a Dodger someday."

Wes improved as a ballplayer, and as a high school sophomore he made the varsity baseball team at the private all-boys Harvard School, located in the Los Angeles community of Studio City, on the edge of West Los Angeles and the San Fernando Valley.

Parker was back on familiar terrain, surrounded by the well-heeled offspring of Los Angeles's elite, who included Doris Day's son, Terry Melcher (in adulthood, to be an intended target of mass murderer Charles Manson), and later two of Gregory Peck's sons. As his Harvard career began, Parker was no athletic star. But in his junior year, his body blossomed. He was on his way to becoming a six-two, 180-pound prospect with speed, grace, and remarkable reflexes. "I suddenly felt like a Ferrari," he remembers. "Like I could do anything." Long-legged, with a gliding swiftness, he was amazed by his sudden ability to run down fly balls in center field and turn them into outs. He excelled at first base as well, regularly diving to rob opponents of base hits. His Harvard High teammate Biff Naylor had never seen a player who made tough catches look as easy: "He had the softest hands you ever saw. He caught anything and everything. It was a gift."

There was nothing Parker couldn't do against Harvard's small private school foes. As a switch-hitter with skill from both sides of the plate, he hit over .400. A few professional scouts began appearing at his games during his senior year. By then, in 1958, he had performed well in major schoolboy competitions against American Legion rivals and California's other teenage standouts, including several who would go on to become successful major leaguers—outfielder Curt Flood and pitchers Jim Maloney, Dick Ellsworth, and Mike McCormick. His father had made another call to Charlie Dressen, who arranged for eighteen-year-old Wes to drop by the Los Angeles Coliseum sometimes to work out with the Dodgers before home games. Whenever he showed up, he had his own locker in the Dodger clubhouse and changed into a Dodger uniform. On the field, he did a bit of everything: pitched a little batting practice to the Dodger players, shagged fly balls in the outfield, and scooped up infield ground balls with his first baseman's glove. Then he returned to starring in his high school games.

The excitement over his play brought him popularity, party invitations, and the attention of pretty teenage girls in poodle skirts. He dated the daughter of the screen star Alan Ladd, sometimes watching films with Alana Ladd at her parents' home in Bel Air. "But my talent in sports didn't make any major change in the way I felt about myself, my lack of worth," he remembers. "It brought me friendships and some admiration. It was the first time in my life I had anything like that. But it didn't make me feel a lot better, not really."

Upon his high school graduation, he received no contract offers from big-league scouts. It mattered little to him. He still wasn't sure what he wanted anyway. He enrolled at Claremont, where his athletic gifts attracted the interest of football coaches who swiftly made him a quarterback on the varsity team. In the spring he flourished in baseball, on his way to becoming the best player on the Claremont varsity. But two years into his college career, his dismal self-image and the memories of his horrific youth still plagued him.

He was seeing a therapist once or twice a week in Hollywood. Striving to improve his relationship with his mother, he sometimes drove the hour from his campus to pay her visits in Brentwood. They watched the telecast of the 1960 presidential election returns together, disappointed that Richard Nixon lost to John Kennedy. But the main event of the evening, like all their time together, was the slim possibility that a bond might still be forged between them.

He wanted to be loved; he wanted peace. It was futile. He could do virtually nothing right in her eyes. Updates about his collegiate baseball successes were largely met by indifference or her observation that he shouldn't let his head get too big. His mother's heart was the block of ice that would never melt.

He couldn't turn to his father, who was living elsewhere now, his parents having finally divorced when he was eighteen. His dad seemed as unhappy as ever to Wes, who viewed him as all that he feared becoming.

His family's desolation turned him further inward, where only baseball provided solace. During his junior year, as an outfielder, first baseman, and pitcher, he hit .400 for Claremont and was selected as a first-team Small College All-American. In an era when no amateur player draft yet existed in professional baseball, a young prospect's best hope was that traveling major-league scouts would notice him. A few scouts had dropped by to study him in games, but none ever so much as talked to him.

Parker thought he understood the basic reason for their lack of interest. "They figured I'd end up leaving baseball in a hurry and becoming a comfortable investor or doctor or lawyer," he remembers.

The lingering question was whether his family's money had made him soft. "I didn't blame the scouts. What they knew is that the game gets hard and frustrating sometimes. You have to be tough-minded to hit a ball pitched at ninety or ninety-five miles per hour. You need to be able to battle back when it's not going well. It's a question of hunger, of being able to hang in. And they looked at me and thought it would be difficult for me to do it from a position of wealth. They thought I might struggle and get so down that I'd just walk away from the game. They didn't think I ever had shown signs of being tough. What they didn't know was how much I needed baseball, how much I saw it as an escape from my family life. How could they know? I wasn't talking to anybody about it."

The scouts' rejections during his junior year only made it easier for him to make the life-altering decision to leave Claremont and give up the game. Despite his hours of study each day, the college's demanding academic requirements had proven difficult for him. He feared he was in danger of flunking his senior thesis if he remained in the school. Academically, he had never caught up with his peers after all those missed school days during his sickly and traumatic childhood. Not even being chosen as a co-captain of the Claremont baseball team could keep him there. "I had nothing to lose," Parker remembers. "Given that the scouts had passed me by, I had no future in baseball anyway."

In 1962, during a quiet senior year without athletics, he fulfilled the requirements at USC for a degree in history, only to feel as lost as ever. Off on his European adventure, miserable in the Paris hotel room, he now awaits the beautiful Annick, his worries mounting.

The thought of his future terrifies him. International diplomacy intrigues him, but UNESCO has rejected him for an entry-level position, in yet another reminder that he has no marketable skills. What does he do now? Every scenario he sees seems to push him toward further reliance on his parents and their money. He dreads the thought of taking advantage of their social and business contacts, having no desire to become a stockbroker or a suit-and-tie trainee at somebody's bank. Only two months from turning twenty-three, he wants out of their orbit for good. And then he has a thought. It hits him with the force of an epiphany.

Why can't I play baseball?

Why can't I play for the Dodgers? Why can't I just call them, tell them I want to play, and ask for a tryout?

He argues with himself, going back and forth.

The scouts don't think I have the talent, or they would've signed me a long time ago.

But what if the scouts are plain wrong?

No, the scouts are never wrong about that sort of thing—that's why they're scouts. They just didn't see enough talent in me.

It doesn't matter what the damn scouts say.

Well, it does matter if they didn't want me.

I don't give a damn. I need to try. I'm going to get myself home, make a phone call, and tell the Dodgers I want to play for them.

Perhaps his life of privilege helps in that instant. Who else but a somewhat indulged young man would ever believe that he could get a Dodger tryout with a mere phone call? Who else but a sometimes pampered child would see this as anything other than delusional? But Parker has a sense of destiny that most human beings don't. Besides, what else is he qualified to do? Nothing. What does he have to lose? Nothing. Baseball is it. Worse, any other professional pursuit will keep him under his parents' thumb for a long time, maybe forever. No, he must do this. He must at least try. He resolves that, if the Dodgers give him a chance, he will do anything asked of him, start however low he must.

He is not naive. This might not work out even if they do give him a look, he tells himself. Few who launch a professional baseball career on the doorstep of twenty-three ever make it to the big leagues. And there is all his rust to worry about. Not having swung a bat for about a year and a half, how can he expect his dulled reflexes to react to wicked sinkers and curveballs?

It doesn't matter, he tells himself. He's doing it. He's already made up his mind.

He races out of the hotel and runs through rain for the four blocks along the Champs-Elysées to the TWA office, where he asks for the earliest flight back to LA. He is gone from Paris the next morning, having written a note to Annick saying he had to leave. He already feels better than he has in a long while. "I had a purpose for the first time in a long time," he will later recall.

The magnitude of his audacity becomes clear only after he touches down in Los Angeles. Wasting no time, he calls the Dodgers and leaves a message for Chuck Dressen, the old acquaintance of his father and now a Dodger coach. Returning the call the next day, a puzzled Dressen can't even remember Parker for a moment.

The old baseball man is befuddled. *You want* what?

"I want to play for the Dodgers," Parker says.

"Kid, that's not how it works," Dressen answers, throwing cold water all over the fantasy. "Prospects don't call us. We call them. You haven't played for a while, right? We don't even know if you still got it."

"I still got it," Parker says, hoping this is true.

Dressen can offer him nothing more than news about a low-key, off-season winter league in Southern California, where a ragtag bunch of dreamers and nobodies—mostly former collegiate and high school players who've never attracted the interest of professional teams—compete in unpublicized games with a few journeymen minor leaguers. Now and then, scouts might drop by for a look. Don't expect anything special, Dressen cautions. The games offer nothing more than an outside possibility you'll get noticed. And few players do. But if you play really well, Dressen says, there's always a chance. If you're interested in playing, I'll see what I can do.

I'm interested.

Dressen calls back in twenty-four hours. He's found a team for Parker.

PRIVATE NIGHTS IN CRENSHAW, AMERICA'S SWEETHEART, AND BAVASI'S WARNING

Sometimes television hosts and producers around Los Angeles, including Dinah Shore, invited him on their shows to play his banjo and chat about music and baseball. Word had spread around Hollywood that, in addition to his base-stealing skills, Maury Wills could pluck a nice tune and banter, too.

But in the ugly paradox of the times, he couldn't live in many Los Angeles neighborhoods without inviting a social firestorm. Inside the ballpark, he was a Dodger; outside it, a black man. The social codes of Los Angeles included an unspoken understanding of who lived where and who didn't, and what occurred when someone, even a celebrity, defied that understanding. Black players on the Dodgers knew well what had happened to the legendary singer Nat King Cole, who purchased a home in 1948 in the city's upscale, virtually all-white Hancock Park community and endured two decades of harassment that included the poisoning of his family dog, the defacing of his property with racial epithets, and a petition drive led by white residents intent on forcing him out of their enclave.

"You want to go where you're comfortable," Wills remembers thinking. While they could probably ride out the tensions and any sporadic insults in a white community, Wills and most other black players didn't see the point in trying, not with so many of Los Angeles's black neighborhoods eager to welcome them. For Wills, the social realities of Los Angeles were merely an extension of his childhood life in stratified Washington, where he had known nothing about another kind of world and was therefore content. Los Angeles would be no different, he believed. As long as people let him live in peace, he thought he could be happy with the duality of his life—a star in a stadium and a careful traveler everywhere else.

Now on most nights, having moved out of the guest house of a church minister and into an apartment in the Crenshaw area of southeast Los Angeles, he had women occasionally come and go. More often he just drank whiskey alone, listened to music, played his banjo, and wished he did not need to be alone so often. It was at all times confusing. He was often crying, by then.

He felt distant from most players and people, white and black. He liked nearly all the guys on his team in one way or another, but that's where it stopped. He just didn't hang out with anybody out of the locker room, really, and—aside from Koufax and maybe Roseboro—his relationships weren't nearly as close as other people's, he thought. It pained him.

He wished it were different, he wished he were wired differently, but he was who he was, and that didn't seem likely to change anytime soon. What he was, he recognized, was someone who had spent his life preferring to be largely alone. He could trace the desire back to his boyhood, back to the Wills family's cramped apartment in the Parkside projects. He and his siblings had slept four to a bed. To the disgust of his siblings, he wet the mattress they shared, and they kicked him out. Shortly later, he received his own bed. A few of his brothers and sisters thereafter called him "Pee-Boy," but he discovered he loved sleeping alone—loved the quiet and sense of specialness that came with being apart from others. He was free to sleep in solitary comfort and to dream alone of a faraway life that never would involve being cramped. He wanted space and privacy, but he yearned for connections. It was a contradiction he would never fully reconcile.

At home and away, he was a man doing his best to cope with his shortcomings, emotional and physical. On road trips, while his teammates rode the team bus back to their hotel after games, Wills often stayed behind to ice his aching legs or receive treatments from the Dodgers training staff. He didn't mind. It just gave him more time in private to think and later, after grabbing a cab back to the hotel, to spend with his banjo. Fame had added to his burdens. On the road, his phone in hotel rooms rang more than ever, with strangers looking to get together. He had stopped answering, leaving his roommate Roseboro to fend off callers while Wills found sanctuary on the banjo or in a blues club. Occasionally a performer persuaded him to come up on a stage and join in playing a number. When it ended, he returned to the shadows.

But increasingly at Dodger Stadium, there was no way to avoid admirers. Many of the best box seats at Dodger games had acquired the look of a Hollywood salon, with Milton Berle, Frank Sinatra, Danny Kaye, and Doris Day among the frequent attendees. The entertainers enjoyed being seen with the star players, whose celebrity in the city rivaled their own.

"They were nice—and they always wanted a piece of you," Wills remembers. Kaye was contemplating making a record about his love of the team. Berle, who sometimes bombastically groused about the location of his season tickets and lack of amenities, chatted up Wills and other Dodgers about the possibility of having them accompany him on a road show. By contrast, the blond, curvy, ivory-skinned Doris Day struck Wills as simply nice—a devoted fan with no agenda, easygoing, free of airs. He viewed her as remarkably down-to-earth for someone regarded by so many lustful men as America's wholesome dream woman.

Although she was married, Day was often at Dodger Stadium alone, and one evening a brief pregame chat between the two of them led to a casual invitation to get together after a game. And it started there, as Wills would later tell the story. She was thirty-eight; he was twenty-nine. Sometimes they went to his apartment, he would recall.

Their relationship, whatever the truth of it, faced challenges, least of which was their marital status. Interracial romances were still taboo in most American circles, and neither could afford gossip about their friendship to turn into a public story that could damage their careers, especially Day, whose pristine image was her calling card in Hollywood.

Day would later deny that a romance ever existed, and no evidence would ever independently corroborate Wills's version of events, no telling photographs or correspondence. But in 1962, there were observers who had arrived at their own suspicions after quiet inquiries. An African American newspaper sought to interview him about Day, eventually publishing a story about a reporter's inability to make contact. The whispers spread until the rumor finally reached Bavasi, who called Wills into his office and asked point-blank whether he was having an affair with Day. Wills was coy. Bavasi was not. Having already privately discussed the matter with others in the Dodgers organization, Bavasi made it clear that the club wouldn't look kindly on the public relations nightmare likely to ensue if white fans learned that one of the team's star black players was dating America's girl-next-door. According to two former Dodger employees with front office ties and direct knowledge of the conversation, Bavasi ordered Wills to stop seeing the actress. Admitting nothing but believing his Dodger future was on the line, a frightened Wills agreed. No sooner did he leave Bavasi's office than he lashed himself for having let the executive intimidate him again. "I was scared," he would admit.

THE INEVITABLE KOUFAX

With the Bavasi meeting behind him, nothing could distract Wills from either the pennant race, in which the Dodgers enjoyed a large lead over the Giants, or his pursuit of Cobb. The mania about the stolen base record had only grown. Much of America, Wills thought, evidently believed he had a greater chance than ever of breaking the mark; the volume of mail and its intensity of passions had both risen, judging by how often Koufax winced when he read some letters. Now and then Wills shared his pain about the hate with Koufax, more grateful than ever that his reticent friend made time to listen to him.

But none of this would matter much if he didn't admire Koufax's character on the mound, a quality that Wills viewed as distinct from Koufax's talent. Behavior in the immediate aftermath of a bad break revealed character, as Wills saw it. He had felt wounded a few times by the current staff ace Don Drysdale and a few other Dodger pitchers, who, whether intentionally or not, lost their cool in the heat of some games and disgustedly kicked the mound after some of his errors. By contrast, Koufax had a habit of reassuringly looking at him after a miscue, slightly raising his glove in a manner that signaled to his friend all was okay—everything would be just fine. In return, a grateful Wills soon found himself playing harder behind Koufax than any other pitcher, diving for grounders and liners with an abandon that he couldn't afford in every game without risking injury.

While Koufax's career as a Dodgers bonus baby began under spectacularly different circumstances, the pitcher's odyssey had been as strange and painful as his own, Wills realized. Koufax ran into his own problems during the 1950s, with resentful Brooklyn regulars convinced he unjustly took a roster spot that ought to have gone to any one of several older, hard-toiling pitchers. Within the Dodgers organization, Koufax did not enjoy close relationships with team officials, a reality not missed by teammates. After the team's move to Los Angeles, Wills and several other black Dodgers players believed that the Dodgers' front office would rather promote Drysdale, a local boy made good from the San Fernando Valley's Van Nuys High School, than New Yorker Koufax.

Koufax never made an issue of the difference in publicity and promotion that he received, Wills knew. As he looked at his friend in the locker room and they put away all their mail, he couldn't think of another Dodger who did so much to avoid the adoration bestowed on ballplayers—or who looked so weary when he received it.

But that was almost beside the point to Wills, who saw the publicity issue as one of fairness: Drysdale seemed to be in far more promotional photos, and featured on the covers of more Dodger publications. Some of this undoubtedly stemmed from Drysdale's successes as a young pitcher; he matured sooner as a performer than Koufax, who earlier experienced the growing pains of control issues with his fastball and the self-doubt that accompanied it. Drysdale was also a more comfortable public figure, so at ease with the medium of television that he appeared on Groucho Marx's quiz show *You Bet Your Life* and several comedy shows. At different points, in the late 1950s and in 1960, as Koufax still struggled to find himself as a pitcher, Drysdale seemed on the brink of superstardom.

But by 1962 Koufax was rapidly catching up. Privately, several black players, keenly alert to discrimination of any kind, suspected that Koufax's Judaism had made some Dodger officials, who had well-deserved reputations for carefully gauging fan reaction to any public relations move, reluctant to use him as a symbol of the team's success and Los Angeles base. "We didn't think there could be any other explanation except that they were worried about him being Jewish and from New York City," Wills recalls. "Here you had Sandy, with all his talent, and he was a good-looking guy, too. But it seemed he was kind of the outsider to them, and Don was the good guy to them who'd grown up there and the guy everybody liked."

The difference in treatment of the two pitchers had the potential to create tensions and divisions, especially as it became clear to most Dodgers, including Wills, that Koufax was the greater talent. He could throw harder; he had a much better breaking ball; he was simply blessed with greater tools. His hands and fingers dwarfed Drysdale's; his back and shoulders were broader, more powerful, than those of his counterpart. In June of that season Koufax had thrown his first no-hitter, leaving observers to gape at what looked to be a limitless talent finally about to flourish.

Until that moment, Drysdale had been the Dodgers' undisputed number-one starting hurler. Now the players had begun to realize that it was only a matter of time, no more perhaps than a year, before Koufax would be regarded as the dominant one, the supertalent. Like a storm approaching, Koufax was an inevitability. The looming change in the pecking order could have unnerved and embittered a less secure number one. But there were few athletes anywhere in American professional sports as free of envy and as easygoing, magnanimous, and comfortable in their own skin as Drysdale. He had a genuine friendship with Koufax. A couple of years earlier, after learning that his teammate had nowhere to go for Thanksgiving, he invited Koufax out to Van Nuys for a family dinner at the house of Drysdale's uncle and aunt, where his younger cousin, Mike Ley, remembered thinking that he was looking at two baseball stars with absolutely no airs and thus perfectly compatible personalities, a natural fit for a friendship.

"There was a poker game after this big dinner, and Don and Sandy played," Ley remembers. "You had these two guys just having a good time. Sandy was the greatest guy, so down-to-earth, so polite. That was Don, too. You couldn't have had two star players more comfortable with each other than those two. It couldn't be any other way with Don. He just wasn't jealous of anybody or anything he didn't have. He was a big man in every way. That's why it worked. Sandy was going to be the more famous pitcher, but Don loved everything about his own life and everything Sandy did."

CHASING A GHOST'S RECORD

The stress mounted in late 1962 for Koufax and Wills. Koufax was struggling physically, a circulatory problem in his index finger and waves of intense pain in his left shoulder leaving him largely sidelined after a brilliant first half of the season, which would end for him with fourteen victories. The workhorse Drysdale, on his way toward winning twenty-five games and capturing the Cy Young Award that year as baseball's most valuable pitcher, tried valiantly to compensate for Koufax's absence. But the Dodgers' first-place lead over the Giants dwindled anyway. Worse, as the season approached its climactic stage, several key Dodgers began slumping.

The club's many problems placed more of a burden on Wills than ever to generate stolen bases and runs. He was hurting badly on some days, an inevitable consequence of all his stealing and sliding. When he launched into a slide at either second or third base, his left leg was typically out front, hooking toward the outfield side of the bag to get away from foes' attempted tags, his right leg slightly tucked and trailing behind, taking the full weight of the impact as he hit hard dirt. All the self-inflicted pounding had left him a physical mess. His right leg, from ankle to hip, looked like one long purple welt.

But the pace of his stealing accelerated. In early September at Dodger Stadium, he stole four bases in a game against the Pirates, bringing his year's total to 82, in the process breaking the fifty-one-year-old National League record of a little-known Cincinnati outfielder named Bob Bescher. Within the next week he stole three bases at home against the Cubs—the sixth time already in 1962 that he had stolen at least three bases in a game. The next night, in another victory over the Cubs, he stole his 90th, just six thefts away now from Cobb's record. He had stolen fourteen bases in the last six games alone, and was two games ahead of Cobb's pace. His two singles in the contest extended his hitting streak to 19 games, the longest of any Dodger all year. He had 15 hits in his last 20 official at-bats, the numbers of a player who had emerged as baseball's greatest offensive threat, at his best now in a tight pennant race. But it was his stealing that mesmerized admirers. Before the season ended, he would have successfully stolen third base alone 33 times out of 34 attempts.

Wanted by no team in baseball just three and a half years earlier, he was a leading candidate to win the National League's Most Valuable Player Award. The Giants' manager, Alvin Dark, helped to fuel the talk by calling him the Dodgers' MVP. Contrary to those who insist a player can't win a game by himself, Wills had won many games essentially alone—certainly without any meaningful offensive assistance from teammates. The pattern had become all too familiar to opponents: after he singled or walked, he stole second base and advanced to third either on a ground out, fly out, or another steal, before coming home on yet another groundout. It wasn't unusual for him to score on no Dodger hits at all. For rivals, it was at once maddening and enviable—they searched for a Wills of their own. He was changing the game nearly as quickly as he was closing in on Cobb.

Dodger officials had long dreamed of employing such speed in the team's new ballpark, which had made its debut at the start of the 1962 season, just in time for Wills's greatness. Dodger Stadium is a pitcher's ballpark—quite deep down the lines at 330 feet, with the heavy evening air of Chavez Ravine conspiring to hinder the flight of the kinds of fly balls that frequently traveled for home runs in the Dodgers' old home at the Los Angeles Memorial Coliseum, where a high fence down the left-field line stood only 250 feet or so from home plate. The Coliseum was a right-handed power hitter's dream. The new ballpark would serve to thwart power, placing a premium on players' ability to generate runs with speed on the base paths.

The Dodgers planned accordingly, even before setting foot in Dodger Stadium. The team's front office had invested its hopes in Wills and other Dodger speedsters—center fielder Willie Davis among them—to have breakthrough years once 1962 arrived. Riding Wills's success, club officials didn't hesitate to boast about their prescience in accentuating speed and seeking to find a player in the mold of their fleet star. "We realized we had to have a different kind of ball club for our new park with its wide expanses of outfield," said Fresco Thompson, a Dodger vice president in charge of minor-league operations. "So we started building early toward the future. . . . I like our kind of baseball, the 'Go-go-go' kind. . . . It is going to be a lot more popular than it was because of men like Wills."

Wills stole his ninety-fifth base during Game 154 of the season, leaving him two games, according to Major League Baseball officials, to match or exceed Cobb, whose 96 thefts came in 156 games that included two makeup contests. Wills tied the record on the same day he broke it, during Game 156 in St. Louis. He stole the record-equaling ninety-sixth base in the third inning, swiping second base off the Cardinals' right-handed starting pitcher Larry Jackson. In the seventh inning, with the Dodgers hopelessly trailing, 11–2, he had another opportunity. After singling, he went through the ritual of taking his lead and diving back to first base, again and again, as Jackson tried picking him off and first baseman Bill White swatted him across the head with his big glove. Thousands of Cardinal fans, suddenly his supporters, chanted "Go, go, go."

Then, with a dash born of inspired improvisation, he moved past Cobb and into history. Remembering a bit of advice from Dodger executive Al Campanis, he executed a delayed steal—a bit of trickery dependent on convincing the Cardinals that he was not stealing at all. He waited until Jackson's pitch had nearly reached home plate before racing toward second base. Caught by surprise, the Cardinal infielders didn't react quickly enough to field a throw from catcher Carl Sawatski, who feebly threw it on several bounces, far too late.

In Los Angeles, stories about Wills's feat dominated the news. It was a heady time that would have been even better if the Dodgers had clinched the National League pennant and the opportunity to play in the World Series. But the team was in trouble. In the season's final couple of weeks, the Dodgers lost ten of their final thirteen games, squandering a comfortable lead in the standings. Wills had to steal home in the ninth inning of a game against Houston just to force the contest into extra innings, after which they lost anyway.

Still, they had a two-game lead over the Giants with only three games to play, a cushion that seemed safe. Then the team closed its regular season by failing to score a run in the final twenty-six innings, and the Dodgers finished in a tie with San Francisco. In early October, a three-game playoff against the Giants began at Candlestick Park with a struggling Koufax, still not fully recovered from his arm problems, getting hammered, as San Francisco won in a rout, 8–0, before a coast-to-coast NBC television audience.

It was an era when announcers still used terms like *coast-to-coast* to convey their awe of the technology. Nationally televised baseball remained something of a rarity in America. Many baseball fans in the East saw Wills for the first time, watching him score from third base on a game-winning sacrifice fly at home in Game 2 of the playoff, beating a throw from Willie Mays in center field. The victory forced a decisive Game 3, in which Wills stole his 102nd, 103rd, and 104th record-breaking bases of the season and scored a run, en route to helping the Dodgers to a 4–2 lead by the start of the ninth inning at Dodger Stadium. He was already allowing himself to contemplate what it would be like to face the Yankees in the World Series.

The Dodgers made a few late and familiar defensive changes, in hopes of protecting their two-run advantage. Alston moved veteran Jim Gilliam from second base to third and brought rookie Larry Burright off the bench to play second. But the biggest question was who would pitch the ninth inning. Alston had to decide whether to stay with reliever Ed Roebuck or turn instead, as many Dodgers privately hoped, to Drysdale, who was warming up in the bullpen. But Drysdale had pitched a subpar five and one-third innings just the day before, giving up three earned runs and seven hits. Without any rest, he might have been especially vulnerable at that moment. Besides, Alston hoped to use him in Game 1 of a prospective World Series.

Then there was Roebuck, who had built a spectacular record of 10–1 in relief during the season, and who had pitched masterfully in the playoff to that point, not having given up a run in seven and two-thirds innings, looking much sharper than Drysdale. But, on this final day, he already had worked three hard innings. He had pitched in every playoff game on three successive days. Players wondered whether he had enough left to work the ninth inning. Yet Alston's options were few. A hurting Koufax was unavailable. No one else in the bullpen looked like any more of a reliable bet than Roebuck.

Coach Leo Durocher, the legendary former manager of both the Dodgers and Giants who had sniped about Alston from the shadows all season, wanted Drysdale. "But Durocher overstepped his bounds with Walt all that season," Wills remembers. "Walt didn't like it that Durocher was trying to do something with Drysdale that he didn't want done. So Walt said no. Walt cut off his nose to spite his face. But the chemistry was bad between Leo and Walt. It wasn't going to happen that day with Drysdale."

This was the cost of a dysfunctional relationship between a manager and coach.

Still, the Dodgers shouldn't have lost, not even after pinch hitter Matty Alou led off the Giants' ninth with a lined single to right field off Roebuck. Up to the plate stepped the right-handed-hitting outfielder Harvey Kuenn, who had a reputation for being an effective opposite-field hitter. Against a hard-throwing pitcher, it might have been shrewd to shade the outfielders toward right field, and the infielders a bit toward first base, to account for the very real possibility that Kuenn might hit the ball to the right side of the field. But Roebuck, who relied on guile and a repertoire of pitches that included a sinker and an excellent slider, didn't throw hard, making it highly unlikely that Kuenn would get a suitable ball to hit the opposite way.

Several Dodgers on the field were surprised to see that Burright, obeying instructions from the Dodgers' third-base dugout, was taking several steps from his usual second-base spot in the direction of first base. Young Wes Parker, back from Paris and sitting in one of his family's season box seats near the visitors' dugout on the first-base side, noticed Burright doing the same thing. So did Dodgers reserve catcher Norm Sherry, who along with other Dodgers would later ask in shock, "Who moved Burright?"

Who moved Burright? It would become the haunting question of their off-season. Even a half century later it would be their common reference to the Dodgers' most important defensive move of the '62 playoff—and a painful mistake.

Kuenn hit a ground ball to Wills. Parker would later have a crystalline recollection of the ball's path. "It's hit like a shot," he recalled. "Two hard skipping hops to Maury—it's almost right at him. It's a perfect double-play ball."

At the crack of the bat, Burright, also recognizing the grounder as a double-play opportunity, sped toward the second-base bag. But he immediately sensed that his earlier shift had presented a problem. He felt himself somewhat out of position. He was so far from the bag. "If I'd been in my normal position, I'd have had no problem turning the double play," he said, decades later. "But this time I had ten to fifteen feet farther to run to second base after being moved. Usually, it was just seven or eight steps to the bag for me. It was more this time, and the way I was coming at the bag, the angle, that was a little different, too. I had to run as hard as I could, catch Maury's throw, then jump, twist, and throw in one motion. It was hard to get my hips and body turned to make the double-play throw because my momentum, coming from where I was, carried me toward left field. Everything was a little late. We got the force out on Alou, but there just wasn't time to get the double play."

Sherry quickly recognized the play's significance. "It's the key play of the inning," he recalls. "You'd have just needed one more out if we'd turned that double play, and the bases would've been empty. And that's why the guys always sort of ask who it was that moved Burright."

The inning now unraveled for the Dodgers. A tired Roebuck walked the next two hitters, and Mays singled. The Dodger nightmare was in full flight. Alston finally signaled for a reliever. But it was the hard-throwing Stan Williams, not Drysdale. Soon the game was tied. Williams eventually walked in the run that gave the Giants a lead. Norm Sherry felt numb, shell-shocked. Wills would later remember a funereal quiet in the stadium. Burright would make an error that he won't be able to recall later, which provided the Giants with their fourth run of the inning, and a 6–4 lead.

The Dodgers went down in order in the bottom of the ninth, and the Giants were celebrating, off to the World Series.

For decades to come, Wills, always protective of younger players, would say he didn't think that Burright was out of position on the game's pivotal play, that his shading toward first base hadn't made a meaningful difference. But most of his teammates would disagree, including Burright. "It was the key play of the inning, not getting that double play," he says. "I still don't remember my error, but I can sure remember Kuenn's ground ball and how we should've gotten that double play. I was thinking about that for quite a while afterward. If I could have just gotten there to the bag a bit sooner, if I just didn't have so far to run: it goes like that in my mind. But there's nothing you can do about it. So people are always gonna say, 'Who moved Burright?'"

Burright himself will supply the answer, finally resolving the mystery. It wasn't Alston who shifted him, he says. Rather the signal that persuaded him to move came from an animated Leo Durocher. "One of his stick arms was straight out and motioning to me to move— motioning hard with his hand: move *over, over, over* that way, *that way*," Burright remembers.

Durocher kept motioning until Burright had moved enough in the direction of first base to satisfy him. "Leo was the guy who moved me. Leo moved players a lot. I moved the way he told me to."

In the locker room after the game, some Dodgers howled about

Alston's refusal to use Drysdale. A few distraught players were trashing the clubhouse in their fury.

Wills was disconsolate. He would only briefly watch the World Series; everything about it was too painful, particularly the sight of the Giants playing in the majestic cathedral that was Yankee Stadium.

With so few games televised, most easterners had only a faint sense of his greatness that season. He had scored 130 runs, the second most in the National League. His 10 triples were the most in the league. He had 208 hits, more than any other shortstop in the league. He had finished with a .299 batting average and surprised his old doubters by hitting 6 home runs. And he had won his second consecutive Gold Glove as the best defensive shortstop in the league. As a whole, his season had outshone that of every other shortstop in the history of the Dodgers, including legend and soon-to-be Hall of Famer Pee Wee Reese.

Wills's run production ranked as high as any home run slugger's that year, except for the Reds' Frank Robinson's, and equaled that of Willie Mays's. In their impact, his stolen bases essentially transformed his singles into doubles and triples; his statistics had invested him with the attributes of the most prolific extra-base hitters. Revered baseball numbers speak to the transcendence of his accomplishment. The single-season major-league record for doubles is sixty-seven, set in 1931 by Boston Red Sox outfielder Earl Webb. Take merely fifty-five of Wills's steals from 1962, realize they have effectively converted his singles and walks into doubles, add them to the thirteen doubles Wills hit on his own—and his total comes to sixty-eight Willsian doubles, exceeding Webb's number. A stolen base attempt becomes a liability only if the practitioner is a poor thief. Brilliant in his thievery during 1962, Wills was thrown out by catchers only thirteen times all season, in addition to being picked off by pitchers three times—a success rate of 86.6 percent.

That winter Wills won the National League's Most Valuable Player Award and received the Hickok Belt as the best athlete of the year in all of American professional sports, ahead of a trio of greats—golfer Arnold Palmer, Green Bay Packers quarterback Bart Starr, and Boston Celtics legendary center Bill Russell. "It all seemed unreal," he recalls.

In a flood of memories during that off-season, he thought of all he had overcome—the eight-plus years in the minors, the devastating rejections at the start of 1959 from the Dodgers and Tigers, the battles with the Brooklynites. How did I do it? he asked himself.

He was the MVP; he had become the greatest base stealer in history; he was among the chief reasons why the Dodgers nearly won the pennant. And now, he figured, it was time, in his contract discussions with Buzzie Bavasi, that he be rewarded. He wanted a salary considerably higher than the $30,000 he had earned in 1962. But already he was worried over how to ask for it. He had to go into Bavasi's office alone; no advisers were permitted to accompany a player during salary discussions. He would need to argue by himself for what he deserved, and he hated arguing with Bavasi about anything. He just didn't know how to do it.

The idol was on top of the world—and already afraid.

WEEKENDS IN THE NOBODY LEAGUE

Wes Parker's winter league began in mid-October. Charlie Dressen wasn't joking. It was nothing fancy—and nothing about it looked very promising. The games were largely played in Southern California public parks without locker rooms or dugouts. Some of the infields didn't have grass—the players called them "skin infields." Some of the outfields didn't even have fences. Little League games drew more spectators. The only onlookers typically were four or five scouts, some of whom didn't always come. Parker didn't care. He showed up wherever a game was being played, out in Culver City or the San Fernando Valley or Compton.

His mother and father hardly mentioned his involvement in this last-chance league. Their dismissiveness reminded him of the stakes here. He felt as though he were playing for his life. Failure would likely leave him no choice but to surrender to whatever his parents wanted him to do. And that would ruin him.

Early during the winter league, America confronted a national emergency. In a televised prime-time speech, President Kennedy informed the country that the Soviet Union had secretly placed nuclear missiles in Cuba. Announcing that American armed forces would quarantine Cuba to prevent any additional Soviet armaments from reaching the island, Kennedy demanded that the Soviets remove the missiles, leaving open the possibility of an American attack on Cuba if the Soviets didn't comply. Any attempt by the Cubans or Soviets to launch missiles against America or its allies would result in immediate retaliation, Kennedy vowed.

Preparing for possible calamity, Americans made a run on grocery stores across the country, emptying shelves of supplies and potable water. American schoolchildren were drilled in ducking under their desks and covering their heads to ward off Armageddon. The White House established tentative plans for the president's emergency evacuation from Washington. Through it all, Parker focused on baseball. "I was a player; I was going to get signed," he recalls. "Nothing was going to distract me. The world could've blown up and it wouldn't have mattered to me. Nothing was going to stop me, not the Cuban missile crisis, not anything. I had to perform."

Over the next few days, the crisis eased. The games in the winter league continued, with Parker exhibiting little of the rust that would have been reasonably expected from a man who hadn't played a baseball game in so long. Whether hitting left-handed or right-handed, the switch-hitter was swinging the bat extraordinarily well, hitting over .400 in the league.

But it was on defense, as he alternated between first base and the outfield, where he separated himself from others. On skin infields all over LA, he made plays at first base that major leaguers would envy—diving snatches, leaping catches, backhanded scoops out of the dirt on errant throws from other infielders. Fielding was his great gift. Beginning with all those years of work in his front yard and on the fields of his adolescence, he had studied the art of catching a baseball the way painters contemplated brush strokes. He had refined a style that was all his own. He played with his elbows relaxed and bent. He didn't stab at balls hit directly at him, like so many other players. Treating the ball as if it were an uncooked egg, he gently brought it toward his body as if to ensure it wouldn't break and slither away.

By then, it was all instinct. All he generally had to do was react and his glove did the rest. For the next decade, his fielding would compensate for the frequent shortcomings of his game—his batting slumps, several years of low batting averages, his waves of self-doubt. His glove was so good that the baseball men wanted him, had to have him, having already recognized the fielding gift that could make him a frontline player if he merely became an average hitter. His defensive gifts were enhanced by attributes not often seen in a first baseman, particularly his raw speed and reflexes. The scouts had discovered that he was more than a first baseman, his glove's versatility enabling him perhaps to handle every position in the outfield.

Twice in one winter-league game, while he played right field, long fly balls were hit toward the gap in right-center. Running at full speed, he caught both balls over his right shoulder. On the second catch, he wheeled around to make a perfect throw to first base, nabbing a baserunner who had wandered off the bag. It was a spectacular double play. He realized that the scouts, including one from the Dodgers named Kenny Myers, were paying closer attention to him. It was Myers's nature that he said next to nothing to anyone, his persistent silence long before having inspired a sardonic nickname: the "Monk." But the Monk had clout: he had signed the Dodgers' heralded young outfielder Willie Davis, fresh out of Los Angeles's Roosevelt High School, in 1958. Parker couldn't read Myers's facial expressions or those of the other scouts. "I just kept playing my ass off in every game," he recalls. "I was so serious. I took Chuck Dressen at his word—that if I played well, somebody would see it. I was playing loose. I had a feeling it might happen. Hell, at least I had a chance."

Along the way, he made friends among some of the other winter-league players, including Clarence Jones, already a minor-league first baseman and outfielder in the Dodgers organization who would go on to play briefly in the majors with the Cubs. Hanging around with Jones offered a window on to a new camaraderie. Parker's life, he remembers, "suddenly felt like I might be going from purgatory to heaven."

In mid-December, as the winter league ended, he wondered how he'd survive if the scouts rejected him. He had heard nothing, triggering the old anxieties. Just as he braced himself for the possibility of crushing disappointment, a call came. The Dodgers offered him a minor-league contract, and officials invited him to come down to Dodger Stadium shortly before Christmas for the signing.

In yet another example of what would forever be the paradox of their relationship, Parker brought his father with him. The pain he had experienced over a lifetime would never stop him from dining with his father, vacationing with his father, and listening to him respectfully. Even amid his hurt and sometimes seething rage, he would search for an elusive connection, and this great day offered another chance. He wanted his dad to experience the jubilation of the event. Fresco Thompson, in his role as director of the Dodgers' minor-league organization, presided over the late morning meeting, which included the two Dodger figures most instrumental in leading Parker to this moment, Dressen and Kenny Myers. The Monk said nothing. A smiling Dressen shook the hands of both Parkers.

Thompson was all business. He reviewed what the contract—a standard bottom-end deal for the least ballyhooed of entry-level minor leaguers—provided and what it didn't. There would be no bonus. "You agree to be paid $300 a month, a $1.50 per diem for meal money, and you agree to keep yourself in shape and do whatever public appearances we might ask you to do," Thompson brusquely told Parker, who signed the contract as his father looked on. The meeting was over in less than five minutes. As with many of the other Dodgers minor-league deals, there would be a short reference to his signing in the local papers, a simple line saying that "Wes Parker of Brentwood" was now part of the Dodgers organization. Nothing could have been more routine for the Dodgers. But the moment was transformative for Parker. He could not have cared less that he received no bonus. He didn't need a dime of the Dodgers' money. For the first time as an adult, he felt he had a real purpose, a chance for escape and fulfillment, a reason for living.

For his part, his father wanted to take him to lunch to celebrate. Within a half hour they were sitting inside the posh Windsor Restaurant, where his father ordered champagne. As the two men toasted the triumph, Parker was struck by a realization: *Dad is even happier about this than I am.*

His father, denied the opportunity to try out for the Red Sox by his own father, had now come full circle to discover his own son seizing the opportunity. "I could see my father had reached his dream through me," Parker remembers thinking. "He must have wondered about his own life."

His father wasn't given to displays of sentimentality. "He never gushed about anything, and he wasn't going to do it around me," Parker says. Just the same, a window opened at the Windsor. That afternoon, Parker detected emotion in the gleam of his father's eyes, which was followed by a proud boast. "My son just signed with the Dodgers," he told their waiter, who asked for young Parker's autograph.

The afternoon served as another reminder of his father's endless charm in the right settings. But Parker wouldn't allow this geniality to obscure their past together, or his desperate need to get away from his parents. In the middle of this scared reverie, he ordered himself to stop and focus on the joy of his big day. For the first time he had control over his fate; finally he could break away. He was assigned to play for the Dodgers' Single-A team in Santa Barbara. The coastal city was only a two-hour drive north from Brentwood, but to Parker it felt like a galaxy away. Freedom, he thought.

Another Dodger official offered congratulations in a phone call. Rival scouts who passed on him during his college career would later rue this day. In time, the Pirates' Rosey Gilhousen would confess that he thought the light-hitting rich kid had no real future in baseball, adding, "But he didn't listen to me."

THE ART OF A BUZZIE BAVASI NEGOTIATION

A few months after his epic 1962 season, the time arrived for Wills to negotiate his 1963 salary with Dodger management. As the owner and outwardly genteel patriarch, Walter O'Malley always left it to lieutenants, serving as his cudgels, to handle such chores, cajoling and threatening uncooperative players when it was in management's interests. His chief lieutenant was Bavasi, his most skilled enforcer.

Blunt, pugnacious, bow-tied, and balding at forty-seven, the rumpled Bavasi was O'Malley's antithesis in appearance and style. The players liked that about him. He could be profane, hilariously so, in ways O'Malley never would, and they regularly looked forward to hearing him mock the vanity or weaknesses of a teammate with a crude but well-timed barb. They liked it that Bavasi could be so loose in their presence; it seemed to grant a license to be a bit looser themselves. They called him "Buzzie" because anything else would've been unthinkable—he was not a "Mr. Bavasi" kind of guy. They knew they could rib him because he'd skewer them in return, and they knew they could complain about things in his presence because he eventually got around to complaining about nearly everything and everybody. He spoke their language, free of bullshit, Wills thought.

Despite Bavasi's candor and style, the players weren't under any illusions. When it came to business, no one thought he was anything other than O'Malley's proxy, there to make certain that players abided by the Dodger Way and caused no embarrassment. Most of all, he was there to execute the owner's wish that the players' payroll not be a dollar higher than necessary. He was not above using the press to deride a player's performance or publicly blast him for not immediately agreeing to what Bavasi regarded as an eminently fair contract offer.

Hoping one day that O'Malley would invite him to become a minority owner of the Dodgers, Bavasi was highly motivated to please his boss. His zeal explained one notable difference between the two men's styles: Bavasi seldom paid a player a compliment. His behavior reflected the worry that to say a player was having an exceptional year would encourage the player to believe he had a greater chance of getting more of O'Malley's dollars, which in turn might damage Bavasi's own reputation as the tightfisted general manager. During an off-season contract negotiation, Bavasi limited most of the discussion to questions about whether the player was staying in shape and what hopes he had for the following season. He wouldn't mention the player's performance in the previous year unless it had been poor, in which case he'd cite it as a reason for denying a raise or cutting pay. At the end, Bavasi typically said that the Dodgers were pleased to welcome the player back for another season. "Here's your contract," he'd regularly say. "Let's wrap this up."

Famously tough and manipulative, Bavasi wasn't above trickery and outright misrepresentations during salary discussions. Occasionally he would scatter fake contracts on his desk and briefly leave his office, leaving the player with whom he was talking tempted to steal a peek at the bogus documents, study the measly salary figures purportedly being offered to other Dodgers, and conclude he was lucky to get whatever Bavasi offered. As Bavasi stepped away one afternoon, the young star Tommy Davis furtively stared at a paltry, fictitious contract with Wills's name on it and soon wanted nothing more than to wrap up a deal.

If anyone had questions about the general manager's methods, he only needed to listen to a gleeful Bavasi boast about his negotiating successes. On another occasion, after wrapping up a new contract for Davis—who had led the National League in batting average and RBIs and finished third in the 1962 MVP balloting, behind only Wills and Willie Mays—Bavasi unabashedly recounted for reporters how he had gotten the best of Davis, whom he signed for a bargain-basement $25,000. Remarkably, Bavasi had sold Davis on the notion that if he took less money now, he would lose less in salary down the road. "Wouldn't you rather have your salary at a steady level," Bavasi persuasively said to his young star, "than to take a big cut if you don't have a very good year?" Davis's salary was several thousand dollars less than the new Dodger contracts of esteemed though fading veterans like pitcher Johnny Podres and reserve outfielder Wally Moon, whose performances in 1962 hadn't come close to matching Davis's. Over the coming years, Bavasi made a habit of feeding reporters the details of his negotiating tricks and the names of other victims who were certain losers from the time they arrived at his office. This was the bargaining atmosphere in which Wills now found himself.

To outsiders still marveling over Wills's Most Valuable Player Award, the new star seemed to possess a rare and enviable negotiating clout. Fresco Thompson's comment on the special importance of Wills's speed in mammoth, homer-unfriendly Dodger Stadium appeared to underscore his indispensability to the team.

But from the start of his meeting with Wills, Bavasi had all the leverage that mattered. He skipped any small talk and made no reference to the past year, instead emphasizing that he and O'Malley expected nothing less than for the club to win a pennant during the coming season. He was full of his usual questions: What are your plans for the rest of the off-season? Are you staying in shape? Are you doing your running? Then he cut to business, saying the club was prepared to boost Wills's salary from $35,000 to $45,000 for the new season. The offer didn't sound all that great to Wills, not after the year he'd just had. He wasn't sure about the best way to say this.

I'm not going a dollar higher, Bavasi declared.

Wills wondered whether to politely say no and ask for something more.

Not a dollar higher, Maury.

Once you have the jitters in life with somebody, you'll always have the jitters, Wills would later think.

He didn't have the nerve to push back. The discussion ended in the next couple of minutes. He signed for about $45,000.

Bavasi wrapped up by saying that the organization was pleased to welcome him back.

"I was feeling fortunate just to be on the team by that point," Wills recalls.

Getting up to leave, he pledged to do everything to win in 1963, and Bavasi was done with him.

A MAN NAMED MUDCAT

Despite the travails of various Dodgers with management, many players around baseball viewed the Dodgers organization with more admiration and envy than ever. African American players in the American League especially wondered what it might be like to play one day for the team that had broken the sport's color barrier and aggressively ushered in a vanguard of black talent ever since, in a sharp contrast to several clubs slow to embrace integration.

For their part, the Dodgers' black players returned the interest, keeping tabs on promising young African American players scattered around the country. They paid attention not merely to the most talented but to those who had exhibited courage and nerve in the face of the harassment all too familiar to black players.

Once in a while a story circulated among the black ballplayers in the Dodger clubhouse about an African American player on another club who had put a mocking bigot in his place, a story that would spark raucous laughter and bolster spirits. In 1959, a twenty-three-year-old Cleveland Indians right-handed pitcher named Jim Grant, known around baseball as "Mudcat," had traveled to New Orleans with the rest of his team for a spring training game against the Red Sox. All the Indians' luggage had been brought to the team's hotel, despite the fact that, in New Orleans, the hotel's management wouldn't permit Grant and other black players to stay there. Accustomed to being turned away from southern hotels, the black players had already made arrangements to stay at a boardinghouse in the area, and drawn straws to see who would have the dreaded responsibility of finding a bellman at the white hotel and picking up their luggage.

This time the task fell on Grant, who over the next decade would become the first black pitcher in history to win a World Series game for an American League club. He would win twenty games in a season, and twice be an All-Star. He would lead all American League pitchers in victories and shutouts during his most glorious year. He would become a formidable Dodger foe in a World Series, and later a Dodger himself.

But in 1959, Grant could see none of this in front of him. He was unheralded, laboring to prove himself during his second season in the major leagues amid racial insults and frequent abuse. Poise was a prerequisite for enduring a season. The last thing a young player could afford was an ugly off-field incident. Yet retrieving bags at a segregated hotel almost always meant a tense, humiliating exchange with a scornful bellman. Grant would remember having made a point of smiling politely as he entered the hotel. He introduced himself to a white bellman in a long green coat, explained the situation, and asked for the black players' bags.

He was instantly rebuffed, with the bellman "using the N-word," as Grant recounted.

Grant sought again to explain: he was a member of the Cleveland Indians, whose black players needed their luggage. It was his job to get all the bags and bring them to a local boardinghouse, where the black players would be staying. The procedure was routine, Grant assured the bellman.

The bellman ordered him to leave, in much the same language.

At that moment, Ted Williams happened to stroll through the hotel. The legend knew the young pitcher and walked over to say hi.

Grant guessed that Williams was wondering about something, so he answered the question for him.

"Ted, we're not staying at the hotel—not allowed to."

Williams nodded. "I know. And it's a damn shame."

Grant then explained his immediate problem: he wasn't able to pick up any of the black players' bags. "This man says he won't let me get them," Grant said, gesturing at the bellman.

"Well, Mudcat, this guy is right," Williams said. "You shouldn't get your bags." Williams paused to stare at Grant before wheeling and pointing at the bellman. "*He* should. He should get all those damn bags." He glared at the bellman and snapped, "Go get his bags."

Grant felt some momentary satisfaction. But nothing could erase the pain of a lifetime of such encounters. He could be doing nothing and suddenly flash on the white policeman, back in his hometown of Lacoochee, Florida, who'd kicked him as a child for not saying "Yes, sir" in response to a question. Some of his most enduring memories as an adult would be of glistening hotels around America, parts or all of which were off-limits to him. Kansas City was another city where he and other black players couldn't stay in the team hotel. "Promising yourself that you'd stay strong is how you survived it," he recalls.

Grant won ten games in each of the '58 and '59 seasons, solidifying his spot on the Indians' pitching staff and receiving attention as one of the few black pitchers in the game. His nickname already had become one of the most familiar in baseball; Mudcat Grant was better known than many of his veteran teammates. But even as his productivity and popularity grew, some things did not change. The harassment of black players had taken on new forms at hotels during the Indians' road trips. "We were getting insulting and threatening calls from strangers at any hour," he remembers. "We became accustomed to it. It was just a fact of life. Somebody would call at two in the morning, wake you up, and say something awful to you. Just one more headache."

Very early one morning on Labor Day weekend of 1960, at the Sheraton-Cadillac Hotel in Detroit, Grant was trying to get some rest in his room before pitching a game against the Tigers. The phone rang. The voice on the other end said that John F. Kennedy wanted to have breakfast with him. "Sometimes the people who called would say something ridiculous to you, kind of a prank, just another way of trying to disturb you," he recounts.

In such situations, the thing to do was to hang up quickly, without saying anything. This he did in Detroit. But the phone rang again. The caller repeated that John F. Kennedy wanted to have breakfast. Grant got rid of the caller a second time without uttering a word. The most cunning racists, he thought, understood that the most destructive thing they could do was to bait you into an argument and mess with your concentration.

He resumed resting, only to hear a knock at the door.

Exasperated, he rose and jerked the door open.

A couple of big, somber-looking guys in suits were standing there.

Mr. Kennedy would like to have breakfast with you, if you're available, the men said.

"I kind of knew then that this was for real," he recalls.

Kennedy was staying in the same hotel. The Massachusetts senator had entered the stretch of his presidential campaign, having come to Detroit to deliver a speech at a Labor Day rally. While scouring the morning papers, he'd noticed that the Indians were in town and that Mudcat Grant was pitching. He'd dispatched aides to find out the location of Grant, who happened to be as close as an elevator away.

The two men shook hands in the Kennedy suite. Someone snapped a picture. As Grant recalls, Kennedy said, "Mudcat, nice to meet you—I'm a big fan." The same man who would later, as president, sit through an entire All-Star game on a hot July day in Washington knew something about Grant's accomplishments and the Indians' season. And he displayed a bit of interest in the Yankees and Red Sox, with Grant later remembering that Kennedy mentioned Mantle and Yogi Berra. But the man wasn't showy, thought Grant, who liked it that Kennedy kept the small talk and baseball stories to a minimum, preferring instead to hear about Grant's off-field interests and his Florida background.

They settled down to breakfast. The candidate apparently had done some hasty research. "How's everybody back in Lockaroochie?" Kennedy asked.

Grant corrected him. "No, it's Lacoochee."

"Oh, excuse me," Kennedy said.

They didn't talk any more that morning about games or pennant races. Instead, they exchanged thoughts about impoverished Lacoochee, civil rights, and the burdens of black athletes. Their impromptu visit went unreported by an unaware national press. But it had a meaning belied by the seeming casualness of their encounter. It and a few other Kennedy meetings that year with notable African Americans, young and old, evinced an effort by the candidate and his advisers to better understand a community with which he'd had scant personal dealings.

Kennedy was facing skepticism from civil rights activists, some of whom had voiced their concerns bluntly: JFK and his brother Robert didn't know black people. The brothers' lack of a bond with the African American community amounted to a potential problem. At stake were millions of undecided black votes on which the presidential election would likely hinge, in an era when neither major political party had a lock on African American loyalties.

The greatest question about the Kennedys revolved around whether the duo had any visceral understanding of black concerns, believed Roger Wilkins, a Kennedy admirer and young African American leader who would go on to work in the Kennedy administration's Agency for International Development. "They didn't know black pain; they were not comfortable with black people," Wilkins observed of the two Kennedys, in an interview decades later with PBS. Their growth, Wilkins posited, had come only later.

Later during the 1960 campaign, John Kennedy would intervene to help free Martin Luther King Jr. when the civil rights icon was jailed and sentenced to four months of hard labor by a Georgia court after leading a sit-in at a segregated restaurant. But on that Labor Day weekend, Kennedy was still feeling his way through even the most basic of relationships with the black community. The young ballplayer sitting across from him in the Detroit hotel suite was no one's emissary. He was not a social leader or anyone with clout. But the player's openness offered the possibility of aiding in Kennedy's education. "I felt he was listening carefully to me," Grant recalls. "He made me feel comfortable. Sometimes he had questions."

For stretches during their breakfast, Grant did most of the talking. He figured it was best if he kept it simple. He shared with Kennedy only the things he knew. He tried to paint a picture of what life was like on the road for black ballplayers. "I told him," Grant remembers, "about the phone calls we sometimes got in our rooms, and about all the insulting names people called us. I talked for quite a while. He could've just said to me how terrible all that was. But after I finished, he was completely honest with me. He said something like, 'Unfortunately, life is that way. But thanks to you fellows, life is changing.' I don't think anybody could have said it any better really. I kind of liked the man quickly."

They talked more about Lacoochee, a poor town in west central Florida where many residents depended on the local lumber mill for their livelihood. Kennedy asked Grant what the town needed.

Grant said that, for starters, Lacoochee could use a real school. A building once serving as housing for lumber mill workers had been converted into a segregated school for the town's black children, he told Kennedy. Nothing about the school was quite right, starting with the classrooms and the blackboards. Given the ways of segregation, the books and other educational supplies of the school were old and outdated, all hand-me-downs from the white schools.

Grant finally asked, "Can you help?"

Before that September was over, Kennedy would debate his Republican opponent, Richard Nixon, for the first time, on his way to winning the presidency. In the years ahead, Lacoochee would receive federal funds that aided in the construction of a new school and more housing for the lumber mill workers. Grant would pay a visit to the new president at the White House, amazed at the impact of a single chance encounter in a hotel.

But all that was in Grant's future. During that September, the pitcher ran into serious professional challenges. He would win only nine games in 1960, a satisfactory season, but nothing that seemed to augur a future as an All-Star. He had temporarily flattened out. He resented what he regarded as the spread of anonymous, whispered innuendo about young black pitchers like himself and the Cardinals' still unproven Bob Gibson. "Black pitchers were thought of like black quarterbacks," he remembers. "Before he became great, Bob Gibson was thought of as someone who might not be smart enough."

The whispers were that a black pitcher required the guiding hands of a shrewd white catcher and manager. Grant suspected that African American pitchers were destined to remain rarities unless he and other black hurlers succeeded and dispelled the biases. "There was a lot on the line. The stereotypes about black pitchers were infecting the game. They were all over baseball."

But not all teams were afflicted, Grant believed. He viewed the Dodgers as the personification of fairness, the franchise that had exposed racial stereotypes as garbage. During the 1950s, with Cy Young

Award–winning pitcher Don Newcombe and eventual Hall of Fame catcher Roy Campanella, the Dodgers had two black men controlling most of the action on every pitch. And if it wasn't Newcombe on the mound, it might be another African American, Joe Black. And if it wasn't Campanella catching, it might be the emerging black star John Roseboro. Grant saw the Dodgers as living examples of how equality translated to victories and good business. "The Dodgers made fools of the racists, even if not everybody understood it yet," he observes. "Black players sure as hell understood it. That's why every black player in baseball would have been proud to wear that Dodger uniform."

It wasn't as if Grant didn't appreciate the history of his own team at that point. In 1947, the Indians had been the first American League franchise to integrate when it signed twenty-three-year-old center fielder Larry Doby out of the Negro Leagues, just months after Jackie Robinson made his debut in Brooklyn. Doby was joined a season later by forty-two-year-old pitcher Satchel Paige, with the Indians going on to win the World Series that same year. Other black stars like Minnie Minoso and Vic Power arrived in the late 1950s. That didn't mean you didn't see a bigot here or there in the Indians organization, Grant thought. Yet on balance, the Indians were far more enlightened than most American League organizations. It was just that no other major-league team, in Grant's view, could compete with the Dodgers' progress, which accounted for its unrivaled charisma in the African American community. "Every year, they seemed to produce some-body new like Maury Wills, who was changing the game," he reflects. "And when you looked at the Dodgers, you always thought of Jackie. The Dodgers pushed things."

And, in pushing baseball, he believed, the Dodgers had contrib-uted to spurring dreams that reached beyond baseball.

Yet aside from the gains of elite African American professionals in sports and entertainment, nothing had much changed in the life of the average black person, Grant thought. Segregation was as insidious as ever, maybe more so. People who protested in 1960 were paying for it. Young black men who sat at a white lunch counter were often beaten. People were plucked off country roads. The man who always felt so free on a pitching mound had come to worry about his life off it. He was no freer when he took his uniform off than any other black person.

Something was brewing inside him. On September 16, 1960, roughly a couple of weeks after his breakfast with Kennedy, he found himself in the bullpen of Cleveland Municipal Stadium before a night game against the Kansas City Athletics, singing along to "The Star-Spangled Banner," as he always did. What happened next was sheer instinct. As the national anthem reached its end, and people in the stadium's stands sang, "O'er the land of the free / And the home of the brave," Grant sang something that basically sounded like this: "This land is not so freeeeeee / I can't even go to Mississippeeeeee."

"I sang it in fun; it was kind of a joke," he remembers. "I hadn't really thought about it. But it showed how I felt."

The furor in the Indians' bullpen was immediate. Indians coach Ted Wilks, who was from Texas, berated Grant with a racial insult. Grant fired back that Texas was worse than Russia, after which he stormed into the Indians clubhouse, changed into his street clothes, and without telling anyone, rushed out of the stadium. Indians management ordered Wilks to apologize for his insult. Meanwhile Indians manager Jimmy Dykes suspended Grant without pay for the remainder of the season for leaving without permission. Grant did not protest. He wished he hadn't fled the very stadium in which he had worked so hard to earn an opportunity to pitch, and vowed to himself that it would never happen again. Yet he felt proud of standing up to Wilks, of refusing to allow an open display of racism to go unchallenged. That just wasn't going to happen around him ever again, he thought.

In the aftermath, he knew something important had happened. Something was in the air. Maybe this was the first time a black ballplayer had said anything like that to a coach, he thought, but it sure as hell wasn't going to be the last time. Something had been turned loose in him; something was being turned loose in the country. Grant could feel it. As if emboldened, he won fifteen games the very next season. He was on his way.

He couldn't have envisioned how much his career, or the country, would soon change. His future in the 1960s would include a World Series in which he would face Wills and the rest of the Dodgers speedsters, marveling over their gifts even as he was beating them twice, all this a prelude to joining them, in what felt like a wonderful fantasy at last realized. By then the whole baseball world would know his name. It was reducible to one name really, the one President Kennedy liked to call him. Some fans would forever struggle to summon his last name, but no one ever forgot Mudcat. He had arrived in the perfect decade, he thought. "Anything was possible for everybody," he said. "It wasn't easy, it was painful, but it was all out there for us. We just had to go after it."

The Frenzy of 1963: The Fearsome Yankees, the Epic World Series, and the Arrival of the Dodgers' Reluctant Idol

THE INVINCIBLE FOE

What happened in a normally quiet Los Angeles parking lot—the rage, the fistfights, the near riot that ensued—revealed a mania new to the city. It was the climax to a frenzied week. On Monday morning, September 30, 1963, about a half mile from Dodger Stadium, the nervous beginnings of a squatters' camp formed in front of the team's small, drab cinder-block ticket office, off a road that Los Angeles had specially built in Chavez Ravine for Walter O'Malley called Stadium Way. Fans had lined up in hopes of purchasing the last available tickets for the 1963 World Series between the Dodgers and the Yankees; the optimists anticipated that the tickets would go on sale that very morning. When they didn't, the more determined among them simply hunkered down in the parking lot in front of the ticket booths and resolved to wait a full four days, until that coming Friday at 11:00 a.m., when about 4,000 tickets for each of three scheduled home Series games would officially become available, the Dodgers announced.

Sleeping bags, cots, pup tents, mattresses, hammocks, overstuffed easy chairs, Coleman stoves, groceries, coolers, pets, transistor radios, and televisions swiftly appeared. The parking lot became the site of an impromptu colony, the communal spirit of the squatters during that week making it easier to endure an afternoon heat wave and the breezy nighttime chill familiar to those who knew autumns in Chavez Ravine. One of the squatters distributed coffee to anyone who wanted it. Another brought an ice chest full of beers. A lunch truck periodically cruised by. Huddling strangers listened to radios together. The Dodgers brought in some portable restrooms and made an electrical outlet available for a television. Decorum prevailed, with everyone respecting the place of others in the orderly line, which had swelled to more than 4,000. Many had taken off work during that entire week to be there. On Thursday night, in the final hours before the tickets would go on sale, the mood of those waiting was festive, with many feeling so secure and relaxed that they removed shoes and boots before climbing into sleeping bags and shutting their eyes.

They awakened to problems. At dawn, packs of rowdy interlopers began arriving, trampling over many squatters and pushing toward the front of the line. Cursing gave way to fights. The mob proved too much for seven Dodger security guards. A squad of nearby Los Angeles police officers chose not to intervene. Overrun squatters, stunned at suddenly being at the rear of a massive line and furious at the Dodgers for not affording them protection, began howling, "Hang O'Malley. Lynch O'Malley."

In the end, according to reports, about half of the squatters were unable to buy tickets. A woman in line collapsed, and an ambulance arrived, though at least her long wait was rewarded by security guards who picked up the money she'd dropped while fainting and bought her a pair of tickets. A woman from the San Diego area who had been in the parking lot since Monday left with tickets too, but not before telling a reporter, "People acted like animals."

The animals included businessmen in suits and women in hair curlers. Respectable people who had never been in a scuffle in their lives were suddenly mauling each other just to get seats to a baseball game. World Series tickets were the new gold in Los Angeles, and people were brawling to get them. Scalpers sold the top-priced $12 box seats for a minimum of $50 in the parking lot, the equivalent of about $500 in 2015 dollars. In a frenzy, prices kept rising around Los Angeles. No one could remember local fans being nearly so delirious or agitated during the Dodgers' inaugural World Series in the city, four years earlier, against the Chicago White Sox.

What had changed was the opponent. What beckoned was a matchup between two longtime antagonists, only one of whom had a history of dominance. The Yankees were the most revered, reviled, and dazzling dynasty in American sports, entering their thirteenth World Series in the last fifteen years and coming off World Championships during the past two seasons. They had won nine World Series in the last fourteen years alone, and twenty World Series during their fifty-year history, which included twenty-eight American League pennants. Their supremacy had even inspired a hit Broadway play and film, *Damn Yankees*, about a frustrated fan of the hopeless Washington Senators, who was willing to risk losing his soul to the devil to see New York beaten.

Any team that confronted the well-heeled Yankees generally did so as a decided underdog. The Yankees were a pillaging army to everyone else's outgunned and underfinanced insurrectionists. They didn't just win, they destroyed; they clubbed their opponents. And no underperforming Yankee ever lasted long. Manager Casey Stengel, who had won a stunning ten pennants and seven World Series in his twelve years at the Yankees' helm, was promptly fired after his team lost to the Pittsburgh Pirates in the 1960 Series, the culmination of an unacceptable two-year span without a World Championship in New York.

In came new manager Ralph Houk, who promptly led the Yankees to successive World Series crowns in 1961 and 1962, restoring order. They were once again living up to their nickname as the Bronx Bombers. Now, in 1963, the Yankees had thoroughly beaten up on the American League, winning the pennant by a lopsided ten and a half games. As always, the team was loaded, with a roster that included three future Hall of Famers and Roger Maris, just two years removed from having broken Ruth's home run record.

Most of all, the Yankees had baseball's most popular player, its blond deity, the one who seemingly had everything, including perhaps the best name in sports. Certainly it was the most pleasurably alliterative. Mickey Mantle, with its clipped, rawboned simplicity and its surname's emphasis on the Man, could not have been more elegantly fitting. To his fans, the name reflected the smooth immortality for which Mantle had appeared destined since his hardscrabble Oklahoma youth.

Mantle had grown up in a dusty mining town near the Arkansas border called Commerce, best known until his stardom as the place where the notorious robbers Bonnie and Clyde killed a local police officer. His father, Mutt, a lead and zinc miner who aimed to make his son into a baseball star, named the boy after Hall of Fame catcher Mickey Cochrane, then obsessively drove him, molding him into a switch-hitter. Once, during his boy's morose minor-league stint, he threatened to bring him home and put him to work in the mines unless he stopped feeling sorry for himself. Mantle's life since had been an American tale of spectacular success and excess. He was a three-time winner of the American League's Most Valuable Player Award, the first of which he had captured in 1956, when at twenty-five he led the league in hitting .353, driving in 130 runs, and slugging 52 home runs, the last player by 1963 to have won baseball's Triple Crown. Now the baseball god drank at Toots Shor's, where Manhattan elites ogled him. Women loved him, men wanted to be him, and children lined up for hours outside stadiums to glimpse him.

It was Mantle's on-field style, rather than his numbers, that fueled his legend. As powerful as a football star at six feet and 195 pounds, he swung so hard that sometimes he seemed to corkscrew himself into the ground while launching white specks deep into steamy Bronx nights. Two of his mammoth home runs had traveled more than 550 feet and completely out of ballparks in Detroit and Washington, to be found across and down city streets, as if they had been mailed there and left on doorsteps for recipients. A third homer had rocketed like a surface-to-air missile against the top of the third deck of Yankee Stadium, almost leaving that edifice, too, which would've made him the first to do it. The volume and wonder of his homers forgave all his lapses and frailties—his routine debaucheries, occasional slumps, and seasonal strikeout totals, an ignominious category in which he led the American League four times. By then all the statistics, accolades, and money were irrelevant. No other player's baseball card or autograph meant half as much. No other name carried the same magic.

But, approaching thirty-two on the eve of the 1963 Series, Mantle was already in his career's twilight. Several of baseball's other star outfielders were clearly more productive now—Willie Mays, Hank Aaron, and Roberto Clemente, just for starters. Injury-riddled, Mantle had missed most of the 1963 regular season, playing in only sixty-five games. Although he hit .314 in his shortened year and could still summon bursts of greatness, time was slowly running out. The World Series would present him with one of his last stages to prove he remained as good a clutch hitter as anyone else in the game, win his eighth World Series championship, add to his fourteen Series homers, and in the process tie or surpass Ruth's record of fifteen.

The Dodgers had no doubt that, at some point in the Series, the god would smite somebody. "Mickey played great in big games," said Dodgers second baseman Dick Tracewski. "All the Yankees did. That's what made them the Yankees. We'd have been crazy not to be a little scared. The Yankees were older, but they'd been there all the time and they all knew how to win."

No one on the Yankees knew more about winning than Whitey Ford, a close Mantle friend, a partying companion, and the Yankees' pitching ace, who would start on the mound in Game 1 at Yankee Stadium. Renowned for his poise and dominance in important games, dubbed the "Chairman of the Board" by sportswriters, and on his way to the National Baseball Hall of Fame, the left-handed Ford was at his best in key World Series encounters. His ten lifetime Series wins were the most in baseball history, and he had claimed a Series record from a former Boston Red Sox pitcher named Babe Ruth, hurling thirty-three and two-thirds consecutive scoreless innings, which included three Series shutouts, against the Pittsburgh Pirates and Cincinnati Reds in 1960 and 1961. He was the Series' Most Valuable Player in 1961, the same year he captured the Cy Young Award, after winning twenty-five games.

On the brink of turning thirty-seven as the Series against the Dodgers began, Ford remained a brilliantly reliable workhorse, having won an American League–leading twenty-four games during the 1963 regular season. Although without an overpowering pitch, he had an excellent curveball and a confounding unpredictability that kept hitters off balance. He ignored typical pitching patterns by frequently greeting frustrated hitters with an overhand curveball. "Most pitchers started you with a fastball, but you didn't swing at Ford's first pitch, because it was probably going to be a sharp breaking ball, something nasty," Tracewski explained. "But if he got it over for a strike, and he usually got that curve over, you were already behind in the count. You were always waiting for something harder from him, because he was never going to scare you with his fastball. Except then he would jam you in a perfect place with the fastball or throw it low and away on a corner. He was tough."

His control of his fastball meant that, even in the autumn of Ford's career, he seldom made mistakes of the kind that frequently plagued harder throwers. The Ford fastball rarely strayed from the corners or crept above a hitter's knees, minimizing a slugger's chance to crush it. Left-handed hitters particularly struggled to homer against him in New York during all of 1963, despite Yankee Stadium's reputation as a haven for home runs by left-handed sluggers, with the seats down the right-field line sitting only 296 feet from home plate, or a full 34 feet closer than in Dodger Stadium. Ford made a living out of enticing opposing power hitters—if and when they made good contact—to hit towering flies to the wasteland that constituted the deepest sections of Yankee Stadium in left-center and center field, which stood 461 feet away in its farthest part, too deep as a practical matter for fly balls to land in the bleachers.

Like a crafty pool player working on a favorite table, Ford knew all the ways to exploit Yankee Stadium's angles. His presence, even more than Mantle's, explained why the Yankees were a 7–5 betting favorite to win the Series, and a slim favorite in the opening game in New York against Koufax. The Chairman of the Board didn't lose big games, argued his believers. He wouldn't fall to a young Dodger hurler who had never pitched in Yankee Stadium and couldn't possibly know the pressure that the ballpark wrought in a monumental matchup. Ford was money.

All the well-known Yankees had reputations for delivering under pressure—it seemed a job requirement. Even thirty-eight-year-old catcher Yogi Berra, the three-time American League MVP and future Hall of Famer who had been largely reduced to a reserve during his last season as a Yankee player, had contributed to big wins in hitting a solid .293 during 1963. The team had no visible holes. Its regular catcher, thirty-four-year-old Elston Howard, was on his way to becoming the American League's 1963 MVP, after batting .287, hitting 28 homers, and driving in 85 runs.

The Yankees had everything: a power-hitting outfield, a coveted pitching staff, and a largely veteran infield regarded as without equal, defensively, in the American League. The team's third baseman, Clete Boyer—a certain Gold Glove winner had it not been for the presence of future Hall of Famer Brooks Robinson in Baltimore—regularly dived to rob foes of extra-base hits.

At second base was Gold Glove winner Bobby Richardson, whose skill and savvy had saved the Yankees a year earlier in the World Series against the Giants, when he made a quick two-out throw to home plate in the bottom of the ninth inning of Game 7 to hold a San Francisco runner at third base and next caught a liner off the bat of Giants' slugger Willie McCovey for the Series' final out. Richardson had joined with Yankees shortstop Tony Kubek to form one of the best double-play combinations in the majors; the duo was known among their teammates as the "Milkshake Twins" for their sedate off-field nights. His eight All-Star appearances and five Gold Gloves obscured Richardson's greatest importance to his team: no other Yankee better personified the team's commitment to doing the small, unflashy things necessary to win. Not once during the 1963 regular season had he struck out twice in a game, fanning only twenty-two times during the entire season, making him among the most difficult players to whiff in baseball history. Typically saving his best for last during championship seasons, Richardson was likely to bedevil the Dodgers while leaving the headlines for others.

Remarkably for a team with so many stars, the Yankees were free of prima donnas and malcontents. No dissension had resulted from the team's on-field changes when old inevitably gave way to young. Years before, Berra had made way for Howard. At the beginning of 1963, twenty-two-year-old Joe Pepitone took over at first base from an aging Bill "Moose" Skowron, who was shrewdly traded to the Dodgers before the start of the season, in a display of Yankee prescience. At twenty-six, outfielder Tom Tresh had emerged as a regular alongside Mantle and Maris, rewarding the faith of Yankee management by hitting twenty-five homers. And twenty-four-year-old pitcher Jim Bouton had won twenty-one games in 1963, becoming an All-Star in his first full season as a frontline starter.

The Yankees made no effort to hide their confidence. Yankee manager Houk penned a syndicated newspaper article in which he predicted victory in the Series. "Now as to why we expect to win," Houk wrote, before launching into a rundown of what he regarded as the Yankees' chief attributes: a lineup "with a run-making potential that should put us on top"; a team "in the best condition we've been in all year"; the return of a healthy Mantle and Maris; "a fine defensive club"; and strong pitching. Houk expressed confidence in the ability of Ford and young left-hander Al Downing to limit the Dodgers' running and base stealing. "It's tough to steal on Whitey and Downing," he added. "We're not going to worry about [the Dodgers] stealing so much. Maybe they won't get on base that often."

Privately, Houk was even more optimistic. He would wait a decade before disclosing his most personal thoughts during a chat with a trusted friend, Dick Tracewski, by then one of Houk's coaches for the Tigers. Houk told Tracewski that he hadn't thought the Yankees could possibly lose the Series, that all the Dodger pitchers had appeared beatable to him. The Yankees had earlier faced Koufax in a spring training game, during which neither his fastball nor his vaunted curve had awed them. He was a solid pitcher but ultimately incapable of stopping the Yankees, thought Houk, who believed that his team's lineup would humble everyone on the Dodgers' pitching staff. Offensively and defensively, their execution would prove decisive, Houk believed. There was no chance the Yankees wouldn't win. They were the Yankees, after all.

It was a very New York attitude. It helped to explain the love and hate for the Yankees. It accounted, at that very moment, for the mania and madness around the Dodger ticket booth. People had to see the Yankees play. People especially had to see the champions if they believed a team of their own had a chance to topple them. And Los Angeles fans did, as confident as New Yorkers about the Series' outcome.

The frenzy over the 1963 Series extended to television viewership. NBC projected that its Series telecasts would be seen by an average of 40 million fans for each weekday game, rising to 60 million for the weekend games, the largest television audiences in history for an American sporting event. The numbers reflected an unprecedented intensity that spanned two coasts now, stoked by civic delirium and old enmities. In Los Angeles, which long had seen itself as the equal of any sports city on the planet, the Series represented, among other things, a chance to demonstrate that a new municipal power had arrived. In Brooklyn, with bitterness over O'Malley and the Dodgers' departure as raw as ever, many jilted fans were rooting for the long-hated Yankees to kick in the teeth of their old team.

Throughout the rest of New York City, the Dodgers' return to the Series triggered joyous anticipation of a Yankees' rout as well as mirth over memories of previous Dodger ineptitude. It would be the first opportunity since the 1956 World Series to see the Dodgers in Yankee Stadium, a happy event for Yankee lovers, like Roman leaders welcoming back serfs into the Colosseum to be eaten by the lions.

HOLLYWOOD AND THE NEW DODGERS

If Brooklyn's sense of abandonment wasn't reason enough to ignite New Yorkers' competitive furies, the indignation spawned by the Dodgers' Hollywood glamour would be. Several young Dodgers stars, whose fame had come only after arriving in Los Angeles, now guest-starred occasionally on major television sitcoms. Suddenly familiar faces in American living rooms, they were reminders to New Yorkers and Los Angelenos alike that the team had been altogether reinvented on the West Coast, expunged of any vestige of Brooklyn.

It was more evidence of a new breed of Dodger, and affirmation in the view of Los Angeles's fans that their city was simply the place to be. Television couldn't get enough of their stars. Just weeks earlier, Koufax, John Roseboro, Willie Davis, and Dodger third-base coach Leo Durocher had appeared in an episode of *Mr. Ed*, the hugely popular CBS comedy about a high-maintenance talking horse who regularly wisecracked and groused about his life to his exasperated owner. Mr. Ed wanted a tryout with the Dodgers, so of course Mr. Ed got a tryout with the Dodgers.

Mr. Ed and his film crew went out to Dodger Stadium to do the scenes, one of which involved a serious-looking Koufax standing on the mound, peering in for the catcher's sign from Roseboro, then going into his windup and pitching to Mr. Ed, who, clenching the bat between his big teeth, naturally hit a home run and trotted around the bases. Young Dodger fans were out of their heads with giddiness. *Mr. Ed in Dodger Stadium. With Koufax.* Was there any cooler team than the Dodgers?

The Dodgers represented the model of the superstar athlete to come, one with a wryer sense of sports as showbiz and quick to see the benefits in moving back and forth between baseball and the entertainment world. Although he didn't have much acting talent, Koufax popped up on other TV shows, playing a cop on a flashy detective series, ABC's *77 Sunset Strip*, and a Civil War cavalryman in a Western. Drysdale did an episode of *The Rifleman*, with Chuck Connors. Always a popular figure, Wills played his banjo on TV variety shows.

The biggest names in Hollywood wanted the players for their shows. Bob Hope already had signed Koufax, Drysdale, and Tommy Davis to appear on a network special with him once the World Series ended. Milton Berle was negotiating with Wills and several other Dodgers to do a string of hotel shows with him in Miami Beach and Las Vegas. The comedian Danny Kaye released a popular song about the Dodgers, simultaneously paying homage and affectionately skewering them. Never had the Brooklyn stars received so much attention.

By then, near the end of the Dodgers' sixth season in California, any emotional bond to Brooklyn had vanished for the Dodgers. Far from feeling like their city had stolen the Dodgers, Los Angeles's public officials, media, and fans made no secret of their befuddlement over how New York had kept the club so long. They gleefully reserved their harshest scorn for the alienating New York bureaucrat Robert Moses, whose absolute power as Gotham's construction czar had permitted him to unilaterally thwart O'Malley's dream of building a new stadium in Brooklyn, thereby guaranteeing the Dodgers' exodus.

The cutting conclusion in Los Angeles was that Brooklyn hadn't been big-time enough for the Dodgers. It was as if the team's presence in Brooklyn, pre-1958, was merely prelude to where the Dodgers were fated to be all along, in a land regarded by locals as possessing superior vision, support, amenities, and climate. For Los Angelenos, the union of their city and the Dodgers—like the marriage of San Francisco with the former New York Giants—was baseball's version of manifest destiny and westward expansion.

Los Angeles had rewarded O'Malley's boldness, city officials pointed out. In Dodger Stadium, the team had already broken the major-league record for home attendance in a single season, welcoming 2.7 million fans in 1962. Brooklyn had never drawn as many as 1.8 million to the bandbox that was Ebbets Field, and the Yankees wouldn't reach even 1.4 million at home in 1963. Los Angeles's baseball market offered riches Brooklyn never imagined.

Los Angeles sportswriters no longer mentioned Brooklyn, except in passing references to retired players or old games. Seldom was a Brooklyn cap spotted in the stands at Dodger Stadium. Even old Brooklyn parlance associated with the Dodgers, like "Dem Bums," was passé. The moniker had never caught on in Los Angeles, where nobody talked Brooklynese.

O'Malley had seen to it that Los Angeles's identity especially asserted itself in his new ballpark, which was the antithesis of tiny and malodorous Ebbets Field and the cramped Brooklyn neighborhood that had surrounded it. Dodger Stadium stood by itself on 300 acres in Chavez Ravine, with a view of rustic hills and 150 acres set aside for parking alone. It could have doubled as several airport runways. Its clusters of towering palm trees behind the bleachers, always visible during national telecasts of games, stood as totemic reminders to Southern Californians of the good life they were leading, as well as a signal to New York observers of all they were missing.

Los Angeles was arguably the first baseball metropolis with a superiority complex over New York and its teams. No other city boasted more of its scenic advantages and its sense of inventiveness and dynamism, with Los Angeles boosters observing that Southern California just naturally spawned winners in every endeavor, as if this were a birthright. As the World Series approached, a wave of prominent Los Angeles entertainment and media figures including many New York transplants coolly predicted that the Dodgers would win.

O'MALLEY'S GOLD MINE

If one Dodger accounted most for Los Angeles's optimism, it was Koufax. He had just finished one of the greatest regular seasons in history, with his eleven shutouts in 1963 breaking the major-league record for left-handed pitchers, set thirty years earlier, by Hall of Famer Carl Hubbell of the New York Giants. He had thrown his second no-hitter in as many years, this time against the Giants. A certainty to win the Cy Young Award as the best pitcher of the year, he led the National League, indeed the entire majors, with twenty-five wins, an earned run average of 1.88, and 306 strikeouts, a trio of statistical achievements that in time would be regarded by baseball analysts as a pitcher's version of a Triple Crown. A half century later he would be only one of three pitchers in history to have won a trifecta of these Triple Crowns.

By 1963 Koufax had emerged as O'Malley's gold mine, drawing an estimated 5,000 to 10,000 extra spectators to Dodger Stadium whenever he pitched. That increase over the Dodgers' average attendance conservatively translated in 1963 to an extra $50,000 in ticket, parking, and concessions revenue per game for the owner, and roughly an extra $1.05 million in total for twenty-one Koufax home appearances that season, in addition to all the extra Dodger income generated by Koufax's role in leading the Dodgers to the pennant and sellout World Series games.

At twenty-seven, Koufax had become the national media's darling that summer. *Life* magazine put him on the cover in August, and if the publication hadn't photographed him in his Dodger uniform, readers might have reasonably thought they were looking at a svelte, dark-haired film star. With an endearingly earnest expression, he bore a resemblance to a young Gregory Peck.

Koufax dated actresses, if quietly. He did everything quietly—and, most of the time, out of sight. He was so often mobbed going into Los Angeles restaurants and businesses that he avoided most public places. The abundance of his worshippers tripped something that thereafter left him acutely uncomfortable with adoring throngs and fiercely protective of his privacy.

Aside from his pitching, his reserve defined Koufax. Courteously soft-spoken, he managed the impressive feat of cogently answering reporters' questions without ever revealing much about his hopes, anxieties, or life. He was the most famous athlete of the sixties to be a blank sheet to so many. There was no hint of arrogance in this. Indeed, the mere possibility that he might ever be seen as arrogant concerned him, to the point that occasionally he would go out of his way to make sure that fans realized their hope of seeing him up close.

Few star pitchers ever deigned to throw in front of crowds between their game appearances. But during an annual pregame Dodger promotion called Camera Day, where anyone with a camera at Dodger Stadium could line up at the railing of the field box seats and snap photographs of his favorite Dodgers, Koufax would step onto a warm-up mound near the team dugout, go into his windup, and proceed to pitch easily to a catcher for about ten minutes, while thousands of admirers rapturously clicked away. He would turn in various directions as his posing session neared its end, responding to howling fans' pleas that he look this this way or that. He wanted to be kind to everybody, Koufax told his good friend Wills. It just wasn't in him to be gregarious, and he didn't need to be idolized. Already he had established an ineffable distance between himself and the world, with fans left to study him as if through a pane of glass.

He was both remote and perfect to them, like a revered royal. He had a charisma born entirely of the possibility that fans might be looking at the greatest pitcher ever, someone as close to perfection at his art as they were ever likely to see. Sometimes just the right photograph captured his elegance on the mound, either his very slow high leg kick or his long, powerful stride to home plate as he released the ball. He looked, when frozen in the images, less like a pitcher than a piece of sculpture, a masterpiece perhaps. And O'Malley owned the rights to the masterpiece—for $35,000 a year.

THE FLAW OF THE INVINCIBLE FOE AND A STUBBORN LEAGUE

That Koufax would be regarded as a slim betting underdog to Whitey Ford in Game 1, even in Yankee Stadium, privately amused the Dodgers, especially Wills, who thought it betrayed easterners' bias and their unfamiliarity with Koufax's dominance. If Koufax had his good stuff, Wills believed, the Yankees were in deep trouble.

We can beat them, he privately told people.

One of the people to whom he said it was Walter O'Malley, whom he always addressed as "Mr. O'Malley." A broadly smiling O'Malley congratulated him on winning the pennant and then, as was the owner's way, ribbed the captain a little, asking whether he was going to get any hits in the Series.

I'll get some hits, Wills said and laughed, playing along with the boss.

Feeling good? O'Malley asked him.

Feeling really good, Mr. O'Malley, Wills said.

He thought he had detected a flaw in the Yankees. It wasn't obvious, it wasn't even visible, but the flaw was there just the same. The Yankees' supremacy had come in a league whose players generally stole far fewer bases and seldom tested defenses by daringly attempting to stretch singles and doubles into something more. Playing a full season, the American League's stolen base leader, Luis Aparicio, had swiped forty bases in 1963, a mark that Wills had matched despite missing a good portion of the year. And Aparicio was the American League's only formidable stolen base threat. Many of the American League's baserunners moved only when safe, just one base at a time, in a deliberate style that came to be labeled station-to-station ball.

The National League could hardly have been more different. The most notable stars in the National League regularly ran, with home run hitters like Henry Aaron and Frank Robinson right behind Wills on the list of stolen base leaders, which included several other black ballplayers, including Willie Davis. Wills privately believed that any inquisitive analyst would need to go all the way back to 1955, when Jackie Robinson successfully stole home in Yankee Stadium during Game 1 of that year's World Series, to find the last time the Yankees had faced an opponent with so many daring baserunners as the 1963 Dodgers. In recent years, the Yankees had never confronted speed like the Dodgers', Wills told teammates—New York had no idea of the unnerving pressure that speed placed on a foe.

Wills thought the Yankees' unfamiliarity with prolific base theivery was just one of the consequences of the American League's long delay during the 1950s in racially integrating many of their teams. Those weaknesses had been exacerbated by the same teams' hesitancy to play more than a handful of blacks as starters over the years. The Yankees had only three black players on their entire roster, aside from Elston Howard. And not one African American had ever played as a regular in the Yankees infield.

African Americans had come to the Yankees late. More than seven years after the Dodgers had integrated their team, the Yankees still hadn't welcomed a black player. Finally, in 1955, the club called up Howard. Several other American League teams had been even slower to accept African Americans. As the last of the established major-league clubs to integrate, the Boston Red Sox waited until 1959 before making infielder Elijah Jerry "Pumpsie" Green its first black player.

Wills thought the American League's social foot-dragging had rendered it an inferior league. "Look at all the black stars that went to the National League," he remembers. "Almost everybody. All the black players on our team talked about it. We'd tell each other it's such an advantage in talent, athleticism, and speed for us and other teams in the National League."

And no team in the National League had more speed than the Dodgers. Speed created chaos, Wills believed. In the ponderous American League, the Yankees had never played against the Dodgers' brand of chaos. It was a weakness, and he was determined to personally exploit it.

To that end, it was important, he thought, that no one on his team view the Yankees as invincible or special. On the day before the Series began, at a Dodgers team meeting and workout in Yankee Stadium, he told his teammates that they were simply going to do to the Yankees what they had done against every other opponent: run.

TRIXIE AND KOUFAX

With the team assembled in Yankee Stadium, on the day before Game 1, Al Campanis, the Dodgers' director of scouting, presented his staff's report on the Yankees, believing he had found a few vulnerabilities: *Pepitone has a weak arm; Boyer doesn't like curveballs; Kubek is vulnerable to being picked off base; Elston Howard can be contained if he's prevented from pulling pitches.*

But mostly, in an admission of the Yankees' prowess, the scouting report was full of warnings for Koufax and the rest of the pitching staff. *Don't throw any changeups to Mantle, because he crushes those pitches. Don't feed Maris many fastballs because he is a dead fastball hitter—and whatever you do, don't let Maris extend his arms on a fastball or he'll hit it so deep in the seats you'll get whiplash watching it. Don't throw a high fastball to Richardson, because he doesn't miss that pitch ever. Don't throw anything inside to Elston Howard or Pepitone, or they'll make you pay.*

Utility infielder Dick Tracewski listened with no small awe. They sound damn good, he thought.

Tracewski fidgeted, preoccupied by the grandeur of Yankee Stadium. He had dreamed of playing there since childhood. The ballpark of ghosts, of Ruth and Gehrig, it was a sacred edifice to him. He felt a bit unnerved. "The ballpark was intimidating," he recalls. "I glanced up at that facade the Yankees have at the top, and I'm thinking, I'm in Yankee Stadium; we're going to play these guys. The ballpark was quirky. It had those monuments and the flagpole right out there in the field of play, in center field. *In the field of play.* Who else does that? But they were the Yankees. Everything there reminded you it was their place. Not that being intimidated was going to matter in my case. I didn't think I was going to play much at all, which was okay."

Tracewski was thrilled just to be on a World Series roster. It was hard to imagine a ballplayer—or a person in any walk of life—more content with his lot than Tracewski. He was twenty-eight, aware he would never be a star, and okay with being a reserve, after eight seasons in the minor leagues.

Four years earlier, as an army private, he sat in a military barracks just outside Atlanta, riveted to telecasts of the Dodgers playing the White Sox in the Series. Once a contender in the battle to succeed Reese at shortstop, Tracewski watched for two years while in the service as Wills, once behind him in the minor-league pecking order, leapfrogged over him and other rivals for the starting shortstop job.

A man known for his equanimity, Tracewski felt no bitterness. That's just life, he'd told himself in the barracks, finding solace in the realization he would resume his baseball career soon enough. He'd studied Wills carefully during the 1959 Series, recalling an old conversation with a gossiping Dodger official who had mocked Wills's defense. Tracewski, believing the scout had missed the obvious, thought Wills was demonstrating quick, nimble feet and a gun for an arm. Wills, a prescient Tracewski had decided, was on his way to big things.

Soon Tracewski realized that Wills was the shortstop of the present and future. He was just fine with that. He was grateful for everything he had in life, unaffected by the demons that haunted some of his teammates. He came from a close family. He'd grown up near Scranton, Pennsylvania, in a little town called Eynon, loved watching baseball with his father, had never struggled with depression or alcohol, had a solid marriage, resented no one who'd climbed above him in the Dodger pecking order, and was an enormously popular figure in the Dodger clubhouse, regarded by teammates as a good listener, easygoing, and willing to play in a pinch wherever and whenever he was asked.

They called him "Trixie." Trixie didn't complain, they said. A few teammates, like Wills, envied Tracewski for his serenity—he just never seemed to get down. Bavasi, never one for lavish shows of affection, expressed his gratitude to him for being such a steady guy. Officials generally didn't call Tracewski a "reserve" or "utility man" but rather an "extra player," which sounded so much more generous, as well as a reflection of how much he meant to everybody.

Finally having been called up to the majors the year before at the advanced baseball age of twenty-seven, with the understanding that he would play only when one of the Dodgers' regular infielders needed a day off or was injured, Tracewski prided himself on being ready when his chances arrived. Nineteen sixty-three had brought his big break. With Wills sidelined early in the season by a leg injury, Tracewski found himself playing shortstop every day for a stretch. On other days, he played second base in place of Jim Gilliam, who found himself forced to move over to third base to fill in for injured starter Ken McMullen. By season's end, Tracewski had played in eighty-one games at short and another twenty-three at second, and though he had hit only .226, his steadiness with the glove had made him indispensable.

But every Dodger regular was seemingly healthy now and ready to play in the Series. Tracewski had returned to his spot in the shadows. He could live with it. It was why men as different as Wills and Bavasi so valued him. He would quietly reassume his role as human insurance, sitting in the corner of the dugout, to be utilized only if one of the regulars came up lame, which wouldn't and couldn't happen, because no regular was going to miss out on a World Series against the Yankees.

On the eve of the Series, during the team's workout at Yankee Stadium, Tracewski was loosening up when Dodger coaches Pete Reiser and Leo Durocher walked over.

It looks like you're going to play, Durocher said.

McMullen had reinjured himself. Gilliam would need to take over at third base.

You're going to be the starter at second, probably for the entire Series, Reiser told him.

Tracewski was stunned. He called his family and shared the news with his father, Joseph, and sister Henrietta, who would be coming to the first game. By then, all the Dodgers, including Koufax, knew of the lineup change. Koufax looked unruffled. He seemed calm about everything happening around him, Tracewski thought.

No one on the team, not even Wills, was as close off the field to Koufax as Tracewski. They often roomed together, ate together, even spent some holidays together with Tracewski's wife and daughter. Tracewski never would be able to put a finger precisely on what accounted for their personal chemistry. "We were just relaxed around each other," he said. "There was just something there. Sandy didn't like being the center of attention. He was always modest, so you had to know that about him. We didn't go to a lot of places or do a lot of things."

Earlier that year, during an off day in Pittsburgh, Tracewski had glimpsed the suffocating attention that enveloped his friend. The two walked into a drugstore, where customers immediately recognized Koufax. "It created a ruckus—there were people all over," Tracewski remembers. He would forever remember the discomfort etched on his friend's face. "It was just wild in that store. And that was Pittsburgh. There was no place in the country he wasn't recognized. I much better understood things after that. He really couldn't go out to dinner."

Even if Koufax had been left alone by fans, Tracewski knew his friend wasn't much for running around: "He just didn't want to do anything to tire himself. He pitched every four days—not five days like most pitchers did in later years—so rest was critical. That's part of why he didn't play golf with anybody, even on off days. He was afraid to hurt his back or neck. He had a job. That's the way he saw it. He wanted his arm right."

As close friends, the two discussed nearly everything, including the art of pitching, the finest details of which Koufax was reserved about with most others, as if to divulge too much about either his philosophy or skills would leave him compromised. Typically power pitchers prided themselves on their ability to prevail with their fastball. They liked the mano a mano feel of it. They relished watching a foe whiffing at air.

But the attitude sometimes betrayed hubris, the very thing that Koufax assiduously guarded against. He had no interest in mano a mano. He preferred to fool and frustrate good hitters when he could. In fact, he didn't mind if the greats of the National League—Willie Mays, Hank Aaron, Frank Robinson, and Roberto Clemente among them—occasionally had success against him, just so long as he kept their teammates off base.

Tracewski listened as Koufax opened windows onto his in-game hopes and worries. Contrary to the popular assumption that he had infinite belief in the wonder of his fastball's velocity, Koufax told Tracewski he had no real confidence in blowing away an opponent with a 98-mile-per-hour heater when the pitch found its way onto the inner half of the plate, in a hitter's wheelhouse. "Sandy always felt that if he made a mistake, it would be on the inside—that it was the only place where he really could get hurt," Tracewski says. "He was just a two-pitch pitcher—a fastball and curve—but they were the best fastball and curve in either league. So he was going to do fine unless his control was off. Being careful was all he had to worry about."

Especially with runners on base and games on the line, Koufax made his career almost entirely on the outer half of home plate. "He could throw it at ninety-eight in a spot as small as a cup on the outside corner," Tracewski remembers. "A cup." After that, the only task remaining was to discourage hitters from looking exclusively for the outside pitch. "He just had to come inside enough to keep hitters honest, to keep them from leaning over the plate. Pitching was mostly about finesse for him. A lot of people didn't understand: he was much more than a power pitcher. And when he got a couple of strikeouts on inside pitches, it encouraged him. He thought it'd be a shutout then, because everything was working. And he'd want those shutouts. He took pride in those kinds of accomplishments and statistics. That was important to advancing, to getting the better money."

His friend's characteristic humility had led observers to overlook his fierce pride, thought Tracewski, who knew of Koufax's tougher side. Earlier that year, Tracewski had joined Koufax, Roseboro, and Alston at the mound, late during a game at the outdoor stadium of the Houston Colt '.45s. It was an oppressively hot Texas day, the climate-controlled Houston Astrodome had yet to be built, and Koufax, drenched in sweat but nursing a lead, looked tired. The time seemed right to remove him. The bullpen had a reliever ready to go. Alston asked Koufax how he felt.

"I feel like shit," Koufax answered. "But I'm better than anybody you have out there."

Alston walked back to the dugout. Koufax finished the game with a victory.

TOMMY DAVIS COMES HOME TO BROOKLYN

No two Dodgers could quite agree on what Koufax was really like. Not truly knowing what he was ever thinking, people tended to see what they wanted to see in Koufax, Tommy Davis thought—it was like a Rorschach test. Wills thought Koufax was forever forgiving of his mistakes in the field. Davis saw a steelier, more demanding Koufax. Once, when Hank Aaron lifted a fly ball off Koufax to left field, Davis misjudged it and the ball landed over his head for a double. Koufax turned on the mound, put his hands on his hips, and looked out at Davis, who thought he detected some not-so-faint irritation in his expression. "He's tougher than you think; you don't really know him," Davis told people. "I love Sandy, but Sandy gets pissed off like anybody else."

Davis would see Koufax's anger on display away from baseball. In later years, Davis and Koufax would join a group of other athletes from a variety of sports on a celebrity basketball team, their games meant to be casual affairs benefiting charities. Koufax, who at six-two had starred on the court as a New York high schooler and later won a partial scholarship and a spot on the University of Cincinnati's basketball team, played the game with a ferocity belying his gentlemanly baseball image. "Sandy was rough," Davis remembers. "Rough rebounder, rough player. He banged guys hard. And if he thought somebody was playing unfairly, it could get bad. We had to stop him once from going after somebody. Fans thought he was easygoing? Shiiit."

The two had much in common, beginning with their Brooklyn backgrounds. Davis had multiple athletic talents of his own—at once a schoolboy basketball star, standout track and field performer, and outstanding third baseman and outfielder who loved the Dodgers and spent much of his boyhood attending games at Ebbets Field. But the Dodgers hadn't pursued Davis with the same zeal as scouts from the Reds, Indians, and Yankees. Trying to accommodate his dual sports interests, an official from the Reds had even offered to make arrangements for Davis to play basketball at Providence University before he began in the Reds' minor-league system. "Black players were getting more attention by then," Davis recalls.

But no team showed the high schooler more attention, during the late 1950s, than the Yankees, suddenly alert to the need to sign more young black talent. Eager officials gave Davis a locker at Yankee Stadium and regularly invited him to work out there. Bill Skowron, by then entrenched as a Yankee starter, loaned him a glove one day. "The money being offered wasn't really big, but Yankee people couldn't have been nicer," Davis remembers. "And I kept thinking: it's the Yankees." Davis looked on his way toward becoming in time the Bronx Bombers' new black star, cast in the mold of a dignified Elston Howard, yet another halting Yankees' step in a slow transition toward a more multiracial club.

In 1956, on the brink of signing with the Yankees, Davis was at home one night when the phone rang. The voice on the other end of the phone said, "This is Jackie Robinson . . ." Davis didn't hear much, if anything, else. He understood the essential message: his hero Jackie Robinson wanted him to sign with the Brooklyn Dodgers.

Another cost of the Yankees' failure to have integrated their team many years earlier revealed itself in that instant: Davis wanted to be with the team that had broken the color barrier. He quickly signed with Brooklyn.

Yet Davis's three-year stint in the minors during the late 1950s had included humiliations familiar to black players. In 1958, even white fans who appreciated his play for the Dodgers' Double-A farm club in Victoria, Texas, sometimes referred to him with the N-word, and he quickly realized that parts of Victoria were entirely off limits to him. Unlike many black players, especially those who had grown up in the South, Davis hadn't previously experienced the daily evils of racism and segregation. He had seldom confronted discrimination during his youth in the Bedford-Stuyvesant community of Brooklyn, better known to residents as Bed-Stuy. There, Davis remembers, he had "Puerto Rican friends, Irish friends, Polish friends, Jewish friends, Italian friends—we got along." Never had anyone in a Bed-Stuy restaurant or shop denied service to him and black friends. He guessed that, if anyone had tried, "We would've kicked his ass. But that never happened to us in Brooklyn."

Growing up largely free of prejudice and harassment had girded Davis with the belief that the overt racism he was enduring in many minor-league cities would not, could not, last in the country; that racial segregation was on its way toward becoming an American relic, and that he shouldn't defer any more than absolutely necessary in the face of it. "I wouldn't take much crap," he said.

The bigotry he experienced enraged and transformed Davis, leaving him to look for a way to strike a blow against segregation after he ascended to the majors in 1960. One target in particular seemed obvious. In 1962, he and several other black Dodgers decided to push the O'Malley family to integrate seating at Holman Stadium, the Vero Beach spring training ballpark.

Until then, the black players had displayed an unwavering stoicism in the face of segregation's humiliations. During spring training games for the visiting Dodgers against the Baltimore Orioles, the Miami hotel that housed the team barred black players from staying there with their white teammates. The Dodgers organization, never publicly condemning the social codes of the hotel or the rest of segregationist Florida, simply responded to the indignity by booking rooms for the black players in a hotel across town, one popular with black entertainers. To spare their ostracized players from having to meet the Dodger bus at the all-white hotel in the mornings, club officials rented cars for them to drive to the ballpark while they were in Miami. Just as in the country at large, "separate" was often treated as "equal" in baseball, and the Dodger brass quietly, if reluctantly, acceded to the arrangement.

For several years, living in a denial of their own, Davis and other black players had sold each other on the idea that their separate facilities during the spring training road games offered advantages. "We told ourselves it was great having those rental cars and going wherever we wanted," he remembered.

The players could live with Florida's everyday racism, they thought, so long as it didn't absolutely trample their dignity or touch their doorstep. They could tolerate discriminatory practices anywhere except in Dodgertown and at the stadium in which they hosted their spring training games. Holman Stadium was more than their doorstep: it was the center of their working home. By 1962, they had become fed up with the ballpark's acquiescence to racism. Racially segregated seating arrangements for white and black fans, and separate drinking fountains and bathrooms, had been constants since the opening of Holman Stadium. "We just thought, No more," Davis remembers. "We were the Dodgers. We were the team that had broken barriers. We weren't going to put up with this stuff Vero Beach was doing with our ballpark. We were going to have to get him to do something about it."

"Him" meant the O'Malley family's scion, young Peter O'Malley. Not long out of college, he was learning the baseball business, in preparation for inheriting ownership of the Dodgers one day. His responsibilities under his father included the management of operations at Holman Stadium and thus the handling of the very kind of issue to be raised by Davis and the other players.

Vero Beach's thorny history with the Dodgers complicated Davis's mission. In 1948, as the team prepared to inhabit roughly 220 acres once serving as an American naval station, players were slated to settle into barracks that, according to a Vero Beach's ordinance, had to be separated by race; the town prohibited privately or publicly integrated housing of any kind. This dictate was unacceptable to a team that had staked out a moral position by signing Robinson, Newcombe, and Campenella. If Vero Beach pushed, black players might not stand for the law. If the team stayed under such circumstances, the charges of

Dodger hypocrisy and the ensuing internal divisions would be devastating. Walter O'Malley issued no public comment about the ordinance. Instead, in his agreement to move into Vero Beach, he and his allies simply saw to it that Dodgertown would be run and overseen by Dodger officials, not by the town's authorities or police force. It was a winning gambit, one that permitted O'Malley and the Dodgers to integrate their barracks while enabling Vero Beach officials to pretend they had no idea what was going on there. It was baseball's version of Don't Ask, Don't Tell.

In cutting a deal to get what he wanted, however, the owner had to accept one onerous condition from Vero Beach officials: in accordance with another city ordinance, spring training games at Dodgertown could only be played before racially segregated spectators, who would be compelled to use segregated bathrooms, entrances, and drinking fountains. The arrangement would endure for the next fourteen years at Holman Stadium.

Walter O'Malley's silence about racial issues always left black players uncertain how he would react if pressed hard about segregation in Florida. When Davis approached Peter O'Malley and demanded the integration of the Dodgertown ballpark, the owner's family suddenly faced an unavoidable civil rights challenge much like that faced by the country's most important leader.

Early in his presidency, John Kennedy told a keenly disappointed Martin Luther King Jr. that there would be no chance for the passage of a civil rights bill during the first two years of his administration. Despite his office, Kennedy at that moment didn't have enough influence within the US Congress to defeat a potential Senate filibuster led by southern opponents. For many establishment Democrats, the political risks of offending white southern Democratic power barons made them cautious on civil rights to the point of paralysis.

The O'Malley family had constituencies of their own to satisfy—millions of white fans to be sure, but also their star black players, on whose talents the team had depended for years. The players' stature gave them a decisive clout by then. Led by an indignant Tommy Davis, a group that included Roseboro, Gilliam, Wills, and Willie Davis went to Peter O'Malley and demanded an end to segregation in the Vero Beach ballpark, which had largely limited blacks to sitting in the right-field corner and in a small area by the left-field foul pole. The shame of the segregated bathrooms, segregated drinking fountains, and separate entrances into the ballpark compounded the wrong, the players added. Holman Stadium was part of Dodgertown, and Dodgertown was not the South, they told the younger O'Malley.

The players asked the heir apparent how a team integrated more than a decade earlier by Jackie Robinson could continue to tolerate segregation in its own facilities, in its own *home*. Several of the players, long having wondered whether Peter O'Malley was anything more than a junior underling cosseted by his family's wealth and privilege, found themselves impressed by his seriousness. "We told him, 'This was the place where Jackie came to play for our team—this is where Jackie stood,'" Tommy Davis remembered. "We told him, 'We are the Dodgers. We don't do this. We don't stand for this. Vero Beach can do what it wants, but this is Dodgertown—we don't do things like that here.' We kept talking and Peter listened very respectfully."

Well into the next century, Peter O'Malley would remember the moment. "Tommy pointed out things we were negligent on," he recalls. "He was eloquent. And I knew he was right."

What Davis didn't know at that moment was the extent to which the young O'Malley had already plunged himself into desegregating the ballpark. In an effort to build support for striking down, or at least rendering unenforceable, the repugnant Vero Beach ordinance, O'Malley had privately met with sympathetic whites from Vero Beach and several African Americans from the nearly all-black town of Gifford, building a coalition.

By the time Davis finished speaking to him, O'Malley had pledged full support. When the team arrived at the ballpark for the next game, a couple of days later, Davis discovered that segregated bathrooms had been integrated. A Dodger employee, operating on orders from the junior O'Malley, had painted over the word *Colored* everywhere he could find it in the stadium. "I think we handled everything smoothly, smartly, rightly," Peter O'Malley remembers. At the start of this new chapter in the history of Holman Stadium, O'Malley found Tommy Davis, updated him on everything done, and thanked him, to which Davis said, "Peter, that's great. Thank you."

Davis thought in that moment that the victory was complete. What he didn't know was that the O'Malley family had acted unilaterally, without the approval of Vero Beach officials. The strict segregation ordinance of the town remained on the books, if Vero Beach wished to enforce it. But Davis was in no mood for anything except the immediate upheaval of the disgraced old order. Stepping out on the field, believing integration was the new way of the ballpark, Davis walked with Gilliam and Roseboro to the restricted right-field seating area and told the black spectators there that they could move—*should move*—to other seats, better seats, around the stadium. The days of segregation around Holman were over, Davis explained. Go grab some nice seats around home plate or anywhere you want. Enjoy the game.

Most of the black fans looked blankly at him, not moving. Their timidity made him ache. Davis realized the truth: after generations of dictates and threats from Vero Beach's white officials, most black fans segregated on their own. The sight of intimidated black men and women infuriated him. He couldn't take any more of their fear. Segregation had never struck him as more otherworldly in its evil. He began dispensing orders to groups of black spectators: *You guys get up and go sit behind home plate; you guys over there go sit behind first base; you guys go behind third base. There's going to be a new way now. You don't have to stay out here in right field. We're integrating the ballpark. Come on. Let's go. Sit anywhere you want. Have fun.*

The small group of fans looked at him, Davis recalled, like he was crazy. "But finally they did it. They got up and sat all around the stadium. They integrated it everywhere."

At any time, Vero Beach's officials could have charged the Dodgers with being in violation of its segregation ordinance. They didn't. Making no fuss, the officials quietly rolled over. By then, the Dodgers' enormous economic impact on the city had made the team's presence critical to Vero Beach's welfare. The ordinance died in time from disuse. The Dodgers' black players had realized a victory uncommon to that point in the civil rights movement. During that spring, with critical assistance from Peter O'Malley, no one in the American sporting world exercised more momentous social clout than Tommy Davis and his small band of teammates.

In such moments, Davis was especially proud of his background. He loved Bed-Stuy, especially for how the community had molded him into a strong and assertive man. But by the time he finally made it to the majors for good in 1960, the Dodgers had long before left Brooklyn behind. Davis was one of the few young Dodgers torn over the team's decision to abandon New York, though he'd also pondered the possibility that its departure from Brooklyn might have been a blessing in disguise; otherwise, he might have hung out with his old boyhood buddies to excess. Too much off-field fun did not go over well with the Dodgers. As it was, he knew Alston in particular harbored doubts about his work ethic, passion, and commitment to team rules. A small incident in 1961 had threatened his Dodger career. Alston, learning that Davis had defied his edict against playing golf, had confronted him, demanding an explanation. Without offering an excuse or apology, Davis simply noted what he thought ought to be obvious to the manager: a bunch of players were secretly playing golf. Alston flared.

"He thought I was a smart-ass," Davis remembers.

At the end of the 1961 season, Davis heard rumors that Alston wanted to get rid of him, but the Dodgers had failed to find an acceptable trade. Davis was proof that some of the best deals in baseball are the ones never made. By 1962, at just twenty-three, Davis had transformed his career and Dodger fortunes by winning the National

League batting crown with a .346 average and leading the league in RBIs with 153. He hit .326 to lead the league again in 1963. Koufax regarded him in that moment as the best pure hitter with whom he'd ever played, a likely Hall of Famer in waiting.

THE ODD NICKNAME

Ready now to play in Game 1 of the Series before family and friends in Yankee Stadium, Davis told people that he had worked out too often in the ballpark to feel intimidated there. Looking around at his teammates, he saw no obvious signs of tension. Koufax seemed especially calm, Davis thought. No other Dodger success story had amazed Davis more than Koufax's ascension, especially given that the pitcher's long, slow climb to greatness had come without the benefit of ever developing his skills in the minors. The Dodgers never had a real choice in the matter. Koufax's $16,000 signing bonus from Brooklyn in 1955 had meant that he—like any player receiving a rookie signing bonus of more than $4,000 in that era—was a so-called bonus baby under baseball's rules, a classification prohibiting the Dodgers from assigning Koufax to the minor leagues without giving other teams an opportunity to sign him for at least two years.

That meant Koufax had no real seasoning at all, no opportunity to make his mistakes and hone his pitches out of the spotlight. Not nearly prepared to pitch to big-leaguers upon his arrival at nineteen with the Dodgers, he rode the bench for weeks at a time, stuck there in limbo for the better part of several seasons, his status plummeting as club officials discovered that he frequently had no control of his pitches. His nonrole infuriated several Brooklyn players who thought he had no place in the club. A few of his bitterest detractors on the Brooklyn club made anti-Semitic remarks about him, overheard by Gilliam and other offended black players, who years later passed the stories along to rookie arrivals, including Wills. Black players, Davis thought, were Koufax's chief allies.

But even among teammates who admired Koufax, their sense of his perfection only added to the perception of his exalted remove. This outlook was, if anything, enhanced by the difference between his religion and most of theirs. In the 1960s, ethnic humor was commonplace on the Dodgers, viewed by its users as a badge of closeness. Koufax and the only other Jew on the Dodgers in 1963, reliever Larry Sherry, had long been hung with nicknames that always ran the risk of giving license to degrading stereotypes and insults.

Koufax's nickname was "the Super Jew." Wills was privately uncomfortable with it. But Koufax's other good friends on the team regularly used it in his presence, and Koufax didn't object, evidently trusting enough in his friends' character and good intentions not to be offended. Sherry, who could be relentlessly grim and blunt during a game, was dubbed "the Rude Jew." His endlessly affable older brother Norm Sherry, a catcher with the team for parts of four years before being traded away after the 1962 season, who never found the nicknames anything but indicators of camaraderie, was called "the Happy Jew."

"We'd tease our Jewish guys, just like we teased our other guys," Tracewski remembers. "Larry and Norm would laugh about it. Whenever Sandy heard 'Super Jew,' he smirked. If somebody asked me who I was having dinner with, sometimes I'd say, 'I'm gonna have dinner with the Super Jew.' Sandy would just have that smirk again. He just wouldn't care."

THE MANAGER AND THE PITCHER

Koufax faced a far greater challenge than the ethnic stereotypes in reading the thinking of key Dodger personnel who enjoyed ultimate sway over his career. No Dodger official had tested his understanding more than Alston, who, as Koufax's manager since his first day in the majors, had been a source of keen frustration for him during the struggles of his early years, when Alston for long stretches declined to use him at all as a starting pitcher. During a period of the 1957 season, Koufax went forty-five days without a start.

Throughout the late 1950s, battling Alston's decisions and his own injuries, losing more games than he won, Koufax was riddled by inconsistency. He led the National League in wild pitches in 1958, but he was sporadically so magnificent that neither Alston nor the Dodgers could afford to give up on him. In 1959 he broke the National League's single-game strikeout record and equaled Bob Feller's major-league mark by setting down eighteen Giants in a game at the Los Angeles Coliseum. That same year, he started Game 5 of the World Series, pitching seven strong innings at the Coliseum against the White Sox, only to lose what would have been a Series-clinching game, 1–0. It was yet another outstanding Koufax performance, but Alston seldom had a compliment about Koufax to pass on to the press.

Their problems weren't helped by a lack of chemistry. Alston never went out of his way to better understand the young prodigy who, as the 1960s began, had yet to master his control or harness all his talents. He was 36–40 in his first six seasons, never having won more than 11 games in a season. Alston had evinced so little curiosity about Koufax's life that, as late as 1961, he still didn't know about Koufax's religious convictions, which included a personal decision not to play on Yom Kippur, the Day of Atonement, the holiest day of the year in Judaism. Unwittingly, Alston scheduled Koufax to pitch on Yom Kippur that year. Only after Koufax reminded club officials that he couldn't pitch that day did Alston agree to take steps to ensure the pitcher wouldn't confront such a conflict again, pledging to learn more about the Jewish holidays.

The two men were courteously professional with each other, though their relationship was never more than symbiotic. Koufax didn't go out of his way to compliment the man who, in private, he often called "Smokey," a nickname that sprang from Alston's habit of smoking cigarettes in dugout runways between innings. He just wanted Smokey to keep giving him the ball, Koufax allowed. For his part, Alston just wanted Koufax to guard against straining on the mound and getting his fastball up in the damn strike zone. They seldom had anything else to say to each other, always respectful, always distant. "They weren't ever going to be close," Tracewski notes. "That wasn't ever going to happen."

In 1961 Koufax's career finally lifted off. He won eighteen games and sat atop the National League in strikeouts. Alston became more attentive. Over the next two seasons, the power subtly changed in their relationship, with Alston suddenly taking pains to pay Koufax public respect. By 1963, in response to questions from reporters covering the World Series, Alston spoke glowingly of his ace, choosing to focus on Koufax's intellect and poise, his responses having become rote. Wrote the *Chicago Tribune*: "Koufax is a calculating, deep-thinking young man. This quality has been emphasized by Dodger manager Walt Alston. . . . Alston says Koufax is so shrewd that he knew all about the science of pitching before he perfected the art."

If Alston might have had any reason left for concern about Koufax, it would have been in the grueling demands placed on his left arm that year. His forty pitching starts and 311 innings during the regular season were the most of his career in either category. Although his workload wasn't regarded at the time as burdensome for the ace of a major-league pitching staff, it was undoubtedly arduous, certain to take its toll if it persisted in future seasons.

With Koufax and other legends of his era regularly pitching on only three days of rest, it was no surprise that some of the titans wilted in the final weeks of a season. An indomitable Koufax had proven to be an exception, as strong in a season's late stages as during its opening weeks. In a series of September performances that delighted Alston, Koufax had pitched brilliantly in the climactic stretch of the 1963 pennant race. The Dodgers traveled to St. Louis for a critical three-game series with the second-place Cardinals, sweeping the contests, with Koufax shutting out the Cardinals in the second game, effectively ending the foes' pennant chances.

In a dominant performance on a hot, steamy St. Louis night, Koufax carried a no-hitter into the seventh inning. Stan Musial, who was playing in his final season, finally singled to center field. Afterward, asked by reporters whether he had made a mistake on the pitch to Musial, Koufax said no. "It was a *good* pitch," he answered serenely, his fastball thrown exactly where he had wanted it, low and outside, where almost no one could touch it. Credit the extraordinary Musial for hitting it, he suggested.

"He's the greatest in baseball this year," said Musial, whose dream of playing in one more World Series was dying.

The next morning, awakening in the St. Louis hotel room that he shared with Tracewski, Koufax was spent. The team still had one game left against the Cardinals. Koufax lay in his bed for a long while, finally eating some breakfast. He turned to Tracewski with a request.

"Tell Smokey I'm not going to the ballpark today," he said.

He could do such a thing now. He had the stature. He also had a very good reason for staying behind: he was flying home so that he could spend Rosh Hashanah, the Jewish New Year, with his parents.

"Sandy told me to tell you he's not coming to the ballpark," Tracewski informed the manager before getting on the team bus.

Alston didn't fully understand. But he smiled, laughed, and said, "Oh, okay, he's staying here."

Tracewski remembers: "Walt didn't care. It was Sandy. And Walt was kind of loose with discipline. But if you gave Walt any indication you didn't give one hundred percent on the field, you had a big problem with him. But Sandy gave us as much as a pitcher could give. That's why he was exhausted so much. Walt knew. Nobody ever questioned Sandy."

The sweep of the Cardinals had made the remainder of the regular season anticlimactic. The baseball world turned all its attention to the Yankees and Dodgers. By then, the approaching confrontation between Koufax and Whitey Ford in Game 1 at Yankee Stadium had the feel of a major New York City prizefight. On the eve of the game, political officials and celebrities pressed to get seats as close as possible to baseball's version of ringside, where Musial (who would throw out the first ball), DiMaggio, and other luminaries would gather in box seats near the dugouts. With a frenzied corps of reporters hungering for any news about the players' moods, the stars of both teams exuded cool, dismissing suggestions that what was coming was anything more than another important game in a season of important games.

Koufax indicated he would do nothing different on the night before Game 1. He'd go to sleep at about midnight, he said, envisioning no special preparation. "I'll start thinking seriously about the game and the hitters when I begin to warm up," he told a newspaper reporter. Around other sportswriters, he denied a rumor that he was recovering from a bout with the flu. What he didn't say was that he had been hit by a cold a few days earlier that had limited his conditioning regimen, his running especially, and that this might come at a cost to his stamina or the pitching power he generated from his legs. "I feel fine and I'll give it my best shot," he said, and was gone.

Tracewski thought his friend appeared relaxed. But Tracewski had worries of his own. He thought that at any moment someone would tell him that he wasn't playing; that McMullen's leg had healed and Trixie would be relegated to the bench. His father and sister, who had driven from Eynon, would be in the stands to see him play—if it happened.

Tommy Davis was spending time with his Brooklyn relatives after a death in the family. A nervous Wills sat in his hotel room, mulling over what he had heard about the difficulty of stealing a base off Ford, resolving to run anyway, to shake up the Yankees at the first opportunity.

Alston was preoccupied by what steps the Yankees might take to hamper Wills. Earlier that day, the worried manager had raised questions in a private meeting with baseball officials over whether the Series' six umpires, a mixed crew from both leagues, would be vigilant in calling balks on Yankee pitchers if they utilized improper moves to hinder his base stealers. Umpires in neither league had shown much appetite for calling balks during the regular season. *Not* to enforce the balk rule would put the Dodgers at a severe disadvantage, Alston pointed out. He pressed the umps and the commissioner's office for reassurances. None came.

Houk expressed no concerns. His calm and confidence mirrored that of his players: they were veterans poised to take care of business. Ford said he was ready. His battery mate, Elston Howard, whose quick reflexes and strong arm made him one of the toughest catchers to steal against, declared he had no greater faith than in the man taking the mound for his team. The Yankees had finished reviewing the scouting report on the Dodgers, written by their super scout Mayo Smith, whose confidence was considerably more restrained than Houk's. Smith warned that Koufax was unlike anyone else the Yankees had faced that season or perhaps any season, summarizing his assessment of the pitcher with three words: "Simply the best."

Nothing remained but to play the game.

The Dodgers' Victory, a President's Assassination, and the First Seeds of a Players' Rebellion

The Series began on Wednesday afternoon, October 2, at 1:00 p.m. Eastern time—10:00 a.m. in Southern California. It was a sunny day in New York, the temperature at game time in Yankee Stadium about 66 degrees—virtually perfect conditions.

In every respect, it was an ideal day for an epic American sporting event. With no crises anywhere in the country to divert attention from its extravaganza, baseball occupied center stage.

From the American perspective, the world was tranquil. A week earlier, the Senate had approved the limited nuclear test ban treaty with the Soviet Union, with President Kennedy scheduled to sign it in the coming days. In a move aimed at further thawing cold war tensions between the two countries, the Kennedy administration, answering the hopes of Russians before a harsh winter, announced the United States would sell $380 million in wheat to the Soviets. The fears sparked in both countries a year earlier by the Cuban Missile

Crisis had eased for now. Although America had 16,000 so-called military advisers in South Vietnam, no American soldier there was officially in combat, and the Vietnamese civil war had yet to preoccupy Americans back home. Many college kids were absorbed at that moment in ritualistic pranks that included fraternity boys squeezing into telephone booths and swallowing goldfish.

Frivolity was in fashion. Fascination with pop culture and television had reached new heights. Annette Funicello, a popular former Disney Mouseketeer, appeared in a carefree film called *Beach Party*, where her excited fans at last saw her in a bikini, on a surfboard no less. The temporary de-escalation of international tensions left room on the front pages of Los Angeles newspapers that October week for an array of stories that reflected the hot topics of local interest: the doings of the squatters who had camped outside the Dodgers ticket office in hopes of getting their World Series seats; the comic stupidity of two hapless Southern California robbers who had decided to make a phone call during their caper; and a sudden epidemic gripping Los Angeles, a raging fever of sorts, a new kind of Blue Flu, which was reportedly causing many workers to leave their offices without explanation around 10:00 a.m. there—the moment of the first pitch in Yankee Stadium.

As with television viewership, the radio audience for the Series was about to break all records, thanks in part to the burgeoning popularity of the transistor radio, which was small enough to fit in a hand, hidden from the view of employers and schoolteachers alike. The *Los Angeles Times* dispatched a crew of photographers to capture people straying from jobs and listening to their transistors as the World Series was about to begin. A man in a suit and tie crossing Fifth Street and Broadway; a uniformed guard at the Ambassador Hotel; a news vendor at Fifth and Spring Streets: all would find their pictures in the paper by the next day, transistors pressed to their ears, their faces rapt.

A multitude of writers and other cultural observers were paying close attention that day to the hooky-playing workers and students making pilgrimages to black-and-white televisions where the game was being shown—in bars and neighbors' homes. The country's mania would in time be most memorably captured by film director Milos Forman's adaptation of Ken Kesey's novel *One Flew Over the Cuckoo's Nest*. Forman saw to it that Jack Nicholson, cast in the role of a career criminal consigned to an asylum and furious over being denied the opportunity to watch the telecast of the Series, would respond to the indignity by gathering a group of delusional patients in front of a blank television screen and vividly delivering an imaginary play-by-play for his new friends, deliriously screaming Koufax's name.

Yet nowhere was America's mania more intense than in Yankee Stadium. During warm-ups, players on each team could hear the indistinct voices of the game's excited radio announcers oozing out of transistors. It was a constant electronic buzzing, a stressful reminder of the stakes here. Wills was looking for a way to calm his nerves. Without telling Alston or anyone else, he and Roseboro had brought a bottle of brandy into the locker room. After taking infield practice, Wills rushed back into the visitor's clubhouse, looked around to make sure no one was watching, grabbed the brandy, had a big swig, and hastily left. Roseboro was taking a few sips of his own when he turned to see Alston directly staring at him.

Roseboro waited for a tirade. Alston smiled. The standard rules didn't apply on this day. Nobody was quite himself. Alston wished Roseboro a good game. In the last hour before the start, several players, including Tracewski, took solitary walks between the locker room and dugout, struggling to stay calm. Tracewski just wanted the damn game to start. He still worried that something might happen that would prompt Alston to pull him from the lineup.

At last, it was time. Ford and the Yankees took the field. Hitting from the right side, Wills stepped into the batter's box to start the game, flush with his dreams about what he would do once on first base. Ford's first pitch was a fastball. Late on it, Wills fouled it off. A couple of pitches later, he was fooled by a Ford curveball that broke and nosedived over the plate for strike three. Gilliam grounded out, Willie Davis struck out to end the inning, and Ford walked back to the Yankee dugout, looking as invincible as ever.

Koufax stepped onto the mound. What would happen during the next two hours would forever change his life and the way baseball and the country viewed him. The game would be one of three in his career most responsible for shaping his legacy, and his most important step yet in what would ultimately be a four-year march toward immortality. These were the Yankees in front of him, and if they humiliated him now, the tarnish to his otherwise extraordinary season would be long-lasting. The majesty of the occasion, the fearsomeness of the opposition, and the legendary stadium in which he found himself would combine with his achievement on this day to infuse Koufax with a mystique unrivaled among pitchers of his era, the kind that comes only by humbling titans on their own turf.

The humbling began immediately. Koufax struck out the left-handed-hitting shortstop Tony Kubek, who badly flailed at a sweeping curveball on the outer half of the plate.

The right-handed Bobby Richardson stepped in, with Dodger memories still fresh about how Richardson enjoyed feasting on high fastballs, according to the scouting report. But Koufax and Roseboro often liked to defy orthodoxy, to pitch "against the book," as Tracewski put it. Unpredictability could be a benefit, the battery mates believed. And if a player like Richardson hadn't been asked for a long while to hit a specific kind of pitch in a specific location, perhaps he might be a tad rusty.

Koufax struck him out on a high fastball.

Koufax ended the first inning by throwing a curveball that looked to Tracewski like it had dropped off a ledge. With no time to react, left fielder Tom Tresh watched it for strike three. Koufax had struck out the side. He slowly strode into the dugout, where teammates excitedly slapped his back, the kind of celebration generally reserved for the end of a game, not one merely an inning old.

Ford, too, looked superb. Into the batter's box stepped Tommy Davis, with radio and television announcers telling America that he had led the National League in hitting and posed a real threat. Ford threw another sharp overhand curve, and Davis hit a weak grounder to Kubek for a quick out. No Dodger had yet to have even a decent swing against Ford.

Everything happening to that point augured a low-scoring pitchers' duel. A long, miserable afternoon was apparently in the offing for hitters from both teams. Ford, mixing up his deliveries, then threw a sidearm fastball to the Dodgers' towering Frank Howard—who crushed it. The ball rocketed on a line to the deepest part of Yankee Stadium's left-center field. In any other major-league ballpark, the ball would have sailed deep into bleacher seats for a mammoth home run. In Dodger Stadium, where center field was 410 feet from home plate and the power alleys only 385 feet away, the ball would have carried into the far edges of the left-field Pavilion. But in the Bronx, the ball was merely headed in the general direction of the unreachable 461-foot sign on the Yankees' outfield wall, way out there on that expanse of prairie grass that never seemed to end. Still, the ball soared over Mantle's head and short-hopped the wall, leaving Howard with the longest double of his career.

Bill Skowron came to bat, which meant it was the moment for a slightly disbelieving Tracewski to step out of the visitors' third-base dugout and kneel on the on-deck circle. He knew his father and sister were sitting in the second deck of seats along the third-base line and that they were looking down at him now, no doubt marveling at what was about to happen. He knew his mother was watching him on television back home in Eynon. All their Eynon neighbors and other Pennsylvania friends would be crowded around their own sets. He looked out at Whitey Ford and thought, Can you believe this?

Skowron, who had fared so poorly all season long, felt as grateful as Tracewski just to be playing. He knew Ford well. Having played first base behind the pitcher for years, Skowron was neither awed nor confused by him. Ford threw a fastball and Skowron hit a bouncer into center field. Mantle rushed to field it, but Howard scored with the game's first run.

It was Tracewski's turn. Shuffling to the plate, waggling his bat in a false show of confidence, he felt sick. Then, as if nothing could make him more nervous, he heard the plate umpire, Joe Paparella, a veteran from the American League, asking, "Dick, aren't you going to say hello to me?"

Tracewski knew Paparella. In an unwelcome coincidence, Paparella was also from the town of Eynon.

He wants me to say hello *now*? Tracewski thought. He wants a chat? Like I need this?

"Please, Joe, not now," Tracewski muttered. "Next time."

Tracewski wouldn't even look at Paparella. He stared out at Ford. He already had put Paparella out of his head. He tuned out 69,000 people. It suddenly became a silent stadium.

He was looking for a fastball. Let Ford throw all the damn curves he wanted to throw; he wasn't about to swing at one of those. He was waiting on a fastball. Maybe Ford would jam him with the fastball or maybe he would throw it hard and away, but he was going to throw that fastball at some point, and when he did he wasn't going to scare Tracewski.

And here came a fastball.

Tracewski hit a liner between shortstop and second, into center field. A base hit. He had a World Series single off Whitey Ford.

In the stands off third base, Joseph Tracewski looked down at his son, turned to his daughter, and said, "I could die right now and I'd be happy."

Skowron had stopped at second base. Tracewski took a short lead off first base. The Dodgers were looking at the possibility of a big inning. But Ford looked as casual as ever, gently smoothing the dirt around the pitcher's mound with his toe, buying himself a little time, in no hurry to do anything. Doubtless he would get out of this jam—he always escaped big jams in monumental Series games, and this would be no different. And now here came the perfect foil, the left-handed-hitting Roseboro, who couldn't have been less suited for success against Ford.

For most of the season, Roseboro had struggled at bat, as reflected by his measly .236 average. He had demonstrated little power, with only nine homers and not one off a left-handed pitcher all year. In Ford, he was facing a left-handed legend who long before had become a nightmare for left-handed hitters. The list of American League left-handed hitters who knew nothing but hitless games against him was long. His domination of them was such that Ford, as the Yankees liked to remind people, had scarcely given up a homer all season to a left-handed hitter in Yankee Stadium.

Then Ford threw a breaking ball that didn't curve or drop. A subpar curveball looks to a capable major-league hitter like a ball sitting on a tee. Roseboro hit Ford's mistake into the right-field stands for a three-run homer. The fly ball landed just inside the foul pole, over the low outfield railing. The Dodgers led, 4–0. Skowron touched the plate, followed by a euphoric Tracewski, who looked like a kid running around the bases, clapping his hands. He had never been so happy in a baseball uniform. Then Roseboro touched the plate, mobbed in the dugout by teammates. The shocked Yankee partisans sat hushed.

But the Yankees had made their livings humiliating foes who had built early leads. As New York came to bat in the second inning, a roar greeted the sight of Mantle, who slowly shuffled into the batter's box from the right side and peered out at Koufax. Here it was, the most anticipated encounter of the Series. Watching his friend kick at the mound, Tracewski wondered whether Koufax would pitch Mantle in the manner that the scouting report urged: no slow curveballs; only hard stuff and preferably low and on the outside part of the plate, where Mantle couldn't kill you as easily.

Koufax was wasting no time, already into his windup.

A fastball on the outer half of the plate.

Mantle swung and missed.

Tracewski thought that fastball had to have been in the upper 90s. Perfectly placed. Low enough to be in that proverbial cup, near the outside corner. A good start.

Koufax was pitching in a hurry. Into his windup.

A fastball on the outer half again, but high.

One ball, one strike.

Mantle waggling the bat.

Here came another fastball on the outside corner.

Mantle fouled it back. Two strikes.

Mantle had been late on the pitch, again. He looked overmatched against that fastball. Just three pitches into his at-bat, it was already evident that Mantle wasn't anywhere close to being *that* Mantle. He looked gimpy somehow, as if swinging with only one decent leg, trying to generate power with his arms alone.

Now, if the scouting report on Koufax was right, he would throw another fastball in that cup on the outside corner.

Koufax threw a dart on the inside corner. Strike three.

It was a fastball at about 98, Tracewski guessed. Mantle, who had been leaning a little closer to the plate, as if expecting something on the outside, never had a chance. His bat did not twitch. One second he was looking out at Koufax, the next the ball was in Roseboro's glove.

Mantle was upset. Several accounts of the moment would have him instantly wheeling on Roseboro and, in an exasperated tone suggestive of awe for Koufax, asking: "How are you supposed to hit that shit?" Doubtless Mantle uttered the line at some point in the Series—he was still alive when his words first made the rounds, many years later, and he never contested their accuracy. But in recounting the line for teammates many times before his death in 2002, Roseboro's recollection of *when* Mantle voiced his disgust frequently changed. Mantle was on his way to a largely miserable Series against Koufax, ultimately to finish with only one hit in seven at-bats against him, with three strikeouts—so there were several apt moments for him to have voiced profane frustration.

What did appear to happen at that moment after his strikeout is that Mantle wheeled not on Roseboro (who had moved out of his line of vision by then) but instead directly toward plate umpire Paparella, as if angry the ump hadn't called the pitch a ball. He appeared to say something to Paparella on his way back to the Yankee dugout. His gesture suggested a belief that the last pitch couldn't possibly have stayed in the strike zone; that it must have been inside. After the game, he told reporters that the Koufax fastball had been an unusual fastball; that it had done something unusual; that it seemed to hop, or sink, or *something*—he didn't know what it did exactly, just that it had moved in some way he wasn't accustomed to seeing.

After Mantle sat back down in the dugout, Maris took his turn. Koufax was taking less time than ever between pitches. *Don't let Maris extend his arms*, the scouting report said. Koufax let Maris stretch those arms, ungainly—and struck him out with a curveball. His five consecutive strikeouts had tied a World Series record.

Crouched at second base, Tracewski thought, This guy is unreal.

In the Yankees dugout, Jim Bouton, the hard-throwing right-hander who would pitch Game 3, was startled by what he had seen. "It wasn't just the speed of Koufax's pitches but the smoothness of his motion," Bouton recalls. "It was easy for him—it was like playing catch. He didn't seem to be throwing hard. The ball just seemed to explode at the last second. It seemed so big coming out of his hand, like it's floating. Then it just explodes—it's like an optical illusion. Wham, it's past you and on the ground."

Elston Howard ended the Yankees' second inning by lofting a high foul off first base, which Roseboro caught near the Yankees dugout. The opposition had yet to hit a fair ball through two innings. His teammates slapped Koufax's back again as he sat down in the dugout. They were excitedly jabbering. He was quiet. He kept something to himself.

He was already feeling a little tired.

Perhaps it was a lingering effect of the cold he had just gotten over, or the running he had missed. Or the pace he was working at. He wouldn't have wanted to worry anybody by talking about it. But had he said anything to his teammates about being tired, they would have felt, if anything, reassured. His control generally became even better, they thought, when he complained of feeling tired. In the past, it was only when he told them how strong he felt during warm-ups that they ever worried he might overthrow and have control issues.

He struck out Pepitone to begin the third inning, retired Boyer on a grounder to Tracewski, and watched Ford foul out. He was even tougher in the fourth. Kubek struck out again, futilely swinging at the same kind of breaking ball that had set him down in the first inning. Richardson swung and missed for strike three on a snapping curve that started at his head and ended at his feet. Tom Tresh was paralyzed by the same curve that had befuddled him in his first at-bat, giving Koufax his ninth strikeout.

For the rest of his life, Tracewski would be able to close his eyes and see this inning, see his friend, see curveball after curveball at a hitter's knees, and fastball after fastball on the outside corner in the cup at 98.

Tracewski thought he already detected a change in Yankee expressions, a surprise bordering on resignation: "They'd known Sandy was good, but those guys were like Ralph Houk: they'd never really believed Sandy could stop them. You could just see it in their faces as the game went along, like, Who is this guy? Tony Kubek was really having a tough time. Richardson wasn't used to striking out, and Sandy was putting him down, too. Mantle, Maris, all of them. It looked like they were stunned. And Yankee Stadium was pretty quiet. Nobody could believe what was happening."

Standing out at shortstop, Wills was as mesmerized as anybody else. He felt in moments like a spectator. He had experienced the same sensation in other Koufax games that season, and it was never a good thing, he told people. Your concentration might lapse, he thought. You could begin staring *too much* at Koufax. You might not react as quickly to a ground ball. Many bad things could happen. He tried reminding himself before each pitch to stay focused, though this was a harder task with Koufax—precisely because he was striking out damn near everybody. As an infielder, you weren't moving an inch, and after a while, that could deprive you of your edge. Wills hadn't touched one grounder yet in this game.

The Dodgers had built their lead to 5–0. In left field, Tommy Davis was glancing at the stands between pitches, then turning back to watch Koufax strike out somebody else. "You'd just start watching Sandy like you were a fan," he remembers. "No fly ball or line drive was coming out your way, so enjoy it."

The Yankees still didn't have a hit as the fifth inning began. Mantle struck out again, this time swinging, overpowered by a fastball, muttering once more. It was Koufax's tenth strikeout.

Maris fouled out to Roseboro for the second out of the inning. Koufax had retired fourteen straight batters, and it was already reasonable to think about the possibility of a no-hitter. He was more than halfway there. But his fatigue had worsened. He felt a little weak now. If anything, his rush of early adrenaline had sped his fatigue. Later, he would admit he had not helped himself by pitching so quickly and throwing so many curves.

Just as spectators had begun contemplating the road to a no-hitter, Elston Howard ended such dreams by singling the opposite way to right field. Seconds later, Pepitone tapped a curve into right field for another base hit. With baserunners on first and second, the Yankees had mustered a genuine threat, and they appeared on the way to their first run of the game when Boyer smashed a liner up the middle. It was headed toward center field, seemingly a certainty to drive in Howard. But in the same instant, Tracewski leaped at the ball. His entire body was off the ground, parallel to the infield dirt, his left arm and glove outstretched, trying to make a backhanded stab. He couldn't. But he got just enough of his mitt on the ball to knock it down and keep it in the infield. It rolled in the direction of Wills, who quickly grabbed it and held a racing Howard at third base. Tracewski had saved a run.

Bases loaded now. For the Yankees, this was likely to be their only chance at a big inning against Koufax. Ford was removed from the game, in favor of pinch hitter Hector Lopez. Lopez had capably filled in for the injured Mantle during much of the season, finishing with 14 homers and a .249 average. Most importantly, he was regarded as a reliable contact hitter who had struck out in fewer than 20 percent of his at-bats. On the other hand, he'd never faced Koufax. And to have never faced Koufax meant having no idea how to prepare for the likes of something you'd never seen, something that couldn't be simulated in any batting cage. Koufax blew him away with a fastball. And the Yankees' best opportunity against him was gone. They wouldn't have another.

Thereafter, he sought to conserve what energy he had left. Limiting his use of a curveball, he was working on a shutout as the eighth inning began. Utility player Phil Linz, thrilled at twenty-four to find himself in a Series, stepped up as a pinch hitter. He had read some stories about the intimidating Koufax. But now, as Koufax delivered the first pitch to him, Linz was pleasantly surprised at how well he saw the ball leave Koufax's hand. This looked promising. "He threw straight overhand with no deception in his windup, and his fastball looked as big as a softball when he released it," Linz remembers. "I saw it great. Then it seemed to pick up speed about three-quarters of the way to the plate. I mean, it just *took off*."

Linz, a fan of the American space program, thought that the fastball reminded him of something. Finally, the image came to him. "You know, it was like one of those rocket boosters separating, like you'd see on the astronauts' flights on TV. When it got close to the plate, it became like a rocket ship: the booster separates and it's gone. And it's rising. It rises the rest of the way. That's what it was like.

The pitch started knee-high to me and ended up at belt high. *Gone.* I missed it completely."

Linz struck out and walked back into the Yankees dugout. Nobody there mentioned either Koufax's name or what was happening. "Guys didn't really say anything to each other," Linz recounts. "Some of them just rolled their eyes and shook their heads a little, like, We're not going to have a good time against him. But nobody openly says anything during a game about their frustration. In our world, the Yankees world, the attitude always was, We'll get him next time, in the next at-bat. But there were some tense looks."

Koufax next gave up an infield single to Kubek, before fanning Richardson on another high fastball. It was the third time Richardson had struck out—never before in nine years of regular-season games and six World Series had he struck out more than twice in a game. That Koufax then gave up a two-out, two-run homer to Tresh seemed not to matter somehow, most of the 69,000 in Yankee Stadium riveted by his utter supremacy. Alston had Perranoski and Drysdale warming up, just in case. But Koufax cruised to a 5–2 victory on a six-hitter, the final out coming when Yankees pinch hitter Harry Bright futilely swung at a fastball, Koufax's fifteenth strikeout, which set a new World Series record.

He appeared reasonably pleased afterward, honored to have the strikeout record, though characteristically restrained, even self-critical. His control was good, he thought, though this was not his "best game," he added. He mentioned his sporadic fatigue and weakness, as well as the loss of his rhythm in the middle innings. That he could have pitched better was perhaps the worst news of all to the Yankees, none of whom thought they had ever seriously challenged him. By the end of their bases-loaded threat against him in the fifth inning, they had felt not encouraged but awed. In the Yankees clubhouse, Yogi Berra expressed shock upon learning that Koufax's 1963 record was twenty-five wins and five defeats.

"How did he lose five?" Berra asked.

O nly one Dodger regular felt disappointed about his performance in Game 1. Wills had gone hitless in five at-bats, and struck out twice. Determined to excel in Game 2, he was studying the scouting report on the Yankees' scheduled starter, the twenty-two-year-old left-hander Al Downing, who was made to order for a rash of stolen bases, Wills told himself. The report had been blunt about the young pitcher: it took a long time for Downing to get rid of the ball when runners were on base and he was pitching from a stretch position. He had a very high and slow leg kick before releasing the ball. Dodger baserunners could take advantage of the flaw, the report said.

If he were to reach first base, Wills decided that as soon as Downing lifted his right leg, he would sprint toward second base, not even bothering to see whether Downing was actually delivering the ball to home plate. Even if Downing at that moment threw over to first base in a pickoff attempt, Wills thought the ball would take so long to get there that he could beat any relay throw from first baseman Pepitone to either Yankee shortstop Kubek or second baseman Richardson. The scouting report's assessment of Pepitone's poor throwing arm further bolstered his confidence.

Wills hit a bouncing single into center field to open the game against Downing, who calmly went into his stretch position as Wills took a large lead off first base. As the Yankees' first black starting pitcher in their history, Downing had enjoyed a wonderful season, winning thirteen games and receiving the honor of this Series' start. Like Wills, he had prepared long and hard for both the Series and this particular moment, assuming that Wills would quickly try to steal.

But he hadn't readied himself for what happened next. Wills sprinted toward second base the instant Downing lifted his right leg and threw over to first base. As the play unfolded, Downing was at first pleased: he thought he had likely picked off Wills for the first out of the game. He knew he had made an accurate toss to Pepitone, who needed now only to make a decent throw to either Kubek or Richardson, who would administer the tag on Wills.

Later, sportswriters would report that Pepitone made a poor throw to second base. In fact, Pepitone's throw was roughly where anyone applying a tag would have wanted it. Wills sensed the throw had him beaten. He had been surprised by its relative swiftness and accuracy.

"They probably would've had me out if they had handled it right," he recalls.

They were Kubek and Richardson. Watching Wills sprint down the baseline, Kubek had quickly moved over to second base to take Pepitone's throw, opening his glove, well positioned around the base. Wills saw him. "Kubek was going to get the throw—Kubek should've taken the throw," Wills says.

On the Yankees' bench, Phil Linz felt the same way. "You wanted Kubek, the shortstop, to handle that throw. It was an easier play for a shortstop."

But Wills had sparked confusion in the Yankee infield. Not once during the entire American League season had Richardson and Kubek encountered a runner who intentionally bolted for second base during a pitcher's pickoff attempt. Successful pickoff throws were supposed to be sure outs. Nabbed runners were supposed to be caught in rundowns until they meekly surrendered. But Wills's style was entirely new to the Yankee duo. Inexperienced at defensing it, they acted now, with the ball in the air, as if they were uncertain which of them should take the throw.

Together, the New York duo had practiced every imaginable kind of infield play over the last few years. But this was not imaginable in their league. The moment resurrected memories of Wills's improbable dash during the All-Star game in Washington just a year earlier, when he had tricked the American Leaguers into trying to throw behind him to second base while he raced to third. It had been Richardson that day who had caught the throw from the fooled outfielder Rocky Colavito and vainly tried to throw out Wills at third. Now Richardson was being victimized for a second time. Wills's speed regularly created chaos, and chaos was bewildering for American Leaguers unaccustomed to dealing with it. Richardson, believing it was his play to make, rushed to the bag, but his momentum was carrying him away from it, which later would create the illusion of an errant throw. Reaching out on the dead run, he caught Pepitone's toss before Wills arrived. But by then Richardson was falling away and over the bag, in the direction of third base. Wills dived headfirst away from him, sliding on his stomach toward the outfield side of the base.

His hands grabbed the bag, and the umpire, Shag Crawford, signaled safe. Wills's steal was yet another reminder, in case any more were needed, of the cost to the Yankees and the American League in not having cultivated, or regularly played against, the likes of a Wills. "We weren't accustomed to seeing the kind of running that came from the Dodgers and Cardinals," Linz observes. "The American League was the long-ball league. We were behind the National League teams in signing black guys."

In the first seconds after the steal, not having moved from the mound, Downing heard a loud buzz coming from the crowd. It sounded like a prolonged *ahhhhhhhhhhhhhhhh* to him, a gasp of amazement. The young pitcher had badly wanted to get Wills out, but over time he would deeply appreciate the significance of the moment. "This was the kind of baseball that we'd missed since the Dodgers left Brooklyn," he recalls. "This was Brooklyn Dodgers' baseball. This was Jackie Robinson's kind of baseball. Except now he's wearing Maury Wills's number 30 and playing for Los Angeles. I remember that buzz. What Maury had just done was Brooklyn baseball, but it wasn't Yankee baseball. The Yankees didn't play like that. The fans' reaction with that buzz was kind of, Wow, this is what we *don't* see when the Yankees play."

Downing steadied himself. But instead of already having an out in his pocket, he was faced with the sight of Wills on second base and nobody out. Gilliam next singled. Willie Davis doubled over

Maris's head, driving home both Wills and Gilliam. Already, the Dodgers had all the runs they would need on this day. Thirty-one-year-old veteran Johnny Podres—eight years removed from having won Game 7 in Yankee Stadium to give the Dodgers their first World Championship—cruised until the ninth inning, when the reliever Perranoski secured the final outs. Mantle went hitless, and Maris injured himself while chasing a triple by Tommy Davis. The Dodgers won, 4–1, headed back to Los Angeles with a two-game lead. Tension had given way to a calm that bordered on cockiness.

The Yankees insisted they were not worried. Ford predicted they would even the Series in California. Mantle said little. On the arrival of the team's flight in Southern California, he irritably tossed a raincoat over a television camera pointed in his direction, pulled it away, and kept moving.

The Dodgers' arrival at Los Angeles International Airport at about 9:30 on that Thursday night was cause for a banner headline on the front page of the *Los Angeles Times*: DODGERS HOME! An accompanying story reported that an aide to Los Angeles mayor Sam Yorty tried to present Alston with a gold key to the city, but that both the aide and the key were swallowed up in a crowd of 2,500 howling fans. The mob "went wild" at the sight of Koufax: "Men roared, women shrieked, and teen-age girls all but swooned. . . . Fans grabbed for his plaid sports coat, especially the left sleeve that clothes the mighty pitching arm."

The Yankees were still loose, having battled back before. On the day before his Game 3 start, which would see him matched up against Drysdale, Bouton walked with Linz into a Los Angeles novelty shop, where the two had a fake newspaper headline printed: BOUTON SHUTS OUT THE DODGERS . . . LINZ WINS GAME WITH HOMER. The two were pleased. It looked like a genuine newspaper. They unfurled it the next day on the team bus during the ride to Dodger Stadium. "Our teammates laughed," Bouton remembers. "Linz and I were two young guys goofing around. I never felt it was life or death going into those things. It was fun more than fear for me. We were in the World Series. I was thrilled."

Linz remembers: "The guys were relaxed. Nobody needed any lift. We thought we could hit Drysdale."

Bouton gave up a run in the first inning, on a bad-hop RBI single by Tommy Davis, but nothing more. In the years ahead, especially after he wrote the landmark book *Ball Four*, which chronicled his daffiness as much as it did his up-and-down career, Bouton acquired a reputation as a sometimes clownish figure. Few images were less deserved. Nicknamed "Bulldog" by his teammates, Bouton was tenacious and resourceful. On that Saturday afternoon, he pitched magnificently, yielding only four hits. "You expect to win those kinds of game," Linz observes. But Drysdale threw a three-hit shutout. So desperate were the Yankees to generate any attack that in the second inning a hobbled Mantle bunted, successfully, only to be stranded on base by a Yankees' offense impotent to that point against Dodgers pitching.

The last out of the game came on a long fly ball from Pepitone to the right-field warning track, where Ron Fairly made the catch to give the Dodgers a three-game advantage. "When he hit it," Bouton recalls, "I thought it was a homer. I thought we were going to win the game. The history of our team said we came back all the time. Even after losing the third game, we thought we could still win the Series; that we were going to score whatever runs were needed and win. The dynasty would continue: that was our attitude. Pepitone, Linz, and I were part of the new blood; we were cocky guys and we were going to keep winning. Nobody ever threw in the towel on our team."

The Dodgers' reaction to the Game 3 victory reflected a different certainty. Watching Pepitone's drive settle into Fairly's mitt, Wills thought, *We've got this—we're going to sweep them tomorrow.*

For Los Angelenos, the next day, a warm, sunny Sunday, represented history in the making. Some of those without tickets that weekend had come to Dodger Stadium anyway, looking for any way to see a game in person, whether that meant buying seats off a scalper or somehow slinking into the ballpark without a ticket.

Among them was a boy named Zev Yaroslavsky, a Dodgers loyalist and devout fan of Koufax. In time, the young Yaroslavsky would become one of the most intriguing politicians in Los Angeles history, never to lose an election in a career spanning thirty-nine years as a city council-man and county supervisor. Before then, he would be best known for his boldness during his years as a local activist. A child of Jewish immi-grants from the Soviet Union, he would establish an organization that frequently staged large rallies against the repressive treatment of Jews by the Soviet government, protests ranging from a demonstration against the visiting Bolshoi Ballet to personally cruising out into the Los An-geles Harbor to deface a Soviet freighter. At fourteen, Yaroslavsky was already as wily as he was determined. Along with a young friend, he successfully sneaked through a Dodger Stadium gate, to be a spectator at what would be the final two games of the Series.

On Sunday, October 6, Yaroslavsky made his way into the stadium early in the morning and wandered down to seats deep along the right-field corner, just in time to see the Yankees exit their bus outside the ballpark and walk toward a concourse leading inside. Off the bus stepped Mantle, who perhaps had been deluged with too much atten-tion for too long. His life had made him boorish in moments. Now, as Yaroslavsky watched, a small child holding an autograph book and a pencil stared up at the hero. "The kid looked about eight years old, and he asked, 'Mickey, can I have your autograph?' And Mantle just glanced at him and said, 'No.' The kid was crushed—he'd been wait-ing there for Mickey and nobody else. Mantle just kept walking. It colored my impression of Mantle. They were down three games to none, so that probably had something to do with his reaction. But it was not a good moment for Mickey."

Another budding Los Angeles politician attended the game. A student at Berkeley, twenty-year-old Mel Levine, who would one day represent West Los Angeles in Congress, sat alongside his mother,

Shirley, in nice seats about midway down the right-field line. The Levines were a prominent Jewish family in Los Angeles, with mother and son equally thrilled on this day about the prospect that Koufax would lead their beloved Dodgers to a championship. But if anyone had doubts about lingering and malignant prejudices, one would have only needed to hear what the Levines heard, not long after the game got under way. "Some guy, a Dodger fan, a few rows behind us shouted, 'Let's see what the Yid can do. How's the Yid gonna do?'" Levine recalled. "It wasn't the kind of comment ever directed at Drysdale. My mother thought it was anti-Semitic. . . . And there *was* a tinge of anti-Semitism to it. There was a taunt-like quality to it. It wasn't entirely a cheer—it was emblematic of something else. . . . It could fall off my shoulder a little in light of what was happening on the field, in light of the Dodgers' sweep that was happening, but it did remind you that the bigotries and biases still existed."

Dodger fans were celebratory from the start, as if, with Koufax on the mound and their team in a commanding position, the Series' outcome was certain. It was the kind of throng that, in later years, would come to be known by outsiders as an "LA crowd"—the fans' mood laid-back, irreverent, inclined toward having fun where they could find it. About a dozen fans in the left-field pavilion happily launched into a yell:

> *Pork chops, pork chops,*
> *Greasy, greasy,*
> *We can beat the Yankees,*
> *Easy, easy!*

In a reprise of the opening game, Koufax made the Yankees look helpless in the first inning. Kubek struck out, Richardson fouled out to Roseboro, and Tresh went down swinging.

Koufax gave up only one hit in the first four innings. Hardly anyone had looked worse against him in the Series than Mantle, who so far on

this last day had flied out and grounded out, having another terrible afternoon, with only one hit in thirteen at-bats to that point in the Series,
and nothing but futility to show for his encounters with Koufax.

As he returned to center field after his latest failed at-bat, the same
chanting fans in the left-field bleachers, now equipped with a bugle,
serenaded him:

> *Who's the leader of the club,*
> *That's made for you and me?*
> *M-I-C-K-E-Y M-O-U-S-E!*
> *Hey there! Hi there! Ho there!*
> *You're as welcome as can be,*
> *M-I-C-K-E-Y M-O-U-S-E!*

Mantle did not move, did not acknowledge them.

If Koufax was confounding the Yankees, so too was Whitey Ford
a puzzle for nearly all the Dodgers. He would give up only two hits
on this day, but one was a missile that Frank Howard launched down
the left-field line in the fifth inning. It landed 430 feet away for a
solo homer, in the distant seats on Dodger Stadium's second level,
better known as the loge boxes. Watching the ball in flight and joyous
Dodger fans leaping, television viewers in New York would have a
good look, too, at the cluster of O'Malley's iconic palm trees in the
background, behind the Dodger bullpen.

As the game progressed into the seventh inning, an invincible-
looking Koufax, protecting a 1–0 lead, seemed on his way to a shutout. Here again was the enfeebled Mantle. Koufax threw him another
scorching fastball.

Mantle hit it into the left-center-field bleachers.

It was not a fly but a bullet. It reached the seats so fast that radio
and TV announcers had no time for their traditional home run calls.

"He killed it," Tommy Davis would remember. "There was no
point in turning around."

"He hit it and it was in the stands—like that," Tracewski would recall. "It was the real him."

Which meant the old Mantle. It was the familiar Mantle corkscrew swing, the one that his hurting body seldom could produce now, the one from his peak years where his knees nimbly bent a little and his swing seemed to twist him into the ground, the one where his body got unfathomably spectacular leverage and he just annihilated the ball. The blast inspired the old awe. It even hushed stunned Dodger partisans, who, as he shuffled around the bases, accorded him the kind of quiet respect reserved for prelates and baseball idols. "I wasn't unhappy," Levine remembers. "It was Mickey Mantle. I felt confident Koufax was going to win, so it was cool to see Mantle hit one out."

His blast had moved Mantle into a tie with Babe Ruth for the most lifetime Series homers, a mark he would break the following year. As he arrived back in the Yankees dugout, his younger teammates rushed him with backslaps, their excitement gushing, as if perhaps his blow could be the one to turn this game and Series around. "We'd tied it up, and we were going to win," Linz recalls thinking.

But in the bottom of the inning, the Yankees gave the run back. Gilliam hit a high bouncer to third. Boyer leaped to stab it and made a strong, accurate throw to Pepitone, who lost sight of the ball amid the background of white shirtsleeves worn by spectators sitting off the third-base line. The ball struck Pepitone in the arm and rolled to the box seat railing on the right-field side, allowing Gilliam to race all the way to third base. Willie Davis drove him home with a sacrifice fly, giving the Dodgers a 2–1 lead they never would relinquish.

Still, the Yankees had their chances. In the eighth inning, Linz, batting for Ford with one out, hit a waist-high Koufax fastball into left field for a single, only to watch as Kubek hit a bouncer to Tracewski, who turned it into a double play to end the inning.

Richardson singled to begin the ninth inning. After Tresh was called out on strikes, Mantle had one last chance. No one in the Dodgers organization had forgotten the scouting report: *Do not give Mantle any slow breaking stuff.* But baseball geniuses, like blues musicians, play by feel, and Koufax threw an off-speed breaking ball so sublime that Mantle was frozen. He took it for strike three, said nothing, and walked back to the dugout, head bowed.

Still, the Yankees hadn't given up. Bouton would forever think the Yankees were the superior team. "Even when Mickey was out in the ninth, I thought, Who's up?" Bouton remembers. "Even with two outs, I thought, We'll find a way to win."

Two batters later, the Yankees expired. Hector Lopez, desperate to make contact with the Koufax fastball, chopped a weak ground ball to Wills, who threw across to Skowron for the Series' final out. The Dodgers had swept the Yankees, who had never experienced such a rout in a World Series. Yet the outcome was somewhat deceptive. The Yankees had lost two of the four games by a mere run. Stellar Yankee pitching had yielded an average of only three runs per game, with the Dodgers' offense nearly as anemic as the Yankees' during many stretches.

The difference in the Series—just as during the National League regular season—had come down to the Dodgers' frontline pitchers, whose ERA for the four games against New York was a stunning 1.00. In Koufax, Drysdale, and Podres, the unfortunate Yankees faced two future Hall of Famers at the peak of their careers, and a money pitcher who had bedeviled them in two different decades. The three pitchers had rendered the Yankees feckless, and in the New York clubhouse, no one bothered to concoct excuses. The losers quickly left for the airport, with a gracious Ford later to say that if he could start only one pitcher in a pivotal game, it would be not himself but Koufax.

Mantle was especially quiet. "Mickey had tears in his eyes," Linz remembers. "We were down; there was no getting out of that. And we had a long flight home. Mickey went to where he lived, the St. Moritz on Central Park South. I don't remember that we talked about anything on the flight. We never talked much about baseball."

A bow-tied Bavasi and a beaming O'Malley arrived in the winners' clubhouse to express appreciation and pose with Koufax, Drysdale, and others. The team was ecstatic, though no raucous celebration occurred among players or fans around Dodger Stadium. Perhaps the Dodgers' dominance had taken some of the edge off the triumph. Jubilant fans filing out of the ballpark did so calmly and quietly, trudging through the immense parking lot in search of their cars. In the Dodgers clubhouse, the restrained party ended early. "We were just happy," Wills remembers. "Really happy and glad it was over. You were always glad when it was over."

A BRUISING FIGHT WITH BAVASI

Overnight, the stature of the Los Angeles Dodgers soared. No less a student of celebrity than Bob Hope recognized the Dodger stars' heightened allure. When asked a few days after the Series ended whether their victory had made Koufax, Drysdale, and Tommy Davis deserving of more money for appearing on his television variety show, Hope quickly and happily said no—the likelihood that they would become bigger stars was precisely why he had made his TV deal with the three players *before* the Series began, he dryly pointed out.

The players didn't have personal agents to negotiate terms with Hope or anyone else. It was no surprise. The players had never needed an agent for anything, including a negotiation of their baseball salaries. This had everything to do with the dictates of Bavasi, who made clear to his players that his scorn for agents and attorneys was absolute when it came to matters of Dodger contracts. Theirs was like a family, Bavasi told players. And no agent or attorney ought to be permitted to violate the family's inner circle by getting between players and Dodger officials who, after all, were looking after the best interests of everyone, Bavasi declared. It was precisely why discussions about salary never needed to last more than a few minutes in his office, one-on-one, face-to-face, in a friendly atmosphere, he explained. Never had a player defied this understanding, with the result that few Dodgers even knew the name of an agent or entertainment attorney.

At best, Koufax and other stars had businessmen friends to whom they could turn for advice once in a while. But the players were on their own when someone like Hope offered to pay them as much as a thousand dollars apiece to perform a funny song-and-dance number together in tuxedos. Was that good money? they asked each other. "It always sounded like easy money when entertainment people talked to you," Wills said. "You just took the deal without questions most of the time. It wasn't a lot different than dealing with Bavasi. You didn't know that there was any other choice with Buzzie or any of the Hollywood people. No one was around you to tell you that you had a choice. If you had ever thought of mentioning an agent or attorney to Buzzie, he would've laughed at you and then gotten angry. Most of the time, you just felt lucky to get whatever you were getting. You were a ballplayer and you'd won the World Series and you had some popularity. And you had all these people saying nice things to you and giving you a little money and by the time you realized the way it worked it was too late to do anything about it. So you just took what you could."

Wills had his own postseason deal with Milton Berle, who was taking him, Koufax, Drysdale, and Willie Davis, among other Dodger stars, out on a road show that would last a week at the Fontainebleau Hotel in Miami Beach, before moving to Las Vegas for a series of performances at the Desert Inn. Berle was a proud Dodger fan and a frequent spectator at Dodger Stadium, but he was irascible too, frequently griping to the Dodgers about his seats or the behavior of ushers or a shortage of amenities, going so far as to list his complaints in a personal letter to O'Malley. But nowhere was he more demanding than in his dealings with those who played parts in his television and hotel shows. He liked the Dodger stars he hired, but once the players were on the road with him, they were his employees. He was manager-boss and they his subordinates, just as if they were playing under Alston, Bavasi, and O'Malley.

After a week of rehearsals with Berle, the shows began at the Fontainebleau. The players sang a few songs in a group before Wills performed a banjo solo and Drysdale belted out an old Sinatra classic written by Bart Howard, "Fly Me to the Moon."

Soon they were off to Las Vegas. One night, between numbers at one show, Wills made the mistake of ad-libbing, casually pointing out to impresario Berle that some notable singers were in the audience.

"I know they're here," Berle snapped onstage.

After the show, Berle was furious with Wills. "Don't you ever break the routine again by telling me somebody is out there," he ordered.

Wills knew that Berle appreciated him, that the entertainer wanted to continue working with him. But the moment served as a reminder of a player's place, even a famous player's. He, Koufax, Drysdale, and the others had stardom—whatever that meant—but they had no clout, and certainly no financial security, either in Bavasi's office or with Berle. As players, they were hired help, glamorous and highly sought-after help perhaps, but help just the same, always subject to wealthy and powerful men's orders, always dependent on their blessing and their money most of all.

Especially in baseball, it was a paternalistic relationship. During the off-season, back home for a couple of months with his family in Spokane, Wills did some promotional work for the Spokane farm club on which he had played, a winter job that Bavasi arranged for him. He long believed that Bavasi had done it out of guilt, aware that the Dodgers organization was badly underpaying him. It was the Bavasi way, he thought: throw a player a few bones to keep him satisfied before saying no at some point to a meaningful salary boost.

Nearly all the Dodger players worked in whatever non-baseball-related jobs they could find during the off-season, stars and non-stars alike. But winter jobs were especially vital for utility players like

Tracewski, whose Dodger salary of $7,500 for the 1963 season was so low that he made more from his World Series player's share, a bonus distributed by the baseball commissioner's office. The Series winners received a little more than the losers; Tracewski was elated to receive a Series share check for $12,794, which meant his total baseball earnings for the year had exceeded $20,000. Never before had he made as much as $10,000.

A nice boost, he thought, but it was also a reminder of a baseball player's year-to-year anxieties and struggles. Money would forever be tight for him. Any salary raises would be meager.

Yet he had learned that if Bavasi liked you, believing you were loyal to the Dodgers, he'd toss a little extra cash your way—within limits—to show his appreciation for your selfless attitude. During the following year, one day around the batting cage, Tracewski would jokingly suggest to Leo Durocher that because money was tight, he and his wife wouldn't be going to Hawaii during the off-season, as they'd hoped, but instead to the little island of Catalina, only about twenty miles off the Los Angeles shore, a favorite destination of Californians living on tight budgets.

A few weeks later he ran into Bavasi, who said, "I understand you're going to Hawaii."

Tracewski was baffled. Then, recalling his joke to Durocher, he groaned. "What the heck are you talking about, Buzzie?"

"You're going to Hawaii," Bavasi said, handing him a check for $2,000.

Tracewski was grateful. But Bavasi's generosity was sparing and always conditioned on the understanding that it was a special gift for someone faithful to the Dodgers family. His star players increasingly chafed under his paternalism. They had tired of management praise meant to serve as a substitute for salary hikes, and gifts meant to mask what Bavasi and O'Malley weren't doing for them.

Koufax made it clear that he simply wanted to be paid what he was worth, like any other productive employee of an American business.

And it was difficult to conceive of any employee in the country who had enjoyed a better year than Koufax. No other athlete had meant as much to his team's fortunes, or earned his owner so much extra money in ticket sales. He had captured every major award for the season. In an unprecedented unanimous vote, he won the Cy Young Award, during an era when baseball limited its selection to a single pitcher in all of baseball. He won the National League's Most Valuable Player Award, only the second time in the past thirteen years that a pitcher had received the honor. Chosen as the World Series' Most Valuable Player, he also won the Hickok Belt as the top American professional athlete.

In Los Angeles his appeal had transmuted into idolatry, evinced by everything from those booming ticket revenues on his game days to the number of Southern California parents naming their children after him, like Philip and Linda Warshauer, whose daughter Sandy was born four minutes after Koufax had triumphed in the World Series finale. The idea for the name had originated with the new mother, who, wasting no time after her delivery, immediately asked, "Who won?" Over the next few years, reasonable analysts would recognize that no matter what the Dodgers paid him, Koufax would earn the organization several million dollars more. In the aftermath of 1963, a salary of a quarter million to a half million dollars for Koufax would have left ample room for Walter O'Malley to profit.

Koufax waited several months after the World Series to broach the issue. "Money is something you argue about after the season ends," he would later explain to a group of local sportswriters. With some of the reporters speculating that he was likely to receive a $20,000 raise above his 1963 salary of $35,000, he already had decided such a figure wasn't anywhere close to what he deserved. Although the Dodgers had never increased a player's salary by even as much as $30,000 in a single season, Koufax wanted about $85,000.

At that moment, Wills and Drysdale were the highest-paid Dodgers, each man earning somewhat less than $50,000. Even before his talks with Koufax began, Bavasi was busy conditioning Los Angeles sportswriters to believe the Dodgers wouldn't be able to pay their greatest star much more than $50,000. He had created a social rationale for his position, telling reporters that his philosophy was to spread the Dodgers' wealth around, helping the many rather than merely satisfying one special player like Koufax. "I prefer two men at $50,000 a year than one at $100,000," he told the *Los Angeles Times*, on another day adding to this explanation and warning of the danger to the club in giving Koufax, Drysdale, or any other player too large a raise: "If I did that, I would have to adjust the salaries of the other players all the way down the line."

In an era when player salaries and team payrolls weren't public knowledge, Bavasi boasted to local sportswriters that he had paid less to assemble his 1963 championship team than the general managers of trailing teams like the Giants and Braves had paid for theirs.

Wills, who also wanted more money, watched to see what moves Koufax would make. "Sandy pushed Buzzie in a way the rest of us didn't," Wills remembers. "I think Sandy was learning as he was doing it. But Sandy was determined in a way we weren't yet. I'd be determined for a while, but then I'd get too scared. But I could feel something coming with Sandy. After we beat the Yankees, Sandy was going to try something. He deserved a lot more money than he was getting, and everybody knew it."

In mid-February of 1964, Koufax met alone with Bavasi for about two hours. Nothing was resolved, and neither Koufax nor Bavasi would disclose the terms of any offers or counteroffers. Operating on his own, Drysdale had encountered similar resistance from Bavasi. "I can tell from the way they talk that it will be impossible for me to give them what they want," Bavasi said of the two pitchers.

The general manager's statement fueled speculation that Koufax was pushing for a salary approaching $100,000. Sportswriters close to Bavasi stressed that Koufax would need several more extraordinary seasons before ever having a remote chance at that. A kind of mysticism attached to the six-digit figure. One sportswriter of the era called it a "golden plateau," which only Mantle occupied at that moment, now that Musial had joined former $100,000-earners Ted Williams, Joe DiMaggio, and Hank Greenberg in retirement. No pitcher had ever been close to the golden plateau. In early 1964, executives and journalists regularly made the case that it was impossible to pay $100,000 to a player who pitched only once every four games.

Not even Koufax would yet ask for $100,000, though what he wanted now was unprecedented for a pitcher.

Bavasi said no when Koufax asked for $85,000, offering $65,000 instead.

Koufax rejected the figure. He asked about the possibility of adding an "attendance clause," a provision that would pay him an unspecified percentage of ticket revenues for games in which he pitched.

No Dodger ever had asked for an attendance clause. To Bavasi, it was an affront. What right did a player have to believe that he could essentially become a partner of the owner and share in revenues?

According to Koufax—who recounted the story a few days later to the *Los Angeles Times*—Bavasi replied, "Mr. O'Malley would never stand for it."

Koufax then asked about players' possible participation in revenue expected to come from the creation of pay television.

Bavasi refused to discuss the matter.

Their discussion became increasingly contentious. Koufax mentioned his league-leading twenty-five wins. Bavasi said he placed more importance "on the number of innings pitched."

Innings pitched?

Koufax was enraged. He remembered the 1960 season, when he had pitched what was then the most innings of his life, only to see Bavasi cut his salary at season's end after he had gone 8–13.

Innings pitched? He would still have the subject on his mind a few days later when he poured out his frustrations to the *Los Angeles Times*.

Bavasi was making the most specious of arguments. The importance of innings pitched paled against Koufax's league-leading numbers in the statistical categories that, aside from his wins, most mattered—earned run average, shutouts, strikeouts, and least hits allowed per inning. Moreover, Koufax had just concluded a season in which he had pitched the most innings of his career and the third most in the National League. A desperate Bavasi was flailing now. Finally, according to Koufax, Bavasi simply threatened to give Koufax nothing more than a "minimum contract" if he didn't yield.

Koufax wouldn't budge. It was a rare display of temerity from a player. Koufax had no real leverage, and no viable baseball options if Bavasi held firm and said no to paying him a dollar more. If Koufax were to play at all in the major leagues, Walter O'Malley and the Dodgers owned the rights to his services. The absolute hold of baseball owners over their labor force, long before validated by Congress and the American courts, was protected by the sport's so-called reserve clause, which generally bound a player to the major-league club for which he had signed his first contract unless the club traded him away or sold his rights. A measure of free agency for players was still a decade away. If Bavasi refused to budge, Koufax had only two disheartening options: accept Bavasi's stingy offer or quit baseball altogether.

Koufax was playing a high-stakes game of poker, counting on Bavasi to worry enough about losing his services for the 1964 season that he would give in, or at least throw a few more dollars his way. Neither man backed down. They argued in Bavasi's office for two and a half hours. Koufax sometimes stepped away to call trusted friends who offered advice or to smoke a cigarette in the corridor. In the end, he compromised, though Bavasi had to give just as much ground, a first in any negotiation between Bavasi and a player. By the end of the day, Koufax signed for about $70,000, double what he had made a year earlier, and the largest raise ever for a Dodger (yet history should note that 19-game winner Drysdale received roughly the same

$70,000 salary, without having to experience either Koufax's anguish or the Dodger management's brass-knuckled resistance). The *Los Angeles Times*, joining in a shopworn portrayal of Koufax, observed that Koufax "never will be accused of lacking business acumen," though noting that Koufax had stressed "his main incentive is Dodger victories, not money."

The Dodgers held a press conference, at which a smiling Koufax posed with Bavasi for photographers. And that would have been the end of their dispute, except that during the same afternoon a story appeared in the city's afternoon newspaper, the Hearst-owned *Los Angeles Herald-Examiner*, which claimed Koufax had vowed to quit unless the Dodgers paid him $90,000. An irate Koufax immediately responded: he had never asked for $90,000 or threatened to leave baseball. He was convinced Dodger management had planted the story to make him look greedy, angry as well with the *Herald-Examiner*'s veteran Dodgers beat writer Bob Hunter, whose article came under immediate attack from a competitor, the *Los Angeles Times*' Dodgers reporter Frank Finch, who labeled it "baseless." The *Herald-Examiner*'s story, Koufax told Finch, "made me look like I was trying to blackmail the Dodgers. It certainly didn't do my public image any good."

Bavasi denied he planted the story with the *Herald-Examiner*, but the acrimony between the general manager and his star pitcher was escalating. "It was made to appear that I was holding up the club with a gun," Koufax told the *Times* two days later. "I've been hurt by people I thought were my friends."

Tracewski privately spoke with Koufax during the controversy. His friend was indignant and rattled, convinced he had been punished for demanding a negotiation with Bavasi. "Sandy was just shocked anybody would do that to him after the kind of season he gave the club," Tracewski remembers. "He just wanted to be treated fairly. And it was nerve-racking for him and other guys when they had to stand up for themselves."

Koufax told the *Times* he had lost about fifteen pounds since his battle with Bavasi began. His voice suddenly had a tremor. The ugliness of the negotiations had come at a cost to Koufax's serenity, but his battle with Bavasi had produced the greatest victory yet for a Dodger player in a negotiation with management. To be sure, it was a small victory relative to what was coming. But it was a start, providing impetus and inspiration.

Others wished they could be as brave and tough. At that moment, still back home with his family in Spokane, Wills had begun a hold-out of his own. He wanted a raise to $65,000. Bavasi said no, sent him a contract for $50,000, and called his home. Wills's wife answered the phone and said Maury had gone fishing. "He has a contract in his pocket and can sign it anytime he wants," Bavasi told reporters. "I don't intend to contact him."

Wills waited two weeks before surrendering in Spokane, sign-ing for $50,000 and getting on a plane headed to spring training. "You get scared," he would say, a half century later. "And if you've been scared about other things in your life, and if they've made you feel scared before, it's easier for them to scare you again. And Buzzie always scared me. I wanted to be like Sandy, but I couldn't be like Sandy. It just wasn't in me. I knew I had to work on that."

He checked into his room in Dodgertown's major-league barracks, the room that had once served as his chief dream. He no longer felt special there. "Here I was on a World Championship team that had just beaten the Yankees—the defending World Series champions," he remembers. "I was an All-Star, I was an MVP, I did television, I had everything. And I felt lousy. Everybody thought 1963 was such a great year for us, but there was this whole other 1963 that fans didn't see. I'd gone through a lot with Buzzie and the Dodgers in the off-season. It made me feel small. Nobody knew any of that, but there were a lot of us who felt that way."

It was the side of baseball that no fans saw, he thought. Those fans who waited so long in front of the Dodgers ticket office, who lined up for players' autographs for hours, who treated him and Koufax like gods: they just had no idea, Wills told friends. "We were champions, but we were kind of nobodies to ourselves," he recalls. "I was a nobody to myself at least. I told myself that had to change. But I didn't know how to change it. I just didn't know how in hell I was going to get there."

THE END OF INNOCENCE

No one, not even Wes Parker, could have foreseen how quickly he would rise in the Dodgers minor-league organization. He was the worst of long shots when he began. The reality was that minor-league players signed to contracts without a bonus and for only $300 per month had only a scintilla of a chance of making it to the majors.

When Parker joined the Class A Santa Barbara Rancheros to begin his minor-league career in 1963, only seven months removed from his pain and epiphany in Paris, he found himself on the same team as his Los Angeles winter-league friend, twenty-one-year-old outfielder Clarence Jones. Parker was twenty-three, old for a first-year minor leaguer, old in a sport where young is cherished, old especially on a team in which twenty-one of his twenty-six teammates that year were twenty-two or younger, and six were teenagers.

The youngsters included the eighteen-year-old New York schoolboy pitching sensation and bonus baby Paul Speckenbach, already regarded by many in the organization as a can't-miss major-league prospect worthy of patience and protection so as not to jeopardize the Dodgers' major investment in him, estimated at between $60,000 and $100,000. No one on the Rancheros received more attention at the 1963 season's start than Speckenbach. He enjoyed a stature among minor leaguers equaled only by the Dodgers' other elite bonus prospects, including Roy Gleason, who would play that season for the Salem, Oregon, Single-A club, and John Werhas, who would hit a solid .295 that year and play third base for Triple-A Spokane while being groomed to become a Dodger in 1964. An All-American at the

University of Southern California in 1959, Werhas had been joined in the organization by one of his collegiate teammates, left-handed pitcher Bruce Gardner, another seemingly golden discovery, signed in 1960 after compiling a remarkable record of 40–5 for USC.

Few Dodger farm babies enjoyed the kind of hoopla surrounding Gardner. Baseball scouts' interest in him dated back to his days at Los Angeles's Fairfax High School, when the Chicago White Sox offered him a $50,000 signing bonus upon his graduation. Choosing instead to attend USC, he had won praise as the best collegiate pitcher in the country by the time the Dodgers wooed him away after his junior year. But as a testament to how collegiate experience in the 1960s sometimes only made a player older and less alluring in the eyes of scouts, Gardner had to settle for a respectable but relatively modest Dodgers bonus of $20,000, or $30,000 less than what the White Sox had offered three years earlier. Ultimately, the figure seemed likely to be little more than an irritation for Gardner. By securing a place in the glamorous Dodgers organization, he would doubtless recoup the lost dollars once he achieved stardom for a team skilled at producing All-Star pitchers and Cy Young Award winners.

In the following years, Gardner's career spoke to the crapshoot nature of trying to predict a prospect's future. After a sterling 20–4 season in Class C ball during 1961 in Reno, he had been drafted into the army, where he injured his left arm. He recovered and resumed his career, but never again would he possess the same magic. After breaking his ankle during spring training in 1964, he returned the same season, only to struggle. With his career flatlining, he was released by the Dodgers organization before the year ended. That is how quickly some baseball dreams are snuffed. Gardner's life would be void of celebrated accomplishments thereafter, though he tried many things. He worked as a broker, did some coaching, and sometimes played the piano professionally.

His last act brought him back to the USC campus and the very college baseball diamond on which he had starred. In June 1971, he stood alone between the pitcher's mound and second base, his USC diploma in his right hand and his All-American plaque resting on the ground nearby. He shot himself dead with a .38-caliber revolver. He left no note.

Gardner's was just the most horrific among the many stories of disappointing careers for Dodgers bonus players. Failure will forever be the norm. So many prospects are signed each year, and there are so few major-league roster spots available. Factor in the many injuries to vulnerable young bodies, along with the reality of how professional ball painfully magnifies a great prospect's slightest flaw, and the failure rate spikes dramatically. Speckenbach, who would compile a record of 5–4 with a 4.86 ERA for the Rancheros in 1963, would encounter arm troubles within a year, never to pitch a game in the majors, eventually to become a high school teacher and coach. Werhas would start the 1964 season with the Dodgers as the team's starting third baseman, but he would struggle offensively and be back in the minors before the season's end, on his way to a short-lived major-league career.

Out of the twenty-seven players on the 1963 Santa Barbara Rancheros, only four would ever become major leaguers. One was Clarence Jones, who would play a bit in the outfield during parts of two different seasons for the Cubs. Two of the others would have short careers as part-time role players. Indeed, the only Ranchero to have a lengthy career in the majors would be Parker, who had quickly confounded the organization's experts by outperforming many of the Dodgers' most coveted bonus players. In July of that year, his father received a letter from Fresco Thompson, the Dodgers vice president in charge of minor-league operations. By then, Thompson knew that Parker would be moving up in the organization. In his note, a pleased but faintly chastened-sounding Thompson confessed to an earlier misjudgment: "No one in the organization expected your son to advance much past the low minor leagues. We knew he had great desire, but no one expected him to advance this far."

Finishing with a .305 average and 11 homers at Santa Barbara, Parker was on his way by August to Double-A Albuquerque. There he shared a place with another player, and quickly signaled his off-field need for serenity. When his roommate displayed a love for playing his guitar into the late hours, Parker abruptly moved out. His singular focus yielded benefits. He was at his hottest in Albuquerque, hitting .350 in twenty-six games there, demonstrating a switch-hitter's skill from both sides of the plate. He knew better than anyone else that he didn't at all understand the art of hitting at the professional level. But he was thriving anyway. He owed his good fortune to his genetic gifts—his athleticism, reflexes, and extraordinary eyesight—and to his luck in being able to feast on mediocre minor-league pitchers who had neither the talent nor the guile of experienced major-league hurlers who were adept at swiftly spotting and exploiting a young hitter's weaknesses. His swift rise would ultimately be his curse, though he could see none of this as his minor-league average kept climbing.

At the end of his 1963 season in Albuquerque, Parker's play sparked speculation that he might be ready to compete for a spot on the major-league roster as early as the following spring training. Looking forward to a few weeks of off-season rest, Parker received news that would necessitate a sudden change in his plans: the Dodgers wanted him to spend most of his autumn in Mesa, Arizona, a suburb of Phoenix, to play in the instructional league there and further hone his skills.

Several other Albuquerque players and future Dodger teammates would join Parker in Mesa, including Jeff Torborg, a collegiate All-American catcher from New Jersey who had graduated only a few months earlier from Rutgers, where he hit an astounding .537 during his senior year. A strong and compact catcher who, at half an inch over six feet and 195 pounds, looked like a power-running tailback, Torborg was as much prized for his sound defense as his big bat. While an ignored Parker had emerged from nowhere to fall into the Dodgers' lap, the twenty-one-year-old Torborg had been coveted by scouts, the object of an intense courting that ended with the Dodgers giving him a signing bonus of $100,000.

If Torborg had anything in common with Parker, it was a sterling athletic pedigree. His six-foot-three father, Bob, had excelled in basketball during the 1940s, where his skills in an eastern league had given him the opportunity to play against several high-profile teams, including the Boston Celtics. Along with the younger Torborg's prodigious physical talent came a deep self-belief. "I'd been fortunate to have success," he remembers. "I just thought it would probably keep happening."

So confident were Dodger officials about Torborg's talent that, instead of starting him in the low minors with a team like Santa Barbara, they immediately dispatched him to Albuquerque.

There, Torborg struggled. He was stymied by the kind of pitching he had never seen before—fastballs in excess of 90 miles per hour and off-speed breaking balls that made him look foolish. Confounded and overwhelmed, he watched his batting average plummet to an embarrassing .230. He was rattled, on and off the field. During his first week in Albuquerque, he saw a black widow spider in the clubhouse shower. One night, as the team sat on a jet taxiing out on the tarmac in Amarillo before takeoff, the plane hit an airport gasoline truck and sheared off part of a wing. What else could go wrong? Torborg wondered. He began striking out more than ever. His setbacks called for a resilience unnecessary during his glory days at Rutgers. "Albuquerque was a rude awakening," Torborg recalls. "I'd been used to succeeding. It was my introduction to how tough the life of a professional ballplayer would be. It probably affected my attitude and play, though I didn't notice it right away."

But his wife, Suzie, did. Early in their Albuquerque stint, during the summer of 1963, she offered a candid assessment—and a terse invitation. "You don't look like you're playing with the same enthusiasm," she told him. "If you don't feel like playing, let's go home. You can do something else."

"It was an awakening," Torborg remembers. "I'd been down. Suzie made me realize it. I was going to need a different attitude. I wanted to be good. I told myself to start enjoying it. I started playing better."

His batting average climbed. "There was pressure, sure, but it was a great life too," he recalls. "I had a job, we had some money. And I had a real baseball career. It seemed like we could do anything. There weren't a lot of concerns. It was a wonderful summer. It was a fantastic time to be young."

Torborg's attitude throughout the summer of 1963 reflected the optimism and pleasures of his country. Most of 1963 felt like one long American summer. The year's most popular new songs emphasized bliss, laughs, and fun in the sun. "Those Lazy, Hazy, Crazy Days of Summer," performed by Nat King Cole, became a hit, as did Allan Sherman's ditty "Hello Muddah, Hello Faddah," in which Sherman channeled the goofy voice of a homesick boy at a mishap-prone summer camp. Surfing songs were the new rage, with the Beach Boys' "Surfin' U.S.A." and Jan and Dean's "Surf City" making immediate stars of the two groups and serving as a reminder that surfing enthusiasts had grown from a few thousand to more than 5 million since the 1950s.

Yet racial tensions had become a tinderbox, belying all of 1963's happy songs and bubbly television variety shows. With critics accusing him of being slow to confront the dilemma, President Kennedy at last declared in a June speech that civil rights had become a "moral issue." Even the plans of the president and his aides were affected by the divisions. Facing an imminent reelection campaign and worried about Democratic disunity in several southern states, the Kennedy team scheduled a political visit to Texas late in the year. The president's press secretary, Pierre Salinger, was scheduled to be away on another assignment during the Texas trip. The number-two man in the White House communications department, a deputy press secretary named Andy Hatcher, would ordinarily have assumed control of press matters in Salinger's absence. But Hatcher was black, southern tensions over issues of race were high, and the White House privately decided not to have him travel to Texas. A white subordinate named Malcolm "Mac" Kilduff would stand in for Salinger and Hatcher.

It was another accommodation quietly made so as not to risk a problem that could be avoided—the kind of accommodation to which major American institutions and private businesses, including the Dodgers, routinely acceded. It was exactly the kind of accommodation that had driven Buzzie Bavasi to warn Maury Wills not to date Doris Day, and the kind that accounted for Wills's submission. It was the kind of understanding that had kept black Dodgers from trying to move into well-heeled all-white Los Angeles neighborhoods.

Such accommodations were simple instinct in 1963. They were so ubiquitous that they constituted a kind of stained old wallpaper in the American house that people had long since stopped noticing. Never having been affected by the accommodations, Parker and Torborg hadn't given them deep thought, though that wasn't to say that a racial disconnect hadn't occurred to each man. In marveling over black National League stars like Willie Mays, Henry Aaron, and Maury Wills, the two young white players sometimes thought how amazing it was—odd, disturbing, and surreal—that even the most famous black players couldn't eat or sleep in certain establishments. They had won Most Valuable Player Awards and led their league to All-Star game victories, but they couldn't get a hamburger in places.

By then, the everyday indignities, coupled with the impatience of civil rights leaders, had reached a tipping point. Leaders would no longer be content confining their demonstrations to the South. This resolve led to the August 1963 "March on Washington," where a crowd of more than a quarter million protesters, black and white, gathered in front of the Lincoln Memorial and listened to a series of speeches culminating with Reverend Martin Luther King Jr.'s "I Have a Dream," with its most famous of clarion calls: "I have a dream that my four little children will one day live in a nation where they will not be judged by the color of their skin, but by the content of their character."

Traveling with the Dodgers at the time, Wills was moved to realize that King's words had been delivered just minutes from his childhood home in the Parkside projects. He wished he could lend his own voice to the struggle—maybe just a few supportive words—before quickly realizing that to do so would likely infuriate Dodger management, which loathed controversy. Wills didn't want to test Bavasi's reaction to any issue involving race. It was not as if anyone in Dodger management had warned black players not to talk publicly about civil rights. But like so much else in the Dodgers organization, Wills thought, it was just understood that you didn't do certain things. By now, the taboo was simply part of that wallpaper you didn't notice.

Meanwhile, Torborg's view of the world could hardly have been sunnier, or more revealing about the differences between his social station and Wills's. Even the tensions accompanying the civil rights movement struck him as a sign of a painstaking progress. He appreciated that a young president like Kennedy was at the helm of the country in such challenging times.

No matter the conflict, a glass was always half full to Torborg. His minor-league teammates had noticed his easygoing optimism and ability to encourage others. He had a sense of command, a useful attribute for a young catcher handling many of the Dodgers' most promising minor-league pitchers. As the season wound down in Albuquerque, he was happy to hear that the Dodgers had assigned him to play fall ball in Arizona. "Going to Mesa for the Instructional League just sounded like it would make me a better ballplayer," he remembers. "Suzie and I took a quick trip home to New Jersey, and then we came back and headed for Mesa."

They drove the desert highway toward Arizona in their used 1952 Plymouth, the backseat of which Torborg had removed to make room for the "TV box," as Torborg called their mammoth black-and-white television: "It was this big box with a small screen, like a piece of furniture. We didn't have a lot, but we had the TV box. Suzie had bought our car in Albuquerque for $175. It didn't even have a heater. We didn't care about anything like that. We were just so young. We were so lucky and having fun. We got out there and saw a Peter, Paul and Mary concert."

Arizona felt idyllic to the young couple. It was as if summer never ended there. Torborg played his ball games during the days, hung out with Suzie at night, and sometimes they watched the gargantuan TV box for laughs. They had friends in Mesa, including Parker, who lived in the same apartment building.

It was, both players realized later, a relatively serene time in their careers. The same could be largely said of the country and planet. Relations between the United States and the Soviet Union remained calm. The only bit of disturbing news came amid the political instability in South Vietnam, where the country's beleaguered leader, sixty-two-year-old Ngo Dinh Diem, was murdered by his own military, along with his brother, Ngo Dinh Nhu, in a coup d'état secretly encouraged by the American government. But Diem's fall had marked the lone disquieting note that autumn. In Los Angeles, bright economic reports and happy updates about the world champion Dodgers quickly pushed Diem off the front pages.

Early on the last Friday before Thanksgiving, Torborg and Suzie were looking forward to their first holiday feast together as marrieds. The country was already easing its foot off the accelerator. Many governmental officials had left Washington. A smiling Secretary of State Dean Rusk and several other Kennedy cabinet officials were in Hawaii, about to fly to Japan for a conference. The president and First Lady were in Texas, appearing before enthusiastic crowds.

It was a terribly slow news day at its start. The front page of the *Los Angeles Times* was reduced to focusing attention on thunderstorms that had hit the region. Overseas, a British band still unknown to most Americans was releasing its second album that morning in the United Kingdom, entitled *With the Beatles*.

In Arizona, sunny skies guaranteed another perfect day. Torborg and Parker had gone to the ballpark in Mesa to prepare for a game when, shortly after 10:30 a.m., a player ran into the locker room and yelled, "Kennedy's been shot."

All too familiar with ballplayer humor, Parker dismissed the remark. "Don't be a jerk," he said.

"Kennedy's been shot," the player repeated. "Check the radio."

About an hour later, speaking from Parkland Hospital in Dallas, White House deputy press secretary Mac Kilduff told the press corps that the president was dead. The Arizona Instructional League announced that it was canceling all its games over the next four days. A stricken Torborg, looking for anything to take his mind off the horror, rounded up some guys for a touch football game. Parker was enlisted to be the quarterback for one of the teams, but they hadn't been playing for even fifteen minutes when he, Torborg, and the others simply stopped and walked off the field. Torborg returned to his apartment, where he and Suzie watched Walter Cronkite on the TV box. Torborg was sickened. He and Suzie were crying. It was horrible to keep watching the TV, but they couldn't drag themselves away from it.

Parker was numb. The president of the United States, he thought. My God. My God. Murdered on a street. If a president's life could be snuffed out like that, before a crowd in broad daylight, what chance did anybody have? What the hell was happening?

Maury Wills was on a Las Vegas golf course when he heard the news. It can't be true, he thought.

It was true, somebody assured him.

A stunned Wills left the course. A Kennedy admirer, he couldn't believe a man so powerful was gone. How could a president with all that damn security around him be shot? How was that possible? Already jittery about his own safety in the face of his new fame, he suddenly felt more in need than ever of taking precautions around strangers.

In Southern California, Tommy Davis, who had a small advertising-related company, was out on an appointment near some railroad tracks when he heard the news on a radio. In a reaction that spoke to his worries and the nation's racial divisions, Davis's first thought was a prayer of sorts about the assassin: "I said to myself, I hope it's not a black guy." Soon, like many Americans, he would begin wondering whether the assassination was the product of a conspiracy.

Tracewski, like many Dodgers, had landed a sales job during the off-season, to supplement his baseball income. On that morning, he drove to work at a Chevrolet dealership at Seventh Street and Central Avenue in downtown Los Angeles. Less than a half hour after his arrival, news of the assassination sped through the dealership. Tracewski didn't wait around. He didn't want to be in an office. He hurried home to his wife, in deep shock. They had voted for Kennedy. "All we did was watch television and mourn for days," Tracewski remembers. "It was impossible to think about anything else. I knew it was going to take all of us quite a lot of time to get over this."

In Cleveland, after another season with the Indians, Mudcat Grant was buying tires for his car. The autumn had been very difficult for him. In September, a group of white supremacists had set off a bomb during a Sunday service at the Sixteenth Street Baptist Church in Birmingham, Alabama. It killed four black girls, ranging in age from eleven to fourteen. The explosion had robbed a surviving child of her sight in one eye. At least twenty other people were injured. Grant had never felt lower in his life. "Small children dying," he remembered. He had recollections dating back to his early childhood of Ku Klux Klan members shooting at black adults just to make sure that anyone who might be disgruntled stayed intimidated—shooting at blacks as if this were sport. Always, Grant had pushed on. But the thought of those four children in graves was more than he could bear. It had torn him up. "I almost couldn't get through it. That was as bad as I've ever felt about things."

On that Friday he had chores at least to keep his mind occupied. He got his new tires. He picked up a pay phone and called home.

His father-in-law answered and said, "They just done shot your president."

He climbed into his car but had to pull off to the side of the road. "It was a day you want to forget. I don't know how else I can put it. There were sleepless nights, a lot of tears. It was a hard few months."

Some Dodgers, like Tracewski, would have days and weeks to grieve and recover; they had no autumn games requiring their concentration. But for Parker and Torborg, there would be only a brief respite before they were scheduled to be back on the field: the Arizona Instructional League had announced that games would resume on the following Tuesday. Parker hadn't been able to stop watching the assassination coverage. On that Sunday, he saw Lee Harvey Oswald murdered on live television during a jail transfer.

Yet Parker had no doubt that he would be able to retrain his attention on baseball. Telling himself his survival was at stake, he resolved not to lose focus. Nothing could be allowed to jeopardize his last opportunity of the year to impress Dodger management. "I couldn't let anything stop me, not John Kennedy's assassination or anything else," he recalls. "I was trying to make a team. If my intensity ever was even a little off, all I had to do was think of my parents and that would bring it back for me—I had to make it. The rest of the world would mourn and I respected that. It was very painful for me, too. But I had to push through all that. I had no time for it. My life felt like it was on the line. I had to play well."

By then, Torborg too was grateful to have baseball as a sanctuary. "Once I got back to playing and competing, that became my priority," he said. "You're a player. That's what you do. You overcome everything; you shut out everything."

So skilled at shutting out stresses since his youth, Parker succeeded in doing it again, exhibiting the same concentration he had displayed a year earlier during the Cuban Missile Crisis. He picked up in Mesa where he had left off in Albuquerque, hitting .300 for the Arizona fall season and hoping he had given himself the best chance to be a part of the Dodgers' spring training plans.

At last he received the call he'd wanted all along. The Dodgers invited him to Vero Beach for spring training. He stayed in good shape over the last winter weeks, determined to impress team officials from the day he arrived in Florida. In early February, he walked out on the tarmac of the Los Angeles International Airport, where the Dodger team awaited their flight. He didn't know any of the Dodger regulars, and he wondered how they would treat him. His nerves eased a little when a smiling Don Drysdale, who had heard something about his hobbies, asked if he wanted to join some guys in a game of bridge during the flight. Parker was silently ecstatic. *I'm going to hang out and play bridge with Don Drysdale.*

People seemed friendly. He strolled toward the plane. It was then that he saw Sandy Koufax in the flesh, Koufax about thirty feet away, Koufax standing on the tarmac alongside another man. It was yet another indication to Parker of his new station in life.

And perhaps he would've looked the other way then, except that something had caught his attention. Koufax looked upset. Koufax was doing all the talking with this other man. Koufax looked very bothered by something the other man had done. The other man was Bob Hunter, the baseball beat writer for the *Los Angeles Herald-Examiner*, the man who had written the story during the winter that Koufax had threatened to quit baseball if the Dodgers didn't give him all the money he wanted. Koufax was really giving it to Bob Hunter.

This was not the Koufax he had seen in television interviews.

This was not the gentle Koufax.

It was his first unguarded glimpse of Koufax, his first sense that the star had his own stresses.

He realized he didn't know any of these players. They didn't know him. He hardened himself for whatever was ahead.

Chapter 4

An Upheaval Begins

While most of his teammates flew on the Dodger plane to their spring training home in Vero Beach, young Jeff Torborg climbed into his old car and, accompanied by his wife, began the long drive from his native New Jersey. Along the way, in need of sleep, the couple found a hotel room. There, Torborg listened to the radio broadcast of a major sporting event gripping the planet—the heavyweight championship fight between a brash twenty-two-year-old underdog named Cassius Clay and the seemingly invincible world champion, Sonny Liston, who had won and successfully defended his crown with a pair of devastating first-round knockouts of the former champion, Floyd Patterson.

The young challenger, a born comic who made a habit of using rhyme to predict the round in which he would knock out an upcoming opponent ("Sonny will fall in eight, to prove I'm great"), appealed to Torborg as a welcome break from the staleness of star athletes' phony humility. A typhoon of mirth, braggadocio, and vehemence, the young fighter had decided that he alone would be in charge of his image. No comment would be too outlandish, no poem too inane. It occurred to Torborg that such freedom was unthinkable in baseball.

"I am the greatest," the fighter happily howled, the personification of self-love. Torborg later recollected, "The guy made you smile."

He loved it that the challenger, a kid his own age from Louisville, Kentucky, was so *different*, so funny, so fresh. It was the winter for new. February had marked the American arrival of an utterly original breed of personalities, in and out of sports. Just two weeks earlier, a mop-haired English rock band he'd never heard before, the Beatles, appeared for the first time on *The Ed Sullivan Show* before a stunning 73 million viewers, the largest audience to that point in American television history. Nine days after the Sullivan show, in a stroke of publicity genius, representatives of the young band brought John Lennon, Paul McCartney, George Harrison, and Ringo Starr to see the young boxer at his Miami training camp. The five horsed around in a ring and posed together for photographs, in what one day would be seen as a historic encounter between the twentieth century's most famous musicians and its most charismatic athlete.

Anyone observing the wisecracking, irreverent twentysomethings and the rapt fascination of the media horde could reasonably have sensed that something larger was afoot here. No one could yet define the change in the air, but a social upheaval was under way. Not even one hundred days had passed since President Kennedy's assassination. Yet already the grieving over his death was giving way to a new restiveness. The self-satisfaction of the 1950s, which had seeped into the early 1960s, was crumbling, along with the staidness of the old order. People were slowly turning the page on an era.

What would come to be identified as the flowering of the '60s, marked by reinvention and turbulence, had fitfully begun. Before spring arrived, twenty-two-year-old Bob Dylan released his third album, whose prescient title track, "The Times They Are a-Changin'," included a line that served at once as a plea and a warning: "Come senators, congressmen, please heed the call." A bedazzling young British band quickly to be labeled unkempt and surly, the Rolling Stones, had arrived with its debut album. Later in the year, Massachusetts authorities would announce the arrest of Albert DeSalvo, who would confess in time to being the Boston Strangler, his rapes and murders one day to animate the Stones' dark masterpiece "Midnight Rambler." It was no longer the decade of Frank Sinatra, Dean Martin, Perry Como, Pat Boone, or Sandra Dee. It was no longer a fashionable time for crew cuts or ducktails, or Vegas lounge shows, or the Rat Pack, or hula hoops, or TV shows that were paeans to traditional values like *Father Knows Best*. Increasingly, in virtually every sector of culture and politics, the old order had little choice but to listen to ascendant new voices.

Several hundred miles away from the Beatles and Cassius Clay, Martin Luther King Jr. and several other leaders of the Southern Christian Leadership Conference, still basking in the resounding triumph of the landmark 1963 March on Washington, ramped up efforts to pressure the US Congress to pass a meaningful civil rights act. Segregated southern communities like Vero Beach, which had dug in their heels against change, faced a social tidal wave.

Sitting in his hotel room, looking for a break from the burden of his own challenges, Torborg was listening to the broadcast of the big fight, which was happening a few hours down the Florida coast, in Miami Beach. Liston was the huge betting favorite. Then the bell rang, and from the opening minute, the lightning-fast challenger dominated. He danced circles around the befuddled older champion, steadily beating him up. A bleeding Liston quit on his stool before the start of round seven, complaining of a bad shoulder. "It was incredibly exciting," Torborg remembered.

The reeling sports world didn't know what to make of the massive upset or the young new champion. Less than twenty-four hours later, as the shock of his victory was finally settling in, the fighter jolted the country anew: he announced he had joined the Nation of Islam and would no longer be known by his "slave name." Briefly, he would be Cassius X, until he settled on a new identity. Nine days later, the Nation of Islam bestowed upon him the name that would be his for the rest of his life—Muhammad Ali. A large body of American sportswriters reacted with puzzlement and scorn. But Ali, on his way to becoming arguably the most important athlete of the twentieth century, had taken control of his destiny, in a transitional moment that would encourage legions of athletes, black and white, to break out in their own ways. Torborg remembered thinking of the fighter: "He's his own man. Things are happening." By then, only nine weeks into 1964, change was already the motif of the young decade. It would place added pressure on an array of American institutions, including major-league baseball, to catch up.

Torborg was acquiring a stronger sense than ever of the change approaching, as well as the human cost of injustice. The recognition did not come overnight. A friendship preceded it. One of the first people Torborg met in Vero Beach was a man capable of making his life either very happy or quite miserable. Entrenched major-league starters sometimes reacted coolly, if not with outright mistrust, to young rookies who played the same position and naturally aspired to take playing time from them. Nothing would have been more un-derstandable than if John Roseboro, the Dodgers' clear number-one catcher and a former National League All-Star, had kept the Dodgers' heralded young bonus-baby catcher (whose six-figure bonus alone was more than double Roseboro's annual salary of $40,000) at a personal distance. For a less secure player, suspicion and resentment might have been natural reactions.

But Roseboro was neither an ordinary player nor an ordinary man. Shortly after Torborg's arrival, having watched the newcomer go through a practice, Roseboro turned to the club's number-two catcher, Doug Camilli, gestured at Torborg, and said, "We have an-other good-looking catcher here." He put Torborg under his wing, sharing his favorite and most effective defensive techniques, including how best to block home plate against onrushing foes, employing a stance he had used in his days as a high school and collegiate football linebacker.

You couldn't ask for more from a mentor, Torborg thought, though for a while they seldom talked to each other about anything other than the game. Actually, Roseboro rarely spoke much to anyone at all—a reality that long before had led friends to dub him "Gabby." Yet on those infrequent occasions when Roseboro offered an observation, what he said carried authority in the team clubhouse.

"Roseboro was the conscience of our club," Tracewski remembered. "He was a steadying influence. He was a bright guy who knew the game and how to handle pitchers. He was fair to everyone. He was a quiet leader. If he said something, you listened. And like Maury, he'd do anything to win."

Anything meant, among other things, playing while hurt. In 1962 a foul tip had broken a weld in his catcher's mask, the ball penetrating the protective bars like a missile and hitting Roseboro above his right eye. Dazed and briefly hospitalized, he was out of action for eleven days. It could've been much longer, but Roseboro insisted on returning, still beset by terrible headaches that plagued him even as 1964 began.

But his toughness had limits. No one could see his emotional pain, which had mounted for more than a decade. He had grown up in Ashland, Ohio, a middling-size town of roughly 15,000 residents, about an hour's drive from Cleveland. Although the Roseboros were one of the few black families in an area whose nods to racial segregation included a movie theater with opposite seating sides for whites and blacks, the young Roseboro felt accepted there, attending Ashland's integrated public high school, where he starred on the football team.

His father, who believed that being tough was essential for a man to defend himself and earn respect, had taught him how to box. Roseboro himself developed a hard-eyed stare that he hoped would deter antagonists. But the stare would seldom be needed in Ashland. He thought virtually all of Ashland's whites treated him well during his adolescence, fondly remembering how once, on a youth team, his upset white teammates had risen to his defense, turning and walking out of an area restaurant that wouldn't serve him.

For a year and a half he attended Wilberforce University, a historically black institution in Ohio, on a football scholarship. Then the Dodgers beckoned. The relative decency of Ashland had left Roseboro wholly unprepared for the humiliations he endured during his minor-league days. Upon his Dodger signing, he'd told club officials that he preferred not to play for a minor-league team in the South, worried about the tales he'd heard of the region's racism. He quickly discovered the North to be little better. In 1952 he began his career in Sheboygan, Wisconsin, playing for a Class D team, in the Wisconsin State League. During a road game in Wausau, he was harassed by a fan who taunted him with the N-word.

Being elevated to the major leagues hadn't brought an end to the racial epithets. A policeman in Houston had mockingly addressed him as "boy." Florida and spring training had sparked the worst memories of all. When a theater in Vero Beach would finally consent to letting blacks purchase seats there, Roseboro had to steel himself when the lights went down and people behind him called out the N-word in his direction.

Roseboro held communities like Vero Beach responsible for the ugliness. But eventually he would "also blame the Dodgers some," he wrote later. Privately, during the early 1960s, he thought that the organization should have made certain that its black players were sent only to cities where they would be welcomed.

The off-field abuses and stresses, coupled with his heavy on-field responsibilities, had taken a toll. He was not even thirty-one as spring training began in 1964, but his sober bearing gave him the look of an older, sometimes world-weary man. Teammate Nate Oliver called him "Dad."

Roseboro was guarded about discussing matters of race with anyone other than a handful of black teammates. He was reminded of the profound difference of the black experience when hearing well-intentioned but often naive expressions of understanding from supportive white friends. This group included Torborg, whose New Jersey background and mind-set bore a strong similarity to those of the white kids who had befriended him on the Ashland teams. One day, wishing to underscore his shared contempt for segregation's evil, Torborg told Roseboro that he had played on integrated teams throughout elementary school, high school, and college, revealing that his head coach at Rutgers once had "read the riot act" to a bigot who turned away Rutgers's black players from a North Carolina sandwich shop.

Roseboro listened quietly for a while before letting his understudy know there were limits to how much any young white man could know about walking in his shoes. He offered a rare glimpse of his scarred heart. "Jeff, that's all well and good," he said gently. "But you'll never know the feeling I've had unless you walk into a room and know that people there don't think you are as good as they are."

"I understood what he meant," Torborg recalls of Roseboro's perspective. "He made me see it in a new way. And I kind of knew, just by the way he said it, that the way things were in the country wouldn't last, couldn't last. People weren't going to put up with it much longer. I think ballplayers—white guys and black guys—could see that before a lot of other people did."

By the late 1950s and early '60s, a different breed of ballplayer had arrived. The newcomers weren't Depression babies overjoyed just to get a paycheck for playing baseball. They did not necessarily feel, as Lou Gehrig had, like the luckiest men on the face of the earth. Some, like Koufax in moments, had the souls of agonizing artists. The most desperate, those not playing as much as they'd like, were as despondent as obscure painters convinced their best work was being ignored. Individualistic and often ascetic, they led off-field lives that in many cases defied the stereotypes of previous generations of ballplayers. Some were averse to big parties and crowds. They had the dispositions of careful, high-strung prodigies. They were monomaniacal about their work. They could be moody and snappish when the work didn't go well.

The intensity of their highs and lows betrayed their worst fears. Like the mercurial artist who destroys his own canvases in a frenzy of despair, the most driven among them could verge on the temperamentally self-destructive, as had a disillusioned Koufax at the end of his 1960 season, when he furiously signaled that he was quitting the Dodgers by throwing his baseball glove and other equipment into a trash can and storming off. Not yet having produced even one notable season after six years, he was perhaps done for good with the game at twenty-four, finished with being underutilized and mismanaged by the Dodgers in his judgment, his mood not helped by his dismal 8–13 record in 1960.

But his fit of petulance, which had all the potential for infuriating the Dodgers and leading to a trade in the off-season, had marked a turning point. It was the greatest sign yet of how much the artist in him cared. Returning for spring training in 1961, he found his discarded glove waiting for him, fished out of the trash bin long before by Nobe Kawano, the Dodgers' clubhouse manager, who had suspected the erratic wunderkind couldn't stay away.

He would give it another season, Koufax decided. The effort was crucial to his self-image, thought close friends like Wills, who knew it mattered to Koufax that he be regarded as a reliable professional and good teammate. He would either win in 1961 or be crushed trying. Yet his swift ascension thereafter did nothing within his own clubhouse to quiet the questions about him. As 1964 began, he was recognized as the greatest pitcher in the game, but the memory of his eruption, three and a half years earlier, was still fresh to some teammates. They knew no one prepared harder for his job or was more monastic in his lead-up to a game. But they also believed his highly sensitive athlete's soul resembled a volatile genius's. If he ever felt disrespected, he would have difficulty moving on until the guilty party had paid a price.

What happened during the first forty-eight hours of the team's 1964 spring training camp revealed the depth of Koufax's bitterness toward Dodger management. He had signed his contract, but he had yet to stop fuming over the indignities that had accompanied it.

Publicly, in Vero Beach, his anger gushed. He couldn't let go of the false story in the *Herald-Examiner* that he'd threatened to quit, convinced that some unnamed team official had set out to turn public sentiment against him and pressure him into accepting a figure under $70,000.

Suspicions about the identity of the *Herald-Examiner*'s anonymous source centered upon Bavasi. Koufax wouldn't be dragged into saying that he thought Bavasi was the culprit, though he revealed that at one tense point in their negotiations Bavasi had threatened to withdraw management's early offer of $65,000 and, as punishment, give him no more than the major-league minimum salary of $10,000. That they had been fighting in the end over so little money especially irked Koufax. All this was over a difference of $5,000, he told people. *Five thousand.* Never before had a player had the temerity to report on Bavasi's tactics and bluster in such telling and acrimonious detail.

Without directly saying so, Koufax's disclosures amounted to an unprecedented broadside from a player against the Dodgers' way of doing things, against the club's ethos. To his close friend and roommate Tracewski, the breach between Koufax and management would never be fully repaired. "There was a lack of respect for Sandy by the Dodgers—that's the way he saw it," Tracewski remembers. "He wanted to be respected for what he did, and part of that respect meant a fair salary and being treated fairly. I liked Buzzie. But I'm not sure Sandy holds the same opinion. It always seemed Buzzie and the Dodgers had some reporters writing what they wanted to be written. Bob Hunter was in bed with the Dodgers, we always thought. It bothered Sandy when he read things in the paper that he knew were just wrong and that had to be coming from the Dodgers. It showed no respect, he thought. The respect to him was bigger than the money."

As spring training began, Koufax was talking to reporters more about his anger than either his pitching or the upcoming season. On the second day of camp, trying to avert a public relations crisis, O'Malley called Koufax into his Vero Beach office and asked him why he was unhappy.

Their discussion lasted an hour and fifteen minutes. Koufax was blunt. The claim that he had ever threatened to quit baseball was ridiculous, he told O'Malley. Then, according to Koufax, he suggested that Dodger management set out to use the *Herald-Examiner* story against him. O'Malley firmly denied it. Along the way, the owner got in his own veiled jabs. He suggested that Koufax was young and had something to learn about the reality of bargaining. According to Koufax, O'Malley urged him to ask his own father about the art of negotiations, as if Koufax's elder would understand something about the dynamics of high-stakes business discussions that young Koufax didn't.

"He . . . didn't change my mind," Koufax said of O'Malley to waiting reporters at the meeting's end.

By then, Bavasi couldn't possibly have doubted that the animosity and bad press weren't going away. Even before flying to Vero Beach, Koufax had called Bavasi at home to tell him that, though he was signing the contract, he was unhappy with the way the Dodgers had handled the negotiations. Feelings were icier than ever between the two men. Arriving in Florida, Bavasi indicated that he saw no need to reach out to Koufax and defuse tensions. "I'll have a chat with Koufax anytime he wants one, but insofar as I'm concerned the matter is closed," Bavasi told reporters. "I'm perfectly willing to listen, but I don't have anything in particular to talk about with Sandy."

An upset Koufax, however, dominated sports section headlines wherever he went. Bavasi couldn't get reporters to concentrate on anything else. Four days after his meeting with O'Malley, Koufax approached Bavasi in the training camp lobby of Dodgertown. A fifteen-minute meeting ensued. Bavasi denied planting the false story with the *Herald-Examiner*. Koufax didn't say whether he believed him, though by then it no longer mattered. Going their separate ways at the end, each man indicated to reporters that their problems had been settled. They had temporarily put the mess behind them, though not the suspicions and antagonisms. There would be an additional price to pay down the road.

I f anything would surprise those he bullied in contract dealings, it would be that Emil Joseph Bavasi was a baseball romantic. He grew up in Scarsdale, New York, where his immigrant father built a good life as a newspaper distributor and where his mother nicknamed him "Buzzie," as her ceaselessly energetic son always seemed to be buzzing around. He attended Fordham Prep School, where he plunged into baseball. He moved on to DePauw University in Indiana, where he played as a catcher on the baseball team. After his graduation in 1938, his mother gave him a car and, as a second present, said he could do whatever he wanted for the next year. He drove south in his new car, sat under the Florida sun, and watched baseball.

A one-in-a-hundred-million connection led to his first job: long before, his college roommate had introduced him to his dad, Ford Frick, the president of the National League, who made use of his glittering contacts for the young Bavasi. Soon he was working as an office boy for Larry MacPhail, the general manager of the Brooklyn Dodgers.

Within a year, he had become the business manager of a Dodger Class D minor-league club in Georgia, the closest thing to a junior executive training position. World War II interrupted his professional climb. Drafted into the army, he won a Bronze Star as a machine-gunner during Allied battles in Italy. Upon his discharge and return home, Dodgers president Branch Rickey made him the business manager of a fledgling minor-league club to be located somewhere in the Northeast, as part of the Class B New England League, in time for the 1946 season. Rickey, who a year earlier had signed Jackie Robinson and sent him to the Dodgers' Triple-A farm club in Montreal, had plans to sign more African Americans who would need to be protected from the many pockets of American racism, North and South. Rickey needed a friendly minor-league city in which his potential stars could develop.

Find us the place, Rickey ordered Bavasi.

Bavasi settled on Nashua, New Hampshire, where soon Rickey sent him a pair of newly signed black players, catcher Roy Campanella and pitcher Don Newcombe, two standouts from the Negro Leagues. The newly established Nashua Dodgers quickly found themselves in a tense rivalry with the all-white Red Sox farm club of Lynn, Massachusetts. With nastiness already brewing between the teams, ugliness erupted when Lynn players and their manager shouted racial taunts at Campanella and Newcombe. After a game in Nashua, a livid Bavasi confronted the Lynn manager in the stadium parking lot and challenged him to a fight. Players separated the two men, but by the time the howling and threats ceased, Bavasi had won the admiration of players and strengthened his bond with the young, little known, and generally impassive Ohioan whom he'd chosen to manage the team, Walter Alston.

Bavasi's ascension was swift thereafter. By 1948 he had his feet on the minors' top rung, taking over as the chief executive of the Montreal team for three seasons. It was his last stop before O'Malley made him the general manager of the Dodgers. As the 1951 season began, Bavasi had putative control over all of the clubs' baseball operations.

In 1954 he put the phlegmatic Alston at the helm of the team. The following year, with young left-hander Johnny Podres shutting out the Yankees in Game 7, the Dodgers captured a World Series title, Brooklyn's first and last. At forty-three, Alston was only two years into what ultimately would be a twenty-three-year stint as the field general of the Dodgers.

When Alston won his next World Series title, four years later in Los Angeles, the man who had launched him won plaudits, too. *Sporting News* magazine honored Bavasi as baseball's Executive of the Year for 1959.

Moon-faced and pudgy, with his sparse hair slicked back and a cigar stub sometimes in his hand, Bavasi could've passed for a bookie subsisting on life's margins. Indeed, some of his working days were interrupted by betting—if he knew a friendly player was going to the racetrack, he frequently stopped whatever he was doing to give the willing Dodger a couple of hundred dollars to bet on a horse or two, inviting the player to pocket a little of the cash for himself. He liked rogues every bit as much as he liked the track, and his favorite Dodgers invariably were partiers who regaled him with tales of their lives, and whom he alternately looked after and chastised. "He treated the younger ones like his own sons," said his oldest son, Peter, later to be the president of the Toronto Blue Jays. No player in the Dodgers organization received more of Bavasi's attention in non-baseball matters than future outfielder and power-hitting pinch hitter Al Ferrara, who, at twenty-two in 1963, was having a great Triple-A season in Spokane when Bavasi began paying closer attention to him.

Ferrara had been first noticed by scouts at Brooklyn's Lafayette High, the same school where Koufax had gotten his feet wet in baseball while starring in basketball, several years before Ferrara arrived. Any similarity between the two players ended there. Koufax was painfully averse to crowds. Ferrara was drawn to nightclubs and any carouser on the team who liked a funny story and a drink. Koufax was prudently saving some of his Dodgers earnings, in time to make investments in a modest motel and a radio station. Ferrara, well known for his devil-may-care streak that would test the patience of Dodger brass, was already on his way to burning through his $9,000 bonus.

Yet no player was better liked by other Dodgers—or closer to

Bavasi. Joining the team in the summer of 1963, Ferrara became the roommate of pitcher Johnny Podres on the team's road trips. The two had gotten to know each other during spring trainings, where they discovered common interests: parties, racetracks, booze. Soon, for a special ballplayer rate of only $2 a night, Ferrara and Podres were living year-round in downtown Los Angeles at the Mayfair Hotel.

The Mayfair was baseball's Animal House, better than any fraternity actually, because being ballplayers meant being a magnet for all kinds of attractive women and fun-loving visitors. Stars from other teams regularly dropped by, the bar stayed open late, and a party was happening whenever Ferrara wanted one. The hotel was an extension of everything limitless and lascivious that he loved about LA. He had room service whenever he wanted it. Best of all, he could charge everything to his tab, without desk clerks hassling him about a bill. After all, how much could you ever owe with a room costing you $2 a night? A guy could run that kind of fuckin' tab forever, he thought. Paradise.

Off the field, Ferrara viewed himself as a periodic screwup. "But Buzzie loved the screwups," Ferrara says. "He was a New York street guy. He lived through me, Podres, the horse players, the drinkers. He liked rebellious guys. He liked the guys with the shenanigans."

To be around Ferrara and Podres was to be reminded that winning didn't need to be a grim task. Bavasi couldn't get enough of Ferrara's stories about dropping in with Podres on Florida's Gulfstream Park during spring trainings. The day finally came when Bavasi asked Ferrara to make some bets at the track for him, too.

By then, Bavasi was calling Ferrara "son." He reserved the term for the players to whom he was closest, the ones whose personal lives, virtually without exception, ran the risk of going awry. He would do special favors for the screwups. During the baseball off-seasons, he came to the aid of Ferrara, who, usually not having saved a dime from his Dodger checks during a season, would be in need of money. "I was always busted in the winter," he remembers. Ferrara's wallet would be even lighter when he'd made a few losing bets at the Santa Anita racetrack. "I loved the racetrack too much not to go. Bavasi would always know where I was headed. He'd give me a check for $300 or so. He'd have me bet $75 or $100 from it on the horses he wanted, and the rest of the money was for me. . . . Sometimes I'd pop by his office and, before I knew it, he'd give me $50 or $100 or $200, hanging-around money. . . . He had fun doing it. He treated me and a few of the other guys like his kids. He didn't want anything bad happening to us. He loved getting us out of jams."

Ferrara's worst jam arose in an unexpected place. The Mayfair had finally asked him to pay his bill, which included a year's worth of bar and meal charges. It came to $4,000. He was making only $8,000 a year before taxes. Can't pay it, he said. The hotel wanted to evict him. Despairing, he turned to an incredulous Bavasi, who howled: "How can anyone run up a $4,000 bill, son? Who does that? What the hell's wrong with you?"

Ferrara had no great answer.

"Goddammit, let me handle this," Bavasi said.

Bavasi called the Mayfair and renegotiated Ferrara's bill down to $400, or 10 cents on the dollar. Ferrara could continue living there.

"Don't ever do anything like that again," Bavasi yelled, but Ferrara's appetites guaranteed that Bavasi would be asked to rescue him often. "There were problems off the field," Ferrara says. "There'd be a girl who wanted more of my money, that sort of thing. . . . Buzzie never said no when you needed help. He even played arbitrator with the girls. . . . He'd deal with the banks and finance companies when I had a problem. He was incredible. I loved the guy. When Buzzie called you 'son,' that wasn't fake. He looked after me like I was a son. . . . He really was like that dad who gets mad at you and then forgives you. He'd do anything for you."

Given Bavasi's many kindnesses, Ferrara thought he had good reason to be optimistic, several years later, when he sat down with Bavasi to talk about his new contract. He hoped for a substantial raise.

Bavasi said no, offering a modest one.

Ferrara was surprised. This was his benefactor. He pointed out that the Dodgers drew well over 2 million fans during an average year; that the team was the most successful franchise in baseball.

Bavasi angrily told him to take the offer or go pump gas for a living.

Ferrara realized he was looking at the other Bavasi, the one he'd heard about from teammates. Bavasi might have regarded them as sons, too, but they all knew now he'd turn on them in a flash if they sought too much of Walter O'Malley's money. "He was always my friend away from the team's business," Ferrara reflected. "I was never going to stop appreciating him. But something changed when you sat down with him to talk contract. He would ream you if he thought you were asking for too much. I guess he thought he had to ream you, that it was his job to ream you, because O'Malley was no-holds-barred when it came to money. Buzzie had to be ruthless. But I never forgot how I felt when Buzzie talked to me about a contract. You felt trapped. You gave in to Buzzie or you were gone. You just don't forget that."

In retrospect, Peter Bavasi—the oldest of Bavasi's four sons and a former baseball executive—believes his late father's outlook on contract negotiations in the 1960s strongly resembled his approach at home with his own children. "Buzzie treated the players like his sons," he said in a 2014 written response to a question, describing his father's attitude toward players he liked. "He was very good to them . . . very thoughtful and caring. But when it came to their salaries, just like when it came to weekly allowances for me and my brothers, he put his foot down: 'Here is what I think is fair. Period.'"

No other assessment of Buzzie Bavasi could have better crystallized the attitude of Dodger management toward its players in the 1960s, or the paternalism of baseball's labor relations in the era. Bavasi typically believed there was an unspoken compact between himself and a player, like that between a caring parent and child. Bavasi would help and guide the young Dodger, in exchange for which Ferrara or any other player would defer to the executive's judgment during salary talks. After all, it had always basically worked that way with Wills and nearly all the other talented young men who had entered Bavasi's office.

Such control, however, fed a mounting anger that Bavasi was slow to see coming. It would give impetus in time to a labor revolution that Bavasi and his fellow titans in baseball would be powerless to stop. "Buzzie and O'Malley just had it so easy for so long—I just don't think either of them could see at all what was gonna happen," Ferrara said. "None of us could, to be honest."

In 1964, at age forty-nine, Bavasi still delighted in players' fury over his ruses. When seated across a table from a player looking for considerably more money, he saw his duplicity as nothing more than a shrewd and sometimes amusing tool, as if it were no different than a clever pitcher's changeup that fooled an overeager power hitter. In the aftermath, he regularly boasted to reporters about his cunning.

Bavasi held many contract meetings with his players prior to the 1964 season, including one with the team's twenty-five-year-old first baseman and right fielder Ron Fairly. An articulate, polished man who would serve as the player representative for the Dodgers when the players union was born, Fairly believed he deserved an ample raise after another solid season, in which he had hit .271 and driven in 77 runs. Since his glittering All-American career at the University of Southern California, he had done everything asked of him in professional ball, rising to become a reliable Dodger regular.

A cheery Bavasi told Fairly at the start of their meeting that he wanted to pass along some good news: Tommy Davis, fresh off another National League batting crown, had just signed a new contract. Bavasi casually gestured at a contract on his desk. The pages rested only an arm's length away from a seated Fairly, who silently wondered what kind of money would be going to Davis, a budding superstar. Fairly knew there was no point in asking for a sense of Davis's earnings from Bavasi, who never divulged such information.

Bavasi got around to the central question: What are you looking for from us, Ron?

Decades later, Fairly wouldn't be able to recall precisely what salary he asked for, only that he hoped for a contract somewhere in the neighborhood of $30,000. What he best remembered was the subterfuge that next unfolded. As usual, Bavasi excused himself, saying he needed to step out of his office for a few minutes to speak with his secretary, inviting Fairly to relax, assuring him they would quickly finish their business upon his return. On his way out, Bavasi closed the door behind him. Without saying so, he had given Fairly the privacy to look around at anything he wished in the office and to contemplate his next move. Fairly was still thinking about Davis's new contract, the one so close to him on Bavasi's desk. He tried imagining the kind of good money the Dodgers' young All-Star must be making—$40,000? More? By then, Fairly's curiosity had driven him to do something previously unthinkable, something entirely at odds with his life's values, which included this tenet: you do not steal glances at another man's private documents. But temptation had made Fairly weak. He leaned forward on to Bavasi's desk, peered down at the contract Bavasi had left there, and studied it to see what Davis was making.

He knew he hadn't produced a season that came close to Davis's wonderful year. But perhaps, in simply seeing what a star like Davis was earning, he could use the figure as a measuring stick for demanding a contract from Bavasi that would be respectable and fair. Upon seeing the Davis figure, a surprised Fairly told himself he would need to revise downward what he had hoped to earn. According to the contract, Davis had signed for roughly the same money Fairly wanted, an amount that led him to think, among other things, that the Dodgers had gotten Tommy Davis on the cheap. Poor Tommy.

Worst of all, he knew Bavasi never would pay him as much as Davis was earning. In that instant, he decided to ask for at least $10,000 less than he had originally intended. When Bavasi returned, he told Fairly what the Dodgers were prepared to pay him, a figure roughly in line with Fairly's revised estimate. Fairly signed his contract. The meeting was over, as always, in about fifteen minutes.

If anyone other than Bavasi had been in charge, no one would ever have known about the deceit. But Bavasi could no more keep a secret about his methods than a glutton can resist a pie. Always eager to share his best cons, he looked for opportunities to burnish his image as a wily baseball executive for whom deception was an art form.

A few years later, with the Fairly deal long behind him, Bavasi told the press how he had hustled the young player, whom he didn't identify. It was so simple, he exclaimed. Before his victim arrived, he prepared a fake contract that had the Dodgers paying Davis far less than what the star actually received and left the official-looking documents on his desk within the gullible player's reach, confident that the unsuspecting foil wouldn't be able to resist having a look once left alone. Bavasi gloated to *Sports Illustrated* that the trick had quickly put an end to the player's hope for a big raise.

Bavasi's public boast stunned a humiliated Fairly, for whom it was no solace that Bavasi hadn't identified him—he regarded both the news of the deception and Bavasi's glee in crowing about the ruse to a national magazine as unconscionable. In a reflection of what was happening among disgruntled players everywhere in baseball, Bavasi's duplicity stiffened Fairly's resolve to support those pushing for reforms. "Those kinds of things created a lot of mistrust," he remembers a half century later. "They hurt baseball more than they helped any owner. I'm sure Buzzie thought he made himself look clever when he told that story. But he made me look like a fool. And he cost me $10,000, when that was a lot of money to a young ballplayer. Players never forgot that sort of thing."

For Bavasi, who never would hear the kinds of cheers lavished on his idolized stars, his negotiating triumphs were the only victories entirely his own. His name would never be in lights around Los Angeles. He would never be in demand at the Hollywood events that clamored for Koufax, Drysdale, Wills, and Tommy Davis, or sought after by business titans in rarefied settings, where Walter O'Malley enjoyed the stature of a royal.

But no player or baseball observer would deny that Bavasi had a unique talent. A shrewd student of human nature, he had a gimlet-eyed view of men's exploitable weaknesses and vanities. It was as if, Wills thought, Bavasi had a sixth sense for who could be intimidated, who could be counted on to blink first in a contract standoff. By then, a sad Wills had concluded that he was one of the blinkers. He beat himself up over this realization. Bavasi had him in his pocket. Wills never could be sure whether Bavasi was bluffing him during a contract dispute or genuinely willing to let him sit out an entire season, and his uncertainty scared him. In the end, it was always Wills—the team's toughest fighter on the field—who folded first.

Without disclosing individual Dodger salaries to players or reporters, Bavasi sometimes revealed the Dodgers' total team payroll, a gesture meant to suggest complete transparency. Before the 1962 season began, he told the press that the budget for the players was a little under $500,000. He noted it had been $540,000 in 1961, but given that the Dodgers had failed to win the pennant, some underperforming players wouldn't receive salaries quite so generous, he declared—and in any event, what Mr. O'Malley could afford to pay to everyone that coming year, he said, was not quite $500,000. It was a payroll that, in 1964, was considerably less than those of several other major franchises, according to a proud Bavasi.

Through the 1963 season, no Dodger in club history had received a contract for as much as even $50,000. In retrospect, even adjusted for inflation by a factor of six, seven, ten, or fifteen times, the player salaries all around baseball were absurdly low, and morally inexcusable. Moreover, what other teams paid their players meant little or nothing to the Dodgers, who, historically, had been miserly. During the 1950s, an epoch that saw Ted Williams, Joe DiMaggio, and Stan Musial each play for $100,000 at one point or another, the Dodgers never paid Jackie Robinson more than $42,500.

Bavasi framed the issue of modest Dodger salaries in the early 1960s as one of fairness. For a Koufax, Wills, Drysdale, Fairly, or anyone else to get too much money from O'Malley's limited budget, he indicated, meant that dollars would be coming out of the pockets of hardworking lesser-paid players.

Bavasi sold many of Los Angeles's prominent sports reporters on his logic. A February 1962 story by *Los Angeles Times* Dodgers beat reporter Frank Finch reflected the prevailing media appreciation of Bavasi. "Most Dodger players will tell you that their boss, Buzzie Bavasi, is more than generous in the matter of negotiating salaries," Finch wrote, before turning to the subject of Bavasi's well-known temper, employing the kind of cultural stereotype common in the era to make his point. "But when he encounters a player with an inflated sense of values at the bargaining table he can be tougher to deal with than a Lebanese rug peddler."

Finch next permitted Bavasi to brag about how he had recently backed down an unidentified player during a contract disagreement, a tale that would serve as a warning to any other Dodger tempted to demand more than what Bavasi offered. Finch wrote this: " 'Okay,' Bavasi exploded, his patience exhausted after prolonged haggling, 'you can have what you're asking for or you can sign for a modest raise. But if you take the big raise and flop this year, you can expect a 25 percent cut—the limit—next year.' The chastened chattel settled for the more modest offer."

That Finch would refer to the player as "chattel," without a hint of irony, reflected just how unified Bavasi and Los Angeles media were in support of baseball's established order.

The ticket sales of Walter O'Malley's franchise, and his coffers, were unrivaled in baseball. But Bavasi made it clear that O'Malley's budget had no room to get bigger without damaging the organization. The bottom line had to be respected. There was no additional money for player salaries.

No Dodger veteran was more preoccupied about money in the early '60s than Edwin Donald "Duke" Snider, on his way in time to the Hall of Fame after a legendary career best remembered for his feats in Brooklyn as a left-handed slugger. Yet at the peak of his career, he'd never earned more than $44,000 in baseball. In 1962, at thirty-five, with his best seasons behind him and a bum left knee that would end his career in two years, Snider was earning only $38,500 as the team entered Dodger Stadium. He had no grudge against the Dodger brass. Part of the real problem, he thought, could be seen in his own dugout. Young, unproven players didn't deserve the big money they'd raked in.

It was the realization of everything that Buzzie Bavasi's approach had put in motion: players turned on each other. Old and historically underpaid players resented the young and seemingly well-heeled.

Snider had become especially perturbed with one unseasoned Dodger, a nineteen-year-old six-foot-five rookie phenom named Joe Moeller, the youngest pitcher ever to start a game for the Dodgers. The phenom, in Snider's view, had made big money with little effort. Just a year earlier, shortly before his graduation from high school, Moeller had signed with the Dodgers for a total bonus package of $105,000, of which $30,000, at young Moeller's request, had been evenly split by the Dodgers between his father and brother.

The wisdom of the Dodgers' investment seemed obvious when Moeller won twenty games during his first full minor-league season. Still, the bonus money O'Malley committed to the kid left Snider enraged: Moeller had signed for more money than Snider had received during two full years of his peak stardom in Brooklyn. It was the era of the bonus babies. In 1961 a gifted teenage outfielder named Roy Gleason had signed a Dodgers contract for a $55,000 bonus, the climax to a feverish competition among several teams that had included a visit to Gleason, on behalf of the Red Sox, by a retired Ted Williams.

Around the clubhouse, Snider's needling of Moeller turned into open scorn.

"It was like he thought I hadn't earned this, didn't deserve what I'd gotten," Moeller remembers. "I'd earned my spot on that team. I had a really good spring training."

In 1962 Moeller made the Dodgers squad. In another week, with the 1962 regular season having begun, he pitched in relief, earning a save in a Dodger win. Six days later he made his first start, at nineteen years and two months, a precociousness that exceeded even Koufax's. His next time out, in Milwaukee on April 23, he pitched a complete game and earned his first victory, in a 5–2 defeat of the Braves.

While never sensational, a steady Moeller completed fifteen of his nineteen starts that season, winning six games and losing five. As a teenager only two years removed from high school, he was surpassing expectations amid a pressure-filled pennant chase.

With the season entering the stretch, and the team enjoying a large lead in the National League standings over the Giants, the thoughts of the Dodgers squad already had turned to the World Series and the significant bonuses that would come to all players on Series rosters, winners and losers alike, from the pool of World Series revenue. The Dodgers met to decide how their share of the anticipated windfall would be split among individual players, coaches, trainers, and other team personnel, including clubhouse attendants and batboys. A vote of the team decided such matters.

As team captain, Snider helped to lead the discussion and vote. The meeting was regarded as routine. Commonly, a player would receive a full share unless he had joined the team late in the season, in which case he would generally receive something less, perhaps a one-half to three-quarters share. But when it came time to vote on Moeller's share, Snider jumped in. "He already got a huge bonus," Snider told the room, making clear his opposition to a full share. "He doesn't need the money."

A shocked Moeller said nothing. No one wanted to argue with the Dodger eminence.

The players voted Moeller a half share.

It would remain, a half century later, the only instance in Dodger history where a yearlong active player, who had won as many as a half dozen games, was denied a full share of a prospective World Series check by his teammates. The moment seared Moeller. That the Dodgers never would make it to the World Series that season, leaving them with only second-place shares of $1,860 for each man with a full share, was incidental to his pain.

Snider's post-baseball life was sometimes a struggle. Money issues still preoccupied him. His lowest moment came in 1995, when at sixty-eight he pleaded guilty to a federal charge of not paying taxes on money he'd made at baseball memorabilia shows. Moeller had made peace with him by then. "Duke apologized to me," Moeller recounts. "We got past things, I think."

Yet some of the memories still sting. A few of Moeller's questions never have gone away. "It was probably envy, the fact that I was making more with the bonus than some of the guys were making in their careers," he says of Snider's motivation. "But why pick me out? I didn't decide salaries. I was just a kid lucky enough to be on the field. Why me?"

The answer was not to be found on any field. It rested high above the players, in the executive suites where Bavasi and O'Malley, in concert with the rest of baseball's rulers, had presided over a pay scale guaranteeing that stars would hit a ceiling far below their true worth. The system had made bitter men of baseball's many Sniders. Simultaneously, it had guaranteed there would be many young Moellers, resented and tormented.

In time, Bavasi would express a wry frustration with his boss's tightfistedness: "If fifteen cents were involved, he became the meanest man you'd ever want to meet. It took me three pennants to get a raise." By then, however, Bavasi would have served his two decades as O'Malley's unyielding enforcer and left. Every day with the Dodgers he had faithfully carried out the marching order O'Malley first gave him in 1950, upon Bavasi's appointment as general manager: "You do the baseball; I'll do the business."

The order meant O'Malley never had to get his hands dirty with the help. In early 1964, it meant O'Malley could rely on his enforcer to handle all thorny issues related to his players' salaries, to serve as the bulwark against any Dodgers pushing to get too much of his money, to browbeat them into submission. It was what the enforcer did best, leaving O'Malley to bask in his role as the Dodgers' courtly visionary.

Walter O'Malley had a gift for putting employees he seldom saw at ease. He had a seductive laugh, a rolling chortle frequently accompanied by a funny story, all of which encouraged listeners to believe they were close to him, part of his family, the Dodger family, and to prove it, here came another story. On the surface at least, he liked to make intimates of his players. On the spur of the moment, he sometimes picked up their families' restaurant tabs; occasionally he included them in his parties. Having heard about his shortstop's skill on the banjo, O'Malley once asked Wills to play some songs at the Dodgers' St. Patrick's Day party, warmly thanking him afterward, even paying him for his time. And though they didn't run into each other often once a season began, there would be moments when, seeing each other in a hallway, O'Malley would excitedly shout "Mauuuuuuury", and drape an arm around him.

To virtually everyone who met him for the first time, O'Malley seemed absolutely benign. By early 1964, nearly everything about the sixty-year-old—his wide face, jowls, ample belly, and omnipresent smile around the players—contributed to his air of affability. None-theless, he would not let anyone, least of all politicians and bureau-crats, interfere with his vision of how the Dodgers did things. It was what finally had made Brooklyn untenable for him. He had exacting standards that the New York politicians didn't share, he thought—chief of which involved the new stadium of his dreams, to be built in the precise place he wanted, in the heart of Brooklyn. New York had said no, and O'Malley said good-bye.

Shortly before, in 1957, he'd taken a ride in a Los Angeles County helicopter. Looking down on a jagged piece of land that was Chavez Ravine, he pointed at it and said, "A ballpark could go right there." The construction of beautiful Dodger Stadium and its surroundings, every detail of which he presided over, was his proudest achievement and ultimate vindication, another way of telling the New York politi-cians to go to hell. It was a challenge sometimes to see the fierceness behind the avuncular facade. But it was always there. It explained his edict that his players remain well groomed. It explained his dark hair that he combed straight back, in the CEO style of Kennedy's and Lyndon Johnson's secretary of defense, Robert McNamara, formerly the straight-arrow president of the Ford Motor Company.

You had to take your eyes off the smile to see the truth about him. It helped to look at his cigar, the one that, when animated by his dreams, he waved around like a scepter.

He was an undeniable futurist. His move to Los Angeles had revealed his talent for recognizing what Southern California could be over the next half century, setting him apart from other baseball men who had merely flirted with moving somewhere more poten-tially profitable. He was also a contrarian, unafraid to do his baseball business in a manner unlike the game's other major franchises. In the early 1960s, that style emboldened him to make a crossroads decision that would help to make his new stadium a gold mine.

The proliferation of TV sets, which by 1960 were in most American homes, had led to nearly daily telecasts of local teams' home games in baseball's leading markets of New York and Chicago. O'Malley's arrival in Los Angeles offered him the same opportunity to exploit the coffers of television and sponsors. As the 1962 season began, he consented to the telecast of the inaugural game at Dodger Stadium, hoping to provide viewers with a flattering view of his new ballpark and all the amenities that fans could experience there, if and when they came.

The sold-out stadium looked majestic, even if, unknown to the TV audience, O'Malley's grounds crew had needed to paint the grass green because the hastily planted sod had yet to grow in. The view from the ballpark of the ravine's hills and the San Gabriel Mountains beyond them was dazzling. The television cameras captured the elation of bleacher fans. Few in the stadium seemed to mind that drinking fountains had yet to be installed, or that the Dodgers lost to the Cincinnati Reds. Television captured the giddiness of the day, the happy images worth millions of dollars in free advertising to O'Malley. The game appeared to be merely a prelude to years of frequent and riveting telecasts from Dodger Stadium for Los Angeles viewers.

Then, without ever talking about it, during the rest of the 1960s, O'Malley didn't permit local telecasts of home games during the regular season. It was the single most important business decision of his tenure in Los Angeles. Anyone who wanted to see the Dodgers play live at home thereafter would need a ticket.

Yet O'Malley's success never would have been realized without the transplanted team's greatest salesman, its play-by-play radio announcer Vin Scully, who was reason alone for the uninitiated to tune in to broadcasts of the games. Raised in New York City, a member of the old Brooklyn broadcasting crew while still a skinny, red-haired kid in his early twenties, Scully had wit and a keen eye to complement a melodious voice devoid of any trace of an eastern accent, his speech and style an amalgam of laid-back folksy and eloquently descriptive.

At thirty-four in 1962, Scully possessed the command of someone twenty years his senior. Never a Dodger lackey who rooted slavishly for O'Malley's team, he casually pronounced judgments about

Dodger strengths and weaknesses, along the way riffing about players' personalities and eccentricities.

He was the game's bard, and Dodger Stadium his theater in the park. Fans by the thousands brought radios to the stadium to hear him, as if his voice alone conferred majesty on a scene. It wasn't long before baseball observers around the country regarded him as the best broadcaster in the sport. He had become the only truly untouchable figure in the Dodgers organization, more important than even Koufax, Wills, and Drysdale.

The reasons for his indispensability were to be found in numbers that constituted broadcasting's lifeblood: radio ratings reported during the 1960s by the *Los Angeles Times* revealed that upwards of 30 percent of all Southern California listeners were tuned in on average to Scully's broadcasts of Dodger games on AM station KFI, an astounding number in the marketplace. With Scully whetting the fans' appetite to see real action in beautiful Dodger Stadium, they would come, O'Malley knew.

Years earlier, from 3,000 miles away, the owner had seen the new gold rush beckoning on the Pacific. By June of 1962 the state's demographers reported that more than 1,700 newcomers a day were moving into California, an unprecedented American migration that by year's end would move California past lagging New York as the most populated state of the union. O'Malley's staff saw each new wave of California transplants as Dodger fans in waiting. Day games would be largely limited to weekends, with eight o'clock weeknight starts designed to give working men and women plenty of time to get to Dodger Stadium.

Hordes of Southern California's newcomers, eager for an affordable taste of Los Angeles glamour, were ready to take advantage. For if there ever was a great secret in the new middle-class communities of Los Angeles during the early 1960s, a secret that flew in the face of the land's image of itself, it was just how little there was to do in many of its relatively new housing developments. This was especially true for the hundreds of thousands of recent middle-class arrivals who lived to the north of downtown Los Angeles, in fledgling communities in the city's San Fernando Valley. In some areas there had been just enough time, as housing tracts were finished there, for developers to erect a chain supermarket, a bank or two, and a small shopping center. Once Los Angeles's stepchild, the San Fernando Valley was in the final stages of a transformation that would have implications for every major corporation and business in the city, including Walter O'Malley's.

Just fifteen years earlier, these had been principally agricultural communities, where Valley ranches were plentiful and citrus reigned. Orange groves and lemon trees had covered much of the Valley's northern communities of Granada Hills and Northridge. About twenty minutes to the west, the Valley community of Canoga Park had its chicken farms and dairy cows.

But by the early 1960s, most of the orchards had been razed; the walnut groves, chickens, and cows had largely disappeared. They'd given way to housing tracts for the influx of eastern and midwestern newcomers who, when finished each day with their white-collar jobs in the new boomland, had little idea what to do or where to go next in the Valley. There were few places to go, really—few entertainment venues, other than a handful of movie theaters.

But the sound of Vin Scully on their radios was ubiquitous. To make that first trip to Dodger Stadium for the new Californians was akin to embarking on an obligatory family pilgrimage to Disneyland.

The drive to the fabled ballpark was not short, a good forty minutes from Northridge and other parts of the Valley. You exited the freeway on an off-ramp called Stadium Way, the road that encircled the ballpark. Only you couldn't see the stadium from the exit. Were it not for the off-ramp sign, you would have thought on your first visit that you'd come upon a barren area, a candidate for urban renewal. Turning onto a long road, you saw nothing to your left but clumps of sagebrush upon tall, dusty hills that looked like a fire hazard, all of it blocking your view of what stood on the other side.

The hills were the outer edge of Chavez Ravine, which major Los Angeles developers had wanted nothing to do with for decades. Many outsiders had dismissed it as a badlands. In truth, it long had been a stable community, the rocky, bumptious province of hard-toiling people who tended sheep and other livestock early in the century, and generations later of working-class Latino families and others who owned and rented homes there. During the 1950s, it was briefly slated to be the site of a government low-income housing project. But politics intervened; the plan was scrapped. Walt Disney looked at it as a possible site for an amusement park before walking away.

Yet city officials never stopped believing there was money to be made in the ravine. Such a large parcel of land, so close to downtown, was not going to sit for long without being acquired by an entrepreneur with pockets deep enough to push aside any dissenters. In the late 1950s, O'Malley told city leaders he wanted it. The passage of a citywide referendum permitted the city to exercise its eminent domain power, seize the ravine, pay off property owners ordered to leave, drag away anyone who resisted, beat back the public rage of evicted residents with the powerful support of the city's business establishment and newspapers, and finally turn all of the ravine over to O'Malley, whose bulldozers and construction crew swiftly reconfigured the land into his vision. All of it would be the future playland of paying fans who, in many cases, had not yet arrived in California and would know nothing about the contentious battle over the ravine when they did.

Heading toward it that first time, a confused Valley newcomer might reasonably have wondered whether the road off the freeway exit had taken him the wrong way; perhaps he'd missed a sign a ways back. Finally the road curved left, and the newcomer began moving up a steep incline in the twilight. In the next half minute, still climbing, he glimpsed the tip of something far off—something bright and high, like a spire. Then he saw, in no particular order, tall banks of lights, the distant left-field bleachers, the back of a scoreboard, a group of towering palm trees, and as he moved closer, one, two, three, four, five tiers of seats, everything in the stadium bathed in the whitest of lights.

Attendants directed drivers into a vast parking lot, the sections numbered by glowing globes that looked like enormous baseballs. You parked and walked into the stadium to see a vibrant green field in stunning contrast to your television's black and white. You looked at the iconic palms, which soared above the bleachers. You soaked in the quietude of the distant mountains, the tops streaked with purple at this hour, the last of the sunlight sinking behind them. All yours, all of it, yours.

Newcomers would stare quietly. For many, this was their first glimpse of anything in their new land that measured up to the fantasy of the Golden State they'd heard about back in their old eastern hometowns. The man who had built this ballpark had given them a taste of beauty and glamour. This was why about 2.5 million people a year on average would crowd their way into the realization of the man's vision.

Their massive presence guaranteed riches for O'Malley. His players increasingly wanted a fair share of his millions. Koufax, Wills, Drysdale, and Fairly—each in his own way—mulled over how to get more. Their frustration was the perfect measure of the confusion over how to best proceed, and an indication of the futility of trying to take on O'Malley alone. They needed a unifying leader and organization of their own. Neither seemed to be coming anytime soon.

Some young players were oblivious to the burgeoning tensions over players' salaries. They felt fortunate just to be a part of the competition to make the club. One scared contender, who cared nothing about money, would forever be grateful to Walter O'Malley for his chance, believing it had given him nothing less than a chance to stay alive.

Coming off his lone year in the minors, Wes Parker genuinely believed he couldn't survive without making the big-league squad at Vero Beach as the 1964 season began. He arrived with his memories of family traumas still driving him. "I didn't have a lot of confidence going for me in 1964, after being vilified by my parents for so long," he recalled. "I had to compensate by having a laser-like focus on the game."

Parker believed he would either triumph and gain some peace or suffer a blow from which he would never recover. There was no in-between, no fallback position.

"If I hadn't made it, maybe I'd have been a street person, maybe one of those people in Haight-Ashbury," he speculated a half century later. "Or stuck at home with my parents. It would've been bad, whatever it was, because I didn't have the people skills or worldly skills to survive on my own. . . . I had one shot to make it in life—not in baseball—in *life*. I was fighting for my survival. Baseball was just the means. . . . So if this didn't work out, I don't know. It would have devastated me. I don't know how I could've handled that. My life would be over."

He recognized how desperate that sounded. "I was never suicidal," he said. Given the misery of his youth, he wasn't about to be a party to his own annihilation. "I had a powerful desire to live. I was determined to continue living, to not let my parents live beyond me. After what I'd gone through with them and what they'd done to me, it was almost my way of avenging their attacks. I never was going to allow them to defeat me. Suicide would have meant my parents won. That was completely out of the question."

In the next few seconds, he put his finger on how baseball saved him. "It gave me worth. I would've had no chance without that. That would've been like dying. So I was fighting for my life. It's the only reason why I had any chance of making it."

Once Koufax had moved on from his standoff with Bavasi, his teammates marveled over how effortlessly he blocked out all distractions. From the time he took the field in Vero Beach, nothing and no one dented his concentration, not golf, women, or playtime. "Other guys would be looking to have a little fun sometimes, would need a little fun," Wills remembered. "Not Sandy. All business. He'd just get settled in and start doing it."

The pitcher was usually serious from the instant he arrived at a ballpark. "He didn't force the funny," Torborg recalled. "That wasn't Sandy. He had that fire from the moment he put on the uniform."

Having wanted to get off to a good start during their first outing together, Torborg asked Koufax where he ought to position himself behind the plate: "On the corners?"

"No," Koufax answered. "Sit in the middle of the plate. If I hit it, then start moving."

Such brief exchanges between them became the norm, along with Koufax's reluctance to talk once their work began. Torborg would see a change then in the star's eyes. "His impatience was there," Torborg recalled. "The eyes would get dark. He didn't want to wait long for you. A lot of times, after he threw a pitch, he would put his glove out. He just wanted the ball back from you right away. If I had anything to say to him, he'd just say, 'All right. I got you.' Then that glove would go up again, like, 'Give me the ball.'"

It stood to reason that at the end of those long days, off the field, a star so serious would want to associate with like-minded dynamos—except that reason never has much to do with baseball friendships. Ballplayers, like the rest of us, gravitate toward whom and what they need, which is often something very different from their own personalities.

This meant that players usually had different sets of friends inside and outside a clubhouse. Inside it, no one could have been closer to Koufax than Wills. But outside stadiums, Koufax had different companions—players with easygoing dispositions, funny perspectives on the absurdities of a baseball life, and a penchant for self-deprecation. Tracewski, with his well-established reputation for defensive prowess and big-game reliability, nonetheless would describe himself as "a humpty-dumpty." The other men in Koufax's coterie had a similarly wry and easy assurance.

Away from ballparks, the group had room only for those who would allow Koufax to relax, contented men with one last thing in common: they weren't at all wired like Koufax. Their ambition never would be a match for his competitive fire. After hours, while he would sometimes brood over a mistake, they could leaven the mood with an amusing story. At his most engaging around them, he opened up, proving to be as skilled as any of them at telling a bawdy joke. "He was very funny," Tracewski remembers. "Not a lot of people saw that part of Sandy, but he had a good time when he could just get away and not have to think about a game."

Koufax's off-field life stood for the proposition that sometimes a serious man needs a break from himself. Necessarily, his group slightly changed over time, given the arrival of new players and the departure of others. In early 1964 the group included Tracewski, Camilli, and Koufax's assigned roommate in Vero Beach, rookie John Werhas, who was battling to make the club and win the starting third-base job. The three men were among the most popular figures on the club— easy to hang out with, quick with a quip or needle, and not above being juvenile. Seeing the trio so often together, Koufax and other Dodgers dubbed them the "Three Stooges," recounts Werhas.

Koufax could be just another guy around the Three Stooges. A great night for his friend, thought Tracewski, was one when no stranger interrupted to tell him he was great. That kind of night had become nearly impossible. At any popular establishment in America, it was virtually guaranteed he would be spotted and besieged. It often left him little choice but to search for some out-of-the-way dive. "We didn't go anywhere special," Tracewski recalled. "Had a beer where Sandy wouldn't have to worry about being disturbed."

For his friends, Koufax's seriousness in a ballpark made it all the more intriguing when his mood momentarily lightened there. After a spring training game, Koufax and Drysdale were having a beer with Henry Aaron, Warren Spahn, Eddie Matthews, and Rico Carty when Koufax, seeing Werhas walk by, invited him to join the group.

Werhas remembers that, at some point, Carty asked Koufax why he pitched against him so hard all the time, as if there might be something personal in this.

Koufax looked Carty over. "Rico, who hits behind you?" he asked and paused.

Everybody in the room knew that the man who frequently hit behind Carty was Aaron, whom Koufax had intentionally walked on many occasions rather than risk being beaten by him. "*Henry* hits behind you, Rico. Which means you're *never* going to be on base when Henry comes to bat."

Even Carty and Aaron laughed. Koufax grinned. In that moment, Werhas—who no one could have known (including Werhas in that moment) would go on to become a Christian minister one day—thought his friend couldn't have looked happier or more relaxed. After Drysdale told a funny story of his own, the informal gathering broke up. The smiling Braves had begun heading back to their clubhouse when Drysdale interrupted, thinking a last point needed to be made. He looked at Aaron and the other rivals and said, "You know, just because we're all having this fun time, don't think I'm not gonna knock you on your ass when you come up to hit."

The Braves looked at him, perhaps waiting for a laugh. Only Drysdale wasn't laughing. He spun around and left without another word, leaving the Braves to realize that nothing about Drysdale the competitor had changed: he would likely throw at or near them soon. In that instant, Werhas understood the difference between the Dodgers' two pitching stars, each of whom he admired. "Don didn't want anyone ever to have an advantage over him," Werhas said. "Don was the blood and guts of our team. Don struck fear into people on a field. Sandy didn't have to do any of that. People knew they couldn't hit him, but nobody feared getting hurt by him. Opponents were just in awe of him."

Werhas understood that Koufax had come to be viewed as that rarest of things in sports—the virtuous figure. After games, screeching fans rushed him as he walked toward the team bus.

Tracewski knew the idolatry had become a greater burden for his friend. Werhas, fulfilling his role as a Stooge, began teasing Koufax about his inability to maneuver past the throngs. "Sandy, you haven't mastered the art of walking through a crowd. You need to work on that. Hey, just watch me. Nobody bothers me at all."

Koufax laughed. Tracewski, Camilli, Werhas, and others with the Stooges' outlook helped to provide him with as close to a normal off-field life as he was ever likely to have. But the life never would be easy, especially when he was preoccupied with concerns about everything from the team's fortunes to how he would next deal with a domineering O'Malley and Bavasi. And he had a new worry at that moment, one that he had hidden from everyone in the top ranks of the Dodgers organization, starting with Alston. His arm hurt.

Teammates had questions about Parker, most revolving around issues of his toughness, given his family's wealth. "Wes came from a sheltered background," remembers teammate Wally Moon, one of Parker's closest friends. "We knew that. There was no doubt he could do the job, defensively, and he had great work habits. . . . But I think there were questions about his mind. Baseball is hard and he wasn't tough mentally or tough physically yet."

Parker sensed the doubts. "I had the feeling some people worried I couldn't ever be as hungry as the players who had grown up poor. I hated hearing it. If they'd known about my family life, they'd never have thought it—they'd have known how much I needed to make it. I was determined that I was going to work harder than anybody else there."

It was his second trip to Dodgertown. A year earlier, he had gone through spring training there with the Dodger minor leaguers. Nearly everything he saw or heard that first time had inspired him. He'd be working out with the other dreamers when suddenly there would be the roar of engines climbing. Like children, the young players looked up into the empty sky, aware of what was coming but transfixed just the same. The Dodger plane, O'Malley's Electra, would appear, lifting over the tall palm trees. Parker would see the Dodgers' royal blue insignia on the plane. Could anything, he'd wonder, look as beautiful, as regal? What he'd give to be on that plane. The Electra would be winging toward a spring training game, filled with the major leaguers.

Now, in spring of 1964, he rode the plane into and out of Vero Beach, fearful he wouldn't be on it for long. A half dozen workout days passed before the team played a game at all, and even then it was just an intrasquad game that Parker started on the bench, the first of four such games in which it appeared unlikely that he would make a serious impression. The intrasquad games were so low-key that Alston didn't even bother leading a team. He let two beat writers from a pair of Southern California newspapers manage the squads. The few spectators had largely drifted off by the seventh inning of the first game. But Bavasi hung around, along with Fresco Thompson, Al Campanis, and Alston.

Parker was called to pinch-hit. On the mound was a tall, hard-throwing right-hander named Doug Anderson, a former Dodger batboy who, like Parker, had come to Vero from the minors, trying to make the most of a rare opportunity.

Hitting left-handed, Parker swung at Anderson's first pitch, a curveball that broke over the middle of the plate.

"I crushed it," Parker remembered.

It isn't a ball's flight that typically alerts experienced baseball men to a good swing. Rather, in that first instant, it is the sound. An exceptionally hit ball sounds like nothing else in sports, with the crack off a wooden bat calling to mind a powerful rifle shot, though with a splintering echo all its own. The effect on knowledgeable spectators is cattle-prod worthy. Drowsy baseball executives with big bellies jerk to full attention.

Parker was running as fast as he could.

It was the hardest hit ball of the afternoon, a screaming line drive to deep right field. Had the ball been accompanied by some loft, Parker thought it would've easily cleared the tall palm trees down the right-field line. But he had hit it squarely and low, and its topspin was bringing the ball down on the front of the ten-foot-high dirt embankment that, running from one foul line to the other, served as the field's outfield wall. The ball skipped over the embankment for a ground-rule double. By then Parker was flying into third base. After he finally stopped, and smiling coaches gestured for him to return to second, he jogged back, glancing sideways and noticing Bavasi, Thompson, Campanis, and Alston suddenly huddled together in seats behind home plate. "I knew what they were saying," he recalls. "I just knew. It was so obvious from their expressions. They were asking each other, 'Where's this guy from again? What did he do last year? What did he hit?' I could feel their excitement."

Parker's future began changing in that instant. He started in the next day's intrasquad affair, on his way to hitting over .700 in the four camp games, with beat reporters telling him that Campanis and Thompson had also expressed delight over his speed, which had enabled him to beat out a ground ball for an infield hit. The young underdog for a roster spot suddenly became a contender. Defensively, his fleetness meant that the first baseman could be utilized in the outfield, too.

Next he hit over .300 in spring training games against Dodger foes, becoming one of the major stories of the spring, with Southern California reporters suddenly pressing for more information about the guy who wasn't a bonus baby. "The newspapers couldn't get enough of me," he remembers.

He learned he had made the squad by discovering his name on the official roster posted on a bulletin board outside the cafeteria.

Yet his rush of pride would soon be accompanied by a characteristic worry. *What if I fail?* He knew, better than anyone else in the organization, just how unprepared he was for this. Since his professional career began, he had produced high batting averages, but against whom? Perennial minor-league pitchers? Largely A-league and Double-A guys? Just a few exhibition games against major-league pitchers had been enough to tell him that they came from a superior class of athletes and tacticians. He was over his head, though he didn't dare confess to this for fear of endangering his new status.

"I'd never learned to hit because I didn't spend enough time in the minors," he says. "You can learn to *field* when you're a kid, because you can have somebody hit you thousands of balls. But there's nobody to throw you major-league sliders and sinkers when you're growing up. You don't see those until you get to the majors. It's just different in the majors—the speed, the breaking balls, the pitchers' control and command, the setting up of hitters by the pitchers, and the relentlessness of it, knowing tough pitchers are going to be out there every day. . . . I needed to learn to hit in the minors and get rid of the problems I had with my swing. I needed to learn not to go after bad pitches. One year in the minors wasn't enough for me to do that. . . . But you're never going to say that to anybody. You can't. So I was worried a lot."

His challenges weren't limited to his inexperience. He had, as critical scouts regularly said of weak hitters, too many holes in his swing to count. Such flaws usually prove fatal, except that Parker's had yet to be discovered by pitchers, so he might still have some success in early 1964 until he was unmasked. The league's ignorance about him could be his friend for a while. But given enough time to study him, experienced major-league hurlers would spot everything about him that greenhorn minor-league pitchers had missed—and when that happened, Parker would struggle for a long while, for the problems with his swing were not easily correctable. In swinging a bat, he often dropped his back shoulder, prone to popping up pitches instead of driving them. He became easily jammed by fastballs, and could not resist swinging at high fastballs that usually blew past him. He had all the makings of a steady out; the only question was when in a season it would happen.

Not even Parker at that moment knew all this. All Parker sensed was his lack of readiness. He had other concerns. The allergies and asthma bedeviling him since childhood had not gone away, making it impossible that he would be able to play a full 162-game schedule without being worn down at some point.

He never would see an upside to telling a teammate about either the emotional scars of his past or the depth of his professional worries. He restricted himself to playing hard, demonstrating respect to everyone around him, and earnestly paying attention to the advice of trusted veterans.

Early in the 1964 season, several of the players had given him a sense of belonging for one of the first times in his life. "I started to like myself," he remembers. "I'd hated myself growing up—I'd felt so worthless and ugly . . . But having friends like Wally [Moon], Fairly, Maury, Drysdale and other guys—feeling that kind of friendship and love—it made me start seeing myself in a new way. I was so grateful to them. It's not the kind of thing you say to guys, but I felt it."

Even the veterans' gruffness and ritualistic hazing warmed him. One afternoon he walked into the trainer's room, where a prone Drysdale was getting a rubdown. The star turned and, noticing Parker, barked at him, "What are you doing in here? Rookies can't be in here. Hodges, Pee Wee, and Duke wouldn't let me into the trainer's room until my third year. Get outta here."

Parker was happy to be worthy of the ribbing, to be that close to the stars' inner circle. He couldn't get enough of Drysdale's ease and confidence. "I'd come from emotional havoc, so I was attracted to people who were secure with themselves," he explained. "Don was so gregarious, so comfortable and down-to-earth in every situation. I'd never known that growing up with the people around me. And I wasn't ever going to be that emotionally secure. I had a hard time laughing at my weaknesses and mistakes—I was just too beaten up by my parents to laugh at those things. But Don could always laugh at his weaknesses and mistakes. If I could've had anybody's personality

One of the first photographs ever taken of then–minor leaguer Maury Wills in a left-handed batting stance, signaling that he had become a switch-hitter and marking the start of his dramatic ascension. In 1959, he would be called up to the Dodgers. Three years later, he would win the National League's Most Valuable Player Award. *(MauryWills.com)*

The Dodgers viewed themselves as destined to win—to the fury of certain opponents. Any young player joining the team was quickly informed of the club's unsparing expectations. *From left to right:* Ron Fairly, Jim Gilliam, John Roseboro, Maury Wills, and Tommy Davis. *(AP Images)*

Hollywood and the Dodgers always had a symbiotic relationship. A demanding and sometimes irascible Milton Berle often included Dodger stars in his hotel shows and television programs. *From left to right:* Berle, Frank Howard, Duke Snider, Maury Wills, Sandy Koufax, Willie Davis, and Don Drysdale. *(Getty Images)*

Maury Wills making a play at second base against the Giants' future Hall of Famer Orlando Cepeda, in 1960. If Giants players dared to come into second base standing up, in an effort to prevent him from completing a double play, Wills wouldn't hesitate to throw the ball at their heads. *(MauryWills.com)*

Maury Wills prepared to bat by staring out at the opposing pitcher and infielders, searching for vulnerabilities and formulating strategies. No other Dodger was more intensely cerebral. *(Getty Images)*

Maury Wills prided himself on discovering his foe's weaknesses, then relentlessly exploiting them. Here, Wills steals his major league single-season-record 104th base on October 3, 1962, during the seventh inning of the final game of a playoff against the Giants for the National League pennant. When Wills scored, giving the Dodgers a 4–2 lead, he immediately began to think ahead to playing against the Yankees in the 1962 World Series. Within the next hour, the Dodgers had blown their lead and the pennant. A crestfallen Wills, who took home the MVP Award and the Hickok Belt that year, would have to wait another season before confronting the Yankees. *(AP Images)*

Sandy Koufax poses for fans at the Dodgers' Camera Day in 1965. Inveterately shy, he gave the worshipful what they wanted that afternoon—an intimate glimpse of a living deity. It was a rare occasion. (*Marti Squyres*)

The ticket stub of Marti Allen, then fourteen years old, from the night Sandy Koufax pitched his perfect game, on September 9, 1965. Five decades later, Marti would say of Koufax: "He was so great, so beautiful." (*Marti Squyres*)

Maury Wills collects an infield single along the first-base line against the Minnesota Twins in Game 4 of the 1965 World Series, a contest in which he went 2–4 and stole a base, as the Dodgers triumphed, 7–2. Also visible in the photo is the Twins' sterling starting pitcher, Jim "Mudcat" Grant. (*MauryWills.com*)

After winning Game 4 of the 1965 World Series, Don Drysdale puts a headlock on the two Dodgers who hit home runs in the game—Lou Johnson on the left, and Wes Parker on the right. For the diffident Parker—frightened that he might let down his team on baseball's biggest stage—his excellent play and .304 batting average in the Series served as a boon for his self-image. For Johnson, his winning homer in the decisive Game 7 made him an overnight Los Angeles hero. *(Getty Images)*

After making a spectacular diving grab of Cardinal Tim McCarver's first-inning grounder, Wes Parker makes a throw to Sandy Koufax, who beats McCarver to the bag for the out, as umpire Tony Venzon watches. That afternoon, August 21, 1966, Koufax went on to win his twentieth game of the year. McCarver regarded Parker's play as the greatest ever made by a first baseman against him. *(Wes Parker)*

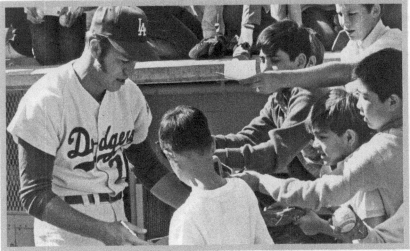

TOP: Sandy Koufax celebrates his twentieth victory of the 1966 season with teammates John Kennedy *(left)* and Al Ferrara (wearing the sombrero) after defeating the St. Louis Cardinals, 4–1. He would go on to win twenty-seven games that year, the last of his major league career. *(AP Images)*

BOTTOM: Wes Parker signs autographs for a group of kids alongside the Dodger dugout after a Sunday afternoon home game. His regular interaction with fans served as a balm for the private pain he frequently felt. *(Wes Parker)*

Wes Parker poses with devoted fan Marti Allen, then eighteen, in the Dodger Stadium parking lot in 1969. The teenager regarded Parker as the most approachable of all the Dodgers. "He would always talk to you if you wanted a moment with him," she remembers. "When you're young, you don't forget that." *(Marti Squyres)*

Surrounded by young fans, Wes Parker prepares to hit fly balls to them in the Dodger Stadium parking lot, following a Sunday afternoon game in 1971. It was a favorite Parker routine after weekend day games. *(Wes Parker)*

Sandy Koufax warms up on the sidelines for the benefit of fans snapping pictures of him at the Dodgers' Camera Day in 1965. The awe of a young fan could affect even his handling of a camera. This grainy photo was taken by the author, then twelve years old. *(Michael Leahy)*

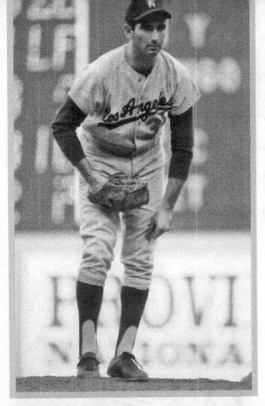

LEFT: Sandy Koufax peering toward home plate, waiting for a sign from his catcher. Such was his dominance that, from the perspective of some teammates, he sometimes seemed utterly alone on the field, while they were merely spectators to the inevitable strikeout. *(Getty Images)*

BELOW: An exultant Sandy Koufax accepts the congratulations of teammates after defeating the Yankees, 5–2, in the opening game of the 1963 World Series. Before a capacity Yankee Stadium crowd, Koufax struck out fifteen, setting a World Series record. *(Getty Images)*

or crawled into a body, it would've been Don's. It just made me feel good to be around someone like that—you could learn from that."

But Parker's new friendships couldn't change some things. His old miseries and fears, especially his terror over possibly failing, still raged. He kept every anxiety hidden from teammates. His friends could be as candid as they wished about their own insecurities. But never could they know about his, or even suspect that he was concealing something. Trust was never the issue—he would have put his life in the hands of these men. But he worried that their confidence in him would be irreparably damaged if he ever discussed his childhood or how his self-doubts sometimes threatened to overwhelm him.

"The reality was that guys were not supposed to be vulnerable," he explains. "Guys needed to feel they could rely on you, no matter what was happening in your private life. Guys might have problems with marriages or other things, but when they got to the ballpark, they had to be focused on baseball. That was our responsibility to each other. You don't bring your personal problems to the ballpark. If I'd said something about what had gone on when I was young and how it affected me, it might have put doubts in their minds about me; it might have been interpreted as weakness."

Besides, he couldn't talk about his problems without jeopardizing his own maniacal concentration. He didn't even see a therapist during the season out of fear it would soften him and ruin his fine-tuned competitive wiring (indeed, aside from seeing a psychologist during the 1965 off-season, Parker would receive no therapy until 1972).

In time, he would liken his preternaturally intense focus to that of zealous police dogs. It wasn't an observation casually arrived at. He rode along one day with some cops and their canine unit on patrol. Before the patrol began, the dogs couldn't have been friendlier. But, on the brink of being deployed, the dogs abruptly changed, becoming as grim-looking as soldiers primed for battle.

"They were ready to be killers," he observes. "That's like us as ballplayers: they're psycho; we're psycho. We go into killer mode when we're on the field. You had to do that to have any chance to hit a ninety-, ninety-five-mile-per-hour fastball every night for six months. You might go back and forth with your personal problems, but you need to keep all that to yourself during a season if you're going to have any chance and keep that killer mode. That was your duty."

The 1964 regular season began for the Dodgers in Los Angeles, with Koufax facing the Cardinals. Ready to play whenever and wherever needed, Parker took a place in the dugout, and waited. He didn't get into the opening game—or any of the next four. But on Sunday afternoon, April 19, seated on the bench in Dodger Stadium, Parker was watching the seventh inning of a tied game against Warren Spahn and the Braves when a coach yelled at him to pinch-run for Roseboro, who stood on second base with two outs. Parker ran out on the field and took a lead off second base. Wills grounded out to end the inning, and Parker quietly returned to his seat in the dugout, to watch the Dodgers lose, 3–2, in twelve innings.

Much later, even he would struggle to remember when and how he had made his major league debut. The event never seared itself into his memory, perhaps because he was always focused—and typically worried—about what was coming next. But in the instant he stepped on second base, he had realized a fantasy. Certainly, the moment would have triggered an ovation had the 30,132 spectators known about the tumult of his life or the speed of his ascent. Just nineteen months since he sat in the Paris hotel room, he had done it. He was the 9,830th person ever to play in the major leagues, and perhaps the most unlikely.

Torborg had made the team as well. He boarded the Dodger plane for the first trip of his life to Los Angeles. A smiling Larry Sherry, unaware of his imminent trade to the Tigers, turned to Torborg as the plane reached cruising altitude and said, "Wait until you see the lights of California. You'll see the lights coming off the desert for a good hour before we get into LA. It'll just get brighter and brighter. It's something to see."

It was true, a mesmerized Torborg thought, as they crossed through the desert into Southern California. He marveled over the lights below. Could anything be more beautiful? After the plane landed, his first days in his new homeland couldn't have been more charmed. He and his wife stayed with several other team members and their wives at the Mayfair Hotel. A generous Frank Howard handed him the keys to one of his cars and said, "I'd like you to use it."

The Torborgs soon found a place of their own in Pasadena, in a nice neighborhood populated by white-collar professionals. It was already his experience that, if you were a Dodger, the whole city and the nicest communities opened their arms to you. Like the rest of the state, Southern California was at its zenith, with its booming economy complementing a glittering infrastructure and attractions—the best new highways, a bevy of young colleges and new schools, glorious beaches and mountains. Los Angeles, Torborg thought, was a dreamland.

For now at least he had made it as a Dodger reserve. He enjoyed a bit of new respect, and friends on the club looked after him. One day, while he was taking batting practice, Willie Davis tried to assert the privileges of a regular by booting him from the batting cage, barking, "Get out of there." Torborg sheepishly complied. Davis entered the cage, ready to take his cuts, when an annoyed Howard shouted, "Don't show up the kid, Willie." Davis swiftly exited the cage, and Torborg resumed hitting.

Life was good, Torborg decided. If his concentration on the game flagged even for an instant, a veteran—Roseboro, Drysdale, Fairly, *somebody*—was always there to remind him of the stakes involved. One day Koufax walked over and offered to hit foul pop-ups to him so he could work on his defense. *Koufax*. Reaching out to work with *him*. It was a reminder, he thought, of how the stars realized that their ability to win hinged in moments on the questionable skills of little-known teammates, even those of a third-string catcher. No wonder they stayed on his ass. I better not mess this up, he told himself.

M aury Wills made a habit of signing autographs after Sunday-afternoon games at Dodger Stadium. In Los Angeles, the Dodgers typically played night games on weekdays and Saturdays, after which Wills—his bruised and sore legs in need of their normal treatment—seldom got out of the ballpark until after midnight. By then sleepy children and their parents would be long gone, with even the most rabid adult fans having slunk off.

Yet on Sundays, hordes of fans routinely waited for Wills in the parking lot behind the left-field pavilion, where most Dodgers parked their cars. The sight of him triggered a frenzied stampede. The most comfortable man in the delirium was always Wills. Unruffled by the fans' pushing, he grinned and held up a hand, taking command as he would on the field.

He regarded these Sunday appearances in the parking lot as a responsibility. It did not matter that the heat was usually intense, and that this was an era before ubiquitous water bottles. He stood there on the hot asphalt and signed and kept signing. If it took an hour or ninety minutes, it did not matter—he signed everything.

It was never lost on him that the vast majority of the children in the autograph line, and their parents, were white. At every moment he knew there was the real possibility that the small child in front of him was meeting a black man for the very first time in his life. "None of that was unusual to me—that was the way it'd been in my child-hood; that's the way it'd been in the minor leagues in some places," he remembers. "But you were aware it was a special situation for them. You wanted to do the right things. You wanted to make sure children and their parents felt good about meeting you. It was important for reasons bigger than being a Dodger."

When finished signing, he thanked everyone and walked toward his car, with admirers tagging along. Curious adults, he sensed, wanted to see what kind of car he owned. He climbed into his station wagon as the last of the kids and their parents waved. He knew people wondered all the time what he and other ballplayers did after they left the stadium—where they were partying and with whom; what beautiful women would be around; who in their celebrity orbit might be dropping by.

Wills had no orbit. Away from ballparks, alone defined him. Being the honored guest at a country club's banquet, where he usually would be the only black invitee, remained as awkward for him as ever. Never would he feel quite as small at such events as when hugely successful white people sang his praises as an outstanding ballplayer, an excellent role model, and a credit to everyone who knew him. Something faintly patronizing about it left him wanting to be gone. Only here at the stadium did he feel at absolute ease and in control. At moments, he wished he never had to leave. He had no real desire to go home; nothing very interesting generally awaited at his apartment. But at least he would be accepted there, in his black neighborhood in the city's Crenshaw district, just as he had been as a child back at Parkside.

He never needed to search long for a place to live. Someone passed along word of an apartment's availability, and soon it was his. But he knew that several of his black teammates had faced obstacles in hunting for housing on their own. A real estate listing that might point a white reader to a suitable house or an apartment would, as often as not, lead nowhere for a black reader.

Although he was content with his own neighborhood, it gnawed at Wills that so many communities in Southern California were impenetrable for blacks. His face was on the front pages of newspapers and the covers of national magazines, but just as several of his black teammates had told each other, this counted for nothing once a black player took off his uniform and put on his street clothes. The unacknowledged segregation in parts of Southern California barred them from purchasing homes in many communities where white team-mates lived or were looking. A few of the white Dodgers lived out by the beach, some in Pasadena, a couple in Orange County, and others like Ron Fairly in the San Fernando Valley, much of which was re-garded as among the areas most resistant to integration.

No law at that point banned racial discrimination in the sale of a California home, with the result that de facto segregation prevailed in large swaths of the Valley. Demographic studies released in 1962 revealed that only about 10 percent of the Valley was nonwhite, with more than 90 percent of the Valley's estimated 16,000 black residents concentrated in the northeastern Valley community of Pacoima, which was fast on its way toward being described, in an early 1960s report from the San Fernando Valley Fair Housing Council to a Cal-ifornia State Senate committee, as a "ghetto," plagued by substandard dwellings and segregated schools.

The Dodgers' black stars were not the only minority athletes to suffer in silence as communities abetted segregation. Bill Russell, a future basketball Hall of Famer around whom the champion Boston Celtics had become an NBA dynasty, bought a home in a nearly all-white Massachusetts enclave, only to have his residence regularly van-dalized and his family threatened. Curt Flood, the Cardinals star, had moved during the off-season into a home in a northern California suburb and encountered much the same ugliness.

While an admirer of Flood, Wills had never possessed the instinct to push back; his childhood had taught him not to make waves. The Crenshaw district gave him the refuge he wanted, yet he couldn't wait on some days to get back to the stadium. All would be better there. He would enter, and ushers would shout his name and rush to get a word with him. The stadium organist would be playing, the excite-ment in the ballpark building. "It was so beautiful," he remembers. "It protected me from everything on the outside, at least when I was there."

He always recognized the tradeoff. He performed for a crowd who came to cheer for him, but would hesitate in some cases to have him as a neighbor. This had been the deal for the best of black American entertainers and athletes forever; Wills realized you had to make your peace with the reality or else be driven crazy. But it was hard enough that he could feel his weariness growing. Don't rock the boat, he reminded himself.

It's just that the indignities wore you down. And you had to hold all that in. You had to take it home with you—the slights, Bavasi's barbs—not to mention all the things out there in the world far beyond the stadium. He felt things festering in himself. But as long as he was in this stadium, on this field, hearing these chants, it was good. He was respected, even loved here. Count your blessings, he told himself. Focus on everything you got.

He kept all this to himself. He didn't want to talk publicly about the racism commonplace to the black players' experience. He didn't want to talk about his own wounds. He didn't want to talk about where he went at night, or his dating life, or Doris Day.

He became nervous at the first hint of a question about any of these subjects from a reporter, black or white. He'd cut an interview short then. He didn't answer phone calls. He avoided telegrams. The thought that hundreds of fans might call the Dodger offices to protest something he did, or that Bavasi might badger him if he said anything controversial to a reporter, frightened him. He resolved to talk only about the good things. Not coincidentally, this was always the moment he felt his lowest. If his banjo was anywhere close, he reached for it.

"I never knew if it all might end for me by the next season—I felt so small," he said. This is what it meant to be the mobbed star in the parking lot but never to feel worthy of the mob.

Parker found it harder to play in Los Angeles than outside it. During the 1964 season, he lived in an apartment on Barrington Avenue in

West Los Angeles, about ten minutes from his childhood home. The proximity added to his stresses. His fear of failure was always greater there. To compound his problems in Los Angeles, he usually didn't have anyone to whom he could turn during the mornings. Friends like Moon, Fairly, and Torborg, who were often breakfast companions on the road and always good for a laugh, were at home with their families, in other parts of the city.

On the mornings and early afternoons of night games, Parker had hours to kill before leaving for Dodger Stadium. Music helped but was no panacea. "I was always fighting my anxieties before going to the ballpark," he said. "I was dealing with the past, with the pain. I had concerns about failing the team. I'd tell myself, 'Don't let the team down. Don't let the past interfere with my game.' It was harder in Los Angeles because there were the reminders of everything around me. I thought there would be more people I knew watching me. There was more of a standard to meet. I didn't want to humiliate myself in front of thousands, tens of thousands, at the ballpark."

As a season ticket holder, his father regularly could be found in his box seats in Aisle 28 on the first-base side, about twelve rows off the field. But Parker usually looked for his brother, the one who had hit those thousands of balls to him.

The day after he made his debut at home with his pinch-running cameo, Parker strode to the plate in Dodger Stadium as a pinch hitter. In his first major-league at-bat, he struck out swinging. The moment was utterly forgettable—three pitches and three strikes against the Braves' right-handed starter, Bob Sadowski, on a night the Dodgers would lose to drop to 1–6 on the season.

The game marked the end of the home stand. The Dodgers flew off to St. Louis to begin their first road trip of the season. On April 22 in St. Louis, summoned to pinch-hit for Dodgers reliever Phil Ortega, Parker hit a hard-bouncing double down the left-field line off veteran Cardinal left-hander Curt Simmons for the first hit of his career. Standing on second base, he turned with surprise to see the Cardinal shortstop, Dick Groat, smiling at him, and wheeled in the opposite direction to notice St. Louis's second baseman, Julian Javier, doing the same. The moment marked the start of his enduring appreciation for games on the road, and for the kindnesses of some prominent opponents. Later that year Groat, a longtime elite shortstop who had won the National League's Most Valuable Player Award in 1960 as part of the Pirates' World Championship team, would tap him on the backside and say, "Good luck in this game, young fellow."

The Cardinals exuded class, he told people. No one competed harder than the Cards, but several of their biggest players went out of their way to show respect for rivals, including young nobodies. They could genuinely like you even while trying to beat your brains in, he thought. The Cardinals had no idea of their effect on him. All his life he had dreamed of finding fulfillment and respect, and in his first year of major-league ball he received it in several baseball cities, though nowhere as keenly as in St. Louis. He would have ten hits against the Cardinals that season, batting at a remarkable .476 clip against them, his highest average versus any rival. He had three hits in one game, including his first major-league homer. That same afternoon, he was on base when Bill White, the Cardinals' All-Star first baseman and a perennial Gold Glove winner, glanced his way and snapped, mock-angry, "You kill us."

Parker chuckled, grateful that White, the very kind of sterling first baseman and capable hitter he hoped to become, had said anything to him. Later, having become relaxed enough to banter with the star, he offered an explanation for his success: "Bill, I don't know what it is, I just like you guys so much."

White groaned. "Dammit, stop liking us."

By that time, several road cities had become refuges for him. "I played more relaxed on the road," he said. "There weren't the hard reminders of my past around. And I had my teammates around all the time—all these guys who were like brothers. As soon as I saw guys in the morning, it was a lot better. Being with ballplayers is good. It's not a down world. It's a virile world. It gives you confidence."

Being on the road with the Dodgers, he found himself making new friends, including some of the veterans. Trying to be one of the guys, he'd happily taken to sprinkling in a bit of profanity now and then. It felt special to call Tracewski a son of a bitch and for Trixie to respond in kind. He loved the road.

He eventually had to come back to Los Angeles, though, where his anxieties were apt to flare at any moment. He was under no illusions. Baseball was a business: if he wanted to remain here, he had to make on-field contributions. He only had to look around the Dodger dugout to see what happened when you fell short. His fellow rookie John Werhas had already lost his starting job at third, soon to be sent back to the minors.

In Los Angeles, on Sunday afternoon, May 24, Parker started a game for the first time. He played center field, in place of a resting Willie Davis, against the Philadelphia Phillies. With the Dodgers languishing in seventh place, Alston managed the game as if he couldn't afford to lose it. Compounding the Dodgers' miseries, the defending champions had to face the Phillies' pitching ace Jim Bunning, an All-Star and future Hall of Famer who would win nineteen games and throw five shutouts that season, including a perfect game just a month later.

On paper, Parker appeared hopelessly overmatched when he came to bat. Bunning had a first-rate curveball, a deceptive fastball, and often employed an unusual sidearm delivery. Never before had the rookie faced a pitcher so formidable. But Parker doubled twice against him, and later tripled and drove in the first run of his career against Phillies reliever Jack Baldschun.

Meanwhile young Joe Moeller, enjoying a two-run lead, pitched shutout ball through the first six innings. But when Moeller gave up a single and a double to begin the seventh inning, Alston yanked him. In a sign of the Dodgers' desperation, the manager turned to Koufax, who hadn't pitched in relief for two years.

Parker watched as Koufax walked in from the bullpen. The rookie and veteran didn't know each other well. Parker, recognizing a man who shared his preference for privacy and space, generally limited himself to saying little more than hi when he ran into the star.

With baserunners on second and third and no outs, Koufax struck out pinch hitter Ruben Amaro and then overpowered Gus Triandos, the Phillies' catcher, forcing him to foul out. To the plate stepped rookie outfielder Danny Cater, a right-handed hitter who had never faced Koufax. Cater connected with the first pitch, hitting an opposite field bullet toward right-center field. Leaving the bat, it looked like a double that would tie the game.

But Parker was sprinting. He stretched as far as possible and caught the ball backhanded, about knee-high off the ground, for the inning's final out. "I robbed them of a couple of runs," he remembers.

The Dodgers won, 3–0, with Koufax pitching the final three innings for the save, Moeller picking up his second victory, and Parker going 3-for-4 to raise his average to .273 on the season. The local newspapers, fascinated with his Brentwood pedigree, treated him as an exotic star in the making. After the game, the *Los Angeles Times*' Frank Finch wrote of the crowd's "intense delight" over his sensational catch, referring to Parker as the "Dodgers' new pin-up boy" and temporarily dubbing him "Walloping Wes" for what he had done against Bunning.

By early June, Parker would be hitting .315. But it was just a matter of time before Bunning and other National League starting pitchers discovered how to render him a feeble hitter. As the 1964 season wore on, pitchers would begin figuring him out, with his batting average falling to .257 in a mere 214 at-bats.

Yet by then, management's judgment had already taken shape: Parker would be a candidate for playing more, having shown promise at first base especially. Unknown to the rest of the Dodgers organization in that moment, his old demons and terrors would intensify over the next year. No one in the organization had a clue about his torment.

But that was in his future. On May 24, he had just played his most impressive major-league game yet. As if his offensive prowess against Bunning wasn't enough, his brilliant catch had rescued Koufax—he had saved the savior. The day was cause for euphoria. Parker savored the memory into the next century: "I have a feeling even Sandy said something about my play that day."

Koufax had no business being on the mound that afternoon. Working on insufficient rest, still recovering from an injury, he needed to be protected, mostly from his own competitive zeal. But there he was, fulfilling what had come to be his chief role in Dodgers lore, which was to defy people's notions of what was possible and sometimes even wise. As regal as DiMaggio, he had something more. He offered the possibility that at any moment you might be about to see a masterpiece for the last time; his injuries spoke to a fragility that hinted his end might always be as close as his next pitch. He wasn't long for baseball. But until the end, he was going to do things spectators had never seen before and might never again. His image thereafter would be frozen in your mind's eye, always young, always enigmatically beautiful. His fans would come to realize they knew him but never really knew him, for he was every bit as reclusive as he was revered.

Just a month earlier in 1964, Koufax had hurt his elbow. He missed two pitching starts, which spurred panicked front-page headlines in the Los Angeles papers about what his injury augured. Returning to action in early May, with the Dodgers pronouncing him healed after a twelve-day break, he allowed himself no time for carefully working his way back into full-time duty, immediately embarking on a breakneck pace. Six appearances later, on May 24, agreeable to being summoned in a surprise from the bullpen, he was daring to pitch on only two days of rest, instead of his normal three.

Ordinarily a sensible manager, Alston's decision to use him was an unfathomable risk. In a 162-game season, how much could one contest matter, even if a team was already far behind in the standings? How could one May game justify the possibility of jeopardizing a vulnerable arm that needed all the rest Koufax could give it between starts? But these are criticisms born of the luxury of historical perspective. In 1964 few managers hesitated to use a pitching ace in relief if, in their view, a critical situation had arisen.

For his part, Koufax needed no prodding to pitch a relief stint, long since accustomed to pushing himself beyond anyone else's limits. Priding himself on his toughness, he pitched with less than his normal rest whenever needed—willing to spring off the bench to save a game, willing to pitch deep into extra innings as a starter, willing to throw a ludicrous 200-plus pitches over thirteen innings to win a contest. He had no idea of the price he would pay for his verve. Famously ascetic and disciplined off the field, he was in the process of unwittingly hastening his deterioration on it.

No one in the organization checked his competitive impulses. If anything, officials stoked them. It hadn't helped that Buzzie Bavasi fatuously pontificated during their tense contract negotiations about how he placed more importance on a pitcher's total number of innings than on figures like Koufax's ERA and win total, a point meant to question his star's durability and will. The truth was, Koufax labored like a plow horse. He had pitched several times over the years on a mere two days of rest. If anything, he was too tough for his own good.

All this stood in front of him on May 24, after he earned his save. His career, which would end within two and a half years of that day, had entered a period of peril that no one around him could see. The May 24 appearance stands out as a signature moment of the folly at work in the organization's handling of him, the most conspicuous example to that point of the team's rashness. The ineptitude could be traced back to spring training, when he casually told a few reporters he felt "lousy" without elaborating on the point. The danger to his left arm had escalated since. The first three months of the 1964 regular season would serve as a harbinger of all his problems to come, as well as a useful textbook on how not to care for an extraordinary pitcher. No period in his baseball life better warrants an examination of how the grind contributed to wearing him down and shortening his career.

His season had begun in mid-April at Dodger Stadium with an artful shutout of the Cardinals on opening night. It was a slightly unusual Koufax performance, more crafty than crushing. He didn't look quite like the dominant pitcher of a season earlier, striking out only five batters. Just the same, he limited the Cardinals to six hits and was never seriously threatened. No one could fairly describe the outing as anything less than masterful.

He received his three days of rest afterward, the customary period in the 1960s for major-league pitchers working in a standard four-man starting rotation. A generation later, the amount of normal rest would grow to four days with what became a typical five-man pitching rotation, an attitudinal shift that embraced the concept of more rest and fewer innings for hurlers. But baseball men of the 1960s never warmed to the idea of five regular starters. How could a fifth starter, they reasoned, be anything other than markedly inferior to a team's ace pitcher? Worse, a fifth starter would reduce the number of starts for a hardworking star like Koufax from roughly forty to thirty-two appearances during a season.

Koufax always liked a four-man rotation. The more starts, the better. He believed he thrived on consistent work. Displaying no visible problem after his opening night win, he lost his next start to the Reds and their ace, Jim Maloney, 3–0. It was a strong appearance on its face, marred only by a three-run homer by Reds first baseman Deron Johnson. But he had struck out only six hitters—a very good number for most pitchers, but by that point in his career, he typically struck out nine or more in a game. Coupled with his opening-day performance, his outing suggested that some of his power might be missing. Koufax recognized it, too. "I haven't had anything on the ball in any of my starts [this year]," he noted later that month to reporters.

It was a rare moment of candor. He was still hiding the deep pain in his pitching arm. Not even Roseboro knew of his problem, though it seemed to him that Koufax was suddenly reluctant to throw his curveball. The catcher was even more puzzled by the poor break on the few curves he was seeing. A mum Koufax, hoping his pain would go away on its own, plodded on. "I was just lucky to get by," he would confess later.

But luck runs out in baseball. The Dodgers traveled to St. Louis, where on April 22 Koufax experienced a painful strain in his left elbow and upper forearm during the very first inning. It felt like something in his forearm had been torn altogether when he threw a curveball to Bill White that bounced several feet in front of home plate. He said nothing to Roseboro or anyone else in that instant. He simply stuck out his glove, waited for a ball to be thrown back to him, and hurled it again.

Although giving up a three-run line-drive homer off a fastball to Cardinals outfielder Charlie James in the next minute, he managed to finish the inning. By then he could no longer conceal his problem. Something in his motion and facial expressions had given him away. An alarmed Alston and pitching coach Joe Becker converged on him as soon as he entered the dugout. They didn't want him throwing another pitch. A resistant Koufax, demonstrating that his capacity for self-denial rivaled his talent, told Becker that he was ready to go on; that he thought he could pitch the pain and stiffness right out of his arm. He wanted the chance at least to try. "Sandy didn't want to come out of the game," Alston would later tell reporters.

Alston removed him anyway, ordering him to pack his bags. By morning Koufax was flying without his teammates back to Los Angeles, where he underwent an examination, his second since the injury happened. In St. Louis, the Cardinals' team physician, Dr. I. C. Middleman, was the first to issue a diagnosis. He informed Koufax that a tendon on the inner part of his elbow was inflamed and that, in confirmation of Koufax's instincts, a muscle in his tender swollen upper forearm had been slightly torn. The forearm was spasming, which was why Koufax had lost all control on his errant curveball. Middleman characterized the root problem as epicondylitis, or tennis elbow, speculating that Koufax would miss "at least one or two" starts. "This type of disorder is tricky and can be dangerous without proper care," Middleman told reporters, though he next downplayed the danger. "This condition is not too serious, in my opinion. One sees it often in pitchers who throw lots of curveballs."

Koufax had opened up to the Cardinals team doctor. He told Middleman that his elbow had hurt him off and on all spring. He seemed to be worried, thought Middleman, who, careful not to heighten his anxiety, said there was no reason for serious concern pending a more thorough examination. The next morning, that second examination occurred in the office of Dr. Robert Kerlan, the Dodgers' team physician and an orthopedic surgeon, who declined afterward to hazard a guess about the long-term implications of the injury, or how long Koufax might be out of action. He described the malady as a strain in the musculature of the "inner side of the elbow and upper half of the forearm," telling reporters that Koufax had undergone cortisone injections at his office, as well as therapy that included ice packs, hot whirlpool submersion, and ultrasound treatments.

A genial Koufax, observers reported, appeared unruffled, going so far as to sign an autograph for the daughter of a newspaper photographer while undergoing a treatment. If anything, Kerlan was the nervously guarded man in the room. It would be at least forty-eight hours, the doctor said, before he could gauge how Koufax's arm was reacting to the cortisone.

Forty-eight hours later, the news was not good. Koufax, said Kerlan, was not responding as well as had been hoped to the cortisone and other treatments. He would be missing a second start. Yet only one week later, he was back. The conditions in Dodger Stadium on that first Monday in May could hardly have been more unfavorable for a pitcher returning from an arm problem, especially one with a history of struggling to get properly loose under the best of circumstances. Rain showers had preceded the night game, and it was unseasonably cool in Los Angeles, no more than 50 degrees as Koufax stepped on the mound.

He was not the type of competitor to ease his way back into things. In defiance of logic, with the quiet approval of Dodger officials, he pitched not a prudent five or six innings but the full nine. Then he kept pitching, with the game deadlocked at one apiece and Koufax locked in an extra-inning duel with the Cubs' left-handed ace, Dick Ellsworth. Improbably, he threw a sensational three-hitter, striking out thirteen Cubs over ten innings, ready to soldier on and pitch the eleventh inning when Wills made it unnecessary by stroking a single that drove in Tracewski with the winning run. Afterward, Koufax told reporters his arm felt better than it had since early in spring training. Dodger management and Los Angeles media alike chose to read his remark as assurance that Koufax was back, as healthy as ever. Delusion about him had reached a new high.

The following Saturday he lost, 3–2, in Candlestick Park to the Giants, seeing his record on the season fall to 2–3 and the Dodgers' mark plummet to 9–15, dropping the team to eighth place in the National League standings. It would get worse for both the club and the pitcher. Koufax lasted a mere four innings in his next outing, giving up four earned runs on May 14 in Wrigley Field, spared another loss only because the Dodgers mounted a comeback. Rest seemed in order.

Instead, the Dodgers gambled. The following Sunday, back in Dodger Stadium, there Koufax was, pitching against the Pirates with only two days of rest, laboring through seven and two-thirds innings, in which he gave up ten hits and found himself in numerous jams. He persevered, escaping with a 3–2 victory, his first win in two weeks. But the triumph came at the cost of foolishly emboldening everyone involved in the decision making about his workload, Alston and Koufax most of all. It sparked a mad rush of Koufax mound appearances over the next month, as if Alston was trying to make up for lost games and Koufax for lost time.

After earning a complete game victory at home against the Mets, in which he gave up seven hits and struck out eleven, Koufax made his relief appearance against the Phillies. It was already the second time in 1964 that he was pitching on just two days of rest.

He wouldn't acknowledge the risks. And Alston was happy to send him out. What ensued was recklessness. After facing the Phillies, he had only two days of rest again before his next outing. He lost to the Reds, 1–0, despite yielding only three hits. Over the span of six games in just seven days, Koufax had made three appearances and pitched nineteen innings. His pace was as self-destructive as it was awe-inspiring.

With his record at 4–4, he could only see all the things he thought he was doing wrong, the things that required him to work not less but more. His four-seam fastball, which ordinarily appeared to rise from the perspective of hitters, was instead mysteriously sinking and acting like a screwball. It didn't have the same pop, no longer seeming to rocket in its final few feet. His strikeout totals and dominance had correspondingly dropped. He puzzled over the problem with Joe Becker, finally determining that he had unconsciously altered his windup motion by stepping too much to his left with his front foot—his right foot—and pitching across his body, in the process severely reducing his power. The task was to regain his old motion, to open up his stride and release the ball while moving directly toward the plate, which was easier for him to describe than execute. Frustrated, he studied photos of himself winding up and delivering pitches, looking to unlock the wonder of the old Koufax. Then he went to work with Becker, resolved to correct the flaw.

His drive left him no room for concerns about reinjuring his arm. It revealed the largest truth about him, the one to which some of the era's sportswriters, who had observed his soft-spoken, deferential nature in media settings, were altogether blind: no fiercer participant could be found in all of baseball. He had become irked by descriptions of him as a "gentle" competitor and man. "It sure as hell isn't 'gentle,' especially playing the game," Koufax said decades later when asked how he would have characterized himself. "Competing to me is being the last man standing."

He had become increasingly disturbed during the 1960s by suggestions that he was conflicted about being a ballplayer. Deep in his heart, some skeptics suggested, perhaps Koufax was less a ballplayer than a budding businessman and bon vivant. Journalists knew of his investments in a radio station and a small hotel on Santa Monica Boulevard, in West Hollywood. Around teammates, he exhibited an avid interest in stereo systems, sometimes sharing news about the latest in state-of-the-art amplifiers and woofers and speakers and record player needles with glazed-eyed teammates, a few of whom thought a career in retail electronics awaited him. Other observers speculated that, were he ever to leave baseball, he might wish to indulge purported passions in architecture and engineering.

Some stories cast him as a closet intellectual, always grounds for suspicion in professional sports. A narrative had taken hold: Koufax possessed artistic and cultural interests not commonly associated with players. It was erroneously reported that his musical tastes ran heavily toward the works of classical composers and that he had a passion for the oeuvres of serious novelists ranging from Thomas Wolfe to Aldous Huxley, the latter of whom, an amused Koufax later said, he couldn't recall having read.

Over the next year, no less respected a publication than *Time* magazine would raise the possibility that Koufax didn't enjoy baseball or even take it seriously, declaring, "Alone among ballplayers, Koufax is an anti-athlete." Dodger executive Fresco Thompson would disparage Koufax without being censured by the Dodgers, telling *Time*: "I don't think he likes baseball. What kind of a line is he drawing anyway—between himself and the world, between himself and the team?" Even some of Koufax's friends and greatest boosters in the press had encouraged the doubts, if unintentionally. He is "a captive of baseball, trapped by his talents, not his instincts," Jim Murray wrote in the *Los Angeles Times*, declaring, "Sandy Koufax belongs in baseball about the way Albert Schweitzer belongs in a twist joint."

No other American athlete in the 1960s endured such highly publicized doubts about his enthusiasm or suitability for a sport. Yet no athlete inspired more pride either. It would be disingenuous not to state what by then was obvious: the pride and the doubts were opposite sides of the same coin, one that had its genesis in Koufax's religion and both the support and virulent biases that, historically, had sprung from it. The ugliest of the doubts turned without directly saying so upon anti-Semitic stereotypes and prejudices occasionally evident in newspaper references to Koufax's supposed business shrewdness and inferences that Koufax might be less committed to the Dodgers than to getting more money, in and out of the sport. (No other player in the game suffered through such veiled and repugnant speculation about his motives—there can be no reasonable doubt about its cause and effect.) However, such cynicism more than met its match in the passionate praise of Koufax as a breakthrough figure of historic importance. The political columnist Morrie Ryskind, in alluding to past European horrors perpetrated upon Jews, observed in 1964, "Had all Jews taken the path of martyrdom, there'd have been neither the Salk vaccine nor Sandy Koufax pitching for the Dodgers."

The association of a baseball pitcher with the genius who had all but eradicated polio wasn't hyperbolic. By then, the two men occupied much the same exalted status among American Jews especially. One had saved countless lives; the other, like the slugger Hank Greenberg and champion boxer Barney Ross before him, had simultaneously enhanced a tribal pride and a nation's regard for extraordinary Jewish athletes. Koufax's prowess was yet another step in lancing the vile stereotype that Jews were brainy nebbishes, generally destined to be inept at sports, more comfortable with watching than playing.

Already immortal, he could have done anything he wished for the remainder of his life—step into an illustrious corporate career, launch a business under his gilded name, enter politics, serve like DiMaggio as a well-paid commercial spokesperson, take a position in baseball, or carve out a career as an actor, having already guest-starred in numerous, if minor, television roles. His abundance of career options perhaps accounted for the doubt in some quarters about his baseball fervor. "Everybody wanted Sandy," Tracewski remembered. "But he loved the game. He liked being a teammate. Sandy had spent his whole career trying to get to this point of pitching regularly—he never would've wanted to give that up. I don't think anything else was as rewarding to him as competing."

His doubters failed to see the essential truth about him: he had not a scintilla of interest in fleeing baseball; he lived for competition. Several major athletic figures from the 1960s would transition from sports into celebrated lives in other sectors, including Jim Bunning and the basketball star Bill Bradley, each of whom won election in time to the US Senate. But for all of Koufax's interests, no occupation or hobby would ever absorb him as much as games.

If he ever had harbored a yearning, sometimes bitterly so, during his career, it was to pitch more, not less. He would forever resent how some of the top men in Dodger management had poorly utilized him early in his career. More than forty years later, at a charity event sponsored by his friend Joe Torre's foundation for combating domestic violence, Koufax poured out the frustrations he had felt during the 1950s, when he pitched seldom and despaired that his superiors had little faith in him. "I'd go warm up in the bullpen, and I'd hear the echo" of another pitcher preparing to come into the game, he recollected, without mentioning Alston by name. He sardonically added, "Really encouraging."

Even after becoming the Dodgers' ace, he sometimes became annoyed by Alston's moves, particularly any adjustment in the pitching rotation that left him being used out of order. One afternoon in Los Angeles, having been surprised by a change, he burst into Alston's office as a nearby Wills overheard their exchange. "Sandy got emotional," Wills recalled. "He was raising hell. There was a lot of shouting between the two of them. Alston basically said, 'Goddammit, I'm the manager.' And Sandy yelled, 'I'm the starting pitcher.'"

Finally the men fell silent, and Koufax emerged from the office.

"Way to go, Sandy," Wills said as he remembered their exchange. "Stand up for your rights."

Koufax snapped: "Yeah, I'm tired of that shit."

Yet neither Koufax's success nor his hard-won respect from Alston could change some things. He remained vulnerable to arm problems. And he wouldn't take any steps on his own to mitigate the danger. Having gone through long stretches in the 1950s when he wasn't asked to pitch at all, he certainly didn't want to pitch any less now.

His stoicism and discipline took over. He pushed on, continuing to work with Becker on his windup and delivery problem. He always seemed to be working, thought Tracewski, who was no longer surprised when Koufax gave him a call on Dodger off days, asking if Tracewski could drop by his home in the Valley so they could play catch together and stay loose on afternoons that fell between the pitcher's starts. "I need you: I gotta throw," Koufax would say.

Tracewski would make the half-hour drive from his apartment in Baldwin Hills to his friend's quiet neighborhood. Koufax's house sat on a slight hill, set off a good distance from his street. As one of his closest and most reliable of friends, Tracewski occupied a unique place in Koufax's sphere—he could be trusted to help, and equally trusted to leave when his friend wanted to prepare alone for the game ahead. "Sandy needed his rest and privacy during the season," Tracewski said. "He didn't want distractions."

Such a sober approach contributed to the perception that he never looked for fun in the game, or found it. Koufax never much disputed the point, insisting that baseball was work, a job, and therefore ought to be approached as seriously as any other profession. After all, who looked for fun in business or finance? He made no secret of wanting to be paid well for his achievements, though he stressed that nothing meant so much to him as feeling professionally fulfilled, which hinged entirely on whether he won. "Personal pride is more the incentive when you're playing than the money is," he said during a television interview in the 1960s with Frank Gifford, the former New York Giants football star. "After [the season] is all over, [if] you think [you've] had a good year, [you] deserve a raise."

It was never that easy. Baseball executives rewarded players for previous achievements. But they paid the most for expectations of stars' ongoing success. It was a distinction not lost on veteran players. Koufax understood that his salary and any additional raises would depend not merely on his past wins but on executives' confidence that his arm had many victories left in it. No pitcher at the time could offer such assurance by playing it safe and competing on a reduced schedule. To prove his prowess, Koufax needed to maintain the appearance of his iron stamina, deliver an abundance of complete game victories, and log so many innings that there could be no question about his future durability. He had his own axiom for describing the importance of going the distance and being present at the end of games to accept congratulations as the winner. "A quality start," he said at the Torre event, speaking in the present tense about the 1960s, "is shaking hands with the catcher."

That had always meant nine innings of work, which in turn commonly meant throwing more than 100 pitches per game, often more than 130, once in a while 150 or more. Many years later, when he would come at last to acknowledge the link between heavy pitch counts, injured arms, and shortened careers, he would speak supportively of efforts by managers and coaches to sustain modern pitching careers by reducing the volume of pitchers' innings and pitches. "I think longevity plays a big part in [decisions about the number of pitches thrown]," he said. "I don't blame them."

But Koufax made clear he didn't have that luxury in the '60s. Winning and pitching a complete game elevated a pitcher to a higher professional and financial status. "You didn't win, you didn't get a raise," he observed.

To earn more money, he would need Herculean output. In the end, that requirement would be the first of three factors that contributed toward his career's early demise. The second would be the absence of multiyear contracts, which meant that Koufax never could pause during his physical struggles to make a priority of his long-term well-being, certainly not without jeopardizing his chance of making greater money.

The third and most critical factor was Koufax himself. He had his own standards, which exceeded everyone else's. His huge competitive heart would drive him to pitch beyond any reasonable threshold of pain; it would drive him into early ruin if it meant winning. As he approached the climax of his career, while still the greatest pitcher on the planet, he knew better than anyone else about the fragility of his arm, but he continued to pitch long innings anyway, because he knew no other way to play. It was why he hid his pain in early 1964. It was why he would keep downplaying his worry, at least for a while.

His work with Joe Becker on his faulty delivery had finally yielded benefits. With his record only at 4–4, he was suddenly pitching with all his body again, the improvement evident in his quickening fastball. His turnaround had begun modestly. On the last day of May in Pittsburgh, he earned his fifth win by pitching seven innings and giving up three earned runs on eight hits, an up-and-down performance that, encouragingly, saw him strike out eight Pirates. He seemed a bit closer to rediscovering his old self, though nothing in his performance could have possibly portended what happened next.

In Philadelphia, on Thursday night, June 4, he threw a no-hitter.

Doug Camilli, the Dodgers' catcher, would best remember just how oddly routine it had felt as the innings ticked by. "He was just out there doing whatever he wanted to do, throwing whatever he wanted, in complete control," Camilli remembered. "You don't expect a no-hitter to be that easy. But nothing was close to a hit. Nobody ever had to dive for anything. The Phillies really couldn't hit either his fastball or his curveball."

He struck out five Phillies in the first three innings. With two outs in the fourth inning, working to that point on a perfect game, he faced Dick Allen for the second time. The count went to three balls and two strikes, and Camilli signaled for a curveball. Koufax shook him off, one of the few times in the game when Koufax disagreed with what his catcher wanted. He waited until Camilli flashed him the sign for the fastball and then went into his windup. Halfway into it, he thought, Doug's right, a curveball would be better. But it was too late to halt his motion. He threw the fastball, another good one, on the outer half of the plate. It was a bit lower than he wanted.

"It could've gone either way," Camilli remembered. "I might have said something to the umpire."

The umpire called ball four.

"It was low, no doubt of that," Koufax would say after the game.

Allen would be the Phillies' only baserunner.

Tracewski remembered the atmosphere in Connie Mack Stadium as "electrifying" as the ninth inning began. "It was a more exciting feel than during Sandy's first two no-hitters," he said. "I think it was because everybody in the country knew who Sandy was by then. He was Koufax. Everyone there wanted to say that they'd seen him do this."

Phillies second baseman Tony Taylor struck out, and shortstop Ruben Amaro fouled out. That left only pinch hitter Bobby Wine, and when the count got to 1–2, Camilli signaled he wanted a fastball. Koufax threw another on the corner, and a flailing Wine had no chance. Later, in a moment of self-criticism, alert to the very end for flaws, he would say, "I hung a curve to Bobby Wine."

It was his third career no-hitter, tying the then-major-league record of the Cleveland Indians' immortal Bob Feller, the legendary Cy Young, and relatively little known workhorse Larry Corcoran, who had accomplished his feats while pitching in the 1880s for the Chicago Cubs.

Among them all, only Koufax had thrown no-hitters in three consecutive seasons. He had reached another milestone that night in Philadelphia: his twelve strikeouts meant he had already fanned ten or more hitters in a game fifty-four times during his career, equaling another major-league record that he would break in short order that season. He was only twenty-eight, a young man destined, sportswriters logically believed at that moment, to shatter many of baseball's most illustrious lifetime pitching records.

In the locker room, he disclosed his frustrations about the previous two months. Candor gushed from him. He vividly detailed his struggles to correct the flaw in his delivery, letting the reporters in on how he pored over his old photos and made a conscious effort during the game to step more to his right when releasing the ball. Descriptive and confessional, he was the best of analysts that night. "It felt fine," he said of the adjustment he had made in his windup. "I had the old pitching rhythm back. As a matter of fact, by the fifth inning, I forgot all about it. Everything was natural again. . . . It was the first time this season I've been able to put everything together." He predicted the night would mark a decisive change in his fortunes, a return to his old form. For the rest of the season, Koufax said, he would be as "tough as ever."

Actually, he would be tougher than ever, having begun two and a half months of unrivaled greatness. His arm remained vulnerable to its heavy workload, but he would win 15 of his last 16 decisions, with a streak at one point of 11 victories in a row. His 1.74 ERA and 7 shutouts for the season would lead the National League. After capturing his nineteenth game on August 16, he would actually find himself ahead of his 25-win pace of a season earlier. He would push himself beyond the breaking point. And then he would break.

On July 2, President Lyndon Johnson signed into law the 1964 Civil Rights Act passed by Congress. Overnight, American life fundamentally changed. No restaurant, lunch counter, hotel, motel, movie theater, gas station, barbershop, or public recreational facility could lawfully discriminate against a black citizen again. "I'd never known a world like that," Wills said. "Everything I'd accepted as a kid no longer existed. I could go *anywhere*. That's what the law said. I couldn't wait to try places. I also knew it wasn't going to be exactly that easy."

The creation of the new law didn't guarantee that white segregationists would obey it, or that there wouldn't be mayhem. The South had become more of a powder keg than ever that summer. Just ten days before, three young civil rights workers had been abducted near Meridian, Mississippi, with the FBI still searching for them. "I thought, It's about time we have a law like this—but I also remember thinking some white people aren't going to like it," Wills remembered.

In Atlanta, a segregationist restaurant owner named Lester Maddox, later to be elected governor of Georgia, brandished a pistol in his parking lot and, joined by a crowd of whites wielding ax handles he'd supplied, ordered three black men to leave, chasing them off and kicking at their car as they fled. In Selma, Alabama, local white police officers abetted avowed segregationists in defying the new law, arresting four black residents when they requested service at a restaurant. Over the next week, a lunch counter in Greenwood, Mississippi, two restaurants in the Florida city of St. Augustine, and fifteen lunch counters and restaurants in Tuscaloosa, Alabama, refused to serve blacks, compelling the federal courts and the Department of Justice to intervene. FBI agents had ramped up their presence in the South, especially in Mississippi, where the search continued for the missing civil rights workers.

The many pockets of southern rebellion, coupled with the imprimatur that scornful officials like Alabama governor George Wallace had lent to the resistance, emboldened other segregationists during that first month. No observer could reasonably predict whether scores of major restaurants and hotels that long had embraced segregationist policies might simply ignore the new law and fight judicial battles, rather than risk offending their recalcitrant white clientele.

In mid-July the Dodgers arrived for a three-game series in St. Louis, a city whose racial polarization belied its self-image as friendly and sedate. The Dodgers regularly stayed at one of the city's best-known establishments, the Chase Hotel, where black Dodgers had been denied rooms for years, until at last, in 1954, an incensed Jackie Robinson went to the hotel's front desk and applied the first round of pressure that eventually enabled all the team's black players to stay there with their white teammates.

The story of Robinson's boldness had become a cherished homily to the club's African American players. By 1964, the courage of many black trailblazers and civil rights activists had come to stir Wills. He felt the first sharp pangs of what he came to view as the birth of his social consciousness. Yet for years, along with Roseboro in St. Louis, Wills had stayed away from the hotel's dining room, not wanting to press the issue and risk a public scene at a time when segregation still enjoyed legal protections. "Our understanding as black players was that we weren't allowed," Wills remembered.

Long resigned to the restrictions, Roseboro savored the hotel's food anyway. Oddly, St. Louis had become his favorite road city, simply because the Chase Hotel served his favorite dish in the country—a "creamed chicken omelet," he said. He could have it brought to him by the hotel's room service whenever he wanted. He just couldn't eat the omelet, or anything else, in the hotel's restaurant.

The indignation that Roseboro had felt during his minor-league days when turned away from restaurants still burned in him. But years of experiencing discrimination in road cities, of enduring hostile looks and epithets here and there, had worn him down, Wills thought. Roseboro chose his battles carefully now. All the while, he looked for modest pleasures. This omelet was one. Solitude in a hotel room was another.

"He was comfortable having room service all the time," Wills remembers. "He was comfortable taking his meals alone. . . . But the thought that I *had* to eat in the room bothered me sometimes. I got lonely eating in the room. Gabby never did. He made his adjustments to the way the world was. It was what all black players had to do— because if you got too upset about it, it was going to affect your play. You had to concentrate on baseball. Those were the two worlds and it was confusing. You told yourself you could live with it. You told yourself it was all right, even though you knew it wasn't all right."

But the adoption of the Civil Rights Act had altered everything. Wills wasted no time in exercising his new freedom. One morning, he excitedly told Roseboro that he was going to have breakfast in the hotel restaurant. "Come on, roomie," he said. "We can go down there and eat. You gotta go with me. I've been down there already. It's fine. Let's go."

Roseboro said simply, "I'll stay here."

"The food's really good. They treated me great. Come on."

"I'll stay here."

Wills returned alone to the restaurant. This became a familiar pattern. By then, Wills recognized a truth nearly as awful as segregation. The passage of the Civil Rights Act had come too late to change the ways of Roseboro and other wary black friends, who never would be comfortable sitting in some places that once had wanted nothing to do with them. This was among segregation's greatest evils, he thought: it had made recluses of hardworking and noble men, who would never experience some of life's everyday pleasures.

Wills told himself he had to get out. "I was tired of being afraid," he said. "When you get some freedom, you need to use it."

In August, after a six-week search, FBI agents found the three missing civil rights workers. Shot to death, buried by their killers in a muddy Mississippi dam, they lay not far from where several members of the White Knights of the Ku Klux Klan had abducted them. The revulsion in the country dominated the networks' evening newscasts. Horrified Dodgers stayed quiet about the subject around strangers. When asked on rare occasions about the turmoil around the country, the players, black and white, continued to take refuge in the same rote response, saying to reporters they were just ballplayers and didn't pay attention to politics.

Yet privately the tumult gripped them. Martin Luther King Jr. announced a renewed effort to push for federal voting rights legislation that would end the systematic disenfranchisement of southern blacks. Behind closed doors, many players cheered on the activists and protesters. Suddenly, nothing about the established order in America seemed so powerful that it couldn't be revamped or toppled in time—no discriminatory law, no unjust business practice, and no unfair salary structure in a game where owners held dictatorial control. "It was nothing but change going on everywhere you looked," Tommy Davis remembered. "It wasn't just black people. Everybody wanted to get some."

The spirit of rebelliousness would soon altogether challenge the oligarchy that was baseball—among the most insulated and slavishly protected of all American institutions—and the ensuing disputes would be among the most important indicators of the sweeping national appetite for change. Club owners still enjoyed the benefits of the so-called reserve clause, which denied players the right to take their services to another team when their contracts expired. In this and other imperial exemptions granted by the US Congress and federal courts, the owners during the 1940s and '50s had possessed a feudal power. But those days were ticking down on baseball as the mid-1960s beckoned. If the owners could be bent to reform their ways, any rebellion in American sports seemed possible.

Players, however, were nowhere near ready as a group to confront the owners. They were athletes, not activists, and needed not only lessons in how to mount a revolt but a measure of confidence that they wouldn't pay for their temerity with their careers. Unlike many civil rights workers, nearly all feared martyrdom, personal or professional.

All along they'd needed a template for believing that the possibilities for success against the owners justified taking on risks that couldn't be predicted. The civil rights victories, achieved against the stiffest odds and dangers, gave it to them, convincing hardboiled players that they might win a future fight all their own. "Change is always hard, but we knew civil rights had come—nobody in the South was able to stop it," Wills pointed out. "You knew all sorts of things could change after that. You were seeing things all the time in the news." Wills's voice went soft with awe. "I remember when they got those Ku Klux Klan people."

Before the year's end, the FBI would accuse a group of KKK members with involvement in the abduction of the three slain civil rights workers, and eighteen men would later be formally charged in federal court with violating the civil rights of the victims. On another front, the Supreme Court, acting speedily to settle any doubt about American resolve, upheld the constitutionality of the Civil Rights Act. The victories heartened a growing number of outspoken athletic legends, including Jackie Robinson, who made speeches in an effort to register black voters and defeat the presidential candidacy of the Republican nominee, Arizona senator Barry Goldwater, a fierce opponent of the Civil Rights Act.

Around the country that summer, people who had never before participated in a political rally or a demonstration ventured outside. A simmering militancy changed the look of even some nonviolent protests. In Los Angeles, 150 civil rights supporters, alarmed over a California ballot measure called Proposition 14 that sought to undo the few protections against racial discrimination in apartment rentals and public housing, picketed a meeting of a white segregationist group. The protest culminated in scuffles and fifteen arrests.

Discord in one place stoked impatience in all places, from streets to locker rooms. The restiveness reached baseball that season, a disruption that caught the attention of reporters and hinted at more problems to come for the owners. In New York, the Yankees' normally mild-mannered shortstop Tony Kubek voiced players' anger over the prospect that the owners would not give them a fair share of a potentially huge future revenue source—subscription television, or "pay TV." Kubek revealed that the owners hadn't even discussed the subject—which was "coming to a boil," he warned—with players. He added that Koufax and Drysdale were among the stars "wondering how it's all going to turn out for the [baseball] performers who make the show something you can sell in a person's home."

Ominously for the owners, Kubek raised a subject previously taboo in many major-league clubhouses. The pay-TV issue, he indicated, illustrated why players needed an organization to bargain on their behalf. "I think we are closer now to a ballplayers' union than we've ever been before," he said, in the next breath rethinking the taboo term. "Maybe the word *union* isn't accurate to describe our banding together to protect our interests. But you can say we're going to be united on this matter if we don't get what we believe is due us. There are many important ballplayers who feel the way I do, particularly on the teams . . . on the West Coast."

Players had begun pushing back against any baseball figure accustomed to ruling by fiat, intimidation, or abuse. In San Francisco, a group of black and Latino players, furious over racist remarks attributed to Giants manager Alvin Dark, threatened not to play, in what would have amounted to baseball's first impromptu players' strike. Dark, having already angered the team's Spanish-speaking players by saying he wanted them to speak only in English at the ballpark, had become a lightning rod when a story published in the New York newspaper *Newsday* quoted him as disparaging the intelligence and character of his minority players: "We have trouble because we have so many Negro and Spanish-speaking players on the team. They are just not able to perform up to the white players when it comes to mental alertness. One of the biggest things is that you can't make them subordinate themselves to the best interest of the team. You don't find pride in them that you get in a white player."

Among the most ethnically diverse teams in the majors, the Giants had five frontline Latino players on their roster that season—two future Hall of Famers in pitching sensation Juan Marichal and slugger Orlando Cepeda, along with infielder Jose Pagan and two of baseball's famous trio of Alou brothers, Matty and Jesus. Giant officials understood their shell-shocked team had no chance of winning without the leadership of its Latino and black stars. On the defensive, Dark denied he had made the controversial statement. But the furor did not die. Only the intervention of Willie Mays, who condemned Dark's words but indicated he could play for him, enabled the manager to keep his job for the remainder of the season—though Dark would be fired soon afterward.

It would also be the final season on the West Coast for another overbearing baseball giant. In Los Angeles, the bombastic Leo Durocher was in the process of losing the last remnants of his clout. Durocher had done nothing to rival the sins of Alvin Dark. But his streaks of boorishness and bullying in the Dodger clubhouse had worn thin among increasingly forceful players. By 1964, those he offended no longer felt the need to hide their feelings about him around each other. He'd made no effort to change. He still ranted that certain players should be fined for their mistakes, ignoring Alston's admonishments to be quiet about such things. He still ridiculed Alston's on-field moves when the manager was out of sight.

Coupled with his bursts of clubhouse abusiveness, Durocher's betrayals of Alston cost him the last shreds of respect among many players.

Even with his stature in the clubhouse plummeting, Durocher acted as if neither the times nor his powers had changed. But several players decided that the days of putting up with his disrespect and abuse had ended, that no coach or manager should enjoy such sway any longer.

Later that summer, holding court with reporters, Durocher lifted a fungo bat and now and then rapped the shins of a seated Frank Howard the way one would tap a ground ball.

"Leo, cut it out," said Howard, a frequent target of Durocher's barbs. "That hurts."

Now Durocher took his ribbing of Howard further than ever. Waving the fungo bat Howard's way and grinning for reporters, Durocher persisted in hitting him, seemingly intent on making a point. "Frank hadn't hit in three or four games, and Leo was on him," Moeller recalls. "He kept making contact with that bat on Frank's shins. Leo wanted to see Frank dance a little. He wanted to show everybody who was in charge."

Characteristically a gentle giant, Howard hadn't moved. But he sounded increasingly irritated, teammates thought. "Leo, cut it out."

Durocher ignored him. It appeared to Moeller and other onlookers that Durocher now wanted to demonstrate he could control the annoyed player or, for that matter, anyone else.

"You do that again, Leo," Howard snapped, "and I'm going to take your head and shove it up your ass."

Torborg recalls that Howard then stood, reached out with a long arm, and slightly lifted Durocher off the floor, shoving him backward while repeating his warning. Durocher put the bat down.

Most coaches by then would've understood the alienation they had provoked. But Durocher continued to search for ways to reassert himself and prove his worth. One afternoon before a game at Dodger Stadium, noticing Torborg working with coach Pete Reiser on the art of blocking home plate, Durocher told Torborg that he was certain he could jar the ball loose from him. The statement sounded like a challenge. "I could score on you," he said. "Wanna try?"

Okay, Torborg said.

Reiser and Torborg had set up some bases on the outfield grass. It took almost no time for the fifty-nine-year-old Durocher to loosen up and say he was ready. He rounded third base and sprinted for home, intent on flattening Torborg. The young catcher, not looking to hurt anyone but eager to show he had mastered techniques learned from Reiser and Roseboro, braced himself for a collision. Reiser threw the ball home, and Torborg tagged Durocher on the head with a forearm so hard he knocked him out cold.

One of Durocher's legs was quivering.

Reiser, who had played under Durocher in Brooklyn, laughed, looked down at the prone coach, and said, "I think you're out."

The effect of seeing Durocher sprawled on the ground, unconscious for an instant, was electric. Gleeful players stared. Torborg felt triumphant. Coming around after a few seconds, Durocher stood and wobbled off without a word.

By then Durocher's future was sealed. Respect is a coach's lifeblood, and by the end of 1964 Durocher had lost it; the players no longer listened to him, as had been Alvin Dark's fate in San Francisco. Each man's fall was a reminder that a new breed of player had its own subtle way of wielding influence and dispensing justice.

Only Alston or Bavasi could've saved Durocher in Los Angeles after 1964, and neither man indicated any interest. Much later, Bavasi would say that he simply wanted to provide a coaching opportunity to someone new, suggesting that Durocher had done nothing wrong and left on good terms. But in a familiar arrangement, a Dodger front office official, who had requested anonymity, spoke after the season's end to the *Los Angeles Times* about the benefits of saying good-bye to Durocher. "Alston is finally on his own as manager," the official said. "Now he doesn't have to defer, subconsciously or otherwise, [to a coach]. . . . There'll be no other 'managers' in the dugout this season. We think it has taken a load off Alston's shoulders."

Durocher's departure was another reminder to Dodger players that the old ways no longer applied. Still living in the Mayfair Hotel, Al Ferrara had begun thinking that the social revolution seemingly afoot everywhere was destined in time to affect baseball, which, when it happened, wouldn't please O'Malley or Bavasi at all. "The sixties got you thinking that some things that used to be standard procedure weren't going to survive," Ferrara observed. "After that, the only thing the players needed was the right guy to show us the smart way to deal with the owners. And that guy was coming."

Less than a week after Koufax's no-hitter in Philadelphia, Dodger Stadium served as the site for "Sandy Koufax Night." An hour after the pregame festivities had ended, the star threw his first pitch of the evening, on his way to beating the Reds, 2–1. In his next two starts, he shut out the Cardinals and Braves at home. His spree of mastery appeared to have no end. He had given up only one run in four complete games. On June 21 he won 4–2 in Cincinnati before heading to San Francisco, where he gave up only one run and struck out ten over nine innings before leaving in a tie game. His record for June alone was 5–0, with an ERA of 0.71.

His July was a match for June. He tossed two more shutouts and won five more games. It should have been six. On July 26 he carried a 2–1 lead into the ninth inning against the Giants at Dodger Stadium, only to watch as errors by Gilliam and Wills led to four unearned runs and defeat. His consecutive winning streak had ended at 11, but his spectacular month seemed to foreshadow a brilliant conclusion to the season.

He next pitched in Pittsburgh, giving up just six hits and winning his sixteenth game, 5–1. Four days later in Milwaukee, on August 8, he found himself trailing, 2–1, in the fifth inning, when he singled against Braves starter Tony Cloninger. After a Wills base hit sent him to second base, Cloninger tried to pick him off when he took a short lead. Diving back to second, Koufax landed hard on his left elbow. He didn't make much of it. "It stung, as you'd expect an elbow to sting when you give it a good rap," he recalled in his autobiography.

By the time Koufax was back on the mound to pitch the bottom of the fifth inning, the pain had all but passed. He won, 5–4, striking out nine, his fastball as effective as ever. The next day he awakened in Milwaukee with a lump on his pitching elbow. The elbow had filled with liquid, the kind that accompanies inflammation of a joint. It was about that time when Tracewski first noticed that his road roomie sometimes seemed in pain while doing very simple things, like combing his hair, brushing his teeth, or putting on a sweater. A Dodger trainer, Wayne Anderson, learned of Koufax's discomfort, but neither Anderson nor anyone else in the organization voiced alarm, and no special measures were taken. By his next start in Cincinnati, the swelling had subsided, and Koufax loosened up easily before the game. He allowed the Reds only five hits and struck out ten, easily winning, 5–1.

Koufax decided that his elbow's problems were simply "another of the little injuries that come and go" for a pitcher. Returning to Los Angeles, he captured his nineteenth victory on Sunday afternoon, August 16, appearing at the peak of his game in shutting out the Cardinals, 3–0, and striking out thirteen. His team languished in seventh place, twelve and a half games back in the standings, its pennant hopes for 1964 dashed. But with Koufax pitching so dazzlingly, an entirely new level of greatness seemed within his reach. The Dodgers still had forty-seven games left to play, which realistically would give him another eleven starts in the four-man rotation, perhaps even twelve or thirteen, if he wanted to push himself and squeeze in an extra appearance on just two days of rest. No one could rule out the possibility that, having won fifteen of his last sixteen decisions, he might win another eleven games that season and reach the epic milestone of thirty victories. Certainly twenty-seven or twenty-eight wins loomed as a highly realistic possibility for him.

His career changed forever the next day. He awakened to discover that his elbow's swelling had spread. From his left shoulder to his wrist, his entire arm looked and felt like "a log," he later observed. As if to emphasize the arm's grotesqueness, he added: "A waterlogged log." The fluid from the elbow's inflammation had made the arm balloon in size. He couldn't bend or straighten it. Still, nothing about the injury convinced Koufax he couldn't go on. Confident that the swelling would ease, he planned to pitch in his next scheduled start, only to encounter Dr. Kerlan, who, after taking one shocked look at the arm, swiftly drove him to his office for X-rays and treatment.

Kerlan's examination revealed that Koufax had arthritis.

At twenty-eight.

More specifically, he had traumatic arthritis. The term means what its adjective suggests. It is a condition triggered by trauma, by injury—in Koufax's case, by damage from the prolonged wear and tear of his affected elbow joint.

Unable to determine whether any single event had precipitated the arthritis, Kerlan and other experts believed that the only certainty was that Koufax's problem had begun long before what happened to him in Milwaukee during August or in St. Louis during April—in short, long before 1964. The prognosis was sobering. The arthritis couldn't be cured. The elbow would only get worse. How much worse would depend on how effectively they mitigated the ongoing damage with treatment and perhaps an adjustment to Koufax's pitching schedule.

In the meantime, the pitcher and doctor decided to conceal the problem from the public until they had a better understanding of the future. During the same week that Kerlan studied the X-rays and possible treatments, Koufax told reporters that he was focused on winning his twentieth game. "I'm feeling fine," he said, going so far as to speculate that he might have as many as thirteen starts left that season. "I plan to keep pitching every four days."

Kerlan began administering treatment. He drew fluid out of the swollen elbow. To reduce its inflammation, he injected it with cortisone and gave Koufax some pills. The pills were phenylbutazone, brand name Butazoladin, commonly called "bute" in the sports world, a relatively new nonsteroidal anti-inflammatory in the 1960s. But the medical community would also learn that phenylbutazone had alarming side effects, including blood count suppression and possible aplastic anemia. Those dangers would eventually lead the federal Food and Drug Administration to ban the use of bute for human beings.

In 1964, and for the remainder of his career, Koufax used the bute. The Dodgers waited until the eve of his next scheduled start against the Braves to announce that Koufax wouldn't be able to pitch. All involved continued to hide the truth from the press. Kerlan simply said Koufax had a swollen left elbow, indicating he might be back in action as soon as the following week. It never happened. Nine days later in St. Louis, Koufax tried to loosen up on the sidelines by throwing to Joe Becker when he felt a sharp pain. His elbow began swelling before he even made it back to the locker room. He was gone from St. Louis within hours, his season over.

Nineteen sixty-four would mistakenly go down in Dodger histories and psyches as a gap year of sorts, the one standing between two of the team's World Championship seasons. In reality, it was the most pivotal year of the Dodgers' 1960s dynasty, the one that determined Koufax's fate.

No one knew it at that moment, but he had only two years left—two years before the pain and drugs would become unbearable. Even with his agonies, not a single teammate close to him doubted he would go on. They knew how fearsome his will could be. They knew that, as long as it was possible, he would get his cortisone shots, take the bute pills, and then go out to the mound every fourth day, along the way probably producing another masterpiece or two. He would do it until he couldn't, and then he would leave so quietly that none of his teammates would know about it until after it was done. "I knew that would be the way for him: he would be here and then one day he would just be gone," Wills said. "I just didn't want to be around when it happened."

Chapter 5

The Riotous Season

losing out the 1964 season in sixth place, with a record of 80–82, the team ended its dreary campaign at home, where it had drawn 2.2 million spectators in the year to lead the league again. Yet, on a somewhat worrisome note, attendance plummeted late in the season, with none of the Dodgers' final seven home games attracting more than 15,000 fans.

Prolonged losing would be bad for business. The troubled front office signaled to reporters that big trades were in the offing, along with a possible shakeup of the roster. Bavasi indicated that most of the players should be braced for the possibility they might be traded. The only genuine "untouchables," he said, were Koufax, Drysdale, Wills, Roseboro, and Willie Davis, who, at twenty-four, had finished his best full season ever, hitting .294 and rekindling belief that he might be a future star. Bavasi also took the opportunity to emphasize he didn't want to blame anyone for the bad year. Then he blamed someone: "There were several big disappointments . . . Everybody knows Tommy Davis had a bad year after winning the batting championship twice in a row."

Davis, who hit .326 in 1963, had seen his batting average fall 51 points during the recent season. Some would argue that a .275 average seemed more than respectable, especially as Davis led the Dodgers with 86 RBIs. But now Bavasi made no commitment to him, merely offering that Davis was at best "possibly" untouchable.

Willing to trade away a great deal of talent to get just the right pitcher, Bavasi had decided to part with the man once regarded within the organization as a possible superstar in the making, but on whom the Dodgers had given up. The front office no longer had room in right field for Frank Howard, who hit only .226 that year. In early December, Bavasi made a deal with the lowly Washington Senators that would change Dodger fortunes. He traded Howard and four other players for a fifteen-win starting pitcher whose name few Los Angelenos knew, Claude Osteen, and a sure-handed infielder whose first and last name virtually everyone on the planet recognized, John Kennedy.

He was John *E.* Kennedy, who, at twenty-three, heard the news of the trade from his mother-in-law while working at his off-season job in a Chicago steel mill, where his paychecks supplemented his $7,500 baseball salary. Kennedy settled into his new town, looking forward to claiming the third-base job. Meanwhile Osteen, the major figure in the trade, flew to Los Angeles for a press conference. The Dodgers front office lavished attention on him, raising his salary from $15,000 to a respectable $25,000, helping him find a home in the Orange County community of Brea, and providing enough money for the down payment. "They really made it clear they were happy to get me," Osteen recalled.

Bavasi announced he had signed Koufax, Drysdale, Tommy Davis, and Willie Davis to contracts for 1965. Koufax posed for a photograph alongside his three teammates, in a sign, if nothing else, that he believed his damaged elbow would likely be all right by the start of the new season.

In South-Central Los Angeles (a part of the city to be renamed "South Los Angeles" in 2003), Wills, aiming to bolster his earnings, devoted considerable time during the off-season to a new interest. Along with a white business partner, he had opened a dry cleaners in a predominantly black area on Santa Barbara Avenue, close to the Los Angeles Memorial Coliseum. At his partner's urging, he agreed to call their store the Maury Wills Stolen Base Cleaners; the name alone was certain to attract customers. He was a long way from being financially comfortable, but for the first time he felt himself on a path that might provide a bit of added security not dependent on the whims of Dodger management.

Even as he took comfort in his vision of a better future for himself, Wills had an uneasy feeling about life around him. He worried in particular about the mood of people in the community. Frustrations seemed high, he thought, though no one he knew ever talked about this publicly. Other players also felt the welling tension. The community's grievances extended beyond racial discrimination and poverty to a deep-seated belief in South-Central that black residents there were being frequently abused by the Los Angeles police. "There were a lot of complaints coming up about the LA cops," Tommy Davis said. "It wasn't a good situation; it'd gotten worse."

Just a couple of weeks before Christmas, Roy Wilkins, the executive director of the NAACP, declared in a television interview that the typical black citizen issuing a complaint of abuse against any Los Angeles police officer felt the "cards stacked against him." The civil rights leader urged that the city establish a citizens' police review board, to provide a "safety valve" for defusing tensions and formally resolving complaints of police brutality and other wrongdoing.

The idea of a review board went nowhere as 1965 began.

"The Civil Rights [Act] and integration meant you could go places, but it didn't take away the tensions that year," Wills recalled. "Things exploded. Some people said they could feel it coming. But we had to keep playing. Even with everything that was happening in Los Angeles in '65, the truth is, we were ballplayers; we still had to win."

The first thing to know about Lou Johnson was that he took no shit. Not even in the Deep South. Not even during an era when not to take shit could get a black man jailed, maimed, or worse. During spring training in 1965, Johnson brought his clothes one day to a Vero Beach laundry, where an appalled white woman, evidently the manager, howled at him for wanting to put his clothes into a washer that was reserved for the clothes of white people. Then, as if things weren't already tense enough, the woman said he shouldn't hang around—his being there would disturb other customers.

That's when Lou Johnson yelled at her. "The shit you had to put up with, come on, man; that couldn't keep happening," Johnson said, a half century later. "They kept you from going into their movie theaters, their restaurants, hotels—you had to stand up for yourself when you could. So I told that woman some stuff she probably didn't want to hear."

But a black man lecturing a white woman? Such a thing didn't happen at the time in Vero Beach. Other players learned later that someone had called the Dodgers organization to complain vehemently about the angry black man with the laundry bag. Dodger officials, privately sympathetic with Johnson, aware of the many Vero Beach indignities that left the organization's black players reluctant to wash their clothes in town or enter a store there, gave the caller the brush-off. Lesson: Do not mess with our guy. It might have been regarded by Johnson, by then an aging outfielder, as a small triumph had it not been for the scar the woman left on him. "People do things like that to you and all that shit builds up," he observed. "Not every person can forget those kinds of things. I didn't forget."

The second thing to know about Lou Johnson was that he was hugely liked by other ballplayers, black and white. That he didn't let anybody mess with his dignity was only part of the reason. What players admired most about him was that he was totally unaffected, "without a phony bone in his whole body," observed Tommy Davis.

Teammates found it hard to imagine another human more comfortable in his own skin. Many envied him for it, given that so much of their own careers had been spent being guarded about everything they said or did around media and club officials. Johnson said anything that came to his mind, which was always direct, often very funny and profane, and usually the very thing that some of the other players were thinking but careful not to say.

"You couldn't be more honest than Lou around people," Wills added. It was a way of saying that Johnson didn't have one way of talking to teammates and another to Dodger management or reporters. Anyone who approached him eventually received the unfiltered Johnson. If he was talking to a reporter, who wouldn't be able to use his interview quotes quite as delivered, he might say something like: "No motherfucker's gonna hit Sandy in the ninth inning, shiiiiiiiiiiiit, game's over. Come on, man." His humor leaned toward the prurient. To a young teammate he'd taken under his wing who looked in need of a break from the unrelenting pressure of a pennant chase, he had simple advice: "Come on, man: peep some fat." This meant the young player, who was Wes Parker, ought to find himself a nice woman; sex was in order.

Johnson was an infectious personality in a generally serious locker room. "Lou could come into a clubhouse and have people laughing in a minute, just because he was Lou being Lou," Ferrara remembers. "You need people like that, people who helped to keep everybody else loose."

But the most important thing to know about Lou Johnson in 1965—a truth that few, if any, of his teammates sensed—is that privately he was seething, at white people especially. His rage over his station as a black male in America had steadily grown since his childhood in segregated Lexington, Kentucky, where, he recalls, he risked a beating if he so much as sat down on the curb of the wrong street.

Young Johnson had a vast athletic talent that in time would set him free from the place. Johnson had starred in three sports at Lexington's Dunbar High School during the early 1950s, dreaming of playing guard at six-one for the all-white basketball dynasty of the University of Kentucky, led by legendary coach Adolph Rupp. It was a wonderful vision, marred only by its impossibility. Kentucky and Rupp, an unabashed racist, were not about to integrate either their famous team or their main university. "It hurt me and haunted me for a long time—because I was just a kid thinking Kentucky was where I was meant to be. So what the hell was I gonna do after that, come on now." The embittered young Johnson had a dismal image of his future: "I already had one foot in the grave and one foot on a damn banana peel."

He found a new dream. Having excelled in softball during high school, he shelved basketball for good and channeled his competitive energies into baseball. During an odyssey that included stints playing for all-black Kentucky State University, a semipro team in Lexington, and lowly Class D teams in the minor-league organizations of the Yankees and Pirates, he eventually landed in the Negro Leagues. There, in 1955, he played for the Indianapolis Clowns before moving that same year to the Kansas City Monarchs, a fabled team led in the past by a pair of future Hall of Famers— Jackie Robinson and pitcher Satchel Paige—before the major leagues beckoned to the stars.

By the time Johnson arrived in Kansas City, integrated baseball had doomed the Negro Leagues. But in the team's twilight, the Monarchs still could boast of having George Altman, a future Chicago Cubs outfielder, and Johnson, for whom the games had become a stage for displaying his talents to major-league scouts. It wasn't going as well as he'd hoped. For all his humor and popularity among teammates, Johnson was developing a reputation as a moody player, easily frustrated with coaches when he thought he was being held back. "Once you got an image in those days, it was pretty damn hard to change it," he remembers.

The Monarchs were led by manager Buck O'Neil, a former Negro

Leagues star, who took notice of Johnson's anger, in and out of uniform. A patient O'Neil tried showing him the fundamentals of succeeding and surviving. "He taught me a lot of baseball," Johnson remembers. "But he also taught me a lot about how to live."

Johnson worshipped O'Neil, who finally told Johnson what other baseball men to that point wouldn't: that his fury was hurting his play, and he needed to harness it, get it under control and use it as a tool for bolstering his performance.

His first major move came in the mid-1950s, when the Cubs bought his contract from the financially struggling Monarchs. He rejoiced. "Here was my chance: a major-league organization where people told me I might have a real opportunity someday," he remembered. But what looked like a turning point was a mirage. He languished for years in the Cubs minor-league system. Finally, in 1960, he received a brief shot in the big leagues. As a utility outfielder for the Cubs, he played in thirty-four games, hitting only .206, without a single home run. He was traded to the expansion Los Angeles Angels, in whose organization he lasted only a year before again packing his bags and playing his way into another major-league utility role, this time in 1962 with the Milwaukee Braves, where he thought he performed well, hitting an impressive .282 in sixty-one games. But already he had acquired a reputation as a minor-league journeyman, someone whose stops in the majors were destined to be brief. The question was why.

"I'd be up for just a few weeks before I was sent down again," he recalled. "I had friends on that Braves team. Hank Aaron was a good friend. But I could tell that some coaches and managers didn't like me much, thought I didn't belong there. They always got around to telling me why. They'd say, 'You talk too much.' They let me know I had a reputation for being a renegade. They said I was angry. The 'angry thing' followed me around."

His teammates, past and future, would struggle to understand how Johnson ever had come to be viewed as disagreeable by baseball's front offices. "Lou was just this carefree, unrestrained spirit—anyone who treated him well had a great friend and teammate: that's the Lou we all knew," Parker recalled.

Johnson spent another two years in the minors, in what had become an itinerant's life. Pushing thirty by then, he was emotionally worn down by the grind. He also bore a scar of his professional travels, having lost the tip of his right ear in a vehicular accident. He had done everything baseball had asked of him, including going down to the Dominican Republic and Mexico to play winter ball. But it was getting increasingly tough to summon the enthusiasm to hold on. By then, he'd climbed all the rungs from Class D through C and B and Single, Double, and Triple A. He had spent his entire adulthood—a decade by then—playing in towns with names like Pampa and St. Jean and Ponca City and Burlington and Lancaster, and all he had really taken from some of the places was a small measure of pride that he had survived them.

It was bad enough what you had to put up with from some cops, he told people. But nobody understood just how exposed and vulnerable a black player was, playing in those small ballparks on the road where that single racist down the left-field line would be free to shower you with taunts.

And even after he'd risen into Triple A, and the towns and crowds got a little bigger, a couple of thousand sometimes, there would be some racist whose voice you'd be able to hear above the beer vendors. In the outfield, he'd stare straight ahead, feeling himself dying a little more.

His fury had grown. Standing at the plate during batting practice, seeing the white ball coming toward him, he sometimes pretended it was a white person and attacked it, swinging as hard as he could. At the time he never shared this thought with a club official or reporter. It was his secret little game, and an emotional release. "I had a lot of hate," he said. "I took it out on that ball. It was the only safe way to take it out."

Concerned about being devoured by the rage, he sought refuge in some of his old defenses. "I was just trying to laugh it off, instead of always being sad and angry," he remembered. "But that was hard a lot of times."

He had other coping strategies. Years earlier, he had begun clapping for himself on the field when he thought he did something good. This absolutely floored people, everybody from spectators to other ballplayers. Clap for *yourself*? But Johnson thought, Why the hell not? Sure as shit, nobody else was clapping. He'd play before a crowd of a couple of hundred people and he'd hit a homer and nobody would make a damn sound. Not one guy applauding, not one old-timer even softly calling out "Nice shot, kid."

Nobody showing the least bit of appreciation, come on, man.

He didn't care that a few people might snicker. As soon as his homer sailed out of the park, he began clapping. It was a series of quick little claps that he performed while running around the bases. He clapped his hands about belt-high. He'd round first base and clap-clap-clap-clap-clap. Round second base and clap-clap-clap-clap-clap.

He never looked anywhere really except at the infield dirt, never stared at the pitcher, never glanced at another soul, just raced around, clap-clap-clap-clap-clapping for a few seconds.

As 1965 began, there was no change in his status. He was thirty now. Nothing he had done in 1964 playing for the Dodgers' Triple-A Spokane team had moved him any closer to a spot on the big club, though he was coming off his best minor-league season ever. He had hit .328 for Spokane, finishing as the runner-up for the batting title of the Pacific Coast League. At the end of 1964, the Dodgers urged him to play winter ball and he agreed, going down to Puerto Rico, where he helped lead his team to a championship. He left the island more hopeful than ever that he would receive a chance to compete for a job on the Dodgers roster in 1965.

It didn't happen. For all his skills, he had done nothing eye-popping. His eighteen homers in Spokane, while a very solid figure, revealed he didn't possess superb power. He ran the bases aggressively, but he wasn't nearly in the class of the speedsters in the Dodger lineup. Defensively, he had a reliable glove and a respectable throwing arm, but he didn't have elite tools. He did many things very well, but nothing great.

Yet if he never made it onto the field in Dodger Stadium in a real Dodger uniform, he was at least a part of the legendary organization now, of Jackie's organization, of Maury's organization, and so a small part of its history, he told himself. "If my career was going to have to end soon, it was better that it was going to end with the Dodgers [organization] than anybody else," he said. "I was happy to be there, even if it meant having to deal with the things I saw in Vero Beach."

He paused. "But, you know, that place wasn't easy, come on now, man. Vero was as bad as it got."

During that spring, a scathing column about Vero Beach appeared in the *Los Angeles Times*. The newspaper's most important and gifted columnist had written it. Jim Murray had come to see Vero Beach for what it was. He let his readers know of his enthusiasm for the wry idea, advanced by black players, that the city should be renamed "Zero Beach." He observed that for nonwhites the lovely coastal city redolent with the scent of Florida orange blossoms amounted to nothing more than "a citrus Siberia."

Murray was just getting started.

He had spent considerable time listening to a pained John Roseboro and Tommy Davis detail their frustrations. He heard their stories about Lou Johnson's inability to get his clothes washed in town. By the time their tales about Vero had ended, so too had Murray's silence about the place. The 1964 Civil Rights Act had been federal law for eight months already, but it was as if Vero never got the message. In a daring move for any Dodger player at the time, Roseboro spoke at length about Vero's sins, as if to say, To hell with the consequences.

Murray wrote this:

It's not that there are police dogs or fire or rubber hoses in the streets of Vero. It is something far harder, in the opinion of Roseboro—a wall of indifference. Vero neither chastises the Negro nor runs from him. It merely insulates itself against him, Roseboro feels.

"It is," says [Roseboro], "the worst city in the South. There are no, or almost no, Negroes in the city limits. If you're a Negro, you come into Vero with a baseball number on your back or a mop and pail in your hands. You get out by dark."

Murray concluded by skewering the hypocrisy of a city that sold itself as forever sunny and sociable:

But Vero has a deceptive smile on its face, a "Who us?" look. It's the kind of prejudice you can't fight, invisible poker-faced rejection you can't lay a glove on, and Negro players on the Dodgers, to a man, just sit there and grind their teeth and put a big red letter on the calendar for getaway day and a return to society. Meanwhile, some of them can't stand the smell of orange blossoms anymore.

Walter O'Malley had no official comment about the Murray piece, nor an official response to Lou Johnson's problems at the Laundromat. But in a quiet change noticed by many at Dodgertown, the team had installed washers and dryers there for use by the players. "The O'Malleys did what they could while we were there, did all they could for us at Dodgertown," Johnson recalls. "But Dodgertown wasn't Florida. Nothing the O'Malleys did was ever gonna help us outside Dodgertown, and nothing was ever gonna make us stop hating that shit in Vero. It hurt. Nobody should have to play in a place like that. People couldn't wait to get their asses out of there."

O nce free of Vero, the Dodgers started the 1965 regular season on a roll, winning twenty of their first thirty games. The most thrilling victory during the auspicious run came in mid-May, during a game at home in which the Dodgers trailed the Cubs, 1–0, in the eighth inning. The Cubs' tough left-hander, Dick Ellsworth, had pitched brilliantly, working on a no-hitter. But after a Cubs error and a botched play on a sacrifice bunt, Ferrara hit a three-run homer, in what would be the Dodgers' only hit of the day, in a 3–1 triumph.

No major-league blast from Ferrara would ever carry more importance. "It was a happy day," he said. "You start believing anything's possible when you win like that. It gets you past some of the tough days."

A tough day had occurred earlier that month at Dodger Stadium. In the fourth inning of a Saturday-night game against the Giants, Tommy Davis slid into second base on a ground-ball hit by Fairly. "The thing was, I didn't have to slide," Davis remembers. "I was on first base, and Orlando Cepeda was playing first base for them and he fielded the grounder, but he wasn't throwing to second. He was flipping the ball to the pitcher [Gaylord Perry] at first base. But I had no idea. I was sliding because I was sure a throw was coming and I was going to take out [Giants shortstop] Jose Pagan when I got to second base, so he couldn't complete a double play. But Pagan could see Cepeda wasn't throwing to him. My whole slide was for nothing. I went in fast and my back right spike caught on that really hard Georgia clay of our infield. That's when it happened."

At twenty-six, Davis had broken his right ankle, a season-ending injury.

After undergoing surgery that night, Davis lay in Daniel Freeman Hospital, feeling his life turned on its head. "There's a lot of shock when something like that happens to you," he reflected. "You don't know what the future is. There's no security. I knew it was going to take a long time to recover. I wondered what the team was going to do."

Wills didn't know exactly what the team would do without Davis for the remaining five months of the season. "I know a lot of people immediately thought that, with Tommy out, we had no chance to win the pennant," he said. "We were dead is what some people said. Dead. The first thing you tell yourself in that situation is you're not dead. And that's how you deal with it; it's your only chance."

Lou Johnson, stuck for good in Spokane, thought for the first time that he could see the end of his career. He tried not to lapse into self-pity. He realized there were hundreds of good players out there whose destiny it was never to get out of the minors for more than a few games. And when their last damn day in baseball passed, not a single fan remembered their names.

He was probably going to be one more of them.

He struggled to tamp down his frustration. "When I got angry before, it usually made me more determined—I usually played better, fought harder," he said. "But I was getting worn down. I'd been up and down so long, I was tired."

The thought of waking up in Spokane at thirty-five scared him. He batted over .300 in his first fifteen games, but it was joyless. One April morning, he made a decision that he kept to himself: he was quitting Spokane and baseball altogether at the end of the 1965 season. "I decided that's it—no more for me after the year ended, no more of going nowhere," he remembers. "I was thirty. I was through. No more of the minors. I was going to get a regular job—it couldn't be any worse than this."

He had started thinking about what kind of job this might be when word came to him one night that Tommy Davis had suffered a terrible injury and was finished for the season. Buzzie Bavasi relayed word to Spokane that Johnson should pack a bag and pick up a plane ticket.

If the Dodgers did not have Koufax in 1965, they were ruined. No Dodger believed otherwise. Koufax had gone through the entire winter off-season without pills, shots, or treatments for his bad elbow, hoping that simple rest might solve his problem. It couldn't. Shortly before the season had begun, the time for concealing the problem from the public had ended. Dr. Kerlan told the press that the pitcher's elbow was plagued by arthritis. In a stark assessment, the doctor added it was too early to know whether treatments would be successful. Koufax was back to ingesting his orange phenylbutazone pills on a regular basis. A cortisone injection straight into the elbow joint brought some relief. Within forty-eight hours, the elbow's swelling ebbed. Koufax could pitch. But Kerlan told him that he didn't believe a regimen of frequent shots would be good in the long run for the elbow; that the arm over a period of several years wouldn't be able to withstand the rigors of frequent pitching, with or without shots. Koufax was on borrowed time now.

Turning to a hot ointment called Capsolin that had aided him during the past in getting his arm loose, he now regularly asked team trainers to slather it on his left shoulder and upper back. If after a heavy Capsolin application and a bullpen warm-up Koufax still felt stiff, he'd often reapply the ointment, the heat already so intense that it reddened his skin after the initial slathering, the scent so strong that people thirty feet away felt it invading their nostrils. The smell served as a reality check for teammates. Anyone who needed to go to these lengths to compete wouldn't be around long. "I wanted badly to win for him every time he went out there," Wills said.

To understand the grind of Wills's 1965 season—perhaps his greatest and most challenging year ever, superior in many ways even to his extraordinary 1962 campaign—it is worth glimpsing the worst of his ordeal. Having pushed his legs and psyche beyond what his body could handle, Wills felt parts of himself breaking down as the season wore on. His right leg, the one on which he landed hard when he slid, the one that always took the pounding of the crushed brick and red clay of Dodger Stadium's rock-hard drag strip of an infield, was bleeding internally, the evidence of its hemorrhaging visible to his teammates in the welts that covered most of the upper leg—his right thigh especially. "You'd see him and say, 'My God,' " John Kennedy remembered. "You'd see the blood and bruises on the *inside* of his leg. You didn't really know how long he'd be able to deal with it."

Typically hunched over after games, Wills often didn't get out of his uniform for long stretches. Teammates became accustomed to seeing him sitting in a stupor in front of his locker, especially after losses, too tired and pensive to move, staring clear through his locker, brooding, his brown eyes drained of their usual fire. "There were days I sensed Maury was troubled, but I didn't know why, I didn't probe," Parker remembered. "I looked up to him—he was a veteran and my friend, so I wasn't going to intrude. He would just get very quiet sometimes, just sit by his locker. He would be staring and staring."

People would leave him be. Finally, he might talk for a bit to a friend like Koufax or Parker. Next he would rise, for it was already time to get ready for the next day's game by receiving the treatments he couldn't do without.

Rare was the night he could get out of the clubhouse without an hour or two of ministrations. If the team was on the road and the bus gone as he continued getting treatments, sometimes he walked alone back to the hotel. He was an obsessive man by nature, and by the summer of 1965 his chief obsession blocked out all else. He had to win. He thought Alston understood this part of him, that it was much of the reason why Alston, two years earlier, had made him the team's captain. He could and would be a badass, if need be. He could and would bend others to his will. He was prepared to fight if somebody challenged his methods. Everything in his play, in his body language, and in his emphatic orders to others said this: they had to push themselves. By the time the season ended, he was going to find a way to drive himself and anyone else who needed it across the finish line.

Such resolve was necessary to compensate for an abundance of

Dodger weaknesses. Even with Koufax's twenty-six regular season wins and Drysdale's twenty-three victories that season—the sum of which amounted to more than half of the team's ninety-seven triumphs—and even with the team's magnificently low ERA of 2.81 (the best in the major leagues), an observer could reasonably argue the Dodgers had no business winning the pennant in 1965. On paper, the Dodgers' collective offense was, to put it charitably, measly. Up to that point in history, the team's batting average of .245 was the worst for a twentieth-century National League pennant winner. Highlighting their struggles at the plate was the fact that the team's highest individual batting average belonged to a pitcher—Drysdale—who hit .300, slugged seven homers, and was sometimes called upon by Alston to pinch-hit, in embarrassing preference to any of the team's available position players.

Hitting .286 in 1965, Wills, the lone All-Star that season among the team's everyday players, led in batting average among all Dodger regulars, some of whom would suffer through awful slogs for long stretches in 1965. Willie Davis—who had envisioned stardom for himself after his excellent 1964 season—would sink 56 points to .238. The dogged Roseboro, who would suffer through nagging injuries and late-season mayhem at the hands of a pitcher who would bloody his skull with a bat, would drop 54 points.

The team's gains in the most important offensive categories during 1965 belonged to select individuals. Wills's average would climb 11 points from 1964, and Fairly's would rise 18 points to .274. While the thirty-six-year-old workhorse Gilliam hit a fine .280 and the Dodgers couldn't have done without the skill he displayed in hitting behind Wills, his bat produced no eye-popping numbers.

But all the numbers hid something. Gilliam was selfless and, like Fairly, at his best under pressure. Parker was at his most reliable when his teetering self-respect hinged on his very next swing. Second baseman Jim Lefebvre, on his way to becoming the National League's Rookie of the Year though hitting only .250, would win several games with key hits. And Johnson, while batting a rather ordinary .259 on the season, had an impact that belied this pedestrian figure, proving to be fantastic in the crunch, winning three of the most critical regular season games with decisive home runs and extra-base hits before striking his biggest blow of all in the most important game of the World Series.

Even amid all the well-timed contributions of others, no pennant that year was possible without Wills. He would steal ninety-four bases (the most ever in the National League to that point, aside from his own 1962 record) and score ninety-two runs on a team whose scant weapons meant he had to take more chances to find ways to circle the bases. In 1962, he had been able in moments to afford the luxury of staying patient and relying on the sterling Tommy Davis and the powerful Frank Howard to bring him home. But in 1965, with the team lacking a player able to drive in more than seventy runs, Wills couldn't afford to be anything less than daring.

Very late into the season, until his banged-up body betrayed him, he would be markedly ahead of his 1962 pace for steals, seemingly on his way to breaking his record. Curtailing his running during much of August and parts of September just to remain on the field, he husbanded what energy his legs had left so he could run in key games here and there—stealing two bases in this game, three more in that game, stealing when it counted most. Meanwhile, he led all National League shortstops with 535 assists—which included the hundreds of ground balls that he converted into routine outs, as well as sharply gunned throws to home plate that cut down runners badly underestimating his arm strength.

Yet his greatest achievements in 1965 would elude box score statistics. They would take the shape of building blocks, erected game by close game, on which a pennant could finally be constructed. His greatness derived from finding ways to score that others couldn't. He took the extra base that no one else in a similar situation dared to take. He would bunt for a base hit before next slapping balls past drawn-in infielders. He would so rattle some catchers that he *knew* he would not only steal on them but also that they were likely at some point to throw the ball away, enabling him to take extra bases. And if the bases were loaded when he stepped to bat, he could sometimes muscle up and hit a long ball down the line to clear the bases.

In every moment, he gave off the air of a man believing he was destined to whip the opponent in front of him. So lean and taut, with rippled forearms that bespoke a life committed to fitness and ferocity, Wills up close resembled an undersize, steely street fighter who would die before he ever quit on his dreams. One night, during a game in Milwaukee, he told Tracewski what he would do during his next at-bat: he was going to drag a bunt down the first-base line, in the direction of the Braves' first baseman, Joe Torre. If the bunt was a bad one, if perhaps he tapped it too hard and Torre had a play on the ball, he had a special plan for dealing with him: "I'll pretend to give up as I'm going down the base path," Wills said. "Then I'll dive into the coach's box and go around him and be safe at first." Tracewski was skeptical. Wills went out and did it. "I was the only person who knew beforehand that Maury had thought about it and then executed it," Tracewski recalls. "It told me all you needed to know about his preparation and belief in himself."

No player was more skilled in spotting and preying upon opponents' weaknesses. Early in the season, on a beautiful, breezy afternoon in San Francisco, Wills told Parker they would make the Giants pay for the audacity of playing a backup catcher, Ed Bailey, at first base: *How can the Giants think they can get away with putting a player like Bailey there?* To start the game, he bunted down the first-base line at Bailey, beat it out for a hit, and promptly stole second. Parker followed with a bunt of his own toward Bailey, who threw the ball away as Wills trotted home with the first of his three runs that day.

The game was not yet two minutes old, and Bailey had already been exposed. Wills was baseball's version of the quarterback who picked mercilessly on a defender until the guy proved that he could play. Later in the game, he drove home a run with another bunt single aimed squarely at Bailey. During the same game, he stole three bases against Giants catcher Tom Haller, who, overwhelmed, threw a ball away that yielded yet another base to Wills, who went 3-for-4 in a 9–0 Dodger rout.

Wills's gambling and guile, accompanied by an appetite for intense study of the opposition, left him largely immune to hitting slumps. During the opener of a Memorial Day doubleheader in Dodger Stadium before 50,997 fans, the Dodgers found themselves confronting the Reds and the fireballing Jim Maloney, who entered the game as the hottest young pitcher in the league, with a record of 5–0. Wills looked forward to confronting Maloney. The beneficiary of a short hitting stroke, he didn't get overpowered by pitchers reliant on fastballs.

What followed was a mesmerizing contest, in which one man's resolve finally prevailed. The Dodgers found themselves down 3–0, before Wills beat out a bouncer to Reds third baseman Deron Johnson that drove home a run. In the bottom of the fifth inning, he had another infield hit, this time beating a throw from the Reds' All-Star shortstop Leo Cardenas. In the next minute, he evened the contest, taking advantage of something he had learned long before the game had begun. He had watched Maloney pitch from the stretch position during his warm-up, detecting a twitch in the pitcher's left side that signaled when he was about to deliver the ball to the plate. Now, with the twitch identified and a jammed ballpark roaring, he stole second base and third base off Maloney. Soon he was home, and the game was tied.

In the bottom of the ninth, climaxing a 4–3 Dodger victory in which he went 4-for-5, he rapped a single to left off Maloney, driving home Lefebvre with the winning run. Sitting on the bench, Al Ferrara told teammates, "This is the greatest offensive weapon in baseball. There is no stopping him when he gets going. He turns singles into home runs. He gets on base, he scores."

In his zeal, Wills sometimes flirted with strategies outside the rules. One afternoon, sitting in the clubhouse, he turned to Parker with an invitation. The Dodgers would be facing the Giants in two more critical series, one of which would be in Dodger Stadium, and Wills wondered whether Parker would be willing to do a little something extra for the team.

He had Parker's attention.

In a key situation, would you be willing to stick out your foot and trip one of their hitters when the guy was running around first base? Wills asked.

Parker just looked at him.

Wills elaborated on his hypothetical: when a Giant hit a line drive, say, in the gap to the outfield wall, everyone in the ballpark would naturally turn to watch the rolling ball and the Dodger outfielder chasing it. The 50,000 fans, the four umpires, the players on the field and in the dugouts, the two teams' radio and TV play-by-play announcers, the media, the security men—all eyes would be on the outfielder retrieving the ball. For a moment, everyone else on the field, including the Giant hitter who had just smacked the ball, would be ignored.

At that very instant, Wills said, as the Giants hitter sprinted around first base, thinking he was on his way to a double or triple, you could just slightly stick out your foot, Wes—and trip the guy. It'd be easy. Nobody would ever see it.

No, I can't do that, Parker said.

Wills said, Sure you can, Wes. It could make all the difference in a tight game. I'm not talking about just any game. I'm talking about a game against the Giants.

I can't, Maury. It'd be cheating.

Wes, if I guarantee you that no one will see you trip the guy, will you do it? Because I can guarantee it: nobody will see you. Everybody will be looking out at the outfield and the ball. Wes, it's the Giants. This could be important. You can do it, right?

I can't do it, Maury. It's not me. It's not the way I'm made up.

Wes, let me start over. Let's say it's September. The game is on the line. Nobody's going to see you trip him. And if you trip him, you can save the game for us.

No, I don't want to do that, Parker repeated.

One more time, Wes. He's a Giant. He would trip *you*. Okay? He would trip *you*, no doubt about it. So now you know what kind of guy he is. Here he comes now. You're going to trip him, right?

No, Maury, I won't do that. I can't.

Wills gave up. He never again sought to have anybody else trip a foe, and never did it himself. Parker's refusal left him wondering whether the band of new young Dodger players played by a different code. "I couldn't ever get Wes to trip a guy—I couldn't rough him up," he said. "He didn't have that dirty side that all ballplayers once seemed to have."

Parker was regularly inspired by Wills's toughness, even if he couldn't bring himself to adopt all of Wills's methods, including his occasional streaks of on-field nastiness. Perhaps the most malevolent of Wills's plays since Parker's arrival had happened a season earlier, with the Giants' power-hitting third baseman, Jim Ray Hart, serving as the target.

Frustration with Giants' baserunning tactics had ignited Wills's rage. On potential double-play ground balls, several San Francisco baserunners had come into second base standing up rather than sliding, as part of an effort to prevent Wills from throwing to Dodger first basemen on a direct line, to complete double plays. Frank Robinson had tried the same thing in 1963. A ground ball hit in front of a sprinting Robinson to second baseman Tracewski had been fed to Wills, who stepped on the second-base bag and, seeing that Robinson had no intention of sliding, pointedly threw the ball at the head of the Reds star, a rugged player who had no problem with others playing just as aggressively. Robinson dipped in time to avoid being struck. Hart was not so fortunate. As the Giant ran upright yet again to second, Wills decided to bypass the double play altogether, in favor of meting out punishment and perhaps forever ending the Giants' practice of thwarting his throws. Pretending that he was throwing to first base, Wills hurled the ball as hard as he could at Hart, striking him in the forehead and leaving the woozy Giant motionless in the dirt for several minutes. A stretcher carried him off, with Hart hospitalized overnight. The Giants did not come standing up into second base again any time soon.

Parker would have a lasting memory of the chilling moment, able to picture trainers putting Hart on the stretcher. But, a half century later, Parker couldn't help chuckling in awe when he remembered it, amazed by the temerity of his friend, who had thrown the ball, he said, *right between Hart's eyes*. Such a leader would stop at nothing, thought an admiring Parker, for whom the incident had revealed the limitlessness of Wills's fury and resolve.

Wills was equally intrigued by Parker. The kid never asked for much. But neither Wills nor anyone else on the team had an inkling of Parker's terrors. The young player was increasingly distraught about his shortcomings as a hitter, convinced he might be exposed at any moment as a hopelessly limited player. Struggling to manage his assorted fears and in need of company, he returned, improbably, to the place where he had suffered the most, moving out of his Brentwood apartment and back into his childhood home.

It was a different, more tolerable place now. His mother, as much of a social butterfly as ever, was hardly around. His father lived in another part of the city. Yet his surrogate mother, the family's longtime housekeeper Judith Coy, was still there, to offer encouragement and look after his needs. Best of all, he was back with his brother, with whom he shared his old bedroom. "It helped so much to have Lyn as a companion," he remembers. "He was very compassionate. I could bare my soul to him. I could weep in front of him about my fears, my pain, and the things that'd happened to us as kids. I never would've been as good without Lyn. I could talk to him about all my massive insecurities. And my worries about my hitting were getting worse."

No one knew it, but sometimes he was barely hanging on. Occasionally his fear of being humiliated in an upcoming home game became overwhelming. A variety of things could trigger his dread, including reading in the local papers that the Dodgers would be facing an especially formidable pitcher that night. One of those foes was Jim Maloney, whom a teenage Parker had first encountered in American Legion tournaments, a colossus quite capable, he thought, of unmasking him.

Sometimes a pitcher had nothing to do with his fright. Just reading at home that a sellout crowd in Los Angeles was expected for the evening's big game could unnerve him. The prospect of failing in the packed stadium sometimes threatened to make it impossible for him to play at all, to even rise from his chair and leave for the stadium. "I'd think to myself, I'm not sure I'm really worthy of being on the Dodgers, I'm not sure all this fear is worth it."

In some of the worst moments, he turned to Lyn. On most days, however, he grappled alone with the terror. Finally, he rose from his chair, walked out of the house in a hurry, got into his car, and drove to the stadium.

Unaware of Parker's torment, Wills appreciated that you never needed to get on the kid about his approach to the game—Parker couldn't possibly practice or play any harder. But some Dodgers, even some veterans, required a chewing-out occasionally from the captain. Wills barked at Willie Davis about his poor positioning and frequent failure to throw accurately to cutoff men. Those were just the beginning of Davis's problems. He didn't always run out ground balls as hard as he could, and wasted too many at-bats trying to hit a pitch deep instead of just putting the ball in play and utilizing his speed.

More than once when criticized for his play, Davis retorted with what soon became a familiar line to teammates, who interpreted it as proof that his profession wasn't Davis's priority: "Ain't my life; ain't my wife." The perception grew that Davis was squandering his talent at a cost to the team, and Wills didn't like it.

Davis sniped to others on the team that Wills thought he was a big shot, that the title of captain had gone to his head. Davis's animus toward Wills reached its height when Wills, in his role as captain, convened a players' kangaroo court that fined Davis $100 for not hustling on an infield groundout. Alston told Wills that no player had the power to fine a teammate; in response, Wills briefly resigned as captain, before getting the position back from Alston.

Davis was alone in his prolonged resentment of Wills. Koufax, never known for dispensing lavish praise, thought Wills ideally fit the mold of on-field leader. "There was an intensity about the way he played, and the guys benefited from seeing it," he said in a 2009 interview. "He made people better. He did things right. He cared that the game was played correctly. He was an extraordinary player, but he led, too."

By the All-Star break, Wills was hitting .275 with 55 stolen bases, and the Dodgers were tied for first place. Players and coaches around the league rewarded him with a starting spot in the All-Star game in Minneapolis.

The hot, humid months had arrived. Tempers always grew shorter then. In early August, the team arrived in Milwaukee for a three-game series, starting with a twilight doubleheader. Wills got off to a fast start in the first game, walking, stealing his seventy-third base, and scoring a run in the first inning.

Then he ran into trouble. Taking his usual big lead on the base paths, he was picked off in the fifth inning when Braves pitcher Hank Fischer threw to the bulky Joe Torre, who, usually a catcher but playing first base on this night, applied a catcher's block and a tag as Wills, diving back headfirst as usual, never reached the bag, impeded by

Torre's knees. Wills was livid, convinced that Torre's block amounted to an obstruction in violation of the rules. A bad game became worse when he was thrown out trying to steal in the ninth inning of a 4–3 Dodger loss. That the Dodgers won the second game of the double-header, during which he stole another base, offered him no solace over Torre's play. "I was just furious," he remembered. "I was going to get even if it happened again. I was going to make sure it never happened again."

It happened again.

The very next night, in the sixth inning, as Wills took another large lead, Braves pitcher and future Hall of Famer Phil Niekro wheeled and threw to Torre, who again applied his block. Wills never could get his hand on the bag. First base umpire John Kibler called him out, and after hollering for a moment, Wills stormed back to the dugout. "Maury had tears in his eyes," Torborg remembered. "We were in a pennant race. He thought he'd let the team down."

But this time Wills was prepared, bent on punishing Torre. He went into the visitors' clubhouse and put on a new pair of shoes with spikes he had sharpened the night before, in a lesson learned from Ty Cobb. After beating out a bunt against Niekro in his next at-bat, and seeing Torre again drop into his catcher's block as he took his lead, Wills immediately served notice that Torre was courting injury. Instead of diving headfirst back to the bag on Niekro's next pickoff attempt, he leaped feetfirst toward an elusive Torre and dug his razor-sharp spikes into the bag so deeply that when he extricated the spikes some of the bag's stuffing came out with them.

Torre didn't back down, convinced his block of Wills was perfectly fair so long as he had the ball while employing it. Their contest became a game of cat-and-mouse, with Wills sometimes leaping to cut him and Torre dancing backward, safely out of reach. Finally, after Niekro had made more than a half dozen pickoff throws to first, Wills dug his spikes into Torre's right leg, right around the knee. Blood spurted. "It was all over him," Wills remembered. The game was delayed more than fifteen minutes as Torre left the field and had his leg taped, not about to give in, determined to finish the game. As the action resumed, Wills worried about being slugged by his bigger nemesis. "He was a strong guy," Wills said. "I thought he was gonna pinch my ears." Retaking his place at first, the bloodied Torre simply patted Wills's leg and said, "Let's go, Maurice," the first time a foe had ever used his formal name.

Wills, who respected tough, stoic men, admired Torre thereafter. An uncompromising Torre would always play hard, and Wills would always do what was necessary. It wouldn't be the last time he spiked somebody. But always, he said later, he thought his victim had it coming. "And it wasn't anything personal; it's just the way you had to play," he added. "It's the way Cobb played."

He imagined Cobb likely had these same kinds of encounters with men he battled. He viewed his slashing white predecessor, by then buried in Georgia, as the odd pioneer of all these fracases. The man apparently had some awful emotional issues and a dark side—and Cobb's alleged history of unabashed racism saddened Wills. Yet nothing the violent man had ever done could alter his belief that he and Cobb shared the same competitive temperament.

He was following in Cobb's baseball footsteps, he liked to think; he'd done his part to bring a raw abandon back to base stealing. The Dodgers won that night, 6–3, with Wills going 2-for-5 and scoring two runs, in Koufax's nineteenth victory of the season.

Lou Johnson felt increasingly stoked by Wills's on-field pugnacity. "Maury would piss off God to win," Johnson said. "We had great talent—shit, we had *Sandy*, the Superman, the greatest of all time— nobody could beat Superman. But Maury was the leader of the band. He showed everybody how to do it. Need a steal and a run? He got the motherfucking steal and the run, come on now."

The veneration of Koufax always obscured his rough edges. It concealed athletic flaws and flashes of anger that, if revealed in his prime years, would have gone a long ways toward illuminating his complexity. His long list of baseball shortcomings involved everything from his poor pickoff move (and thus his occasional struggles to foil steal attempts) to his own slow baserunning. It covered virtually everything except the act of pitching itself, though somehow this sounded beside the point, like saying Sinatra couldn't do much of anything except sing. But even otherwise admiring teammates saw the deficiencies for the defects they were, wondering if they might have an impact at some point on a game. "Sandy had absolutely no pickoff move to first base," said Parker, who sided with those who viewed Koufax as a "specialist," a player with a singular talent that compensated for all the areas in which he didn't excel.

Wills, to be forever a bit pained when having to critique his close friend, observed: "He was an amazing pitcher, but he didn't do everything great. He didn't have a great move to first base. He wasn't a very good fielder. He couldn't bunt really. He did the most important thing a pitcher can do: he kept people off base. But he could have done some things better, like holding runners on base."

Koufax's short stint in college baseball and utter absence of minor-league ball meant he'd never received adequate schooling in holding runners from a stretch position. He never looked entirely comfortable when he needed to do that, taking signals from his catcher with his left foot entirely off the pitching rubber, before finally lifting the foot and deliberately placing it on the rubber as opportunistic baserunners took liberal leads. He had a habit, teammates thought, of badly telegraphing his rare pickoff attempts to first base, leaving good baserunners immediately aware they could run against him.

The flaw, at first glance, seemed like such a small thing, especially when measured against the struggles of hitters against Koufax. But in a 1965 game at home against the Cardinals, he ran into the player who, next to Wills, posed the greatest baserunning threat in the league. At twenty-four, left fielder Lou Brock had begun his march toward one day succeeding Wills as the game's most renowned stealer.

Already he exhibited the qualities necessary to get there—speed, cunning, relentless ambition, and a Wills-like passion for studying foes. Brock would successfully steal on about 66 percent of his attempts that season (as opposed to Wills's roughly 75 percent), on his way toward collecting sixty-three thefts as the runner-up to Wills. But Brock was doing everything possible to close the gap. Dodger players had noticed that Brock brought with him a small eight-millimeter camera to film opposing pitchers, apparently in hopes of probing his rivals' weaknesses.

Nothing seemed out of the ordinary as the game began. Koufax, looking in superb form, struck out St. Louis's leadoff hitter, second baseman Julian Javier. Up to the plate stepped Brock, who bunted in front of the plate, slightly on the third-base side, in a place where only Koufax could pick it up, wheel, and try to make a play.

Koufax scrambled off the mound. He moved as he usually moved in such situations, a bit ungainly. Some skills don't necessarily translate from one sport to another: the athleticism that he had displayed during his New York schoolboy years as a quick, strong, leaping basketball star was largely absent on a baseball diamond. If quick in his first step or two, he never would be fast. It took him considerable time to grab Brock's bunt. Tentatively cocking his arm, he at last made the throw to Parker at first base, by which time Brock had easily beaten the ball to the bag.

It was just the start of Koufax's difficulties. Now Brock made him his prey, quickly stealing second base. With Curt Flood soon at first base, Brock prepared to steal third base. Much of Dodger Stadium was riveted by then. It was impossible not to be fixated on Brock. He had a way, when taking a lead off any base, of slowly and rhythmically swinging both arms across his body, to and fro. The movement seemed to be nothing more than an unconscious tic, a way to keep loose and relaxed, not at all intended to taunt a pitcher or catcher. But still it was unusual (by contrast, Wills customarily kept his arms quite still once having taken his lead). In the eyes of some Dodgers, who overlooked the fact that the young Cardinal usually kept his feet absolutely rooted once he assumed his lead, all this conspicuous arm swaying made it appear that Brock was showboating, bent at once on drawing attention to his successful steal and to his bold belief that he was about to steal again.

Sitting in the dugout, Drysdale remarked to a teammate that Brock was dancing at Koufax's expense. He wondered aloud how Koufax, a proud man, would react to it.

By then, Brock's arms had drawn the attention of everyone. To the Dodgers, this could only mean that Brock was signaling he was in control here, ready to take another base: *Here I come.*

Brock took off and stole third base.

On the same play, running behind Brock, Flood stole second, the rare time anyone had executed a double steal against the Dodgers. Koufax had given up three stolen bases in a single inning. Brock was still swinging the arms, still dancing, indignant Dodgers thought. As if he might try to steal home. When Ken Boyer hit nothing more than a lazy fly ball to Willie Davis in center field, Brock tagged up and trotted home with the game's first run. A paltry 30-foot bunt, two Brock stolen bases, and a sacrifice fly had given the Cardinals the lead.

Koufax was as angry as he ever would be.

Brock next came to bat in the top of the third inning, with one man already out and no one on base. It was the perfect moment for a pitcher who wanted to exact payback against a young player guilty of embarrassing him, several Dodgers thought. Koufax already had decided what he was going to do—and not do. And he wasn't going to forewarn Brock.

Koufax did not, as a rule, throw at hitters. Batters would crowd the plate against him sometimes—the very thing that would be perceived as a dare and an insult by some pitchers, notably Drysdale, who would drill offenders in the back with a fastball. Koufax would let the transgression go.

A sympathetic Wills thought Koufax didn't want to harm anyone;

that he knew the damage that his 95- to 100-mile-per-hour-plus fast-ball could do to a skull or face, and couldn't have lived with that. His friend had a kind and decent streak, Wills believed, and that wasn't going to change—Sandy wasn't going to risk hurting somebody just because some Dodger might be furious that another pitcher had hit him. To the public, the trait said everything about Koufax's restraint, good sense, and decency. He'd earned a reputation as noble, which was entirely deserved, and as genteel and forbearing, which absolutely wasn't.

If he felt disrespected, a switch in him flipped. Tommy Davis believed he saw it flipped during the pickup basketball game in which an irate Koufax, as Davis told the story, wanted to go after the guy who'd bumped him hard and unfairly. Teammates had seen it on display during his contract fight with Bavasi, and the lingering bitter feelings afterward.

Brock, who had settled into the batter's box, seemed to have no idea what was coming, Torborg thought.

Koufax, pitching out of a full windup, threw a hard fastball at Brock that struck him just below his right shoulder, in the broad muscles known as the latissimus dorsi, or lats. From Torborg's perspective, the ball momentarily seemed to stick and bury itself in Brock's lats and ribs. "The ball took a while to fall to the dirt," Torborg recalled.

Then Brock dropped to the dirt.

Teammates remember Koufax staring hard at Brock, as if to make it clear that this pitch had been no accident.

So uncharacteristic was Koufax's action, and so pristine his image, that some sportswriters didn't recognize what he had just done, their failure to write about his real motivation reflecting a belief that his control over his fastball had simply failed him.

But to a man, the Dodgers knew better. Drysdale would later tell people exactly where Koufax had plunked Brock—and why. The lesson, he said, was simple: Don't embarrass Sandy.

Brock got up and slowly made his way to first. Immediately, he stole second base again. But he was hurting terribly; Cardinals catcher Tim McCarver later heard from a teammate that Brock had suffered a hairline fracture somewhere around his right shoulder. Brock played two more innings. After striking out in the fifth inning, unable to continue, he left the game, which the Cardinals won, beating Koufax, 2–1.

Brock would be out of the Cardinals' lineup for the next five games. Two weeks after the incident, when Brock next saw Koufax in St. Louis, he would steal another base. "Brock still couldn't fully raise his right arm," Torborg remembered. "But he was running."

Each man, Torborg thought, had made his point.

For decades, Koufax didn't publicly comment on the incident, leaving some fans to doubt that he had ever purposely struck a batter with a pitch. Finally, at the Torre charity event, he acknowledged that he had intentionally thrown at Brock. "If you're going to hit someone, you never tell them," he said.

By mid-1965 a fascinated Lou Johnson, who revered Koufax, thought he recognized what many people didn't. "He was the best and kindest teammate you could have," Johnson recalls. "But people didn't know everything. One thing you gotta know: you didn't fuck with Sandy on the field."

Johnson had quickly grown to love everything associated with his new team, even the blunt orders from management that, in the beginning, sounded miserable to him. After Bavasi summoned him from Spokane, Johnson met the Dodgers on a road trip in Cincinnati, where soon he was informed he would room with the team's eighteen-year-old bonus baby, Willie Crawford. It was suggested that perhaps he could keep an eye on the youngster, extending help and advice when the need arose.

Johnson groaned. "Shit, I don't want to room with the baby. I like to go out on the town, man. I like to have a good time. I don't want to be babysitting the baby."

Somebody in the Dodger front office informed him that Crawford had received a $100,000 signing bonus.

"No shit?" Johnson experienced a change of heart on the spot. "Shit, give me his bags. I'll carry them, I'll go with him, I'll feed him."

He and the youngster became fast friends. "We were together all the time. I wasn't ever lonely around Willie. It was a great way to get started off with the team."

He sensed that reporters, outsiders, and Dodger foes didn't expect much from him, viewing him as an inadequate substitute for the mending Tommy Davis. But all that mattered to him was what his teammates thought. "Ballplayers never let you know they're worried, but, come on now, nobody knew if I could really do it," he said. "If I was bad and couldn't fill in for Tommy, we were finished. I had to show everybody."

On May 10, less than a week after his arrival, he had his first start, in a home game against Houston, during which he went 1-for-5, the beginning of a weeklong stretch of sporadic appearances as a left fielder. Three nights into his new baseball life, he was playing, unbelievably, with Koufax. "You don't get more nervous than that, playing with Sandy the first time," he remembered. "Come on now. This is real." In the second inning, he hit his first homer. Wills stole a pair of bases and scored a run, as Koufax tossed a three-hit shutout, in a 3–0 home victory over the Astros.

In a night game at the Astrodome on May 19, he had made his biggest impression yet on Alston, going 4-for-6, with an RBI double, during a 4–2 victory in fourteen innings. By the game's end, he had become the regular left fielder. He would be one of the Dodgers' leaders that year in home runs, with a modest twelve.

Through it all, he employed his customary hitting style. He crowded the plate, putting outside pitches within reach of his bat, though in the process inviting more pitchers than ever to throw at him. He was on his way to being hit sixteen times by pitches that season, the second most in the National League (behind Frank Robinson's eighteen). He couldn't back down, he said. "If I did anything different, my career was gonna be over," he remembered. "This was my chance. I could take anything coming at me."

The media wrote flatteringly about his contributions and the enormous affection he enjoyed from teammates who, swept along by his infectious spirit, would one day love it when he raucously led them in a song on a parked team bus that literally swayed as the players belted out a tune and rocked from side to side. He had a gift for making others happy. But he thought that if you looked deep enough, you'd still see his rage.

About a half century later, he would still be thinking about his young self. Sitting high in Dodger Stadium on the third-base side, he looked beyond where he'd played in left field, beyond the left-field bleachers, beyond the ballpark and vast stadium parking lot even. He stared out toward the vista and pointed in the general direction of distant communities once off-limits for him. "The hardest part of life for me was out there," he said. "Some places didn't want you around. You ran into things that hurt you, made you angry. I was very safe playing here; I loved every minute playing here. But out there? Come on now."

He kept his anger to himself for as long as he could in 1965. But one summer afternoon at the stadium, it spilled out after he had gone through his typical routine of ferociously swinging at batting practice pitches. A white reporter asked him, "Why do you attack the ball so hard?"

It was the first time he had ever heard the question.

"Because it's fuckin' white," he answered.

He meant it. "I had anger," he remembers. "I had hate."

The reporter quickly moved away. Johnson never worried that the man might write about the comment. Sports reporters typically avoided all topics having to do with race or anything else that might hint that ballplayers weren't altogether happy Americans. At about the same time, Johnson had discovered a use for his rage, channeling it to his advantage during games. "I had a lot of opportunities that year to use it," he remembered. "The way I hit, the way I stole bases, the way I was sliding to break up double plays: I just let my anger come. I couldn't do anything with my anger outside a ballpark or I was gonna be in trouble. But, in games, I could use it all the time. I'd see that white ball and I'd just get angry and do it, swing at all that white."

Race is a weird thing, he thought. He liked his white teammates. Some, like Koufax, Torborg, and Parker, were among the best people he'd ever met. You could be a young man furious at a race, he thought, and still love many of its people, especially the guys playing ball with you. Like Wills, he often wished he didn't ever need to leave Dodger Stadium.

Johnson lived near the busy corner of Hoover Avenue and El Segundo Boulevard, in South-Central, only a few blocks from Roseboro, with whom he often rode home after games. While Johnson alternated between being gabby, funny, grim, and fiery on their rides, Roseboro was usually subdued. Sometimes at night they rolled down the windows. The August afternoons had brought frying hot temperatures in the nineties, but the nights were usually pleasant enough, the thermometers registering mid-seventies. The evening temperatures would later be described by the *Los Angeles Times* as "uncomfortably warm"—the suggestion being that an oppressive heat may have served as a trigger, or aggravating factor, for the sudden troubles that had descended on the city. In reality, the evenings were balmy in downtown Los Angeles and South-Central—perhaps a touch muggy on a couple of evenings, but comfortable. And the dry, sometimes scorching Santa Ana winds hadn't yet rolled into the city. The weather couldn't be blamed for the volcano about to erupt.

The heat was inside people, Johnson thought. Tensions in places like this had been building for years; everybody could feel it. For more than a year, black leaders within the community had been raising concerns about the Los Angeles Police Department's relationship and tactics in the community. Civil rights leaders had warned that things were getting worse; that the LAPD's continued opposition to an independent police review board or any enhanced civilian oversight had exacerbated local anger. South-Central had so little clout that it couldn't even get a hearing on the matter. What happened next was inevitable.

On Wednesday, August 11, at 7:19 p.m., as the Dodgers prepared to take the field at home against the Mets, a California Highway Patrol officer named Lee Minikus, alone on patrol in South-Central, learned from a passing motorist that an apparently drunk driver was cruising nearby. Minikus pulled over a suspect at the corner of 116th Street and Avalon Boulevard, on the edge of a Los Angeles community known as Watts, a name soon to symbolize all that was wrong with America's racial relations. Located just a few miles from where Johnson and Roseboro lived, much of Watts was a ghetto. Overwhelmingly black, poor, and suffused with the familiar tensions between South-Central's residents and the police, Watts had run out of patience.

Minikus would later say he administered a sobriety test that the driver, a twenty-one-year-old black man named Marquette Frye, failed as Frye's twenty-two-year-old brother, Ronald, watched. By then a crowd had gathered. Soon the Frye brothers were joined by their upset mother, forty-nine-year-old Rena. According to Minikus, in an account published the next morning by the *Los Angeles Times*, Marquette resisted arrest, refusing to get into Minikus's squad car even after Minikus drew his revolver. "Go ahead, kill me," Marquette reportedly screamed. Rena Frye jumped on Minikus's back, the *Times* wrote.

By then a second highway patrolman had arrived to provide backup, soon to be joined by a pack of LAPD officers in eight squad cars. A cop pulled out a shotgun to restrain the crowd. Officers began placing the three Fryes into cars. Incensed neighborhood witnesses believed the police had brutalized the Fryes, a claim rejected by arresting officers.

After the Fryes' departure, stories swiftly spread through Watts about what had happened to the family. The news had an incendiary effect. The swelling mob erupted, with an estimated 1,000 rioters moving in different directions from 116th and Avalon throughout Wednesday night and into Thursday morning, pelting police and motorists with rocks, bricks, bottles, and pieces of concrete.

It was just the beginning. By late Thursday night, an estimated 7,000 rioters had overrun Watts and nearby neighborhoods. The intersection of Imperial Highway and Avalon had become a mass of overturned automobiles. Over six days, what would come to be known as the Watts riots, or the Watts rebellion, would claim thirty-four lives. More than 1,000 people would be injured, and roughly 3,400 arrested. The riots engulfed a roughly forty-five-square-mile area, including several blocks where arson and looting devastated most white-owned businesses. More than 250 buildings in the area were destroyed. Martial law and curfews went into effect. Still, nothing slowed the rioting during the first hundred hours, not even the presence of nearly 4,000 National Guardsmen. Within a few days, the estimated number of rioters exceeded 20,000. Some observers thought that figure was ridiculously conservative.

Johnson learned about the start of the riots on that Wednesday night, following the last out of a Dodgers victory at about 10:35 p.m. By then, the violence had engulfed much of Watts. In the clubhouse, sportswriters gathered quotes from players about the game. With Drysdale pitching a shutout, and Wills scoring the Dodgers' only run on a Gilliam single, the Dodgers story line would constitute the rare bit of normalcy in Los Angeles over that next week.

Hearing about the rioters' rampage as he sat in front of his locker, Johnson wasn't at all surprised. He knew Watts well, and regarded what was happening there as an insurrection. *You can't hold people down forever.*

That Friday night, about forty-eight hours into the rioting, Johnson was in left field, while Roseboro, given a night off, spent the game quietly in the left-field bullpen, a transistor radio pressed to his ear, listening for the latest from Watts. Between innings he walked over to the bullpen gate and, in a murmur, passed on riot updates to Johnson, then turned and repeated the same news to Tracewski and a couple of other reserves hanging in the bullpen. "We were playing a game and people were getting killed," Johnson recalls. "That got me worked up even more later."

Johnson rode home on several nights during the riots with Roseboro and young Willie Crawford. To avoid danger, they departed from their normal route, trying to stay away from the worst of the melees and fires. They wore their Dodger uniforms during the drives, so as not to be mistaken for rioters if they were stopped by police. Teammates worried about them. Fairly urged Roseboro to gather up his entire family and stay with him in Northridge. Roseboro thanked Fairly, but assured him he was safe in his own home. In reality, he wasn't at all sure about that; he had no idea how far the destruction might spread. Arriving home one night during the riots, he heard a rumor that some protesters might be coming through his neighborhood. Not taking chances, he gathered his guns and sat by his front door, ready to guard his family and property.

Roseboro wasn't going anywhere. A leader at the ballpark and away from it, Roseboro didn't run, thought Johnson, who liked riding with him, thinking there might be safety in numbers if they were to come upon either cops or rioters. What neither man knew at that moment was that top officials of the LAPD, estranged from the very citizenry they were sworn to protect, would ask Roseboro before the year's end to be a consultant for the department, to do what he could as a local celebrity to rebuild trust between the cops and skeptical inner-city residents. His hiring would amount to an acknowledgment that the police needed to chart a new course. The Los Angeles City Council's view of the police's tactics would change, too, with a council committee condemning the LAPD's failure to build confidence in South-Central: "The Department has not in the past placed sufficient emphasis on its community relations activities and recognized the necessity of having support from the community."

But all that would come later. In those first days, the sight of so many stores being burned to the ground prompted one white businessman to call his black partner, with whom he owned a dry cleaners.

I need you, the white partner said.

This accounted for why, on mornings and afternoons during the riots, Maury Wills could be found standing alone in front of the Maury Wills Stolen Base Cleaners on Santa Barbara Avenue (one day to become Martin Luther King Jr. Boulevard), a few miles from Watts.

The riot hadn't spread to Santa Barbara Avenue. But no one could be sure that it wouldn't. Wills's partner stayed inside the shop, taking care of the dry cleaning. Wills remained outside, his presence meant to remind everyone in the area that this was a black-owned business; that it should be left alone. Some residents waved and said hello, as if to show support. Wills spent two to three hours in front of the shop each day during the riots, before heading to the ballpark. His business—and the immediate neighborhood—would go untouched.

Other than playing ball and keeping watch over the cleaners, Wills stayed at home during the riots, worried that he might encounter trouble if he stepped outdoors. One afternoon that week, before leaving for the ballpark, he ran into a serious problem. He called the Dodgers clubhouse manager, Nobe Kawano, who in turn telephoned Wes Parker at home.

Maury's car won't start, Kawano said, adding that no taxi would come into Wills's neighborhood.

Could you pick him up? Kawano asked.

Sure, Parker said.

Parker would later recollect that he climbed into "this little 1955 Mercedes I had," setting out on a drive of about fifteen miles to his destination. It might as well have been 150,000 miles; it was another world to him. In his quarter century of life in Los Angeles, Parker had never set foot in Wills's community. As a youth, he had spent much time at the Los Angeles Memorial Coliseum, both watching Dodger games and later, thanks to his schoolboy athletic skills and his father's connections, participating in pregame workouts there as a teenager alongside Dodger players. During his abbreviated 1962 winter-league season in LA, he had played ball several times on the city's south side. But most of this community was as unfamiliar to him as Mars.

Arriving in Wills's neighborhood, with an address scribbled on a piece of paper, he stopped in front of an apartment building. In an era without cell phones, he waited for Wills to emerge. "I was a little tense," he remembers. "I was in a real target car. I'd been worried about somebody maybe shooting at the car or throwing rocks at it. Nothing happened. But I still felt good when Maury came out."

For their part, Tracewski and his wife, Dolores, didn't know what might happen next. Living in Baldwin Hills, a few miles from the riot area, they were far enough away to believe the mayhem wouldn't reach them, but close enough to be forever altered by it. After attending a church service that Sunday, they saw a battle tank belonging to the National Guard sitting near their church, in the parking lot of a shopping center they frequented at the corner of Santa Barbara Avenue and Crenshaw Boulevard. "The tank was right there behind the Broadway department store and the May Company," Tracewski recalled. "It was upsetting."

Then, like most of his teammates, Tracewski got into his car and drove alone to Dodger Stadium. "You knew the riot was still going on," he recalls. "All that smoke: you could see it from the top of the stadium. Coming home at night was eerie. I remember driving alone through the stadium parking lot after one game—a totally empty lot. People had gotten out of there in a hurry. Then I got out of the stadium and the whole downtown was quiet. I'd never seen it like that. You didn't know what was going to happen next. Yet I never thought of getting a gun, just didn't occur to me."

The idea had occurred to Torborg, though, who was living in

South Pasadena. He was taking no chances. A friend loaned him a shotgun. Torborg made sure it was loaded before getting in his car and making the short drive from Pasadena to Dodger Stadium. "Lots of guys on the team were carrying guns during the riots," he observed. "There was this hump on the floor of the car by the backseat. That's where I kept the shotgun. Never had to use it, but just having it there made me feel a little better, I guess."

But like Parker, Wills, Tracewski, and Johnson, Torborg had the ability to tune out all else and concentrate on the game once he came through a stadium's gates. Even when Roseboro passed along a riot update through the bullpen gate to Johnson, it was so swift that Johnson processed it as he simultaneously positioned himself for a hitter. "You know if you don't do it, you might not have a job, come on now," Johnson said. "So you don't stop concentrating for nothin' out there. Not even the riot. I waited till later to get angry."

Then he and Roseboro drove home. Getting closer to his place, Johnson heard on the radio about more people dying. He had no place to put all this rage, he thought.

And then it was over. Around the Dodger clubhouse, no one would even mention the riots by week's end. In what came as a surprise to his teammates, the only Dodger who would be publicly talking about the subject, six months later, was the quietest of them.

As the LAPD's new consultant, Roseboro spoke bluntly to meetings of blacks and whites. If anyone thought he was going to whitewash anything about the police's behavior, he said, they better think again. He knew there had been misconduct on the part of some LAPD officers, resulting in the mistreatment of black residents. After recruiting a couple of young black men for the police department, he said he wanted to see more black officers hired, and more of those officers deployed to black communities.

But Roseboro didn't feel support from everyone in the city bureaucracy or the LAPD. He later recalled that some veteran officers let him know they weren't admirers of his brand of community work, which they viewed, he recounted, as part of a misguided LAPD effort that involved "romancing the same people who created the riots and committed crimes." Increasingly uncomfortable in his position, Roseboro reluctantly stepped down. The police department looked as much like a white institution as ever to South-Central residents, including Johnson, who just wanted to play baseball.

In the first days after the riots' end, Johnson thought it was a nice coincidence that the team was ending its home stand and preparing for a road trip. The Dodgers could benefit, he thought, from some time away from the strife. They were headed to San Francisco, and nothing ever felt better than winning there. It was just the right time for a fracas.

For a few hours during August 1965, America's most compelling sports theater emanated from San Francisco. There, on a sunny Sunday, with the two teams battling for a pennant, the Dodgers-Giants four-game series culminated with an infamous brawl, sparked by a fight between Roseboro and the Giants' star pitcher Juan Marichal, who clubbed Roseboro on the skull with his bat. In the aftermath, observers would wonder whether factors outside baseball contributed to the principal combatants' fury. They pondered the effect of stresses suffered by Roseboro during the Watts riots, and the worries gripping Marichal about the well-being of family members back in his homeland, the Dominican Republic, which had been engulfed that summer by a civil war that prompted a Lyndon Johnson–ordered American military intervention to effect a truce between the warring factions.

But in reality, all the theories about how social traumas might have sparked the on-field rage would largely miss the point. It wasn't the trauma suffered by South-Central that had compelled Roseboro to rise from his catcher's crouch and confront his antagonist, his teammates thought. Nor was it because of anything happening in Santo

Domingo that Marichal brought his bat down like a sledgehammer on Roseboro's head. It was because each man at that moment was in the grip of baseball's ugliest rivalry, which sometimes made even highly principled Dodgers and Giants do uncharacteristically unfair and vile things, or contemplate doing them. Like spike a maddeningly fast little baserunner as he slid. Or ram a glove in the face of that fast baserunner. Or spike the guy who just spiked you. Or trip a big clumsy slugger as he rounded a base. Or knee him in the groin as he slid. Or throw balls at the heads of hitters or onrushing baserunners.

These were the *Giants*, Wills would say. This meant that you had license to do to them what they would undoubtedly try to do to you—things you would never think of doing in any widespread manner against any other team in baseball, for no other rival incited such contempt.

Most Dodgers struggled to remember a specific episode to explain how and when their dislike for the Giants originated. The scorn simply got inculcated—in a hurry. "It kind of begins in the minor leagues, almost as soon as you get there," Fairly said. Before players knew it, they had come to despise such things as the orange in the Giants' uniforms, so much so that some players would forever be uncomfortable on Halloween, surrounded by pumpkins and decorations in the Giants' trademark color.

The most infuriating Giant was Marichal, whom Wills described as "the guy who always had that shit-ass grin."

But no Dodger ever thought that Marichal, on his way to the Hall of Fame, was anything less than a remarkable pitcher. That year he would win twenty-two games and post a 2.13 ERA. He would compile six twenty-victory seasons during the 1960s, twice leading the league in wins and once, after Koufax retired, winning an ERA title. Had he not played in the same era as Koufax and the Cardinals' Bob Gibson, he would have taken home a shelf full of Cy Young Awards. As it was, he received none. But over time no opposing pitcher would win more grudging respect from the Dodgers.

His pitching delivery alone made the right-hander an artistic wonder. Midway into his standard windup, he kicked his left leg so high that it resembled a prima ballerina's, the leg soaring above his head as he cocked his head toward the sky. For a long moment, Marichal seemed to take his eyes off the plate entirely. In a feat of improbable balance, he paused for an instant at the top of his windup to rock a little, in what felt to many victims like a bit of impudence. Finally, with an overhand motion, he whipped himself toward the plate, the ball seeming to come right out of that lofted left leg, which made it all the more difficult to discern what kind of pitch was coming, because by that point he seemed to be all legs anyway. It was like hitting against a spider.

Parker regarded Marichal as the greatest and most confounding pitcher he'd ever faced. He didn't have the best fastball or curveball in the league, but no other pitcher possessed more savvy, imagination, or control of his pitches. Parker regularly felt himself being "picked apart like a butterfly" by his foe. He came to believe Marichal was capable of reading his mind, of knowing exactly the kind of pitch Parker expected him to throw. "He was always one step ahead of me when it really counted."

On a whim, Marichal could switch to any of his other baffling pitching motions, among them a windup in which he spun, momentarily turning his back on the hitter entirely so that his uniform number, 27, was exposed, before twisting back to the plate with a three-quarters or sidearm delivery, depending on his mood. He had what the Dodgers commonly regarded as a minimum of five pitches, including a screwball, a sinker, and a variety of off-speed pitches that complemented his fastball and curveball. But for the Dodgers, his pitches would always be overshadowed by that swagger and grin. "Marichal had as close to an arrogance about him as you could have," Parker says. "No other pitcher in the league would ever smile at you. Then he'd go into his windup and that leg would go even higher. And sometimes when he got you out, he smiled some more."

The series finale between the two teams featured a hugely antici-pated duel between Koufax and Marichal, the only time that season the two pitchers would face each other.

Marichal struggled early in the game. Leading off, Wills dropped a perfect bunt down the third-base line. He had won the game's first battle of skill and wits and now stood on first base.

A Gilliam groundout advanced Wills to second base. With two outs, Fairly doubled, Wills trotted home, and the Dodgers had the lead.

In the Dodgers second inning, Parker doubled the opposite way to left field. Roseboro singled him home. The Dodgers had two runs, and the second inning hadn't ended.

Predictably, the old tensions flared in the next couple of minutes. In Wills's second at-bat, with the memory of his game-opening bunt still fresh, Marichal threw a fastball at his neck. Wills jerked out of the way, falling on his back. In the third inning, Fairly found him-self sprawled in the dirt after a Marichal pitch just missed his chin. "He knocked me down," Fairly recollected. "Marichal and those guys tested your mental toughness. But I got up, like always. There was a psychological advantage in it for me with those guys: I'd get up and hit the ball hard. And it was kind of flattering to me that Marichal knocked me down. It meant I was hitting well. But we still didn't like it. We gave it to Marichal pretty good."

To Roseboro, retaliation now seemed in order.

In the bottom of the third inning, the Dodgers would target a Giants hitter to receive much the same treatment that Marichal had given to Wills and Fairly. Roseboro decided Marichal himself would pay.

Wills listened, he said, as Roseboro and Koufax huddled around the dugout water cooler and discussed what to do about Marichal. "Let's get him," Roseboro told Koufax, inviting him, Wills thought, to take care of the issue. But Koufax's subdued reaction betrayed a lack of enthusiasm.

Roseboro did not push, as if unsurprised by Koufax's reaction. What the catcher said next conveyed an affectionate understanding of his friend's nature and limits. "I'll do something about it—I'll take care of it," Roseboro responded, as Wills remembers.

"I decided to take matters in my own hands," Roseboro wrote later.

For many years thereafter, the question of his willingness to throw a knockdown pitch on that day would be a highly sensitive one for Koufax. Tracewski remembered Koufax later telling him that he had said to Roseboro, "I'm gonna take care of this," meaning he would be glad to target Marichal, to which Roseboro said, "No, I'll take care of this." Nobody had ever told him to throw at Marichal or anybody else, Koufax emphasized to Tracewski.

Years later, after Wills had shared his recollection of the Roseboro-Koufax discussion with a couple of people, Koufax expressed sharp disappointment. It was a rare disagreement between the two devoted friends. "When he heard what I'd said, Sandy was hurt," Wills remembered. "He said to me, 'Why did you do that, Maury? Why did you say that?' Sandy always said to people that nobody told him to throw at Marichal. But I know what Roseboro said to him by the water cooler. That's all I was saying."

For Koufax to feel pained by his recollection was the last thing Wills wanted. "I would never want to hurt Sandy," he said plaintively. "He's a wonderful person and he didn't want anybody to get hurt. That's all I meant. He just couldn't do it, didn't want to do it, not even against the Giants. He couldn't hurt somebody or want to risk that. The only person he ever really threw at was Brock because he got mad."

As the Dodgers took the field for the bottom of the third inning, Roseboro had decided what to do. After the second pitch from Koufax to Marichal, Roseboro went through the pretense of dropping the ball, picking it up near Marichal, and then, while behind his adversary, gunning it back toward Koufax, his goal being, he recounted, to "buzz" Marichal, to rattle him, having the ball come within a couple of inches of Marichal's nose as it passed his head.

He succeeded.

Insults were exchanged. Roseboro moved toward Marichal, who backed up in the direction of the mound, raised his bat, and in a flash struck Roseboro on the head.

It was the first of what would be three blows to Roseboro from Marichal's bat. One landed squarely on the left side of Roseboro's head. It was sickeningly audible. Blood immediately spurted from his skull. Roseboro dived at Marichal while throwing punches, but he was already half blinded by the blood. He made decent contact only once with Marichal's face, clearly getting the worst of the fight, his head a crimson mess.

A terrified Mays, having run out of the dugout to intervene, was crying. He had seen the wounds to Roseboro's skull and, with blood pouring down his old friend's face and into an eye socket, was convinced that Roseboro's left eye had been knocked out. Tracewski, noticing Roseboro momentarily down on the ground, thought his injuries might be mortal. Mays put his arms around a scrambling Roseboro in a gesture meant to rescue and restrain him, begging for him to stop struggling, telling him his eye was out (Roseboro learned later that Alston had feared the same thing, reasonably enough, for it appeared there was only blood where an eye ought to have been visible). "Baseball was Mays's family," Wills said. "Roseboro was his buddy. It killed Mays to see this happening. He couldn't stop crying."

Mays, hoping to lead a stumbling Roseboro into the Dodger dugout, was doing his best to quell the madness. But he was among the few pacifists on the field at that moment. The brawl had been going on for several minutes by then.

Now Lou Johnson made his presence felt, having made a long run in from left field. He had his first good look at his close friend. Roseboro's wounds had appeared bad to him from the outfield. Up

close, blood still gushing from them, they looked disfiguring and perhaps permanent. Johnson exploded. Among the first Giants he saw
was second baseman Tito Fuentes, who was holding a bat of his own.
"You take a step toward me, I'm gonna kill you," Johnson told him.

At about the same time, Fairly and other Dodgers confronted
Fuentes. "We let Tito know: 'You put that bat down right now or
else,'" Fairly remembered.

Fuentes complied. Johnson already had rushed on. Sprinting
around a phalanx of Giants, he bolted toward Marichal. A half dozen
Giants tried unsuccessfully to restrain him. "I was duking it with a
bunch of sons of bitches," he remembered. He tagged Marichal, who
kicked and spiked him in return before scrambling backward in full
retreat. Johnson hit a couple of more guys. The fight moved toward
the Giants dugout. Giant fans leaned over the box seat railings, some
looking poised to run out on the field and join the battle. Johnson
wanted more of Marichal, but at that moment a strapping six-foot-
four Giant who generally never spoke to any Dodger appeared.

Willie McCovey plucked Johnson from the mob and lifted him
off the ground. It occurred to Johnson that nobody had ever been able
to do this to him before.

"Come on, Lou," McCovey said.

It was the first time Johnson had heard the big man speak. He
struggled in vain to get away. McCovey was too damn strong.

"Come on, Lou," McCovey kept saying. "Don't do that, Lou.
Come on, Lou."

McCovey's tone told Johnson that he wasn't threatening him, just
trying to break things up.

Marichal did not get away unmarked. Tracewski remembered that
somebody briefly put him into a headlock. Marichal's eyebrow was
scratched, and it was a bleeding a little. Tracewski had an up-close
look at him, by then caught himself in the eye of the fast-moving
storm, not quite sure how he had gotten there, but finding himself
swept along by it. "I don't remember doing anything to anybody," he

recalled. "I was just in it. There was no way to get out of it until it was over—it was just too big."

Mays had never stopped attending to Roseboro or shouting for calm. At one point, Mays cradled Roseboro's head in the dugout, in a scene visible to unruly fans as well as to the warring players. "If it hadn't been for Mays," Parker said, "there would've been a riot in the ballpark."

Finally the brawl died out, the players spent.

A weary and disheveled Marichal, his jersey out of his pants, was brought into the dugout to learn that he had been ejected from the game. The police were still on the diamond, just in case. Roseboro was assisted off the field. Boos rained down on him from Giant partisans.

The teams had a game to finish. The Dodgers returned to their positions on the field to resume the third inning. Torborg took over for Roseboro. A shaken Koufax gave up a three-run homer to Mays in the inning, and the Dodgers lost, 4–3.

In the immediate aftermath of the game, reflecting the view of many Dodgers, Parker wanted Marichal arrested and thrown in jail. In St. Louis, hearing of an attack on a fellow catcher, a furious Tim McCarver hoped, like Fairly, that Marichal would be suspended for the rest of the season. The ten-game suspension handed down by the commissioner's office—which translated to two missed pitching starts for Marichal—infuriated the Dodgers as ludicrously insufficient. But in such a tight pennant race, those two missed starts would loom large, their impact underscored at the end of the season when the final standings revealed the Dodgers had prevailed over the Giants by only two games. ("Absolutely, it had an effect," Giants outfielder Len Gabrielson reflected.)

The suspension had done other damage. When he finally returned to the mound in late August, Marichal wasn't the same dynamo. He was reduced to a largely mediocre hurler for the remainder of the season, losing four of his final seven decisions. Subjected to death threats, he wouldn't pitch in Los Angeles.

By contrast Roseboro, initially thought to need weeks of healing, would miss only four games after the brawl before returning to the lineup. Soon his attorneys would file a lawsuit against Marichal, eventually settled out of court for a mere $7,000 for Roseboro. Roseboro became a hugely popular and sympathetic figure, cast as the brave warrior who had persevered in the face of the villainous Giant's assault. As time passed, however, the characterization increasingly bothered some Dodgers, who thought it failed to account for all the tension on the field that day. "Nobody was very surprised there'd been a fight," Tracewski remembered. Several players, hearing about Marichal's expressions of regret, were uncomfortable with seeing him marked as a pariah. "This was out of character for Marichal," said Tracewski, who viewed the old rival as a special talent and competitor. "I think he expected to get hit or thrown at that day in San Francisco."

The stain would cling to Marichal into the 1970s. By then Wills had accepted him, welcoming Marichal to Los Angeles during his brief Dodger stint in 1974. But it would take the intervention of Roseboro, who had forgiven him and grown to like him, to make observers and fans set aside the old ugliness and focus on Marichal the marvel. At Roseboro's funeral in 2002, which drew stars including Hank Aaron and Bill White, Marichal was an honorary pallbearer.

Wills believed he understood what, down deep, had triggered the bloody fight. "It really was just the history of the Giants-Dodgers things," he said. "It was crazy. That rivalry got all of us to do things we'd never do against anybody else."

After the game, the Dodgers headed for the San Francisco airport. Remarkably, Roseboro was on the plane with them, winging toward the East. The Dodgers had a game the very next night in New York, on a road trip taking them through Philadelphia, Pittsburgh, and Houston before two games at home (both losses) against the Giants. The Dodgers were in the midst of a grind that saw them play twenty-five games in twenty-six days. By the time they finally had an off day, on September 8, they were exhausted. They trailed the Giants by a half game in the standings. But Wills thought they would be recharged by the following day, cheered by the realization that Koufax would be on the mound.

In Northridge, a future television costume designer, fourteen-year-old Dodger fan Marti Allen, whose school year had just begun, wanted to see Koufax pitch. After her classes ended on Thursday, September 9, she went home, waited for her father to step through the door at the end of his workday, and pleaded with him to take her and her younger brother, Kevin, to the game.

Her father said he was beat.

She wouldn't accept no. She told him she had a feeling that something great was going to happen. We *have to go*. We all have to go.

Her father gave in. He said she could bring along a friend. They had to hurry. Had games not begun at the later hour of 8:00 p.m. in 1965, they never would have had a chance of making it on time. She told her little brother that they were all going, and he asked if he could bring his own friend.

Yes.

Kevin Allen picked up a phone and called me.

To be in attendance with the Allens at Koufax's perfect game has meant, during the fifty-one years since, to be a part of a small, ever-dwindling group: those spectators still alive who possess visual images of the night, by which I mean simple memories, as opposed to photographs, video, or an old tape of a television broadcast (there was no telecast). Indeed, only one short piece of film exists of the game. It is an amateurish black-and-white bit of footage largely limited to showing Koufax, his catcher, and Cubs hitters, and it supposedly lasts for only the opening two innings.

The absence of useful video about a masterpiece that a 1995

survey of the members of the Society for American Baseball Research deemed to be the greatest pitched game in history means that Koufax's feat lives today in romantic shadows, where verifiable history melds with mythology. It remains to baseball chroniclers what the Gettysburg Address is to Lincoln scholars, a transcendent event that, though tracked by a prodigious paper trail and deeply chronicled by journalists and historians, stubbornly eludes efforts to picture and feel it.

The game marked the apotheosis of Koufax. Even the era's newspaper sportswriters, a breed typically worshipful of retired giants like DiMaggio but customarily restrained in their assessments of players they had to cover, couldn't hold back their awe. Koufax, they posited, was no longer merely the best pitcher of his era. In a typical assessment, the *Chicago Tribune*'s Richard Dozer in his postgame story described Koufax as "the most electrifying pitcher of all time." The *Los Angeles Times*' Frank Finch called him "a Michelangelo." Off the field, the latest wave of adoration, butting up against Koufax's need for privacy, would steadily add to his discomfort, leaving him soon to resist questions about the masterpiece, pushing him toward a hermitage of his own making. In his autobiography, to be released a year later, he would devote merely half a page to the perfect game. It was as if he put his achievement into a sealed vault.

But not on that first night. "I think the stuff I had tonight was the best I've had all season," he said to reporters, adding that he had begun thinking he had a genuine shot at the perfect game during the seventh inning. "I had a real good fastball, and that sort of helps your curve. I thought the fastball was really working best the last three innings. . . . The last three innings I had the best stuff I threw all night."

Seldom had he ever been so talkative about his own success. He disclosed that, in the midst of his past no-hitters, some rival coaches—in violation of a quaint but silly baseball tradition that asks both teams to refrain from mentioning a creeping no-hitter to the pitcher involved so as not to rattle or jinx him—had pointedly told him about his prospective gems. "The opposing coaches said something in those other games, but not tonight," he revealed. Between innings, he reported, the Dodgers' dugout was very still. "For the first time, nobody on the bench said a word to me," he said. "At least I didn't hear anything."

His concentration was absolute. Along the way, the game served as a reminder that nothing on a baseball field is more thrilling than the sight of a power pitcher blowing away All-Star hitters. Three future Hall of Famers—left fielder Billy Williams, third baseman Ron Santo, and first baseman Ernie Banks—occupied the third, fourth, and fifth spots of the Cubs' lineup. Collectively, they struck out six times that night, in nine failed plate appearances against Koufax. That he needed to throw as many pitches as he did (113, of which 79 were strikes) was a simple function of the Cubs' many futile swings and his fourteen strikeouts. No Cub who made an appearance escaped being struck out. Characteristically, Koufax became stronger as the game progressed, fanning eight of the last ten Cubs hitters, and the final six. After the last strike, he had thrown his major-league record-breaking fourth no-hitter—one in each of four consecutive seasons.

The signs before the game had been anything but auspicious. It was a bit cool in Chavez Ravine (which often sees temperatures dip at night in September), while Koufax preferred warmth. Torborg, who was getting a start so that Roseboro could have a night off, noticed as Koufax warmed up that he seemed to have problems getting loose. His fastball didn't have its usual pop.

Torborg called for an abundance of breaking balls in the opening inning. The Cubs' leadoff hitter, center fielder Don Young, playing in his first major-league game, took a curve in the dirt before popping out to Lefebvre. Then came rookie Glenn Beckert, the Cubs' second baseman, who hit a breaking ball just foul down the third-base line. "It was no more than an inch or two foul—actually, I thought it was going to be fair when he hit it," Torborg said. "It was close."

Torborg realized Koufax had a problem. That had been a very poor breaking ball, he thought. It wasn't Koufax's typical sharp-breaking, 12–6 curveball but rather a "rolling curve," as Torborg described it. In its ineffectiveness, the rolling curve is very little different than the dreadful pitch known as "a hanger," the kind of ball that hangs in the air like a piñata, ready to be clubbed.

Beckert settled back into the batter's box. Torborg needed to see the sharp breaker in a hurry, he decided. Only it wasn't coming. And Koufax couldn't turn to the fastball, because he still wasn't loose. Many years after the game, a puzzled Santo would tell the *Los Angeles Times* that during the early innings, Koufax "was pitching a different game than he usually does," noting that at one point Koufax "threw me four curves in a row."

But Koufax had no choice at that point. Koufax was not yet Koufax. And Beckert would now get another look at a breaking ball. In a reminder that luck counts even on nights of athletic genius, Beckert froze as a rolling curve found the plate for strike three. Then Billy Williams—crusher of hangers—watched another rolling curve for strike three. Remarkably, Koufax was out of the first inning unscathed.

And the opposition was hitless.

In Dodger Stadium, this last detail—rather unremarkable on its face, given that Koufax had pitched only an inning—nonetheless had a profound impact on spectators. By the time Koufax made it through the first inning of any home game without giving up a hit, the dreamers in the crowd had already begun envisioning the possibility of a no-hitter. After all, this was the reason why many of them had bought tickets. It was part of why Marti had brought us here. We sat on the third-base side in Aisle 27, Row S (Marti kept her ticket stub), of Dodger Stadium's fourth deck, the so-called reserve level, part of a crowd that included sixteen-year-old Zev Yaroslavsky, the future councilman, who, unwilling to miss the possibility of Koufax magic, had ridden a bus to the ballpark and bought a general admission ticket.

Memories are capricious. I wish I could say that I have in my head an image of every key play, but I don't. My images of that night are cluttered with odd and juvenile moments, which had everything to do with the twelve-year-old brain that stored them.

But I can still clearly see a few things from the game, a couple of which truly matter. In the second inning, I saw something so alarming that my brain must have immediately burned the image onto my mind's eye, where it has remained since. The moment was not an odd or small thing. In fact, it is something that ought to involve a correction of a widespread mistake in historical accounts of the game. With two outs in the top of the second inning, after cleanup hitter Santo had fouled out to Torborg and Banks whiffed at strike three, a rookie in his first major-league game, right-handed-hitting outfielder Byron Browne, stepped into the batter's box and smacked a line drive. Koufax's fastball still wasn't quite itself, and his curve still hung. Now Koufax had thrown a high hanger that sat up in the strike zone, and Browne ripped it toward center field.

To this day, I can see the ball moving on a low line. I can see the tall, left-handed center fielder Willie Davis, in whose direction the ball was speeding. Aisle 27, Row S, afforded a perfect view. I've long wondered why it is that I remember this at-bat, as opposed to those of Banks and so many other Cubs. The only reasonable explanation I can offer is that, like many others in the ballpark, I was stunned, afraid that Koufax had lost his no-hitter and that I would be denied yet again an opportunity to see one. The alarmed spectators included the young Yaroslavsky, who would later simply recall a sharp line drive being struck somewhere into the outfield by an unidentified Cub ("My heart sank," he said). When it left Browne's bat, the ball had the appearance of being a certain base hit, a rather routine single to center field that would drop in front of Davis. But luck intervened. Browne had hit the ball so hard that it hung in the air. It was a rope, as ballplayers commonly call such a shot, a tribute to the quality of contact made and to its beautiful look, a ghostly white blur that stays at the same height for a considerable distance, as straight as a taut rope.

Published accounts over the last half century have varied as to where Davis positioned himself before the pitch, and where he had to run (or not run) to attempt a play on the ball. The discrepancies are understandable: there is no film, after all. Many journalists and historians, who didn't see the moment for themselves, have had to rely on the accounts of others. Most day-after accounts of the game had the ball arriving on a line to Davis, though few reporters specified where he stood exactly. One school of thought speculates that Davis was more or less in shallow center field, from where he never moved or moved only a few steps, the liner hit essentially right at him. Another account, from a highly respected baseball website that is generally flawless on such matters, has Davis running to the ball in "deep CF-RF"—deep right-center field.

Neither description is accurate, which does a historical disservice to the man who caught the liner.

Davis wasn't positioned in shallow center field, but instead was playing the newcomer Browne—whose offensive abilities he didn't know firsthand—in medium center, from where he would have a reasonable chance on a deep or shallow ball.

At the crack of the bat, Davis had to race in. Never in his Dodger career, not even now, would Davis look like he was sprinting on an outfield play. Although he was acknowledged to be the fastest player on the Dodgers, his speed was terribly deceptive. He could appear to be coasting in the outfield when in fact he was covering ground like a deer. His long-legged gait had everything to do with this. A former Los Angeles high school sprint champion, his stride resembled that of the future Olympic 200-meter gold medalist Tommie Smith. It was fluid to the point of loping. But the stride ate up ground. And it gobbled up the Dodger Stadium outfield grass now, as he chased Browne's shot.

Over the years, Davis's problems in the outfield had included his notorious habit of getting horrible jumps on balls as they were coming off opponents' bats. Sometimes he would position himself abysmally, playing toward right-center when he should have been shading a hitter toward left-center, or vice versa. Now and then he would make Wills want to scream when he lost concentration, failed to hustle, missed a cutoff man with a poor throw, or dropped ordinary fly balls. Amazingly, in the 1970s, Davis would win three Gold Gloves. But in an eighteen-year career that saw him play for six teams, he also would lead the National League twice in errors at his position. He had a deserved reputation for being a maddeningly erratic fielder. Within another year, he would let Koufax down by dropping two easy fly balls in a critical game, resurrecting old doubts among his teammates about his focus.

But on this night, on this play, he did everything right. He got a terrific jump on the ball. He approached the tricky liner at just the right angle. And he was flying, a twenty-five-year-old at the peak of his speed. With a few long strides, he had closed in on an unpredictable ball that would have posed a very stiff challenge for slower outfielders, who would have had difficulty reaching it before it began sinking, at which point it might have required a difficult catch beneath their knees. Davis's speed permitted him to reach the low liner while it was still a rope. He caught it on his glove side, about thigh high. He made the tough play look so easy, so ordinary, that he would never receive his just due in newspaper accounts or histories.

Eight years later, as a twenty-year-old college kid who had finagled a press pass, I spoke to him before a game. I didn't take notes of our brief conversation (I had come to stare at Hank Aaron in a batting cage), but I remember basically what he said in his slow, deep voice and how he said it: *I had to make that catch for Sandy—what if I didn't?* Just the possibility of "didn't" triggered a sigh that conveyed the pressures of that night. *Not a lot of guys wanted the ball hit to them. That wasn't an easy play I had. You can get fooled on a liner. But I was good coming in. What if I didn't catch it?*

But he had caught it. And Byron Browne was out.

By the third inning, a finally limber Koufax had found his best fastball and 12–6 curve. Thereafter, the strikeouts mounted. With his fireball sizzling, the contrast of his curveball became all the more deadly. In Aisle 27, Row S, twelve-year-old Kevin Allen, a future Colorado attorney who even as a kid was careful in voicing observations and arriving at deductions, thought with amazement that for the first time in his life on the reserve level, he could make out the break of a pitch. Koufax must have a really great curve tonight, he thought. "I started thinking this was going to be different than any other game I'd seen," Allen recalled. "His curve looked unhittable. He had everything that night."

By then Torborg thought so too. Between innings, he wondered whether he should seek out Koufax for the briefest of chats, and then just as quickly decided against it. "Sandy didn't need my input," Torborg remembered. "I just deferred to him like I always did. Between innings, I was on the other side of the dugout from him. I figured if he wanted to talk to me, he'll come see me. He didn't . . . I wasn't at his level. He knew what he wanted. He didn't need to talk to anybody about it. I didn't hear anybody talking to Sandy during the entire game."

The game was important to Torborg for reasons that extended beyond Koufax to issues of his own future. Just as during the 1964 season, he had spent much of 1965 frustrated over his inability to prove to the Dodgers that he could be a worthy successor to Roseboro. By the season's end he would hit only .240, bearing no resemblance to the collegiate phenomenon who had hit close to .400. So often had he screamed and flung helmets in disgust over his failures that Tommy Davis finally said to him, in a remark that cut deep, "You have the worst temper of anybody on the field." Torborg knew that Davis was right. Alston, who was increasingly weary of his outbursts, sometimes called him "Red Ass." The chiding changed nothing. Torborg couldn't dial down his fury any better than he could produce base hits. His frustrations mounted. "Jeff got angry over not being able to live up to his standards," Parker said. "He wasn't the only one with a temper—I certainly had one—but Jeff just couldn't hide his a lot of the time."

Catching Koufax on this night was another chance to show that he could capably handle a big pitcher in a critical moment. Increasingly excited as the perfect game moved along, his adrenaline surging, Torborg fired the ball back to Koufax between pitches. In the middle of the game, Koufax paused to admonish him: "Will you calm down? You're throwing the ball harder than I am." Later, when asked about the most formidable challenges of the night, Koufax would joke, "The toughest guy to pitch to was Torborg."

But Torborg wanted this nearly as badly as Koufax. The periodic starts that Alston gave him were to end when the pennant race reached its climactic weeks. By then, the manager would want only Roseboro behind the plate. "I'm going with John the rest of the way," Alston told Torborg, who calmly replied, "Sure, John has won for you in the past." Still, the decision stung, if only because it was yet another reminder that he hadn't lived up to the stardom forecast for him. By now his reputation around the league, the good and bad of it, had begun to solidify. "Torborg didn't have much power and wasn't a big hitter, but he was an excellent defensive catcher," recalled his Chicago counterpart that night, Chris Krug.

Krug, a twenty-five-year-old rookie, faced the same doubts as Torborg, the challenge compounded by the high hopes that had been building for him since his teenage years. Born in Los Angeles, a high school star in Riverside and a product of Southern California youth ball, where his rivals had included Wes Parker, Krug wanted to succeed in front of a crowd that included many friends and family members.

But he committed a key error. It happened in the fifth inning, after Lou Johnson walked to become the first baserunner of the game. Soon standing on second base, thanks to a Fairly sacrifice bunt, Johnson next tried to steal third. Krug fired the ball toward Santo, but his throw was high. Johnson took away any chance of Santo leaping up to reach the ball by sliding hard and getting tangled up with the third baseman's legs. The ball sailed into left field, and the Dodgers had manufactured a run. It would be the only run of the game. "I ran home and we had what we needed," Johnson said. "We did what we always did: we ran, we stole a base."

Krug felt awful. He was certain that Johnson would've been out if his throw had been accurate. He thought he had let down the Cubs pitcher, twenty-six-year-old journeyman Bob Hendley, who would give up only one hit the entire night—an opposite-field bloop double by Johnson just over the outstretched glove of first baseman Banks. Although Hendley would later try to convince an apologetic Krug that it wasn't his fault, the catcher had already begun beating himself up. He would spend the rest of the game trying to atone for it.

In the sixth inning, Krug came to bat for the second time against Koufax. Working the count to two balls and two strikes, he saw another Koufax fastball and hit a sharp ground ball to shortstop, where Wills fielded it cleanly and turned in the direction of Parker at first base. "I was not a fast runner, so Wills had time," Krug recounted. "But then he hurried his throw."

Wills's toss fell alarmingly short of first base. As Krug ran down the line, he saw the ball in his peripheral vision. "It was in the dirt, at least a good foot to a foot and a half in front of Wes," remembered Krug, who felt a rush of excitement as he neared the bag, thinking the Dodgers' mistake might be the Cubs' opening. At that instant he glimpsed Parker—his old rival from their Pony League days—stretching and plucking the ball out of the dirt. "Wes just *picked it*—I was rung out on a bang-bang play, very close," Krug added. "I don't think many first basemen could've made that play. But that was Wes."

Some journalists present that night thought that Parker, in averting disaster, had helped to save the masterpiece. Having overlooked Davis's play, United Press International declared that the only threat to the perfect game had come on Krug's grounder: "Wills' throw to first base was into the dirt, but Wes Parker made a scoop pick up to retire the Cub catcher." The *Los Angeles Times* said, "Parker had to make a pickup catch" of the low throw.

Characteristically, Parker would have no memory of doing anything exceptional. Having executed the same pickup countless times, his mind made no note of it. A half century later, upon hearing of Krug's observation, he radiated puzzlement: "Chris said that? I don't remember it really." What he better recalled was the tension in the air. Even Parker, always so confident with his glove, was not eager to have the ball bouncing his way.

In the late innings, Alston wanted his best defensive players on the field. Kennedy prepared to replace Gilliam at third base in the eighth inning by warming up in the tunnel with Ferrara, whose anxious pacing around the dugout drew the attention of Vin Scully during the announcer's play-by-play account.

Alston made another change. Tracewski would take over in the ninth inning at second base for Lefebvre, who was supportive of the move. Tracewski didn't feel the same enthusiasm. "I wasn't too thrilled to be playing," he recalled. He warmed up by nervously running up and down the runway. When he took the field, he heard Vin Scully's voice coming from transistor radios all over the stadium, which only compounded his stress. "It was torture," he said. "I was a Humpty Dumpty. I was so nervous."

Nothing is good about being a defensive replacement, he thought. *If you make all the plays, well, you were supposed to. If you don't, you're a goat. It's no place for a Humpty Dumpty.* "I was thinking, what if something goes wrong? I know you're supposed to want the ball hit to you, but I didn't."

For the first time in many years, neither did Wills. "You don't want to mess up," he said. "You're hoping the ball will be hit to someone else. If it's coming to me, I want a good hop."

During the final three innings, Koufax would relieve all teammates of the need to make a difficult play. He faced his greatest danger with two outs in the seventh, after falling behind three balls and no strikes to Billy Williams. At that point he had more than a perfect game to worry about, with only a one-run lead and Santo on deck.

He put his next pitch across the middle of the plate. "I tried to throw it as hard as I could down the pike," Koufax told reporters after the game. "I was thinking first of protecting the lead."

After two strikes, Williams flied out to Johnson in left field.

Koufax had never felt stronger all season, he would say later. In the eighth, Santo, Banks, and Browne struck out in quick succession.

Krug was the first Cubs hitter in the ninth. Loosening up in the on-deck circle, he heard Scully describing the scene. By the time he reached the plate, he had tuned out everything except for Koufax. He had nothing to say to Torborg or plate umpire Ed Vargo.

The first pitch was a curveball for a strike. Krug watched it, and Scully called it.

"Torborg told me later that he knew I would be a little more determined because of my throwing error," remembered Krug, who took this to mean that Torborg thought it would be clever for Koufax to take a little off the first pitch, to take advantage of a hyperaggressive Krug. "Torborg was right. I was more motivated. The breaking ball was a good pitch to call. I was looking for a fastball. I wanted to do something badly."

Down a strike, he then saw a fastball and missed it.

No balls, two strikes.

Krug stepped out of the batter's box, took off his helmet, and collected himself. Koufax was throwing harder than ever. But on the good side, nothing about that last pitch had fooled him, Krug thought. He'd just missed it.

He had so quieted his mind by then that he might as well have been with Koufax in an empty stadium. He took a pitch for a ball. Then he fouled off two fastballs, the second one straight back. He'd liked his cut on that last one. His head was right on that swing, he thought.

I'm seeing the ball well. I can do this.

Down at third base, Kennedy was playing close to the foul line. If the score had been 8–0 instead of 1–0, he could have positioned himself closer to the shortstop hole and had a better shot of taking away a ground ball there. But, in need of guarding against an extra-base hit that would place the tying run in scoring position, he had no choice but to hug the line. If Krug hit a shot between shortstop and third, it was going to be a hit—nothing he could do about that. At second base, a nervous Tracewski was shading Krug toward the middle of the diamond. He still didn't want the ball, but if it was hit anywhere near him, he wasn't going to let down Koufax. He heard Scully everywhere around him. He felt like there were 29,000 radios in the ballpark.

Torborg could hear and feel nothing but his thumping heart. He called for another fastball to Krug.

Koufax threw a rising heater.

Outside.

Ball two.

The crowd groaned.

The collective roar blew down the sound wall Krug had erected. He suddenly heard everything. "It was loud. They wanted a strike."

Scully told his listeners, "A lot of people in the ballpark now are starting to see the pitches with their hearts. The pitch was outside. Torborg tried to pull it over the plate, but Vargo, an experienced umpire, wouldn't go for it. Two-and-two the count to Chris Krug."

Krug made the stadium quiet again.

And Koufax was into his windup.

Krug saw the fastball well as it left Koufax's hand. He liked everything about it. He especially liked its location, which was right in line with the bottom of his knees and a bit on the inside part of the plate, in his power zone.

Fifty years later, he would still be able to see it. Every time he replays the image in his head, every time he begins swinging at it, he thinks, *I'm right on it.*

"I remember what I was thinking as it was coming. I'm thinking, 'I'm gonna hit the snot out of this thing.' My head was *on* that swing. I felt like Superman.

"I swung right through it."

He heard roars.

"I still can't believe I missed it. I had one hellacious swing. If I'd hit it, it would've been a home run."

One out.

The first of two pinch hitters, the right-handed Joe Amalfitano, stepped into the batter's box. Scully reminded listeners that Amalfitano was a former Giants bonus baby. At thirty-one, Amalfitano, a utility man in his playing twilight, had never enjoyed a great career. But Torborg and other Dodgers were leery of him. Amalfitano had beaten them earlier in the season with a liner off a fastball, so Torborg would make sure that, at some point in this at-bat, Amalfitano was forced to contend with a breaking ball.

In a hurry, Koufax overwhelmed Amalfitano. He threw a fastball for a strike, a curve that was tapped foul, and another fastball for strikeout number 13.

Two outs.

The Dodger infielders would do nothing different now. Outwardly, Tracewski, Kennedy, and Wills affected the calm of men going about their ordinary business. But their jitters had some of them contemplating nightmarish scenarios. What if there was a terrible hop on a grounder? What if they had to make a long throw? Silently Wills pleaded for another strikeout, while preparing to do anything to help Koufax. He decided he would dive at any hard ground ball in the hole and come up throwing, not hesitating for an instant, just unloading from his knees if necessary. Across the diamond at first base, Parker smoothed the infield dirt around him with a foot before settling into his stance. In moments of intense pressure, he immersed himself in routine.

Among them all, only Tracewski permitted himself to marvel. He couldn't help it. This was his close friend on the mound, and he realized his friend was an out away from ascending to a rarefied place in baseball history. Now, just as in Philadelphia a year earlier, he thought for an instant that, in his dominance, Koufax seemed alone. He had struck out the last five Cubs. Chicago couldn't touch him, a good thing, thought Tracewski, relieved that he hadn't seen a fair ball since entering the game. But a bad bounce and all this could be ruined, he realized. And the Cub's next pinch hitter, who had begun walking toward the plate, was no Humpty Dumpty.

The Cubs' last threat was thirty-four-year-old Harvey Kuenn—the same Kuenn who, during the infamous 1962 playoff loss to the Giants, had hit the seemingly certain double-play ground ball to Wills for which second baseman Larry Burright had been shifted out of position by Leo Durocher. Kuenn sparked all kinds of bad memories and spooky omens. A former Rookie of the Year and ten-time All-Star who, in 1959, had led the American League in hitting with a .353 average, Kuenn had gone from being a star to an aging role player. But few hitters could possibly have known more about how best to give himself a shot of scratching out a base hit. Koufax had every reason to fear him.

One of the few players on the field who sounded highly doubtful about Harvey Kuenn's chances was Harvey Kuenn. "See you soon," he said to Amalfitano, as the latter man headed back to the dugout. But Torborg knew Kuenn was a battler. "He wasn't afraid," Torborg said.

During that last at-bat, witnesses saw and felt different things. Torborg reminded himself of a fundamental: *Hold on to the ball.* Tracewski heard Scully's voice booming louder than ever. Sandy's got 'em, come on now, Lou Johnson thought.

In Aisle 27, Row S, Marti Allen shared Johnson's sense of inevitability. "I just thought Sandy was going to do it," she said, fifty years later. "That's just what our team did. That's just what happened in Los Angeles. We won. We always won."

Koufax threw a quick strike to Kuenn.

Now the fate of his masterpiece hinged on his ability to keep his nerve. He was, if anything, suddenly working too quickly, and throwing harder than ever. On his next pitch, he threw too hard. Overstriding toward the plate, he unleashed a fastball high out of the strike zone.

"He really forced that one," Scully told his listeners. "That's only the second time tonight where I have had the feeling that Sandy threw instead of pitched."

The strain of the pitch sent Koufax's cap tumbling off his head. But the moment forced him to slow down. He bent, picked up his cap, put it back on, and paused to collect himself before pushing toward the finish.

His final pitch was a 2–2 fastball.

"Swung on and missed—a perfect game," yelled Scully, who then stopped talking for nearly forty seconds, letting the roar fill his broadcast. When he next spoke, it was to let his listeners know where all this had happened. He referenced the city that Marti and others—natives and transplants alike—viewed as the land of dreams. It was his home now, too. "On the scoreboard in right field," the former New Yorker solemnly intoned, "it is 9:46 p.m. in the City of the Angels, Los Angeles, California."

The interviewed players sounded like they had won a World Series. Later, newspapermen would hear from both teams. Sounding more like a teammate than an opponent, Ernie Banks said of Koufax, "The man was just great. It was beautiful." A beaming Koufax answered every question. He made time to praise teammates and pose for pictures with Lou Johnson before saying, "Don't forget the other fellow did a pretty good job out there . . . we were lucky to get the run we did." This was a sympathetic reference to Bob Hendley, who had arguably hurled the best one-hitter ever from a losing pitcher.

Hendley, who had been down in the minor leagues earlier that year, was doing just fine, receiving what would turn out to be his only moment in the spotlight. The man suffering was Hendley's catcher, who couldn't forget his unfortunate throw. After the final out, Krug sat alone in the Cubs' first-base dugout, watching the Dodgers celebrate on the field. Numb, he didn't move for twenty minutes. "Not until Kuenn struck out did I accept it was over," he remembered, in 2014. "Then the wind gets knocked out of you. I knew I'd made the throwing error that had cost us the game. . . . The fault was mine. One bad throw did all that to me. People like Hendley couldn't have been more understanding. But it stuck with me; it was kind of a struggle."

Late in 1965, Krug mentioned it in passing to Torborg. During that winter, he found himself at a Palm Springs charity golf tournament when Koufax walked up to him. "I guess Torborg said something, because Sandy was kind of concerned," recounted Krug, who was moved that Koufax would make time to talk to someone he really didn't know. "Sandy just told me, 'It wasn't your fault—it was a tough play.' He wanted to make sure I understood that. It mattered to him. Sandy didn't talk about himself or the game. He just wanted me to know what he thought about my play: '*not your fault*.' He was trying to bolster me. I just basically said, 'Thanks—I appreciate it.' But you never forget something like that. You think to yourself, So that's Koufax."

Torborg felt his life had changed, too. In the first days after the game, Scully jokingly dubbed him "The Perfect Catcher." For a little while he enjoyed a new stature. A celebrity couple, Cary Grant and Dyan Cannon, reached out to him via a telegram: "Congratulations on the perfect game . . ."

After their retirements, Torborg began making a point of calling Koufax—whom he frequently calls "Sanford" in private—nearly every year on the anniversary of the perfect game. "When you're not around, Sanford, I take credit for it," Torborg said one year.

"So I've heard," Koufax answered.

But they don't talk much about the game. Even around the elites he encounters on those rare occasions when he consents to being honored somewhere, Koufax resists being lured into a discussion of his no-hitters. The impression left is that of a man weary of being caged in the 1960s. At the White House, after he was feted along with others during Jewish American Heritage Month in May 2010, a young guest excitedly told him that a close family member had seen him pitch his 1962 no-hitter against the Mets. Koufax, recounted someone with knowledge of the conversation, "looked stricken." The subject was hastily dropped.

I have some sense of what that exchange was like. In 2009 Koufax called me, in response to my request for an interview about Wills, who was the subject of a newspaper story I was writing at the time. At the start of our discussion, he clarified a point: he wanted to answer only those questions related to Wills, whom Koufax wished to see elected to the Hall of Fame. He then spoke for about twenty minutes in illuminating detail about Wills's career and their close friendship, along the way making a few passing references to other Dodgers, including Tommy Davis and Wes Parker.

At some point, I mentioned that I'd attended the perfect game as a kid.

There was an uncomfortable pause. He didn't voice irritation over my rather transparent attempt to get him to talk about a subject that was supposed to be off the table. He didn't sigh or cluck his tongue or do any of the things that annoyed subjects sometimes do. In fact, he didn't speak at all. There was complete silence on the other end of the phone for several uneasy seconds, until I got the point and changed the subject. Then, as if nothing unusual had just happened, he answered more questions about Wills, thus supremely tactful in rebuffing me and moving on. Nonetheless, the moment served as a reminder that for the time being at least he'd closed the book on any lengthy interview about the perfect game or his life, closed it as certainly as J. D. Salinger had closed himself off from talking about *The Catcher in the Rye* or anything else. And that should be no surprise. We ought to allow the men we turn into deities to have their sanctuaries.

n Texas, the fervent sports fan Bob Oswald knew well of Sandy
Koufax's successes during the mid-1960s. Bob's life had changed
considerably since that family Thanksgiving back in 1962, when he'd
happily spent time with his kid brother and talked a little about football. Within a year after the dinner, people he'd never met—complete
strangers, journalists, social commentators—regularly referred to him
by his formal name, Robert Oswald. Nearly always by then, they identified his kid brother not as Lee Oswald but as Lee Harvey Oswald,
appending that extra name for the same reason that Lincoln's assassin
never would be merely John Booth—infamy invites flourishes; history books need villains to be as big as their atrocities.

Bob mourned his dead brother, though he believed there was no
question that Lee had murdered John F. Kennedy on November 22,
1963, and acted alone in doing it. After the assassination, he gave himself two weeks to grieve over the madness before returning to his sales
job at the brick company outside Dallas. All over the country, Oswalds
unrelated to his family were changing their names for fear of becoming lepers. But as a matter of pride in his father, grandfather, and an-
cestors whose roots in America dated to colonial times, Bob refused.

On orders from Lyndon Johnson, Bob, his wife, Vada, and their
two children, Cathy and Robert Jr., had received Secret Service protection for a couple of weeks after the assassination. Then they were
on their own.

The world was a decent place, Bob thought, if you gave it a chance.
During the following summer, his company transferred him about
two hours away to north Texas and the small city of Wichita Falls,
one day to be a preseason training camp of Bob's beloved Cowboys.
He would still be there with his wife more than a half century later,
in no small part because, as his friends would attest, Bob Oswald
couldn't have sparked more admiration from local residents moved by
the quiet decency with which he had lived his life.

After the horrors of November 1963, he derived solace and strength from everyday pleasures. He loved any time he spent with his children and Vada. He enjoyed fishing, hunting, golfing, taking a walk, and turning on the television to take in a ball game or a golf tournament. He traveled down to Dallas to see a Cowboys game in the middle 1960s, a thrill that lifted his spirits. The smallest things could make him feel a little better and take his mind off the nightmares for a while. "Football, baseball, playing some golf—it could be anything," he remembered. "Whatever it was, it got you doing something; you were concentrating on that. Seeing a game on TV: it was always good for me. Any sport helped when I was going through things."

Some athletes stood out to him. He liked watching the New Zealand golfer Bob Charles and Koufax for much the same reason: they were left-handers, and Bob was naturally left-handed (though he had taught himself to throw and golf right-handed).

"Koufax was special to watch," he said. "Oh, my goodness—Koufax was good."

But Bob Oswald, with his twang that was equal parts Texan and Cajun, did not say the word "good" quite like this. When talking about Koufax, he put an emphasis on the word, so that the line sounded like this:

"Oh, my goodness—Koufax was *goooooooood*."

And anyone or anything that good made him feel a little better. "It didn't get better than Koufax."

Sports served as a slice of tranquillity. Some years later, Bob would finally cross paths with his favorite Yankee. He was at a Houston-area golf course, at a promotional event, when he met Mickey Mantle at a tee box. They spoke briefly. "It was mostly like any moment between a star and a fan, I guess," Bob remembered. "That's what made it special. It was just very easy, very casual and natural."

Watching Koufax, meeting Mantle, seeing a Cowboys game, playing a round of golf, relaxing with his fishing pole by a stream: each of the moments lifted Bob Oswald. They spoke of the power of athletics and recreation, along with that of family and close friends, he thought, to help a hurting man momentarily put aside miseries never to be forgotten, and to slowly heal, to move on. As time passed, the small pleasures of watching a game reminded him of the daily wonders of life. That was the greatest value of baseball and athletics during the turbulent 1960s: the big games were totems of normalcy, reminders that the good times hadn't altogether disappeared. "Koufax was gooooooood," Bob Oswald said. "Mantle was gooooooood. You never forgot that. It was all a good thing."

The most memorable pennant races are all about streaks, the good and the ugly. During the afternoon of September 4, 1965, the Giants embarked on a 14-game winning streak. San Francisco's spectacular run gave the team a hefty 4½-game lead over the Dodgers and Reds, with only 16 games left for the Giants. In a span of about two weeks, the Dodgers' chances had gone from excellent to terrible.

But the Dodgers captured 15 of their final 16 games. Koufax and Drysdale each had 4 victories in the final two weeks. Koufax threw shutouts in 3 of his final 5 starts, closing the year with 26 wins. On October 2 at Dodger Stadium, pitching with only two days of rest, he struck out thirteen and beat the Braves, 3–1, in the pennant-clinching triumph.

That Koufax was pitching again with so little rest carried risks. But the last two years had involved nothing but risk. Now he was ending the regular season with league-leading numbers in the three major pitching categories, his victories burnished by his 2.04 ERA and his major-league record 382 strikeouts. He had thrown eight shutouts, and if anyone in the Dodger front office were ever again to raise the matter of durability, he had led the league with 335⅔ innings pitched.

Yet immediately after securing the pennant, he focused much of his attention on the man almost no one in Los Angeles had known at the season's start, the one who had a caught a fly ball for the game's final out. Koufax gave Lou Johnson a hard hug and whispered something to him.

"He said he was proud of me," Lou Johnson remembered. "He said they couldn't have won it without me. It was one of the best moments of my life—this is my friend Sandy telling me. Here I was thinkin' when the season started that I was gonna be out of baseball, and now we're goin' to the Series? We didn't celebrate long. That wasn't the Dodgers. We had to win. We always had to win."

The opening game of the 1965 World Series against the Minnesota Twins took place in Minneapolis on Wednesday, October 6, the same day, coincidentally, as Yom Kippur. This meant Koufax wouldn't pitch the game, couldn't pitch the game. His teammates hardly could have been more casually supportive about it. Nothing had changed, they pointed out to anybody who asked. Koufax had never pitched on Yom Kippur.

Koufax's quiet decision had won him admirers around the country, including Mudcat Grant, the ace of the Twins' pitching staff. Yet as the Twins' Game 1 starting pitcher, who had led the American League with twenty-one victories and six shutouts, Grant was disappointed not to have a chance to compete against Koufax.

The man who breakfasted with John F. Kennedy had contemplated the social significance of a black American pitcher sharing the World Series stage with a Jewish American pitcher for the first time. It would be an American milestone, he thought. That it wouldn't happen now was a bit of a letdown.

With Koufax out of Game 1, Grant shifted his focus to Drysdale, who would be the Dodger starter. "I knew I'd be in a dogfight with Drysdale," he recalls. "He didn't get as much attention as Koufax, but he was another great pitcher. He was known even in the American League for pitching hitters tight, for giving them a close shave. It wasn't going to be easy for us."

Although oddsmakers regarded the Dodgers as slight favorites to capture the Series, the power-hitting Twins, who had won a hefty 102 regular-season games, were confident. The American League leader in team batting average and runs scored, Minnesota had six players who hit fifteen or more home runs in 1965. Their shortstop and leadoff batter, Zoilo Versalles, who won the American League's Most Valuable Player Award that season, had slugged 19 homers. Third baseman Harmon Killebrew, nicknamed "Killer," had hit 25; left fielder Bob Allison, 23; first baseman Don Mincher, 22; and outfielder Jimmie Hall, 20. Then there was the fabulous left-handed-hitting Tony Oliva, who, in addition to his 16 homers, had led the American League in hitting at .321, on the verge of becoming a superstar. Oliva had driven in 98 runs, merely one of five Twins with more than 70 RBIs. The Twins were loaded.

Grant believed he had identified the two biggest keys to winning the Series. "We knew we had to keep Maury off the bases, because he could score runs all by himself," he said. "And we knew at some point in the Series we were going to have to beat Sandy, at least once."

Playing before a national television audience, he thought, would also be another opportunity for him and the Twins' All-Star catcher Earl Battey to show what an all-black battery could do, in the process perhaps lancing a few more stubborn prejudices.

The Twins triumphed in the opener, as Grant went the distance and became the first African American pitcher to win a World Series game for an American League club. Aside from Wills getting a pair of hits and Fairly hitting a solo homer, the Dodgers' bats were quiet. The Twins teed off on Drysdale in the third inning, scoring six times, the biggest blow coming on Versalles's three-run homer. Alston had seen enough, quickly removing Drysdale, with the Twins on their way to an 8–2 rout.

It rained on the morning of Game 2. An hour and a half before the game's start, it was still cold and damp in Minneapolis, the worst possible conditions for Koufax, who had trainers slather an abundance of Capsolin over his shoulder and back. No one might have ever known exactly how much had it not been for the Twins' Game 2 starter, left-hander Jim Kaat, who, while posing alongside Koufax for the pregame photo of the starting pitchers, felt his eyes involuntarily watering and his nostrils filling with the fumes of the Capsolin. Kaat had used a similar treatment a few times himself, but never as much as Koufax had. This was unbelievable, he thought. He couldn't help himself. He began sniffling.

"Whooooooo," he exclaimed.

As Kaat remembers, Koufax said softly, "I've got two tubes of that stuff on me."

Photographers from newspapers and the wire services clicked away as Kaat and Koufax went through the World Series ritual of the starting pitchers' pregame handshake. The two men said little to each other, never having met before. "Players didn't know each other as well in those days," Kaat explained. "Agents hadn't come along yet, so nobody shared the same agents or had similar endorsements. There wasn't much chatter. Shake hands and then you play."

A disturbing possibility had struck the nervous Kaat. Before the game, he shared it with the Twins' pitching coach, Johnny Sain: "I give up a run today and the game might be over."

But Kaat pitched superbly. The game was scoreless into the bottom of the sixth, when Gilliam committed a two-base error on a Versalles grounder and Oliva doubled Versalles home. A Killebrew single scored Oliva, and the Twins and Kaat were cruising to a 5–1 victory. If they could win Game 3 in Los Angeles, the Dodgers were almost certainly finished.

The Dodgers knew it, too. On the plane ride home, one Dodger after another approached the only pitcher who could save them now from a swift demise.

Claude Osteen, who had won fifteen games that year in his first year with the club, was resting in a center-aisle seat, next to his wife. Teammates came by to exhort him. By the time the plane landed in Los Angeles, Osteen had so much adrenaline coursing through him that he was ready to pitch. "I was a nervous wreck," he recalled. "But I knew I'd been six–oh against the Twins when I was with the Senators. I think that gave me confidence. I relaxed as the game got closer."

Osteen threw a five-hitter at home, and the Dodgers won, 4–0.

The next afternoon Mudcat Grant, ready to pitch against Drysdale again, met Doris Day, with whom he fell into a quick chat by the box seat railing.

"We're going to get you today," she said, as he remembers.

An amused Grant loved it: Doris Day trash-talking. Doris Day trash-talking to *him*. What do you even say to Doris Day? He thought it over and kept it simple: "No, you're not."

Day chose to interpret this as a dare. "That's a bet."

What were they going to bet?

She thought a hot dog sounded right.

Fine. A hot dog.

What a city this was: celebrities chatting you up, making bets.

It occurred to Grant he still had a game to pitch.

The Dodgers had a new starting infielder for Game 4. Just as in 1963, when an injury to a regular had forced him into the World Series starting lineup against the Yankees, Tracewski found himself back at second base. The rookie Lefebvre had badly bruised his heel the day before and couldn't run.

Tracewski felt awful for Lefebvre. The kid was going to be the National League's Rookie of the Year. He deserved to be playing. The game never stopped dishing out bad breaks, he thought.

Neither man knew it, but Lefebvre had played his last inning in the Series.

Lefebvre's absence wouldn't help Grant on this day. In the fourth inning, with the Dodgers already leading, 2–1, Parker hit a fastball for a homer and the Dodgers began rolling, with Drysdale winning, 7–2. The teams were even now, at two games apiece. The next day, paying off on their bet, a smiling Grant presented a grilled hot dog on a bun to a happy Doris Day as photographers snapped away.

That afternoon Koufax won Game 5, shutting out Minnesota and

Kaat, 7–0. The Twins trailed three games to two, as the two teams headed back to Minneapolis for Game 6.

The Dodgers announced that Osteen, fresh off his shutout, would be their starting pitcher. One game away from elimination, the Twins believed they had no choice but to turn to Grant, who pitched magnificently on only two days of rest, hurling another complete game and beating the Dodgers, 5–1. He had evened the Series at three games apiece.

Never had Grant felt so good about baseball or his place in it. He'd even blasted a three-run homer that day against Dodger reliever Howie Reed, the first time in forty-five years that an American League pitcher had homered in a Series.

Within an hour, Grant and his teammates had begun thinking about Game 7. Would it be Drysdale or Koufax? If Koufax pitched, he would be working with only two days of rest. By his own admission, the season had worn Koufax down. When asked after Game 5 how he felt, he had confessed: "Like I'm a hundred years old." Logic indicated he was a risk now. Logic said his curveball might not have its normal bite; his fastball might be a touch slower, and his control over his pitches suspect.

"To hell with logic," Johnson recalls thinking.

Even many of Drysdale's devoted admirers on the team privately wished for Koufax. "The night before, we'd thought, how are we going to score seven or eight runs to beat those guys?" Parker recalled. "When we heard Sandy was pitching, I thought, Maybe we'll only need to score one run to win."

Drysdale made the choice easy on everyone. Accompanied by Roseboro, he went to Alston after Game 6 and urged that Koufax be the starter, volunteering to go to the bullpen.

The next morning, both Drysdale and Koufax arrived at the ballpark unshaven, the way of pitchers believing there is a serious chance they might start a ball game. Whether Drysdale, after his initial suggestion that Koufax be the pitcher, was in the dark about what Alston already had decided is unclear. Gathering his players before the game, Alston told them that he would "start the left-hander."

When the meeting ended, Tracewski said to Koufax, He didn't even say your name.

No, he didn't, Koufax said.

"That rubbed Sandy the wrong way," said Tracewski, who believed that Koufax regarded Alston's announcement as yet another slight in a relationship that "wasn't going to be warm and fuzzy ever."

In the last hour before the game, everyone prepared in his own way. Wills was grateful to do a taped interview to be used in NBC's game telecast. It might help him, he thought, put his hopes and tensions into proper perspective. He desperately wanted to win. No one, aside from Koufax perhaps, needed this as much, he imagined. Sometimes he thought he lived for winning alone. He'd given so much. Winning seemed the only fair and logical outcome. *We have to win. We will win.*

Wills was exhausted. If you're in a seven-game World Series, you're playing roughly 190 games from the start of spring training, he figured—what with all those intrasquad contests and exhibition games they make you play, it's too much for a body, it just seems like it never ends. But it does end. You play so hard for seven months, and it all begins to blur, and then you're asked to settle it with one game? *One?* With his thoughts formulated, he went out and gave the NBC people a statement. He kept it as short and upbeat as he could. A half century later, he wouldn't be able to recall precisely what he said. But he remembered the gist of it, and how it summed up his torment at that moment, and how he had boiled it all down to expressing his pride in his teammates and why they should all be proud, no matter what happened that day.

He said this to NBC: "When Tommy Davis broke his leg in May, we knew that it would be a tough season ahead for us. We had to scratch for everything. Regardless of how the game comes out today, I feel that every player on the club should be proud of the season that we've had."

He wondered how his teammates, particularly the younger ones, were holding up. Parker was playing well, on his way to hitting over .300 in the Series. His defense had been superb. In Game 6, he had made a sprawling backhanded grab of a lined bouncer off the bat of Earl Battey that was headed down the right-field line, robbing the Twin of an extra-base hit.

But Parker remained as terrified as ever about his hitting. What if he failed in a crucial at-bat with the Series on the line? Would he ever survive it? *I cannot fail.* "I thought I had to be the guy to do something extra," he remembers. On the team's flight back to Minneapolis before Game 6, he poured out his worries to Drysdale, who provided reassurance, telling Parker he had to do nothing more than to play his usual game; that everything would be okay. It was like a mantra by then. *You're going to be fine*, Drysdale repeated. Parker wasn't sure. Besides his emotional havoc, he was physically worn down after seven months of ball, playing at twenty pounds under his normal weight. He had doubts that he could handle a first-rate fastball any longer.

Lou Johnson, who was having a good Series in which he'd homered once already and was hitting around .300, had no doubts. He couldn't wait to play Game 7. The night before, after happily hearing that Koufax would likely be pitching, he'd hung out with old friends visiting from Kentucky. It moved him to think they'd made the trip all the way up from little Paris, Kentucky, to give him their support. Their night together had been a good one, so good that his morning was slow in getting started. He was late getting to Metropolitan Stadium. Incredibly, he missed a large portion of batting practice.

"Where the fuck have you been?" Alston demanded.

Johnson was already scared. He offered a rushed explanation. He could tell Alston was buying none of it. If anything, the older man was getting angrier.

Johnson wondered what was about to happen. "I always seemed to have one foot in the grave and one foot on the banana peel," he recalls. "Here it was again."

"You little son of a bitch," Alston snapped.

Johnson had never seen Alston so upset. That the two men got past the moment had less to do with anything Johnson said than it did with Alston's utter lack of choices. On a team with so little power and only a few reliable bats, Johnson would need to be Alston's cleanup hitter in Game 7.

Be ready, Alston snapped and walked away.

"I was still kind of shook up a little," Johnson remembered. "But nothing was going to get in my way that day. I'd worked too hard. Walt Alston had done a lot for me. I didn't want to let him down. Didn't want to let the team down."

Before the game, he telephoned his mother in Kentucky. She told him she had said a prayer for him and would be watching the game. No conversation could've stirred him more. His odyssey had taken thirteen years and carried him to eighteen teams, but here was the proof he had made it, he thought: his mother would be seeing him on a television.

Shortly before game time, he went down into the visitors' clubhouse to be alone for a few minutes.

The reserves were doing what they could to help others. Torborg warmed up Koufax out in the visitors' bullpen in right-center field. It was only 60 degrees, but Koufax didn't seem to have any difficulty getting warm, he thought. Even on only two days of rest, he basically looked okay. But you just never knew, Torborg realized.

Koufax finished his warm-up, put on his Dodger windbreaker, headed out of the bullpen, and made the long walk across the outfield toward the Dodgers' third-base dugout, where teammates waited for him. Johnson had never felt so ready. It was hard to explain, he would say later. He just felt so lucky to be there. So damn happy. He was going to be a part of this game somehow.

A record Metropolitan Stadium crowd of 50,596 filled every seat. The two teams were ready now. On the mound, Kaat finished the last of his warm-up tosses, and Wills prepared to step into the batter's box. At that instant on Thursday, October 14, 1965, as Game 7 began, contentment reigned in most of America. With creeping worries about Southeast Asia and the troubled, sometimes burning cities, no one at that moment could have reasonably called 1965 a year of innocence. Yet never again in the '60s would the country feel this carefree. It wasn't because of anything that was happening. Rather it was because of all the things that had yet to happen. Five hundred thousand American troops had yet to arrive in Vietnam. There had been no protest marches on the Pentagon. There had been no revolts in the ghettos of Detroit and Newark. There had been no takeovers of university administration buildings, no sit-down protests on Wilshire Boulevard, no mass burning of draft cards. There had been no rise of the SDS, the Weathermen, or the Black Panthers. There had been no televised shots of police officers beating antiwar protesters on the streets of downtown Chicago during a political convention, no loud chants from protesters that "the whole world is watching." There was no reason yet to know Jerry Rubin, Abbie Hoffman, Yippies, Eldridge Cleaver, or Huey Newton. James Earl Ray and Sirhan Sirhan were not names that provoked tears. Few in the nation had ever heard of LSD. Haight-Ashbury had yet to become a state of mind.

It was all coming.

No one knew it, but tumult was speeding toward the Dodgers, too, along with every other team in major-league baseball. The game that was about to begin in Minnesota would be the last in the sport's history played under the old assumption of how things were supposed to work—of how players were to be reflexively subservient to management's whims, of how players were to be grateful just to have the chance to play, of how one-year contracts were a player's fate because an owner said so, of how a player couldn't leave a team on his own because baseball said so.

By the following spring, players and a surprising new leader would take the first organized steps to resist. The established order of dominance in baseball would be toppled within another decade, the change to turn on its head the fundamental relationship between owners and players.

The change would come too late for most of these Dodgers. The greatest pitcher who ever lived would never make as much as $150,000. Had he been born fifteen years later, he would've earned tens of millions. In future generations, many stars would make more in salary for one game than Koufax would make during an entire 162-game season.

But Koufax achieved one thing that future stars wouldn't: he'd arrived at an ideal point in history to become unforgettable, a moment when baseball was still for a while longer the leading sport in the country, and America still yearned for athletic deities from its ranks.

Having won the rights to telecast the Series, NBC, through Vin Scully, trumpeted the network's pride in bringing "America's Game" that day to the entire country. The only pregame suspense turned on the Dodgers' choice of a starting pitcher. Less than a half hour before the game, NBC broke the news to a rapt country: it would be Koufax.

On such days, for better or worse, players' reputations can be forever sealed. Koufax was about to deliver a performance that would take its place alongside his 1963 World Series domination of the Yankees in New York, and his perfect game, as his third and final masterpiece—and the strongest evidence of his brilliance. He would do it without proper rest or his best stuff.

He was in the dugout now, prepared to go, looking out toward the diamond, where Wills was ready to hit. NBC was ready, too. For the Series, the network had hired the two teams' top play-by-play broadcasters—Scully and another giant of sports broadcasting, the Twins' Ray Scott, best known as the voice of the Green Bay Packers. Like Scully, Scott had a style all his own. He had built a reputation as the Packers' broadcaster for the economy of his descriptions, which were so sparse at times as to be reducible to a few words: "Starr. . . . McGee. . . . Touchdown." He was as huge in the Midwest as Scully was in California. Each man had powerful gifts of observation and analysis, to go along with an abhorrence of partisanship. Their expertise rivaled the players'. Viewers could scarcely be in better hands. Scott would announce the first half of the game; Scully the last half. As NBC's cameras locked in on the Dodger captain, Scott told viewers, "The Dodger leadoff batter is Maury Wills. He has had a great Series. He has eleven hits in twenty-six at-bats; he has knocked in three runs; he has stolen three bases."

As Scott spoke, a rolling graphic on the bottom of television screens informed viewers that Wills was the Series' leading hitter through six games, batting .423. NBC ran the tape of Wills's short, stoic statement.

Kaat threw a pitch inside for a ball, and Game 7 was under way.

From the start, Kaat nibbled at the plate. Wills was called out on a fastball that caught the outside corner. In the bottom of the first, Koufax quickly encountered problems, showing the effects of an arm handicapped by scant rest. Although he struck out the leadoff man, Versalles, and watched the Twins' young center fielder Joe Nossek ground out to Wills, he was already fighting to control his curveball. With two outs, he walked Oliva and Killebrew. For the Twins to tally the first run, in what was expected to be a low-scoring game, would be huge, Kaat thought. Oliva stood at second, ready to race home on any base hit. But Koufax struck out Battey on a chest-high fastball to end the inning. He had escaped his first jam.

Thereafter, he was without a functional curveball.

In the third inning, Versalles hit a high hanging curve to center field for a leadoff base hit. Scott told the national audience: "I think Sandy tried to turn that one over. But *nothing* happened."

The fifth inning presented the greatest danger. With one out, Twins second baseman Frank Quilici doubled. Then Twins veteran Rich Rollins, who had seen nothing but fastballs, worked the count to 2–2. Koufax finally threw another curve. It was just out of the strike zone for ball three. Koufax's head jerked in exasperation and Scully, who had taken over in the broadcasting booth, saw it. His voice rose:

"*Curveball*—and he missed with it. And he *wanted it*. That's the first curve he's thrown in quite some time and, oh, did he want it."

A Koufax fastball was well off the plate for ball four. The 50,000 in Metropolitan Stadium howled. The Twins had two runners aboard, with the inning long from over and the big-hitting Versalles coming up.

Scully let viewers know that Koufax now faced steep odds. "So Koufax is struggling. It's almost impossible to do it on one pitch in the big leagues, and he does not have a curveball. . . . Koufax appears to have only the fastball."

Roseboro went out to the mound and—as Tracewski would later recall—coolly talked with Koufax about what they ought to do next, given the curveball's impotence. Koufax finally shrugged—and here, recollections of players like Tracewski, Wills, and others slightly diverge. All remember Koufax essentially saying he would turn to his fastball to get them out of this jam and win the game. What some remember is that, in his resolve, he said this: "We'll just have to fuckin' blow them away."

Before he could pitch to Versalles, he had something else to think about.

Alston was walking to the mound.

Drysdale was throwing in the bullpen.

Drysdale had already warmed up amid Koufax's struggles in the first and third innings. Drysdale was ready to go, if Alston wanted him.

Alston didn't.

No matter what else would ever be said about the Koufax-Alston relationship, the two men showed each other enormous respect in such moments. There was a pecking order here that Koufax keenly understood. As Alston spoke to him now, Koufax could be seen dutifully nodding and nodding—sending the signal, consciously or not, that he was on the same page as his manager. For his part, Alston spoke casually. His facial expression and body language evinced a cool leader who had lost no confidence in either his star or anybody else around the mound. He looked no more concerned than a man talking to some people on a street corner. As he would recall later, he simply urged Koufax "to pitch your normal way," not to try too hard, because that was when pitchers tended to make mistakes. It was not an order but a simple, useful reminder. It was basically the same advice Norm Sherry had given Koufax during the 1961 spring training camp, advice that had helped the erratic young pitcher launch his turnaround as a big-leaguer.

Alston nonchalantly turned and walked back to the dugout.

Versalles stepped into the batter's box. No Twins' at-bat that day would prove more important. Having singled in the third inning, Versalles came to the plate with justifiable confidence—Koufax had been no puzzle for him. The Dodgers took special care now to guard against an extra-base hit by having Gilliam play closer to third base, where hopefully he would be better positioned to field a ball hit down the line. If it had been late in the game, the Dodgers would likely have had the excellent glove of Kennedy at third base, rather than Gilliam. While he was the superior offensive player, Gilliam's skills at third base were no match for Kennedy's. Gilliam had the lowest fielding average of all Dodger starters. He had made two errors in Game 2 alone, one of them on a leadoff grounder hit by Versalles that had triggered Koufax's downfall in the game.

Gilliam took a few steps closer to the third-base line.

Koufax was still visibly frustrated by his lack of control. After throwing a fastball high out of the strike zone to Versalles, he conferenced again with Roseboro. He was throwing nothing but fastballs now. With a 1–1 count, Versalles fouled off two more.

But he hit the next one on the button.

It was a grounded shot, headed on a low line over the third-base bag and toward the left-field corner, seemingly certain to score at least one run and perhaps two. But Gilliam reached across his body and made a backhanded stab at the ball, robbing Versalles of an RBI double. Gilliam quickly tagged third base, just ahead of the sliding Quilici, to get the force out.

"Oh, what a play," Scully exclaimed, later declaring that Gilliam had "saved" Koufax.

But there were only two outs, and still two runners on base. At the plate now was the right-handed-hitting Nossek, who felt like he'd had some success against Koufax from their very first encounter in Game 2, when he'd flied out deep to Johnson in left field. He'd gone 1-for-2 against Koufax that day, and 1-for-4 against him in Game 5, on an afternoon when Nossek thought he easily could have gone 3-for-4. ("Maury just nipped me on a ball I hit deep in the hole. And I lined into a double play in the ninth inning—hit it hard. I wasn't a hitter to be feared, so maybe I was getting better pitches to hit than some of the other guys.")

Koufax kept throwing hard fastballs. The first to Nossek was very high for a ball.

"He pressed that time," Scully told his audience. "That was about the second time today that he did not pitch but *threw*. He forced himself on that one."

The next fastball badly missed, too.

"And he forced *that* one," Scully declared.

Nossek knew Koufax couldn't afford to walk him and load the bases. He told himself he was going to get a good pitch to hit with a 2–0 count. For damn sure, it wasn't going to be a curveball.

If any quality about Koufax ever went undervalued, it was his combination of prudence and brains. Fans tend to associate power pitchers with unchecked machismo and ego. But Koufax made a habit of being conspicuously cautious against the game's great hitters; on several occasions he had intentionally walked Hank Aaron rather than be beaten by him. In dicey situations, he took nothing for granted against even the unknown and ordinary player. Hubris never would be permitted to get the best of him. Nossek, who was on his way to hitting .200 in this Series and .218 on the season, would never be confused with Aaron. But any major-league regular, with a 2–0 count and a virtual guarantee that a fastball is coming, becomes a dangerous hitter.

As soon as the pitch left Koufax's hand, Nossek knew it wasn't a curveball, which was a very good thing, because it left only one possibility, he told himself.

Nossek could see the pitch was a little down and moving slightly away from him. But very hittable. He could pull this pitch. It was the predictable fastball.

Nossek's arms started moving. It was very late in his swing when he first realized he had a problem. He was out in front of the pitch—*way out* in front of the pitch.

This wasn't a curve, but it sure as heck wasn't a fastball either, he thought. It was too slow to be a fastball.

Trying to save himself, he attempted to slow down his swing. Only it was much too late—he was already committed. The bat was coming through the strike zone much too quickly to stop it. He couldn't keep his top hand in its proper position on the bat. All his power was spent now, his swing almost complete. He was fortunate just to make contact with the top half of the ball, which he hit weakly on the ground. It was fielded by Wills, who flipped to Tracewski for the force out that ended the inning and the Twins' threat.

For the half century since, during which Koufax has never talked about that at-bat, Nossek has wondered what his foe did exactly.

"I could handle the bat pretty good, but I was young and dumb that day," he recalled. "I had a lot of adrenaline going. I shouldn't have tried to pull the pitch. I should've just gone with it, been patient. But it was a great pitch, a smart pitch. He fooled me pretty completely. But he's Sandy Koufax. I guess that's going to happen." He thought about it some more. It was as confounding as ever to Nossek.

"I still can't be sure what he threw me."

For his part, Kaat badly fooled most of the Dodgers through the first three innings. At the start of the fourth, he faced Johnson, who had put his scolding from Alston out of his head. Kaat had gotten Johnson out in the first inning on an off-speed breaking ball, but now Kaat threw him a fastball on the outer half of the plate, intending for the pitch to be well away from Johnson. But a ball simply thrown on the outer half of the plate to Johnson was, in practical terms, a pitch down the middle, given Johnson's habit of crowding the plate. If you wanted Johnson to see a genuinely outside pitch, you had to place the ball well outside.

"It felt pretty inside to me—and it was between my knee and thigh," Johnson remembered. "Just where you want to go looking for something."

"I tip my cap to him," Kaat reflected. "He stood on top of the plate, and he went out there for the pitch, squared up his shoulders, and he got it. He hooked it."

"Uh-oh," Ray Scott said on NBC as the ball left Johnson's bat.

The blast hit the left-field foul pole for a home run: 1–0, Dodgers.

Metropolitan Stadium went silent. It was impossible for 50,000 people to be quieter.

"You could hear a cat pissin' on cotton after I hit it," Johnson recalled.

"I could actually hear Lou's footsteps as he rounded third base," Tracewski remembered. "It was that silent."

Of course Johnson clapped as he trotted around the bases. One clap as he rounded second base, another as he rounded third, and a last quick one just before touching home. "Nobody was making any sound at all," he remembered. "I might as well clap."

Meanwhile, Kaat couldn't get his mind off what had just happened. Usually, if he held the opposition to a couple of runs, he and the Twins won. But to have given up a mere run in a game against Koufax had put his team in a tough position, Kaat realized.

This sense of foreboding was always an added problem for a pitcher matching up against Koufax. Now, thinking about that run and Koufax, Kaat lost his concentration. Although he didn't know it, he wouldn't be in the game for longer than two more pitches. "You realize you're out there pitching against Sandy Koufax," Kaat recalled, "and you get down a little and lose some of your focus. And you have a little lapse and throw a couple of more pitches and boom, boom, you're out of there."

Fairly and Parker were the next batters.

Fairly, who would end the day with the Dodgers' highest Series average, immediately hit an off-speed pitch into the right-field corner for a double. The Twins' infield prepared next for Parker to lay down a sacrifice bunt. Minnesota's first baseman, Don Mincher, crept in, hoping to field the bunt and throw out Fairly at third base. But, swinging away as a right-handed hitter, Parker hit the first pitch, a sinking fastball. On one big bounce, it went over Mincher's head into right field, driving home Fairly for another run. When Oliva bobbled the ball, Parker took second base.

Kaat felt awful. He already realized the cost of losing focus. Manager Sam Mele walked out to the mound with a wry little smile on his face. The smile said that the fates aren't always fair. Kaat's day was done. He gave Mele the ball and headed off the field.

Parker didn't feel he had done anything special in his at-bat ("I think Mincher would've caught my ball if he wasn't playing in for a bunt"). Yet he was having an outstanding Series, on his way to hitting .304 for the seven games, a full 66 points above his regular season average.

Koufax allowed only one hit over the game's final four innings, retiring eleven Minnesota hitters in a row at one point. Kaat realized that Koufax was doing all this with one pitch, having basically given up on his curveball. The Twins hitters knew it, too. "They were ready for that fastball and they still couldn't hit it," Kaat observed.

While his foes were downcast, Koufax was fidgety as he began the ninth with a 2–0 lead. He repeatedly tugged at his jersey, grasped the bill of his cap, reached down to touch the resin bag. He had reason to be tense: he would be facing the heart of the Twins' lineup. Scully had left for the Dodgers' clubhouse, in anticipation of doing postgame interviews with the winners.

On television, Ray Scott said, "Meanwhile, the man generally recognized as baseball's greatest pitcher, Sandy Koufax, in the last of the ninth, must face one of the fine hitters in the game, two-time American League batting champion Tony Oliva; one of the premier long-ball hitters in the game, Harmon Killebrew; and another long-ball threat, Earl Battey."

If any of the three batters reached base, Bob Allison would have another chance to bat.

No hitting foursome in the middle of an American League lineup had so routinely beaten up on pitchers during the regular season. But against Koufax in the Series, they collectively hit .179—on seven hits in thirty-nine official at-bats. Of the four, only Killebrew had a measure of success, going 4-for-9 and striking out but once. Koufax enfeebled the remaining three. Oliva had only one hit in nine at-bats against him, striking out five times; Battey went 1-for-11, with three strikeouts; and Allison finished 1-for-10, with seven strikeouts. It was an annihilation of the heart of the Twins' order. But the foursome had one last chance now. Koufax was not yet home. Without his curve or great control, no one could be sure he would get there. Drysdale was throwing again in the bullpen. If Koufax made a single mistake with a runner on base, the Twins might benefit from a wind blowing out to left field at about 10 miles per hour. It could be just enough to turn a warning track fly ball into a game-tying homer.

He would throw fifteen pitches to the foursome in the final inning—fourteen of which would be fastballs. Oliva saw only fastballs, four of them, not one of which he was able to get fully around on. He slowly grounded the last one to John Kennedy, who had taken over from Gilliam at third base.

One out.

Now Killebrew stepped up. Koufax started the slugger with a curve that landed in the dirt. After falling behind in the count, 2–1, he put a fastball down the middle, and Killebrew singled to left. Despite Koufax's earlier crises, and the sense that he had been under siege for half the game, it was only the third hit for the Twins. But it brought the potential tying run to the plate. Tracewski walked to the mound and said something to Koufax ("It was just about how we were positioning guys"). Into the batter's box stepped Earl Battey, who swung at and missed two letter-high fastballs before being frozen on the last one for a called strike three.

Just one out away now. The Dodger infielders thought different things. Wills was pondering the positioning of everyone, as focused on small details as ever.

Kennedy felt fortunate for this opportunity. "I put myself almost right on the third-base line. I wasn't going to allow an extra-base hit."

Parker cleared his mind. "I didn't think about anything more than making a play. I didn't allow myself any indulgence."

"I thought Sandy would get them," Tracewski recalled.

Up came Allison. In the dugout, Claude Osteen was mesmerized. Koufax was not only overpowering these guys, Osteen thought. He was *outthinking* them. Osteen realized that, in an approach that slightly resembled his own, Koufax was now pitching to some batters' strengths, daring them to take a swing at what they thought they liked to hit.

Allison was regarded as a dead high-fastball hitter. The conventional wisdom was that he would hit a high fastball into the Dakotas if anyone was dumb enough to give him one. He had hit a high fastball off Osteen only the day before for a homer. But now Koufax was starting off the at-bat by throwing a high fastball to him. Osteen observed, "It's like Sandy was saying to him, 'Okay, here are some fastballs *up* and a little more *up*. See if you can hit them.'"

Allison was late on the first one, fouling it straight back into the stands. Strike one. Then Koufax threw a pitch inside and high—just under Allison's chin—for a ball.

His next fastball was inside for ball two.

Koufax fidgeted a little more and then looked at Roseboro. He threw the next pitch so hard that he stumbled slightly on his follow-through. But the pitch was exactly where he wanted it, Osteen thought. It was on the outside of the plate—and, in terms of height, was right where any power pitcher trying to tempt a high-ball hitter to swing would want it.

Allison went up and tried to kill it. Strike two.

Koufax was on the pitching rubber. Then, thinking better of it, he stepped off.

Now Koufax bent, touched the resin bag, then straightened upright, stepped back on the rubber, and brought his hands into the stretch position. He hurled another high fastball on the outside part of the plate.

Allison swung and missed.

Ray Scott did not scream *The Dodgers win the World Series*—or anything like it. His voice was solemn. His thoughts were entirely on Koufax.

"He did it," Scott said. "Sandy Koufax gets his tenth strikeout, his second consecutive shutout of the Twins. On Monday, on a four-hitter. Today, on a three-hitter. Every pitcher, of course, likes to finish a game with a strikeout. This, of course, was not *a* game. This was the seventh game of the World Series."

The awed among the Twins included manager Mele, who knew that a single player had accounted for the difference between the two teams. Koufax's statistical line for the Series said as much: only 1 earned run yielded in 24 innings; a microscopic ERA of 0.38. Years later, Kennedy would run into a smiling Mele, who wisecracked, "If there had been one more Jewish holiday, we'd have beaten you guys."

At the moment of victory, Kennedy yelled and ran toward Koufax. Koufax hurried toward no one. On the grass between the mound and the third-base line, Roseboro shook his hand. Koufax smiled broadly but never stopped moving toward the dugout. By then, Kennedy and Wills had converged on him. Parker raced over, ready to see players jumping and piling on each other, eager to join in a raucous celebration.

Except nobody was jumping or piling on anybody, he realized. Noticing the restraint of Koufax and the others, Parker thought, I don't want to make an ass of myself. As others shook Koufax's hand, he patted Koufax's back until the star turned his way and tapped his chest, all the while striding purposefully.

Relief bathed the idol's expression. He looked like nothing so much as a young man who had survived an ordeal. By then, the Dodgers crowding around Koufax included a beaming Alston, who gave him several backslaps and draped an arm around him. Moving, moving. Parker guessed at why guys weren't leaping on each other: this was the team's third World Series championship in the last seven seasons, their second in three seasons. This is just what the Dodgers did.

But he was out of his head with euphoria. The pack spilled into the dugout. An ecstatic Lefebvre and Johnson—like Parker, newcomers to all this—threw their arms around each other. A radiant Drysdale was grinning and embracing people. In the next minute, Koufax was in the visitors' clubhouse.

In the press box of Metropolitan Stadium, a dazzled Jim Murray wrote, "A Koufax-pitched game is a work of art, a tribute to the craftsmanship of Man—like the Kohinoor diamond or a Greek statue."

Scully climbed atop a storage trunk in the clubhouse to do interviews. "Here's the fellow who gave the Dodgers the championship," he said and put an arm around Koufax, who was reminded of his comment about feeling like he was "a hundred years old" after his Game 5 victory.

Scully asked him how he felt now.

"A hundred and one," Koufax said. Smiling, laughing, he swiftly added: "I feel great, Vinny. I know I don't have to go out there for about another four months."

He said he'd had no curveball at all, reduced to trying to place his fastball in tough spots for the Twins. But he'd felt stronger as the game moved along, with his fastball at its best in the closing innings. "Which I didn't figure [happening] on two days rest," he admitted.

He was at his most expansive in talking about Johnson. Sportswriters, he noted, had written off the team after Tommy Davis suffered his injury: "They thought we were going to finish eighth. . . . Lou Johnson, who hit the home run today, came up when Tommy got hurt and did a great job. He carried us for the first ten days to two weeks he was with us. I think that got us over the hump."

Standing nearby, Johnson had never felt so emotional. Koufax stepped off the trunk. "You're the greatest, Sandy," he called out. "You're the greatest, baby." Johnson talked to Scully for a while about his homer before blurting, "I want to cry. But it won't come out."

Eventually Alston walked over. Aside from his smile, he was as stolid as ever; it might as well have been a spring training game in March. Pressed by Scully, he said that starting Koufax over Drysdale had been his toughest decision of the year, before lavishing diplomatic praise on both of the stars: "I'm glad Sandy pitched a great game. . . . Don pitched nine innings in the bullpen."

Parker was blissful. Later, seeing a photograph of himself alongside Koufax, he thought it captured everything: *Look at the smile on my face*. It was nothing less than the best day of his life. In winning, he felt that at last he had climbed out of his personal purgatory. "I made it," he recalls thinking. "Winning this told me I'm not a piece of crap. I thought to myself, I have value—what I've done has value." Opinion among his parents would be divided on this last point. His mother would be unimpressed. "But my dad was so proud. I was a World Series champion. I loved seeing his expression."

No set of interviews for a Dodger broadcaster after the game could be complete without getting a statement from Walter O'Malley, who happily joined Scully on top of the trunk. What followed was notable for what the owner didn't say, and whom he didn't mention. He didn't mention Koufax. He didn't mention Wills or Drysdale. He didn't mention Roseboro or Fairly or Gilliam or Johnson or Parker or Osteen or Lefebvre or Willie Davis or Tommy Davis or any other player.

What O'Malley said to Scully was this: "You never know what's gonna happen with these boys. I wish it could've been finished in Los Angeles so all our wonderful fans out there could've been in on the end of it. But they got the picture. It was a great Series. We're very proud of our manager, our team, and Buzzie. And you, Vinny. And Jerry, too."

"Jerry" was Jerry Doggett, the team's second play-by-play broadcaster.

That week, back at Dodger Stadium, O'Malley hosted a private party for the team in the Stadium Club. Before speaking, he sidled up to Fairly with a smile and said, "Ron, I want you to speak to everybody here on behalf of the players who won't be here next year."

With comments like that, the owner had a unique talent for throwing you off balance, Fairly thought. Most of the time, Fairly much enjoyed bantering with O'Malley, whom he found charming, affably mischievous, and typically very kind in their personal dealings. "When he said something like that to me, it was just his way of agitating," Fairly remembered. Just the same, O'Malley liked to keep everybody a bit on edge. Bavasi did the same thing, only Bavasi got on players' nerves, because his manipulation and tricks came at a cost to players' livelihoods. Fairly didn't know how that arrangement could be changed, only that it couldn't be allowed to last forever.

But you couldn't dwell on such matters, he thought; soon it would be contract time, time for Bavasi to bring you into his office again, ask what you were doing to stay in shape and say that he was pleased to let you know the team was offering you another very good one-year contract to play with the Dodgers. Standing there in the Stadium Club, players were already nervously thinking about it.

Tracewski got his phone call not long after the Series ended.

Bavasi asked him about his plans for the off-season.

Tracewski said he was going to Pennsylvania at some point to see his family and relax a little.

Bavasi reminded him to come into the office before he left to sign his contract.

Tracewski said sure. He was in no rush. He was enjoying himself after a long season. Even though he hadn't hit as well as he'd hoped in the Series, he was grateful he'd had a chance to play so much and be with another group of winners. Nineteen sixty-five had been a good year all around, he thought. Although his Dodger salary of about $20,000 was nothing more than respectable, he'd supplemented it again with a World Series check, the winning player's share this time coming to $10,297, which boosted his income on the year by more than 50 percent, a very nice windfall. He was looking forward to 1966, when he hoped he would get a shot to play more at third base, as no one knew how much longer the thirty-seven-year-old Gilliam could hang on.

As his Pennsylvania trip neared, he gave Bavasi a call about coming in to sign his contract. Bavasi was suddenly in no hurry either, reassuring him it wasn't a big deal when he signed.

Nothing to worry about—you can go on your trip, and I'll be in touch, Bavasi said.

Tracewski went off to Pennsylvania, where he was having a great week when, on December 15, Bavasi's lieutenant Red Patterson telephoned to say he had been traded to the Detroit Tigers for a relief pitcher named Phil Regan.

Tracewski was stunned. He'd had no inkling. He didn't want to go to Detroit.

In the next twenty-four hours he called a sympathetic Koufax, who talked to him about it for a while.

Tracewski remembers, "Finally, Sandy and I just told each other, 'That's baseball.'"

The upheaval in Tracewski's life and career struck no one as unusual. The Dodgers' player representative, Ron Fairly, whose job it was to talk to O'Malley or Bavasi when the players had a request or a gripe, thought it was simply another baseball trade, business as normal: after all, a team owner and his general manager could ship you wherever they wanted, whenever they wanted. What most players were wondering about, he knew, were their contracts for the upcoming season. Although joyous over the Series victory, Fairly was pondering his own contract discussion with Bavasi and the next possible screwing. "You always started worrying about that as soon as the season was over."

Fairly had no idea of the revolution approaching. Neither did O'Malley or Bavasi.

Chapter 6

Baseball's Watershed

Two weeks after the Series, Parker checked himself into the Mayo Clinic, in Rochester, Minnesota, to undergo a series of tests for his lifelong allergies. He also had X-rays taken of a shoulder injury he'd suffered during a home plate collision early in the year, against Cincinnati. The good news was that the shoulder had suffered no serious structural damage. But the clinic's doctors informed him he had the third worst case of allergies they'd ever seen—it was no wonder he'd been so worn down as the 1965 pennant battle moved along, he realized. That assessment would force a change in the way Parker coped with the malady. During the following season, Dodgers trainer Bill Buhler would see to it that he received desensitization shots from a team doctor, with the added hope that, in tamping down the allergies, Parker would also be less vulnerable to asthma attacks. The ailment that had stalked him since his frail childhood was still there even as he had become tall and robust. Some things about your past just don't leave you, he thought.

What he most needed, he believed, was rest. He sought to recuperate after an exhausting seven-plus months of relentless pressure. The off-season was also giving him and other Dodgers a chance to catch up on a world about which they felt somewhat out of touch. He heard about a few more guys from his old school who'd been drafted and sent to Vietnam. He knew their ranks would never include him. Long before, his chronic asthma meant he couldn't be drafted; he was officially 4-F.

Parker and Lefebvre, having achieved a measure of their dream, now faced the task of holding on to it. "If the Dodgers ever had somebody better, that person was going to play," Lefebvre recalls. "The pressure was always there. You had to get ready for the next season. Buzzie called you in and you signed your contract and you pretty much took what they gave you—unless you were somebody like Koufax or Drysdale."

The three most critical one-year contracts to be negotiated during the off-season were those of Koufax, Wills, and Drysdale. The thirty-three-year-old Wills hoped for a substantial raise, dreaming of a $100,000 salary but privately willing as the talks began to settle for $90,000, which would reasonably put him within reach of a $100,000 contract one day. With his 94 steals, he'd had another year unique in the history of infielders, leading the National League in thefts for the sixth consecutive season. In a conservative assessment, he had single-handedly ignited the Dodger offense in more than twenty-five games that year. His team-leading combination of runs scored and RBIs during 1965 (the sum amounted to 125) meant he had factored into more than 1 in 5 of the Dodgers' runs. Had the club been deprived of even a small fraction of his generated runs, a pennant wouldn't have been a possibility.

All this ought to have meant far more in time than a hefty salary hike. His peerless run atop the shortstop position since the start of 1962—resulting in two World Championships, a league MVP Award, and the introduction of a game-changing style of play—should have made him a lock for the Hall of Fame.

A half century later he would still be waiting for the honor.

When at age forty he ended his fourteen-year career after the 1972 season, he would have a lifetime average of .281, part of an array of personal statistics that compare favorably to three shortstops who preceded him in the game and were later elected to the Hall of Fame—the Yankees' Phil Rizzuto, the White Sox's and Orioles' Luis Aparicio, and the Dodgers' legendary Reese.

As a teenager growing up in northern California, Joe Morgan—his era's preeminent second baseman, who was inducted into the Hall of Fame in 1990 after a twenty-two-year career with five teams—watched Wills on telecasts of Dodgers-Giants games. Later, as a young player with Houston, Morgan encountered firsthand the chaos and quandaries that Wills created. He still remembers pregame meetings when getting ready to face the Dodgers: "They began and ended with talk about how we were going to try to stop Wills, because if you didn't stop Wills and keep him off base, you weren't going to beat the Dodgers. . . . He dominated games as much as Willie [Mays] did. . . . Koufax and Drysdale were winning 2–1, 1–0, and getting most of the publicity, and Maury was getting them the runs. He manufactured the runs; he just reconfigured those games. . . . I meet baseball guys who already think Maury's in the Hall of Fame—they can't believe he's not in there."

Koufax is among the incredulous. "People thought Cobb's single-season stolen base record would never be broken," he said in 2009. "Before what Maury did, people were really not stealing bases much. Maury made it all right to steal. . . . Maury was in scoring position so often and then somebody like Tommy [Davis] would drive him home—that's what all of Maury's steals gave us. And that doesn't even account for all those times when Maury would get on, steal a base or two, and score without a hit. He changed the way the game is played. If the Hall of Fame is judged by someone's impact on the game, there can be no question about him."

But as 1965 ended, the Hall of Fame was the furthest thing from Wills's mind. Besides, he had a pressing concern at that moment: he wanted to get a fair deal from Bavasi, a contract worth far more than the roughly $60,000 he'd earned in 1965. It was overdue, he thought. He was determined to be firm this time.

Buoyed by a recent stay in Japan, where people had been so kind and he'd played his banjo and guitar before appreciative audiences, he wanted to feel something approaching the same respect from Dodger officials. Koufax was right, he thought: the whole issue of money came down to respect. When a team's officials didn't pay you what you were worth, it sent the message that not only did they fail to appreciate what you had done but they thought they could bully you. He was tired of being an easy mark.

So when Bavasi presented the Dodgers' offer that off-season— something in the neighborhood of $70,000—Wills said no. That isn't even close, he thought. Bavasi would have to come up, way up. For the first time, Wills decided not to report to spring training in Vero Beach until his demands were met. Let them get a feel for what it would be like to play without him, he thought. He wasn't giving in.

The off-season following the 1965 World Series would be a watershed in baseball history. Two incidents sparked headlines on sports pages everywhere. The first involved Koufax and Drysdale, who, rejecting salary offers from Dodgers management, refused to get on the team plane to Florida, beginning a prolonged holdout. At the same time, an organized labor movement led by an outsider with no real baseball ties was quietly under way in the major leagues. The reactions of Dodger executives and other baseball leaders to these episodes would expose the complacency of the game's rulers at a point when the sport was about to confront a serious challenge to its standing as the national pastime.

The dominance that baseball had enjoyed since its nineteenth-century inception had left its barons self-satisfied and vulnerable. As major-league executives unwittingly undermined their sport's appeal by discounting the value of some legends during salary negotiations, professional football—in the grip of internecine warfare between the NFL and the young American Football League—was escaping baseball's shadow by pursuing a very different course. That year football feverishly promoted a bevy of new, well-paid young players, including the New York Jets' charismatic rookie quarterback Joe Namath, as if they were movie idols. The stunningly effective marketing offensive turned the players into stars overnight, which ultimately had dramatic effects on everything from expanding football's fan base to winning lucrative television contracts.

By contrast, O'Malley and other baseball titans seldom acknowledged having stars, as this would mean having to pay them like stars. O'Malley commonly referred to his Dodger standouts as "the boys," lavishing praise instead on Bavasi and Alston. The smug unwillingness of baseball to trumpet its great talent, coupled with pro football's inventiveness in exalting its own, would contribute by late in the decade to a sea change in the fortunes of the two sports. Football became sexy, the province of liberated players who included golden-arm quarterbacks wearing mink coats and shades. Baseball was the game presided over by the many Bavasis, in which no single player would receive too much money or attention. Football would be seen as the game perfectly suited to the rollicking times, having acquired the image of a sport dominated by daring innovators, free spirits, and renegades, in contrast to baseball's tired orthodoxy.

That perception had already begun to infect baseball by the early months of 1966. Neither Koufax nor Drysdale—each of whom by then had played more than a decade in the majors—had yet been able to get a multiyear contract or money anywhere in the neighborhood of Namath's three-year deal for $427,000; O'Malley didn't believe in multiyear deals, and had never paid a player even $100,000.

O'Malley's rationale? It was simply not the way he and the Dodgers did things. The interests of the team took priority over any player, he and his lieutenants emphasized. O'Malley's implicit message was clear: a team was bigger than any single star; the game could survive the loss of a Koufax, Drysdale, Wills, or anybody else who didn't appreciate the contract Bavasi offered.

In case O'Malley's ethos wasn't clear enough, Bavasi made it plain to Dodger players that, per his boss's instructions, the 1966 budget for salary increases would be limited to $100,000 for the twenty-three players signing new contracts. If Koufax, Drysdale, or any other player received too large a chunk of that $100,000, it would leave that much less for other players, Bavasi emphasized. Players were appalled. *One hundred thousand dollars* was supposed to cover raises for *everybody*? O'Malley made far more than $100,000 in ticket and concession sales from one home game alone, the players knew, and there were eighty-one home games in a year. Did Bavasi expect them to support such a ridiculously self-serving budget? *This* was the thanks they were receiving for winning a World Series and packing Walter O'Malley's stadium?

O'Malley's budget was proof to players that, fundamentally, nothing had changed. Yet what could they do? they asked each other. No one among them, aside from Koufax, had negotiating clout. With the reserve system in place, a dissatisfied star had only two choices: play with the team or sit out the season without a paycheck.

But near the end of January, Koufax and Drysdale stunned O'Malley and Bavasi with a decision that rendered all the executives' assumptions worthless and suddenly gave both pitchers a new weapon. Having earlier entered into separate contract discussions with the team, Koufax and Drysdale informed Dodger officials that they'd decided to hold out together. Each pitcher pledged that he wouldn't sign until the other was satisfied with his deal, marking the first time in history that a duo of baseball players had united to bend a team's chieftains to their will. Koufax and Drysdale had become a union of two.

The bargaining advantage swung dramatically in that instant, and an angry Walter O'Malley knew it. Peter O'Malley was a witness to his father's exasperation. "His attitude," the younger O'Malley remembers, "was, 'You can't negotiate with *two* of your four starting pitchers—that's *half* of your pitching staff.'" The elder O'Malley saw dire ramifications if the Koufax-Drysdale pact became a precedent for joint holdouts in the future. "My father said, 'The infielders could all come in together. . . . Our bullpen could come in together.'" By then Peter O'Malley, heir to the Dodger throne, understood that the prospect of many more alliances of star players in protracted hold-outs was a far greater concern to his father than whatever additional money might be spent on Koufax and Drysdale. "To an owner, this was breaking a new ceiling," Peter recalls. "The biggest thing was, they were doing this together."

The Dodgers couldn't afford to be without both pitchers, and no one understood this reality better than an assured Koufax, who came to believe that it protected him and Drysdale. "I never doubted for a minute if Don or I had been in it alone, we would have been chewed up and thoroughly digested," he wrote in a 1966 article for *Look* magazine. "Before the Dodgers would have given in to me alone, they'd have traded me or let me sit it out. You can trade one player and get in return equivalent value. You can't trade two of your top players."

Wills, standing firm in his own holdout, was observing the two pitchers' progress from afar. "Sandy and Don could only pull that off and win against the Dodgers by sticking together," he reflected. "Buzzie was furious about it—I remember that. Being together meant they couldn't trade them—you couldn't lose Koufax *and* Drysdale and have a team that could win. The only way Sandy and Don had a chance was if the Dodgers really thought Sandy might just leave."

Parker remembered something that Koufax once said on the team bus during a road trip. *If you don't like your salary, you have to be willing to quit the game—it's your only leverage.*

Yet no teammate could possibly have known the true depth of Koufax's resolve. Unlike most bargainers in a baseball dispute, Koufax wasn't bluffing. He wanted to play another season, but he didn't need the game any longer. In a secret shared with no one, he had already decided, given the pain of his arthritic elbow and all the medication he needed just to compete—pills and injections that sometimes had left him with a pharmaceutically induced high and posed a risk to his long-term health—that 1966 would likely be his final season under any conditions. In 2010, at the Joe Torre event, he disclosed the truth about his thinking during that period. If O'Malley and Bavasi hadn't given him a contract he regarded as fair, he would have been comfortable walking away from the game that winter for good, knowing his stance had deprived him of only one season.

Money was not an immediate worry for Koufax. By early 1966, he and Drysdale had contracts with Paramount Pictures to appear in films and television; the two players were already scheduled for small roles in a film starring Dodger fan David Janssen. Koufax didn't see a great future for himself as an actor. But the studio contract at least meant he would have an income if Dodger executives refused to yield. He had investments, money in the bank; he was risking nothing more at that point than a short-lived conclusion to his career.

O'Malley and Bavasi eventually blinked. All along the only real question involved the shape, timing, and exact dollar amount of O'Malley and Bavasi's capitulation, and how much face-saving Koufax would permit the two men during their bargaining.

Publicly, Bavasi did his best to hew to the company line throughout the dispute, echoing the magisterial O'Malley's unruffled pessimism about the situation, coolly offering good wishes to Koufax and Drysdale and voicing perfunctory hope that they would have successful film careers. The Dodgers would be just fine without the boys, he implied, for no duo of players was bigger than the game: "If they can make more money in the movies—and they tell me they're independently wealthy—I wish them the best of luck." But privately Bavasi was fuming, close to panic. Peter O'Malley had come to view Bavasi as a highly sensitive man prone to erratic shifts around his father and other executives. One day, Bavasi furiously told a group of club officials that Koufax and Drysdale were acting irresponsibly. Then, behind closed doors, his position underwent a sudden transformation: he thought it best now to give the pitchers what they wanted. Within the executive offices, Bavasi was acquiring a reputation as a man vulnerable to troubling mood swings. Peter O'Malley remembers the confusion around the table: "During the holdout one day, Buzzie said, 'Two pitchers have never held out together, never asked for so much money and multi-year contracts . . . It's not right; it's crazy.' Then the next day, Buzzie would say to us, 'These are the two best pitchers together in baseball—they deserve it.' The overnight change was disconcerting. . . . Buzzie was a complex guy with many talents . . . But he was an emotional man." Yet, regardless of his volatility, as long as he worked for the Dodgers, Bavasi's fealty would always be to O'Malley's bottom line. In his dealings with players and the press, he was never anyone other than the iron-fisted lieutenant.

As spring training in Vero Beach was about to end, with Koufax and Drysdale still back in Los Angeles, the pitchers proceeded as if they wouldn't be playing, embarking on their new careers. They began rehearsing at Paramount for their roles in the David Janssen film, which would commence filming on April 11. Their schedules were busy. Drysdale agreed to a meeting with Bavasi, though the point of the get-together seemed murky at best, as Bavasi and other Dodger executives insisted they had made their final offer and that the matter was closed.

At their meeting, Bavasi made a new offer to Drysdale, who liked it. It amounted to $12,500 more for each pitcher: $125,000 for Koufax; $110,000 for Drysdale.

After Koufax said fine, the deal was done. The pitchers signed the same day.

In a swift, private message to his negotiator, a vexed O'Malley reacted with humor and needling sarcasm. It was "the only note he ever sent me," Bavasi would recall, decades later. Alluding to the salary boost that Drysdale in particular had received, the owner wrote: "Congratulations on another fine year. Nice of you to give your raise to Drysdale."

No one around baseball failed to recognize what had just happened: O'Malley and Bavasi had yielded to two players. No Dodger could ever remember such a thing happening. "The Dodgers got scared," Wills would later observe. "That's what brought the whole thing to an end. Sandy made it happen."

In the coming years, baseball figures would react in different ways to Koufax and Drysdale's victory and the labor changes slowly under way. Peter O'Malley recalls that his father was largely philosophical in the face of the game's coming revolt, having already privately conceded that a new era was approaching. Bavasi would slowly change with the times, too, though his evolution would be more grudging, his reflections on his past struggles—including his battle with Koufax and Drysdale—tinged with a bitterness that seeped into his comments and writings. A general manager is largely defined by such battles, and Bavasi had been humbled in what would forever be seen by observers as his best-known defeat. He couldn't resist the impulse in time to seek payback. "They unknowingly took money out of the pockets of the 23 other players," he wrote of Koufax and Drysdale. "We had budgeted $100,000 for salary increases for the entire club, and when Koufax and Drysdale took $70,000 of that, it left just $30,000 in raises for the rest of the team."

The sourness of that observation mirrored both the enduring antagonisms of Bavasi and the limits of baseball's vision as the 1960s moved along, an aversion to change that ultimately came at a cost to the game's image and vitality. In the spring of 1966, Bavasi would not allow any other players to get the best of him and O'Malley. There would be no more prolonged holdouts, front-office humiliations, or public relations disasters. Which meant Wills was about to become a victim, again.

D uring a March phone call, as Wills's holdout showed no sign of ending, Bavasi asked him what he wanted.

"Whatever they get from you is what I want," Wills answered.

"They" meant Koufax and Drysdale.

When Wills heard the two pitchers were asking for $166,666 a year and a three-year deal, he knew he couldn't get that much. On the positive side, $100,000 or something very close to it certainly didn't sound at all out of the question now.

He and Bavasi couldn't agree on a number. They hung up, with Wills feeling proud about not surrendering at least. Certainly the Dodgers would know now that he wasn't messing around. He had no plans to pick up the phone and plead for anything. And he wasn't about to travel to Florida and begin spring training until his contract was settled. Bavasi would just have to call back with a fair offer.

Bavasi phoned him a few days later with news.

"Mr. O'Malley *knows* you're in cahoots with Koufax and Drysdale," Bavasi snapped, as Wills would later remember. "Mr. O'Malley *knows* it."

Instantly, Wills was scared. He hadn't spoken with Koufax and Drysdale since their holdout had begun. But this somehow sounded very bad, even career-threatening. His heart pounded. He knew Mr. O'Malley didn't put up with disloyalty.

Bavasi added: "And you know *you* can't get away with that."

This scared him even more. *And you know YOU can't get away with that.* What did this even mean? The *YOU* jumped out at him. It made it sound as though his situation was somehow different from Sandy's and Don's, as if Sandy and Don had some special standing that he didn't; that he should've understood he was in some second-class position. He wondered if the statement had a racial meaning, or whether it was simply intended to intimidate him. Whatever it was, it had worked. He was terrified. What would Mr. O'Malley do to him?

In the next couple of minutes, he heard himself backing down. He said he was ready to come to spring training.

"I'll be there tomorrow," he told Bavasi. "I'll pay my own way to Vero Beach."

The next morning he was on a plane. Bavasi picked him up at the airport and told him everything would be fine. When they arrived at Dodgertown, he said, "Put on your uniform. We'll work it out."

Wills said okay and got dressed.

He signed for about $75,000. Although it was nothing close to what he wanted, the contract would make him the fifth highest paid player in the majors that year, behind only Mays, Koufax, Drysdale, and Mantle—the four active players in the $100,000 club. Still, Wills felt humiliated, unable to forget how Bavasi made him surrender. "It was the same old thing," he remembers. "Buzzie used scare tactics on me. He tried to do that with everyone. But Sandy didn't back down. He had leverage to do that. The scare tactics worked on me. After I signed, I told reporters I was ready to win another pennant and play hard, and all that was true—I always played hard. But the whole thing hurt. The way they could scare you like that: it hurt your pride as a man. That was the worst thing: what it took out of you."

In the midst of the Wills holdout and the Koufax-Drysdale maneuvering, a short, mustachioed, nattily dressed, frail-looking man with an enfeebled right arm began visiting the teams' spring training clubhouses, one by one, for lengthy discussions with players, most of whom never before had heard his name. At once a gifted labor negotiator, economist, and organizer, forty-nine-year-old Marvin Miller so impressed his listeners with the message that they needed a strong union to assert their interests that, by the following September, they would overwhelmingly elect him as the executive director of the Major League Baseball Players Association, a choice that would prove to be the beginning of the end of the owners' absolute rule. Miller arrived from sixteen years on the staff of the United Steelworkers, where he had risen to become the union's chief negotiator.

The day before Miller's meeting with the Dodgers, Bavasi had told the players all the reasons why they should be afraid of a union. John Kennedy and Al Ferrara left with a similar recollection of Bavasi's words, the theme of which was that a union would be a scourge. "Buzzie said to us, 'You got families to feed; you got clothes to buy; you got kids going to school—you need to make money. Unions mean strikes and no work. You guys won't get paid,'" recounted Kennedy, who, listening intently, had an epiphany. "I thought, If Buzzie is this much against it, it's gotta be good for us. And that's when I thought, This union guy is *in*."

Ferrara, so often the beneficiary of Bavasi's help and kindnesses, remained close to him. The young player had been subjected to Bavasi's private entreaties: *Stay out of a union, Al—a union is no good*. But as he listened to Bavasi's attempt to persuade his teammates of the evils of a union, Ferrara sensed management's fear. No spiel from a baseball executive, Ferrara thought, could have been more counter-productive than Bavasi's. "We all knew Buzzie was a mouthpiece for O'Malley and that Buzzie was there to make money for O'Malley," he recalled. "You could tell Buzzie and O'Malley wanted no part of Miller educating us. Buzzie's attitude was: 'Who is this guy?' Well, that did it. Now we're *really* interested in what this guy has to say."

Although he was a lover of baseball, a Dodgers fan since his Brooklyn boyhood, Marvin Miller didn't talk a lot about the game. Arriving in the Dodger clubhouse, he immediately began talking about business, in a voice so soft that many players had to lean forward to catch what he was saying.

After reviewing the state of labor in baseball, focusing on the players' few rights and their many challenges and grievances, Miller talked specifically to the Dodgers about what he viewed as gross injustices in the game, big and small. No detail about the players' lives seemed to have escaped Miller's attention. Among other things, he was very disturbed, he said, by the treatment the players received from the Topps baseball card company. A player, Miller pointed out, received only about $125 a year from Topps for permitting his photo to be used on a Topps card. Topps made *millions*, Miller said. His voice began rising. "You don't understand," he went on. "You're not getting your fair share." Then Miller said something profane that got Ferrara's attention.

"He said to us, 'You big dumb son of a bitches,'" Ferrara remembers. "I liked him—I liked his competitive fire. He grew on people. We needed Marvin. A lot of us were dumb fucking guys when it came to all that stuff. We weren't businessmen. I was an uneducated guy. We were getting screwed by all kinds of people, starting with baseball owners and all the way down to Topps. We were looking for someone smart and tough to lead us out of the woods, because we didn't even know where the woods were."

Miller's talk to the Dodgers presaged a tectonic shift in baseball's labor relations. He wouldn't leave his post as executive director until 1982, by which time his achievements had altogether changed the economic station of players, who could boast of a profession where the average salary had risen from less than $20,000 in Miller's opening year to more than $300,000 by his last. In 1968 he would carve out the MLBPA's initial collective bargaining agreement with the owners, which increased a player's minimum salary from $7,000 to $10,000 and established a formal process for the arbitration of player grievances. Subsequent collective agreements led to more protections and greater opportunities for significant salary increases. A 1972 MLBPA-led strike would end with the owners agreeing to make larger payments into the players' pension fund and establish a formalized procedure spelled out in the agreement for salary arbitration. Arguably, the greatest moment of Miller's sixteen-year run would come in December 1975, when a landmark decision by arbitrator Peter Seitz effectively abolished the reserve clause, paving the way for a measure of free agency.

But on that first day in the clubhouse, Ferrara couldn't see anything that was coming, only that he liked this guy. In time he decided that Marvin Miller—whom he just called Marvin by then—could handle Buzzie. He liked the idea that Marvin wanted to show the players how to handle all the Buzzies out there.

You had to love what was happening all over the country, Ferrara told people. Nobody could hold you down anymore. You wanted something, you just took it. You wanted to do something, you just did it. It'd been one helluva spring, he decided. But exhausting in its tensions. Just damn stressful all the way around. It'd worn people down, he thought. And they hadn't played a single real game yet. They still had the whole 1966 regular season ahead, and a World Championship to defend. Six months. One hundred and sixty-two games. Exhausting.

Chapter 7

The Last March

The many years of historic baserunning had taken something out of Wills's thirty-three-year-old legs. This new reality left him no choice but to ration his steal attempts now, to make sure his legs weren't so drained by the 1966 season's midway point as to leave him unproductive during the brutally hot days of July and August and the stretch run in September. Even in limiting himself, he would steal thirty-eight bases—third in the National League—during a season that saw his six-year run as the stolen base king end, with Lou Brock becoming the game's top baserunner. During the first half of the year, Wills compensated by raising his average from the previous season. Hitting .292 in early July, he was again an All-Star.

By then, he was already a bit worn down and vulnerable. In New York, during the Dodgers' second game back from the All-Star break, he suffered an injury that, within a few more months, would lead to the greatest crisis of his career. In the fourth inning, after Mets' starting pitcher Jack Fisher doubled off Drysdale, Wills, noticing that Fisher had taken a large lead off second base, momentarily removed his glove from his left hand. This was a signal to Drysdale for a pickoff throw. To acknowledge the sign, all Drysdale had to do was slightly tip his cap. When he did this, Wills waited a few seconds and then bolted for second base behind an unaware Fisher. Wills's move to the bag and Drysdale's throw to him were perfectly executed, leaving Fisher picked off by about ten feet, a certain out, it seemed. Fisher didn't even attempt to dive back to the bag, so badly fooled that momentarily he just stood there in the base path, caught now in a routine rundown play, waiting, it seemed, for Wills to rush toward him with the ball and apply a tag. At third base, Gilliam prepared for a throw, in the event Fisher ran that way and Wills wished to throw across the diamond.

The best kind of rundown play involves as few throws as possible. Ideally, the man with the ball sprints toward the baserunner and attempts to tag him, while perhaps along the way faking a toss or two in hopes that the fooled runner might come to a sudden stop and try to reverse direction, making him run directly into the tag. This particular rundown had all the makings of an especially easy play. Few baserunners had ever looked as hapless to Wills as pudgy Jack Fisher, best known around baseball by his nickname, "Fat Jack."

The moniker seemed to say everything about Fat Jack: he would doubtless be slow and easy prey. Despite its unflattering ring, the nickname reflected considerable affection for the twenty-seven-year-old pitcher, in much the same way that those who loved billiards referred to the great hustler of the era as Minnesota Fats. Jack Fisher was comfortable enough with his alternative identity that, long after his baseball retirement, having come to live and work in Easton, Pennsylvania, he would call his sports bar Fat Jack's.

Wills looked at Fat Jack, faked a throw, and began chasing him. Fat Jack turned and ran in the direction of third base.

Only Wills wasn't closing in on Fat Jack as fast as he would have liked. They were more than halfway to the bag already. This had the potential of being hugely embarrassing.

Shit, Fat Jack can run, Wills thought.

"I don't want to be beaten by Fat Jack," he said. "I didn't want to have to throw the ball. My ego was involved. He was still ahead and getting really close to the bag. I got a little closer and finally—I had no choice—I just dived at him."

Wills made the tag, but the effort left him sprawled in the infield. "I was a little dazed and the worst thing was I'd landed on my right knee. My problems that season started right there. The knee kind of hurt right away. It was scraped and cut up. They tried to put gauze and tape on it, but the gauze didn't hold. I told them just to put the tape on it, to try to cover the cuts and scrapes. I'm all right, I was telling myself. I'm able to walk fine. I'm okay."

But he wasn't. In the top of the fifth inning, he bunted down the third-base line against Fisher. Halfway to first, he heard a pop in his right knee. A terrible pain shot through the leg. He never made it to the first-base bag. The future of his season was written in that moment: he would steal only eight bases over the remainder of the year. Immediately, he missed the next four games, as doctors told him fluid had crept into the knee, symptomatic perhaps of a greater problem. They urged a long rest. He ignored their advice, iced the knee, and was back in the lineup within a week.

The knee's cuts were an entirely separate problem. Each day, with gauze and bandages having proven to be worthless during a slide, he simply had the trainers put more athletic tape on the wounds. Soon he had no skin on the knee. "It was just red and raw," he remembered. "The knee was twisted. It hurt to run, hurt to slide. We were in a pennant race, so I kept playing. I was the captain. We wanted to be back in the World Series. But it was all going to get me eventually. All my difficulties later: they all began right there with the knee and chasing Fat Jack. He was faster than anyone knew. That was a shock. A lot of things about that year were a shock."

Parker faced his own crisis. Alston benched him in mid-July for not hitting. At first, he didn't complain, knowing he had given Alston little choice. Benching him meant Alston could turn over the first-base job for a while to Dodger newcomer Dick Stuart, a major-league veteran and an established power hitter. Parker resolved to do what any baseball professional does under such circumstances: support his teammates, never sulk, and patiently work his way back into the lineup. But over the next month he received few chances to play anywhere. As his benching extended into the middle of August, with Stuart and Fairly seemingly having taken over at first base, Parker panicked, terrified his major-league career might soon be over. His desperation evoked memories of his childhood.

Stuart, who had starred for several years with the Pirates, was a fine veteran, he thought. But Stuart hadn't made much difference for the Dodgers, on his way to hitting only .264, in 38 games. The offensive upgrade for which Alston was searching hadn't come with Stuart's stint at first base. More worrisome, Stuart had a history of woefully spotty defensive play, which had earned him the nickname "Doctor Strangeglove." Parker didn't think Stuart was the answer, all the more reason for Alston to reverse his decision and give him his position back. Fairly could return to playing exclusively in right field, just as he had in 1965, Parker thought. But less than two months remained in the season. The games kept ticking away as he sat. He had never felt so miserable in baseball.

With his torment leading him to think that nothing less than his life was on the line again, he received news of the death of his old benefactor Charlie Dressen. On a Saturday morning he attended Dressen's funeral service in Westwood, where he ran into Bavasi. He hadn't planned on discussing his problems at a funeral, but with Bavasi right there and momentarily away from the funeral crowd, he couldn't help himself. Upset, he began venting. He made clear to Bavasi that he wanted his job at first base back.

"If you want to win the pennant again," Parker said, "you better go with the lineup that won for you last year."

Bavasi didn't say a word. He was patiently listening, Parker thought. "I think Buzzie saw my fire and felt my sincerity," Parker

THE LAST MARCH   359

remembers. "I'm sure he saw it in my eyes. I wasn't trying to be rude. I was just mad. I was scared. Buzzie handled it well. Usually, Buzzie talked a lot. But I don't remember a comment or question from him. He just listened, very carefully."

When Parker's rant ended, Bavasi moved on. Parker had no idea what impression he had just left on the general manager, or what, if anything—good or awful—might ensue.

Two days after the funeral, Parker found himself back in the starting lineup, never to leave it again for the remainder of the season, despite hitting only .253. "I might not have been playing much during the rest of that season if not for Buzzie doing whatever he did," Parker remembered. "Once I got back out there I was happy. I wasn't coming out again."

Having already stood up once for himself, Parker did it again the following Sunday, August 21. Koufax was on the mound at home against the Cardinals on a warm afternoon. The game began routinely. The Cardinals' leadoff hitter, second baseman Julian Javier, was late on a fastball and tapped a bouncer down to Parker, who fielded it and casually ran to the first-base bag for the out. Koufax's nemesis Lou Brock then stroked an opposite single to left and, quickly challenging Koufax and Roseboro, stole second base.

Up to the plate stepped the right-handed-hitting third baseman Charley Smith, a .267 batter with fairly good speed. Koufax went to the stretch position, glanced back at Brock, and threw another fastball. Like Javier and Brock, Smith was late on the pitch, hitting a grounder deep at first to Parker, who immediately noticed that Koufax had gotten a late start in sprinting over to cover first base and field the throw.

As Smith got close to the bag, Parker could see that the rival had Koufax clearly beaten. There was no point in making the throw and risking a miscue, he decided. He held on to the ball as Smith crossed the bag for the hit.

Koufax was furious, as Parker remembers.

"Why didn't you throw me the ball?" he yelled.

"Because he had you beat," Parker firmly answered, not about to back down here with Koufax. He was an established player now, not a kid anymore. What was Koufax doing yelling at him like this?

Koufax's disgust was obvious. "Next time throw me the ball and I'll run faster," he snapped.

Parker wasn't about to apologize. *He* was the first baseman, not Koufax. He alone would make the decision on when or when not to throw the ball to the bag. For all of Koufax's extraordinary assets as a pitcher, the truth was he didn't field his position well, thought Parker. He sure as hell didn't need a lecture from Koufax on how to play first base.

Smith had an infield hit, and that was the end of the matter. Koufax would just have to accept it. "Sandy always played the part of the good guy, the modest guy," Parker said. "But he was short-tempered sometimes."

Neither of the two men said another word to each other. There was no point in escalating their disagreement. They'd already put the momentary spat behind them.

Charley Smith took a short lead off first base. Brock, who had advanced on Smith's hit, moved from the third-base bag a ways down the line. After Orlando Cepeda struck out, Curt Flood singled to drive Brock home with the game's first run, and right fielder Mike Shannon walked to load the bases. Koufax was in trouble. Up to the plate came All-Star catcher Tim McCarver, who, proud of being one of the relatively few left-handed batters in the league to have homered against Koufax, thought he'd devised a realistic approach for hitting against him.

"Your best chance against Sandy was to get ahead of him in the count," McCarver explained. "Sandy would try to get ahead of you with his fastball, high fastballs. A lot of guys just fouled them back and fell behind in the count right away. If he did get ahead of you,

you were in big trouble, because then he'd probably throw his curve-ball, and his curveball was unhittable. You only had a chance against his fastball. You hoped he'd missed on a couple of pitches to start off against you. Then you'd try to sit on his fastball. You'd hope for a low fastball. . . . His high fastball was harder to handle. You'd look for that low fastball and that would be your best shot. And that's exactly what happened to me that day. The bases were loaded and I got ahead two and oh in the count. Here comes a low fastball. And I was sitting on it."

McCarver anticipated pulling the ball hard to right field. As the fastball neared the plate, Parker saw McCarver's legs and waist swiftly pivot. The batter's hips "flew open," Parker would later remember. In the same moment, instinct told him everything that would happen next. "I thought, if he hits it, it's coming this way."

McCarver ripped the pitch on one hop, several feet to Parker's left. "I couldn't have hit it harder," McCarver remembered. "It probably would have gone into the right-field corner and cleared the bases. . . . We already had a run in. We had Sandy on the ropes, in real trouble. It probably would've been four-to-nothing. That might have been it for Sandy that day."

The shot took no more than a tenth to two-tenths of a second to travel the 90-plus feet beyond the first-base bag. Parker remembers that he glimpsed not so much a ball as "a gray blur." The blur moved faster than conscious thought. Parker would have no memory of what he did in that tenth of a second. No memory of diving. No memory of catching a ball.

All he knew was that he was on his stomach, conscious only of his chest and belly having collided with the dirt and aware that his glove was extended, as if the glove on its own had attempted to make a backhanded stab at the ball. His eyes had dirt in them. "My mind kind of caught up then with what was happening," he recalls.

He had no idea whether he had caught the ball. "I hadn't felt any impact of the ball in the glove, probably because I hit the ground with my chest. It's hard to feel two impacts at the same time. I fumbled with my glove a little, reached into it, and felt the ball. The ball had hit right in the glove's pocket. McCarver was running. I didn't have time to get up, no time to get to my knees. I rolled over to my left side in the dirt, lifted my legs to get some leverage, and I just threw it. I thought I'd thrown it over Koufax's head."

Koufax wouldn't make the same mistake he had committed earlier in the inning. As the ball was hit and Parker dived, he had begun running toward first base, ready for a throw. McCarver was sprinting down the line. Among the fastest catchers in baseball, he would steal a base against Koufax later that day. Now Parker's throw arrived at the same moment that Koufax touched first base, less than half a foot ahead of McCarver, who struggled to believe what he had just seen. Parker had robbed him of an extra-base hit and the Cardinals of three runs on a ball that he'd thought had no chance of being caught when it left his bat. "It was the best play ever made by a first baseman against me," he recalled. "It was the best play I ever saw made by a first baseman in a game I was ever in. I just couldn't see how he came up with the ball."

McCarver's out ended the inning. Koufax had escaped, giving up only a run. The threat would be the last chance for the Cardinals, who were shut out the rest of the day, collecting only three hits over the final eight innings, with Koufax striking out ten and winning his twentieth game of the season. At its end, much of the focus was on Parker's play and the press's growing recognition of him, at twenty-six, as already one of the most gifted defensive players in history, though, oddly, it would be another year before he won the first of his six Gold Glove awards. The *Los Angeles Times* noted with awe that Parker, with his chest still pressed to the dirt after grabbing McCarver's smash, had rolled before making his throw. A gracious Koufax, sounding as amazed as anyone, noted that the remarkable grab was the contest's pivotal moment ("It might have been the play that kept me in the game"), informing reporters that he'd told Parker, "Boy, you saved the game for me."

Few witnesses to the play, including McCarver, would ever be able to understand how someone could possess the hair-trigger reflexes necessary for reaching such a shot. But Parker suspected he knew what had given birth to the skill. "My fear and angst gave me my wiring," he explained. "I'd had that wiring since I was a child. The adrenaline was always inside me. I was always just below the boiling point. My fear and angst stoked my worries, my adrenaline, my reflexes. . . . It was hard in my life, but it helped me on the field. The play I made that day wasn't even my best one ever."

Yet one man was especially amazed over his extraordinary play and others like it. His father never exactly said he was proud, but Wes could feel it; his father's eyes lit up whenever Wes showed up at his house in Mandeville Canyon, where the elder Parker had been living since his divorce from Wes's mother.

Beaming, he would excitedly ask his son to describe how he had caught the ball.

Parker would do more than talk about it. He happily got on the floor to demonstrate for his father, flopping on his stomach, rolling around, twisting a little on the rug, pantomiming a toss. *This is how I do it, Dad. This is all you have to do, Dad.*

Having already asserted himself with Bavasi and Koufax, Parker soon found himself in an office at Dodger Stadium with Walter O'Malley. The owner had heard a troublesome story from someone in the Dodgers organization: Parker didn't want to accompany teammates on a postseason trip to Japan, where the Dodgers were scheduled to play a long series of games that would extend into November against a group of Japanese All-Stars.

"We want you to go—we want you to go for the good of baseball," O'Malley told him, as Parker remembers.

"I'm exhausted," Parker replied.

He meant it. He was bone tired. And the regular season still had a month to go. If the team reached the World Series, there would be more games. He didn't want to be pressured into playing any more baseball than necessary. He let O'Malley know he was too tired for extra games—he would need serious rest when the season finally ended.

O'Malley politely listened, then resumed his wheedling. He dangled a carrot, indicating the Dodgers organization had plans for Parker beyond his playing days.

"Wes, we want you to be a part of our organization, many years from now."

Parker recognized the carrot here and didn't bite. He didn't need a job down the road from the Dodgers; he and his family already had money, plenty of it. But he wasn't at all offended by O'Malley's methods. He liked the owner. And he would forever be grateful to O'Malley and the Dodgers organization for having given him a chance when no one else in baseball would.

Just the same, he didn't want to play any baseball games in Japan that year. He hoped that O'Malley would understand; he'd already made up his mind.

O'Malley kept pressing his case. Although feeling a not-so-subtle pressure, Parker received no threat, veiled or otherwise. Other players were not as fortunate. Fairly had told O'Malley he didn't want to go. By then, several players were grumbling. Some already had made vacation plans. Others asked why they were being pressured to go *anywhere* during what was supposed to be their free time. O'Malley didn't brook dissent. He wanted a display of loyalty to the organization and an appreciation for this wonderful opportunity in front of everybody. He found it hard to imagine why anyone would wish to pass on a chance to see Japan, especially when he was paying each player $4,000, in addition to their travel expenses.

Fairly thought his off-season ought to belong to him alone. Like Parker, he looked forward to nothing so much as a good long rest. He was not about to be coerced or bamboozled.

"Ron, I really need you to go to Japan," O'Malley told him, as Fairly later recounted.

In as respectful a voice as he could summon, Fairly said he was tired and really didn't want to go.

O'Malley next resorted to a casually delivered warning. He and Fairly had long enjoyed an excellent relationship. Even so, O'Malley made it clear that the player would give him what he wanted, or there would be consequences.

"Ron, we can play *with* you next year or we can play *without* you next year," O'Malley said.

"All of a sudden, I couldn't wait to go to Japan," Fairly remembered.

"Ron and my father had some very good times together," Peter O'Malley would say, nearly a half century later. "They never had a difficult discussion."

They never had a difficult discussion largely because Fairly, like nearly every other Dodger, had absolutely no negotiating leverage with O'Malley. In the following days, Fairly realized that all players understood the choice about Japan. "You could decide not to go and risk being traded," he said. "I didn't know anybody willing to take that risk. Mr. O'Malley was going to get what he wanted."

Aside from rookie and future Hall of Famer Don Sutton (who had a strained pitching arm and a military commitment after winning twelve games that year), the only players excused at that point from the Japan trip were Koufax and Drysdale, who, it was commonly believed, were now free to do whatever they wanted. Every other healthy player, including Wills, would be expected to be aboard the Dodger plane when it departed in late October. From the view of management, a young player like Parker had no grounds for an exemption. O'Malley had called him into his office to secure Parker's pledge and end this nonsense.

But Parker had yet to be persuaded. O'Malley was pushing hard enough that it occurred to Parker he might be traded if he refused to go. If the owner shipped him off, he would probably continue to play ball. Yet, then again, he might not—he might just quit altogether, especially if he wasn't interested in playing for the new team. O'Malley could do whatever he wanted to him; Parker wasn't going anywhere. If O'Malley gave him an ultimatum about Japan, he would just say no. He was the rare player whose personal wealth meant that no owner would ever have leverage over him. And nobody knew how determined he could get when cornered.

He tried to explain his thinking as simply as possible. "Mr. O'Malley, if you want me to help you win the pennant next year, I'm going to need to rest. I'm just too exhausted."

"We still would like you to go," O'Malley said. "We'd like you to think about it."

Bred to be courteous, Parker said he would think about it, though in the next breath he politely made clear that this wasn't going to happen.

He never again heard from O'Malley about Japan. The issue disappeared, just like most of his other headaches that summer. He'd discovered the pluses in being more forceful. "I felt like I was coming into my own as a person that year," he recalls.

Away from the ballpark, he took sanctuary in familiar places. When his miseries about anything resurfaced, he still turned to his brother Lyn, with whom he was sharing an apartment now in Century City. On off days, he still went off alone, sometimes to Disneyland, to hear legends like Harry James and Count Basie perform. He sometimes dropped into a Westwood theater alone late at night after games to watch movies. One day, as part of a small group of visitors, he saw Doris Day on the set of a new film she was making, telling his old crush how much he'd liked her in *Calamity Jane*, a Western released back in 1953, when Wes Parker was thirteen years old.

He was at heart an earnest 1940s and '50s child playing an exceedingly difficult game during a stormy decade for which he never would be the most natural fit. But he was surviving—thriving even.

He'd fought through the game's hazards and his own monsters with a ferocity that no observer had a clue about. Doubters and even some friends thought he was a genteel and possibly soft boy. Always, they underestimated him.

At some point, Parker let loose his inner teenager. He noticed the many attractive, well-dressed women who made a habit of hanging out around the box seat railing near the Dodger dugout—models, actresses, coeds. He quickly soured on actresses ("Too self-involved—you'd be somewhere and they'd be looking around to see who else was there"). No group of women appeared as abundant as local beauty pageant winners, who regularly made the pilgrimage to Dodger Stadium to pose for photos and do publicity, along the way making no secret of their desire to meet him and other Dodgers. "It seemed I was dating every pretty woman who came to the Stadium," he remembers. "It was like a smorgasbord for me for a while, like dying and going to heaven. And the women had class and good manners. I couldn't believe they wanted to go out with me—I had such bad self-esteem. I could've had a hundred women loving me, and it wasn't ever going to be enough. I couldn't take the next step."

He had concluded that all his relationships were destined to end: "There were the old fears from my childhood. There was the fear of being hurt, criticized, humiliated, held to impossible standards. There was terror in that. I was silently pleading all the time that I was with them to be treated kindly. So the relationships would just fade or stop."

A half century later, the subject of relationships reduces his voice to a murmur; he suggests there are some doors he can't open, as it dredges up too much misery. And that takes him back to baseball.

"It wasn't always bad," he said. "I had plenty of good friends and teammates." Sometimes he double-dated with Lefebvre. And he had the camaraderie of Wills, Johnson, Torborg, and others in the clubhouse. He had Lyn back at the apartment. He had his tickets at the

Music Center, especially during his off-seasons, and his limitless love of film. "I lived as full a life as someone in my situation with my background could," he reflects. "My days and nights were full. It could've been a lot worse."

D uring 1966, the Dodgers' best hitter of the decade returned to the team and his position in left field, after nearly a full season away. The team said the star's broken ankle had healed and that he was ready. At first glance, this seemed to be the case, but only because of the inherent gifts of Tommy Davis.

Because he could rise from a couch, pick up a bat, and immediately rip pitches, Davis was on his way to hitting .313 in 1966. Yet there was a problem: his mended ankle wasn't anywhere close to being right, in serious need of more treatment and rest, with the result that he played sporadically. He started in only about half the games that season, his limited action translating to limited productivity. He did not run like he had in the past. He did not seem to have the same explosiveness. He had only three homers and 27 RBIs for the entire season, reduced to being largely a singles hitter. "I needed more than one season to rehab," Davis recalled. "The doctors said it was going to take more than one year."

Only the Dodgers didn't have that kind of patience. This was going to be Tommy Davis's last season in Los Angeles.

I f 1965 had been an ordeal for the Dodgers, 1966 was a debilitating march. Fatigue, injuries, and anxieties frayed nerves as the season wore on. It hadn't helped Wills's mood one night when, after raising a couple of fingers toward Tommy Davis in left field to signal two outs, his teammate didn't acknowledge it, believing he didn't need Wills to remind him of something so simple, in what was an old source of friction between the two.

But Wills, always a believer in reminders and attention to the smallest detail, was furious over what he regarded as a breach of respect. At the end of the inning, the two exchanged words in the dugout, their anger escalating to the point where only the intervention of several teammates prevented a fistfight. "Maury was always my captain, my friend," Davis remembered. "It was a love-hate relationship between us because we were both proud, both competitive. But he was the one who made us go. That time I got angry: that was in a big part of the season and those games had a lot riding on them. I know Maury just wanted to win so bad. He pushed people to win: that was his job. I know he had a lot of pressure on him."

With the stresses building, even the mildest mannered found they were not immune from tense exchanges with the captain. Getting off the team bus one day during a road trip, Parker was good-naturedly ribbing Wills about a subject that neither would be able to recall, decades later, when suddenly his close friend snapped: "Wes, if I want any shit from you, I'll just kick it out of you."

Parker could see that nearby teammates were stunned. "Guys kind of let out a *Whoa! Whoa! What was THAT? Whoa!*" Parker remembered.

The young player felt terrible. "I just backed off. Maury was my buddy. I was sorry I'd upset him."

The incident simply spoke to the costs of a two-year physical and emotional grind that had begun in early 1965, as the players first sought to win a championship and now to defend it. Some of them felt their bodies breaking down. On the verge of turning thirty-eight, Gilliam would play in only eighty-eight games that year, his average plummeting 63 points to .217 and necessitating the acquisition of a new infielder during September, which the Dodgers began in third place. The team picked up thirty-one-year-old journeyman Dick Schofield from the Yankees, quickly making use of him at third and giving Gilliam some time to rest and recover from nagging injuries. But the absence of the once steady, now aging veteran only ratcheted up the pressure on everyone else to raise his game, if possible.

Characteristically, Wills was scratching out victories any way he could. On Saturday afternoon, September 10, collecting two hits in five at-bats against the Astros, he scored the game's only run when he led off the bottom of the tenth inning with a lined single, advanced to second on Gilliam's sacrifice bunt, and came home on pinch hitter Ferrara's two-out, game-winning base hit to left. The two teams played a doubleheader the following day. During the first game, going 3-for-4, Wills scored the first and only run Koufax needed. In the fourth inning, he dragged a bunt past the Astros right-handed pitcher Larry Dierker, the ball rolling toward Houston's gifted twenty-two-year-old second baseman Joe Morgan, who couldn't make the play in time. Wills had himself a single. "You would always know he was going to try something like that, and people still couldn't stop it," Morgan reflected later.

Advancing to second base on another Gilliam sacrifice bunt, Wills scored on a Fairly single to center. Koufax threw a six-hit shutout. Winning the doubleheader, the Dodgers took over first place.

The Dodgers' final eleven games were on the road. Reliever Phil Regan, enjoying a spectacular season, won his fourteenth game during the Dodgers' sweep of the Cubs in a doubleheader at Wrigley Field. In St. Louis, after Osteen beat Bob Gibson to win his seventeenth game, and Drysdale threw a four-hit shutout in his best performance of the season, Koufax defeated the Cardinals' Al Jackson, 2–1, giving up only four hits and striking out thirteen. "Sandy was at his toughest when it counted," Wills remember. "That's what I think of most when I think of him that year."

N o other pitcher in his final season, before or since, has ever had the success that the thirty-year-old Koufax did. No other departing pitcher has won a Cy Young Award. Or had a year that in full was the equal of Koufax's utter mastery: he captured twenty-seven games, seized the ERA title (Koufax's fifth in a row, a major-league record, with his 1.73 ERA his best ever for a season), led his league in shutouts (his five that season marked the third time he led the National League in that category), and won pitching's equivalent of the Triple Crown, by leading the league in wins, ERA, and strikeouts.

As final acts go in sports history, Koufax's 1966 campaign is unsurpassed. It is a virtual certainty that, had he wanted nothing more than a large paycheck the following year, Koufax would have become the highest-paid player to that point in baseball history, earning as much perhaps as $200,000 for 1967. That he would walk away from an enormous payday in favor of safeguarding his health would reflect not merely good sense but his ethical standards. He would not pitch feeling doped up or in agony; he wouldn't take a pile of money if there was any possibility he couldn't live up to the expectations of those who would give it to him.

Privately, by then, he had all but made up his mind to quit after the season. Bavasi would later recount that Koufax told him he was pondering retirement, a claim Koufax has never disputed. Yet he kept his tentative plans a secret from those closest to him, in and out of the organization. Teammates, including Wills, have no recollection of Koufax ever discussing the subject.

Such reticence was perfectly consistent with Koufax's aversion to doing or saying anything that might spark distractions, fuel gossip and worry, or interfere with his carefully honed preparation and routines. Besides, for him, there could only be something liberating about knowing the end was likely near, a freedom that would serve to embolden him during the pennant fight's final month. With his departure imminent, he no longer risked anything, professionally, if he were to push himself to his limits, and beyond. If he badly hurt his arm, he had the rest of his life to recover.

While no Dodger player had a clue about Koufax's plans, Wills knew that his friend had made clear to Alston and the coaches that they ought to feel free to use him as often as they wanted. If they needed him at any point on only two days of rest, he would be there. If they needed him in relief, he would do it. "Sandy wanted to go out a winner—we know that now," Wills observed. "Sandy was doing everything possible those last couple of months—he pushed himself harder than any other pitcher could."

From the start of September, Koufax would win six of his final seven decisions. During the season's final weekend, the Dodgers traveled to Philadelphia, only a victory away from winning the National League title, with three games to play. The Phillies were out of the pennant race, on their way to finishing in fourth place. But they had immense pride and, led by a familiar antagonist in Gene Mauch, would enjoy few things more than derailing the Dodgers. Their team now included two All-Stars and former Cardinals, Dick Groat and Bill White. Nothing would be a sure thing in Philadelphia.

On Friday, September 30, determined to clinch the pennant that night, Wills singled three times and stole three bases, pushing himself through his pain in a last great burst. But his supreme effort wasn't enough: the Dodgers and Osteen lost, 5–3.

After a rainout the following day, the two teams met in a Sunday doubleheader, the last day of the regular season. A Los Angeles win in either game, or a loss by the second-place Giants against the Pirates in Pittsburgh, would give the Dodgers the pennant. But Drysdale, who entered the first game with a disappointing record of 13–16, having struggled most of the season after his holdout with Koufax, lasted only two innings. The Dodgers led into the eighth inning, but the Phillies rallied to win, 4–3.

Now the Dodgers and Alston were down to the one option they had feared all weekend. Had either Osteen or Drysdale secured the pennant with a win in Philadelphia, it would have made it unnecessary for Koufax to pitch again until Game 1 of the World Series against the Baltimore Orioles. Had it happened, Koufax would have begun the Series with five days of rest, more off time than he had enjoyed all season. But now, with the pennant perhaps hanging in the balance, Alston had no reasonable alternative to using Koufax, which meant he would be unavailable to pitch the World Series opener, assuming the Dodgers got that far. Compounding the challenge in Philadelphia would be that, yet again, Alston would be sending out Koufax to pitch on only two days of rest. It was, in many ways, the worst of all scenarios for a club looking to repeat as World Series champions. Only a Giants' loss now in Pittsburgh could spare Koufax from having to pitch the second game of the doubleheader.

As the Dodgers sat in the visitors' clubhouse of Connie Mack Stadium before their doubleheader's nightcap, the Giants' game had entered the late innings. Good news suddenly came out of Pittsburgh. The Giants trailed, 4–3, in the top of the ninth inning, against the Pirates' tough left-handed starter Bob Veale. Players huddled on benches, waiting for word that the Giants had lost, with no one more riveted than a quiet Koufax, who would be able to settle back with a beer and forgo having to set foot on the field at all if the Giants fell.

Someone rushed into the clubhouse and said, "Pirates, 4–3."

Yeahhhhhhhhhhhh.

"Top of the ninth."

Collective groans. A few curses. The players settled back again.

Here came another update. "The Eagles just kicked a field goal," reported Dick Stuart.

"What the hell?" Lefebvre muttered.

It was perhaps lucky that they didn't know exactly what was transpiring in Pittsburgh, for it would have sounded like the most maddening of curses. The trailing Giants were down to their last out against Veale. With Jim Ray Hart standing on second base, the Giants, in need of a pinch hitter, had no better option than utility man Ozzie Virgil, who'd hit only .213 that year.

Virgil singled to center to tie the game.

In the bottom of the ninth, the Pirates had the winning run on third base with two outs, the bases loaded, and Roberto Clemente at bat against Giants reliever Lindy McDaniel. Clemente grounded out, and the game went into extra innings.

Finally, the player with reason for the greatest concern had heard enough. It was getting too close to game time to wait any longer. As Lefebvre remembers, Koufax turned and mumbled, "Fuck it, I'm gonna warm up—let's win the goddamn game."

He had made a prudent decision in not lingering a second longer. In Pittsburgh, Willie McCovey hit an eleventh-inning homer with a man aboard off Pirates reliever Steve Blass, part of a four-run inning for the Giants, who would wrap up the contest in the next few minutes. The Dodgers' lead now was down to a single game. If they lost their nightcap, the Giants could deadlock the race and force a playoff with a victory in a makeup game the following day in Cincinnati.

The Phillies played the game as if their own World Series hopes depended on it. Philadelphia's pitching ace, Jim Bunning, was eager for the battle; the start would give him an opportunity, among other things, to capture his twentieth game of the season. No Phillies regular wanted to sit out the contest. Groat showered between games and put on a fresh uniform, ready to go. Taking a seat in the Phillies dugout, he began hearing, over and over, a loud smack of sorts coming from the Dodgers bullpen, a noise he instantly identified without ever moving his head. "It was the pop of a glove, only it had a different sound—it was a much louder pop, much sharper," he remembered. "You knew it was Sandy. You knew it couldn't be anybody else. Only one person could make a sound like that. We knew he had to be tired, but he was still Sandy."

Bunning was sharp at the start of the game, striking out Wills and retiring the Dodgers in order in the first inning. Koufax had immediate problems. Just as when he had pitched on two days of rest against the Twins in 1965's ultimate game, he struggled to find his curveball, forcing him to rely almost exclusively throughout the afternoon on his fastball. In the Phillies' first inning, Jackie Brandt led off with an infield hit and moved to second base on a sacrifice bunt, before Groat hit a one-hop liner into the gap between shortstop and third base. "I thought we had a run and the lead," Groat remembered.

But Wills stretched out, knocked down the ball, kept it in the infield, and forced a flying Brandt to stop at third. "Wills saved them a run on that play," Groat recounted. "It would've been big to get that first run. But we still had Dick Allen coming up that inning. Except that Sandy then just took control of the game."

Koufax struck out the slugger Allen. Next came left fielder Harvey Kuenn, who had a chance to avenge his ninth-inning strikeout against Koufax in the perfect game. But Kuenn grounded out to end the inning. As the game moved along, the Phillies would be reminded of what the Twins had learned: a foe that failed to capitalize on an early opportunity against Koufax would be made to regret it. Koufax would give up only two hits over the next seven innings.

The Dodgers scored the game's first runs in the third. Parker walked, stole second base, and scored on a two-out single by Schofield. History ought to note that Willie Davis—who would be the source of so much pain for fans of Koufax within the next week—then homered, to give Koufax a 3–0 lead.

"We were already celebrating when Sandy got those runs," Johnson remembers.

"It was just three, but that's a lot of runs when you're talking about Sandy," Groat observed.

By then, the Phillies' chances of winning were remote, and they knew it. (The esteemed website *Baseball Reference* would later calculate the "expectancy" of a Dodger victory at this point in the game to be 79 percent, the figure steadily climbing as the Dodgers moved toward a 6–0 lead in the ninth inning, eventually to top out at a seemingly unfathomable 100 percent as the Phillies came to bat for the last time, the kind of prognostication ordinarily reserved for rainstorms that have already arrived.)

The Phillies' veterans especially were philosophical over what was happening. Finding himself in a familiar position, Bill White struck out in his first at-bat in the second inning and his next at-bat in the fourth. Away from the ballpark, he would have a line ready when people asked him how he fared against Koufax: "How would I know? I never could hit his curveball or his fastball."

As usual, Koufax was competing with physical challenges that day. He would later say that, inexplicably, his back "popped" in the fifth inning, necessitating a fresh application of hot Capsolin before he went out to pitch the sixth. He dominated the Phillies with fastballs through eight innings, on his way to striking out ten on the day. Dick Allen fanned in three consecutive at-bats. Groat struck out once, going a quiet 1-for-4.

At the start of the ninth, Allen finally hit a ball into fair territory. Rolling toward second base, it reached the glove of Lefebvre, who booted it for an error. Finally tiring, Koufax now ran into problems. Kuenn cleanly singled to left field. Next, Tony Taylor singled to center, with Allen scoring. Into the batter's box stepped Bill White again, in what would be his last at-bat ever against Koufax.

Nearly everything was a last for Koufax now. It was the last inning Koufax would ever pitch in a National League game, and the last time he would ever throw a pitch to White, who hit a fastball hard into the gap in right field, his second hit of the game, driving home both Kuenn and Taylor. So long baffled and powerless against the legend, White would forever have the distinction in record books of being the last player in the National League to get a hit against Koufax, or drive in a run. He would hardly be able to recall the event a half century later, still preoccupied by memories of Koufax's rising four-seam fastball, the one that his bat always struggled to touch. "What I just remember is the feeling that—during that whole last game—we really didn't have a chance against him," he said. "Even when we scored."

With White's double, the Phillies had cut the lead to 6–3. There was still nobody out. Roseboro went out to the mound to talk.

Koufax rubbed a ball and listened. On the bench, Groat thought Koufax had to be wearing down, especially on only two days of rest. He had pitched brilliantly, but enough was enough, Groat believed. Alston should get him out of there. Later, Groat would observe that he thought Alston had let Koufax throw too many pitches in the game; that Koufax was bound to feel the effects of this heavy load in the World Series. Groat wanted the Phillies to come back and win, but he also frowned on poor baseball decisions. He thought Koufax had done all he could, and that it was time for Alston to let a reliever finish the game.

But that kind of approach never was Alston's. The manager liked his great pitchers to finish games. Besides, if he removed Koufax now, he might have faced a rebellion. Out in left field, Johnson didn't think it was possible that Koufax would be replaced. "Sandy never came out of a big game in the ninth," Johnson said. "Never. Don't care how tired somebody thought he looked. We'd be worried to have anybody else out there. It was more than just Sandy being the best pitcher. He was Sandy. He never let you down. So what if he gives up a couple runs. We go down fightin' with him if we go down. And we weren't goin' down. This was Sandy pitching. Come on now."

Each of the others had his own way of saying it, but Wills, Fairly, Lefebvre, Parker, Torborg, Moeller, Ferrara, Osteen, Oliver, and Kennedy felt the same way. You did not need to be personally close to Koufax to want to entrust the team's fate to him, one later observed. It said something about his teammates' awe of his doggedness that not one among them ever doubted that Koufax would remain in the game and win, even as the Philadelphia crowd, smelling blood, howled. "You got to the ninth inning with him and you knew it was a sure thing; you just knew it was a laydown with him," Ferrara said. His comrades saw no possibility that he could fail. Their faith was absolute.

Phillies catcher Bob Uecker, who had hit Koufax reasonably well during his career, was next. Koufax struck him out. Pinch hitter Bobby Wine tapped a grounder to Wills for the second out. That left

Brandt. Koufax threw a four-seam fastball for strike three and the pennant. It would be the last game he ever won.

In the clubhouse afterward, the scene was subdued.

"We'd been all jacked up and excited when we won the pennant in 1965—it was loud afterward," Lefebvre remembered. "Not in 1966, not in Philadelphia. I remember just mostly sitting there around the lockers. There was some champagne. We had a couple of drinks. But there was no celebration. There wasn't much to say. It was more like, Goddamn, it's over, finally. We won, but it was totally exhausting; we were all exhausted. The last thing on our mind was playing a World Series. We were out of gas. We knew it."

Johnson was spent. But he and Oliver took one look at a slumped Wills quietly sitting in front of a locker and realized nobody was more drained than the captain. Wills was trying to gather himself, to find the energy to push off a chair and stand. He pondered the satisfaction of having seen the team pull off what had felt improbable at several points that season. Back-to-back pennants: the achievement was a first for the team in Los Angeles. He hadn't started thinking about the World Series. It was hard for him to get past what had just happened and all it had taken out of everyone. He stayed down on his chair.

Meanwhile, Oliver looked across the way at Koufax. "He just looked exhausted to me," Oliver recalled. Koufax dutifully smiled as Tommy Davis poured a bottle of champagne over his head.

"Thank God it's over," Koufax told the press.

He added that his back would likely be stiff the next day but assured everyone he would be ready for Game 2 of the World Series. Nearby, when asked how he felt, an impassive Alston told reporters that the victory meant another pennant—not much different from the others, he added—and that Drysdale would start Game 1.

A grinning Ferrara strided around wearing a sombrero and smoking a fat cigar. He could feel the collective fatigue in the room. "Our

World Series felt like that last game in Philadelphia," he reflected later. "We were ripe for somebody to sneak up on us. But I still was thinking there was no one in baseball who could beat us."

What the players hadn't told the press in Philadelphia was that the subject of the Japan trip was on many of their minds. Those obligated to make the trip had received the travel and tour schedule, with several players appalled over how little time they would have after the Series ended before needing to get on a plane that would take them overseas for the start of eighteen games against the Japanese players. The games would begin on October 22 and not end until sometime during the second half of November. Parker, relieved at having secured his release from the trip, listened as some of his less fortunate teammates privately fumed about O'Malley's edict. "They were basically ordered to go," Parker remembered. "'Ordered' would be too strong maybe. Let me put it this way: people were *told* the team was going." It was a distinction without a meaningful difference. "The message was clear to everybody: the guys had to go."

Parker thought the distraction only complicated an already tough World Series task for his tired teammates. He had no illusions about the Baltimore Orioles, a superb team led by a trio of veterans and future Hall of Famers: third baseman Brooks Robinson, shortstop Luis Aparicio, and right fielder Frank Robinson, who won the American League Triple Crown that year as well as his second Most Valuable Player Award.

Baltimore's pitching staff included a tough long reliever with an awkward delivery, Moe Drabowsky, and a wunderkind, twenty-year-old Jim Palmer, yet another Oriole on his way to the Hall of Fame, who had won fifteen games in 1966. A power-hitting first baseman, Boog Powell, gave the club a regular long-ball threat, and one of their rookies, Paul Blair, already was building a reputation as perhaps the best defensive center fielder in the game.

At Dodger Stadium, Game 1 wasn't five minutes old when Frank Robinson crushed a two-run homer into the left-field pavilion against Drysdale. It wasn't ten minutes old when Brooks Robinson launched a solo shot off Drysdale into the same vicinity for a 3–0 Orioles lead. As the inning continued, the two Robinsons playfully argued in their dugout over whose ball had traveled the farthest. "Back-to-back homers were proof we could beat them," Brooks recalls. "We'd had confidence all along that we could hit them."

In the bottom of the first inning, Wills walked against the Orioles' left-handed starter Dave McNally and swiftly stole second base. But three Dodger outs left him stranded there. It was just the start of the Dodgers' epic frustration. Wills would not score a run in the Series, on his way to collecting only a single hit in thirteen at-bats.

Lefebvre hit the Dodgers' last homer of the year, in the second inning. McNally, struggling with his control, left the game with the bases loaded in the third inning, giving way to Drabowsky, who walked Gilliam to force home another run.

Remarkably, it would be the last time the Dodgers scored in the entire Series. During the final 33 innings, a span of three and two-thirds games, they would be shut out, a streak of futility that would remain a World Series record a half century later.

The next afternoon, Koufax lost, in his final game. Even as the Orioles and young Jim Palmer beat him, he amazed them. With the game scoreless, the Orioles' rookie catcher, twenty-three-year-old Andy Etchebarren, batted for the first time in the third inning. Koufax struck him out on three fastballs. "You got a good look when that thing left his hand, but you didn't get a good look at it when it went by you," Etchebarren recalled.

Wow, so this is Koufax, Etchebarren thought. As he walked back to the Orioles' dugout, he passed Palmer, who, with a bat in his hands, was slowly making his way from the on-deck circle to home plate. Palmer murmured to Etchebarren with youthful awe: "Those were the three hardest fastballs I've ever seen."

The Orioles would always be a tad sensitive about the subject of Koufax's possible fatigue. Decades later Zev Yaroslavsky, by then a prominent Los Angeles official, was visiting Baltimore's Camden Yards when someone introduced him to a retired Boog Powell. Yaroslavsky, never known for his shyness, needled Powell, in the process touching a nerve: "You must've had a good time batting against Koufax in his last game when he was tired and crippled."

"Bullshit," said Powell, who had two of the six Orioles hits off Koufax that day. "He had the best stuff he ever had. It was almost impossible to get a hit off him."

In the fifth inning of a scoreless game, Powell led off with a single, which looked as though it would be meaningless as Davey Johnson fouled out and Paul Blair hit a lazy fly ball toward Willie Davis in center field. But Davis, battling the sun, dropped it for the first of his three errors in the inning, with Powell moving to third base and Blair taking second.

Now Etchebarren had his second at-bat. "I got a fastball a little up from Koufax and hit a fly ball to short center field," he recalled. "Willie Davis misplayed it again."

After dropping the fly, Davis threw to third base, trying to nail Blair. The ball sailed high and wide, and the Orioles had two runs, with Etchebarren stopping at second. He too would score before the end of an inning that saw the Orioles pick up three unearned runs off Koufax.

At the end of the inning, with Davis fast on his way to being cast as the goat, Koufax patted his back and shook his hand, as if to make clear he blamed no one. "Sandy was always a kind guy in those kinds of situations," Johnson remembers. "But we knew we were in trouble."

In the sixth inning, Etchebarren had one last at-bat against Koufax. By then, Baltimore led, 4–0, having loaded the bases with one out. In what was his unmatched forty-second start of the season, Koufax threw another fastball. The ball had too much speed and movement for Etchebarren to catch up with it. "Nobody ever got many good swings against Koufax," he observed. He hit a bouncer to Gilliam, who started a double play that ended the inning.

Koufax did not return for the seventh inning. He had just thrown his last pitch ever.

After the Orioles wrapped up their 6–0 shellacking to take a two-game lead, the Dodgers got on their plane and headed for Baltimore. Parker thought that many of his exhausted teammates were thinking with dread about Japan. "After we lost game two, guys realized that if we get swept, people get time off before they have to go to Japan," he said. "Nobody ever said it, not once. I just think it was an unconscious thing."

But Parker stressed that he didn't think a flagging commitment had accounted for the Dodgers' coming defeat. The Orioles simply were the superior team that week. "I don't think we were going to score much under any circumstances. We were just so tired. We'd have kept getting shut out no matter how many games we played."

In Baltimore, Claude Osteen pitched a masterful three-hitter. But Paul Blair hit Osteen's only bad pitch of Game 3 deep into the left-field bleachers with two outs in the fifth inning. It was the game's only run, as the Orioles' Wally Bunker, pitching as superbly as Palmer, threw a six-hit shutout.

The Series would end the following day, with McNally thoroughly stymieing the Dodgers. Drysdale was nearly his equal. But in the fifth inning he threw a fastball in the fat part of the strike zone to Frank Robinson. At the very instant Robinson's bat made contact, Drysdale disgustedly kicked the mound, not even bothering to watch the ball's flight. He knew.

The homer gave the Orioles a 1–0 lead, which McNally carried into the ninth inning. He struck out pinch hitter Dick Stuart. Then Ferrara, batting for Drysdale, singled to center. The speedy Nate Oliver entered the game as a pinch runner for Ferrara, representing the potential tying run. He and Ferrara still believed the Series was winnable, with each man carrying the same vision of how it could happen. If they rallied and eked out a victory now, Koufax would win

Game 5. "After that, we'd need just one more victory before Sandy pitches game seven," Oliver said.

Wills walked, with Oliver moving down to second. But Willie Davis lined out to Frank Robinson in right field, before Lou Johnson hit a fly to Blair in center to end it.

The flight home was a quiet one. Most players slept. Ferrara fell into a brief conversation with Koufax. They'd never really hung out together, but now and then they would talk a little baseball, swap stories about their Brooklyn roots, and catch up on their lives. There had never been any intimate disclosures between them—they weren't close enough for that. But they got along well, liked each other, and would forever have New York in common. Ferrara was still wishfully thinking about what it would've been like to have Koufax pitch a Game 5. Then he stopped himself. *It's over*, he thought. *Accept it. It's not the end of the world.* Koufax would be back next year, and they'd sure as hell be in contention for another pennant and World Series. Relax. He noticed that Koufax seemed unperturbed. It was just one more enviable aspect of Koufax, he thought. The guy always seemed to have everything under control. It'd be nice to bottle some of that.

He was talking with Koufax about the off-season. The conversation hardly could have been less important.

This is it, Koufax said then, very casually. He was retiring.

A shocked Ferrara didn't know why Koufax would say something so earthshaking to him, until he realized that Koufax hadn't really chosen him. "He wasn't confiding in me," Ferrara remembered. "I think I was just there and he said it. It just came out. There weren't any throwaway lines from him. He kept it simple. Knowing him, the decision wasn't spur of the moment. He didn't do anything spur of the moment. But he just said it to me and that was pretty much it."

Already, Koufax had stopped talking about it. The disclosure had taken all of fifteen seconds. Something in Koufax's tone told Ferrara that, for the time being, he wasn't sharing the news with the rest of the world, perhaps not even with other teammates. Ferrara would say nothing about it to anyone. It would remain a secret from other Dodgers for the next month. "I wanted what was best for Sandy, but I knew everything was going to change for everybody," he remembers. "This wasn't going to be good news."

S oon, the Dodgers had set out on their eighteen-game goodwill tour of Japan. A half century later, the official website of Walter O'Malley—ultimately overseen by his son, Peter, and dedicated to the achievements of the late owner and his team—provides an abundance of factoids about the tour.

Readers learn that the Dodgers won nine games, lost eight, and tied one against the Japanese players.

Among other things, they also discover the following: that the Japanese emperor and empress, who had not attended a baseball game for years, watched the Dodgers play on November 6, 1966, in Tokyo; and that Walter O'Malley received a "high honor for a non-Japanese," in the form of the "Order of the Sacred Treasure Gold Rays with Neck Ribbon" from the prime minister's office. Notwithstanding the website's colorful and exhaustive chronicling of the tour—of game scores, player statistics, cultural exchanges, exotic sartorial splendors, tourist visits, meetings with prominent Japanese officials, and deeply affecting ceremonies between representatives of the two nations—one thing is curiously absent: any sense of the tensions between Dodger management and several of O'Malley's key players.

Wills thought he had made it clear to Bavasi during the season that he didn't want to go to Japan; that his bad right knee wouldn't be able to handle any more games for the remainder of the year. But O'Malley and Bavasi emphasized, on the eve of the tour, that his absence was not an option.

Wills and other players recall that he arrived at an understanding with Bavasi: he would sign autographs in Japan, pose for photographs, and dutifully participate in pregame ceremonies. But he wouldn't be expected to play often, nothing more than a couple of innings here and there, to protect the right knee from becoming any worse.

Once in Japan, he learned he would have to start at shortstop.

As Wills recalls, he said to Alston, "I talked about this with Buzzie. I can't play that much with this knee. I was told I'd just pose for pictures, hold babies. I can't do this."

Alston, who nearly always in Wills's career had come to his aid, could offer no help now. "I knew Walt was stuck, and that I was going to have to play."

Early during the series, finding himself on base, Wills heard the Japanese crowd chanting in English: "Go, go, go . . ."

Goddamn, I got a bad knee, Wills thought. *I can't run. They have no idea what I'm going through.*

But he prided himself on giving fans what they wanted. "Once you're in the lineup, you can't say you have a bad leg or a bad arm—it's unprofessional."

He stole second base, immediately writhing.

The tour soon took the team to the city of Sapporo, where it was drizzling and cold. Worse, Sapporo had an infield devoid of grass and with ample sand mixed into the dirt, as Wills remembers. Still in pain but with no way out of the lineup, he hit a liner into an outfield gap. As he rounded first base, some of the infield's sand gave way, and his right knee buckled. He felt it popping again, just as it had during the day in New York when he first injured it against the Mets and Fat Jack. The knee was twisted worse than ever. He hobbled into second base before dropping to one knee and clutching his head in agony.

Third-base coach Preston Gomez rushed to him. "You all right?"

"I'm hurting," he answered.

His gaze found Alston, who said nothing. "I'm sure Walt knew what I was thinking and felt awful about it. I wanted out of there right away. It was as if Walt was saying he couldn't help me, that he had nothing to do with me being out there, but that his hands were tied."

He finished the game. The Dodger trainers said they could help him, but Wills, fearing for his knee and health, wanted no more of the tour. Later, back at the team hotel, he fell into a discussion with his roommate on the trip, Nate Oliver.

If you were me, what would you do? he asked Oliver.

There's no question what you should do, Oliver said.

As Oliver would later remember, he said this to Wills: "First and foremost, I'd think of self-preservation. I'd want to continue my career. If an injury was affecting me significantly, if I couldn't perform, I'd go home and get medical attention and take care of myself."

Oliver's comments merely served to affirm a conclusion Wills already had reached. His right knee had locked up by then. He made reservations to fly to Honolulu, and then, sensing the danger he was inviting, decided to call Walter Alston and beg him for permission to leave.

However, something was lost in translation with the hotel operator, who connected him to the wrong Walter. Suddenly he was talking to O'Malley himself, trying to explain that his knee was killing him, that he must go home and get it fixed.

No way, O'Malley responded, as Wills recalls. You can't leave. I won't allow it.

The conversation soon ended. In the future, Wills would experience regrets over what he did next. But mixed with those regrets would be his conviction that the team's management pushed him toward this moment.

"They'd been bogarting me my whole career," he'd explain.

Not anymore, he decided in Japan.

Soon he was on a plane and gone, having played only four games on the tour.

"I wasn't conscious of being defiant in Japan," he remembers. "I just reacted that way after being pushed around so much. In Japan, something made me strike back. I took a stand."

To be a ballplayer in the 1960s meant always having to reconcile defending oneself against a club owner's abuses while taking pains not to trigger his wrath. Wills would soon pay a price for standing up to O'Malley. "These days I regret leaving Japan without permission," he said in 2014. "My leg was banged up. I thought I had to leave. I just didn't think at that time I had any other choice. When you get treated badly too much by some people, that's going to happen."

If Wills made a tactical mistake, it was in going to Hawaii for a few days, instead of immediately traveling home. He woke up in Waikiki, hung out on Oahu, saw some shows. One night a popular Hawaiian entertainer, Don Ho, called him up onstage, and Wills joined him in a few numbers, strumming a banjo. He hung out one night with Sammy Davis. Bavasi reported to O'Malley on what he had learned about Wills's movements. Wills was concealing nothing. He told local reporters in Hawaii that he was simply hoping to relax a little and play his banjo, among other things, before heading back to Los Angeles, where doctors diagnosed his knee as badly strained but fortunately free of cartilage damage.

In Japan, O'Malley decided to let the press and public know of his fury, revealing that he had felt obliged to apologize to Japanese officials for Wills's action, suggesting the transgression rose to the level of an insult against the team's hosts and an entire country, and signaling that there would be serious repercussions for the AWOL player. "It is a breach of contract on his part," O'Malley told the *Los Angeles Times*, indicating that he viewed Wills's departure as nothing less than an act of insubordination. "But there will be no discussion of any possible disciplinary action until we have had to time to evaluate the situation after our return to Los Angeles. As the captain of the team, a higher degree of devotion to duty was expected of Maury."

Characteristically, Alston distanced himself from the disputants: "Leave me out of this. It is a matter between Mr. O'Malley and Wills."

Alston had his own problems as the tour moved along. O'Malley's insistence that the Dodgers perform well in the exhibitions translated to a demand for wins. Early in the tour, O'Malley gave each player a bonus of $250 (with the bonus, a player's total earnings on the trip would come to $4,250 for the 18 games, or $236.11 per game). Nothing O'Malley did, however, could motivate the weary and disinterested. Soon a long losing streak ignited concern among Dodger officials that reached the ears of Alston, who warned the players against underperforming. "All this talk from O'Malley and Alston about needing to win these games—we couldn't give a shit about that," remembers Ferrara. "The games didn't count to anybody, except maybe to O'Malley."

For some players, the trip was more than unpleasurable, amounting to a personal burden. Osteen wanted to be home with his wife, who was due to give birth to their third child. O'Malley had made a deal with him: Osteen could leave Japan after pitching the tour's opening game, which, O'Malley informed him, was to be telecast by ABC. "In the meantime, I'll pay for all your phone calls home to your wife," the owner said. Osteen beat the Yomiuri Giants but ABC showed not his game but the next one, in which the Dodgers were shut out by Yomiuri, 3–0, a thrashing that called to mind the Orioles' domination. O'Malley's embarrassment mounted. Soon Wills had fled, which prompted the owner to summon Osteen to his suite at the New Otani Hotel and briskly tell him that the team needed him to remain in Japan. "If your wife has an emergency, I'll immediately fly you home," O'Malley promised.

"I didn't want to be there, but what I was going to do?" Osteen remembers of his reaction. "I stayed. I didn't win again in Japan. I didn't do well; the team didn't do well. And my wife gave birth while I was over there."

Everything seemed to be unraveling by then. Less than a week after his son's birth, on November 18, Osteen and his roommate on the trip, Jim Brewer, heard a knock at the door of their hotel room. Seconds later a Japanese reporter was asking for a comment about the retirement of Sandy Koufax.

Retirement?

"Yes. Retirement."

Osteen was stunned. "I never suspected a retirement was in the offing."

Aside from Ferrara, no Dodger player in Japan or anywhere else had apparently received advance warning from Koufax. Not even friends as close as Tracewski had been forewarned. Fairly was convinced that the report was either erroneous, misunderstood, or an impulsive decision that Koufax would quickly reverse. For Koufax to retire at the peak of his skills and performance was impossible. He quickly told teammates in Japan: "That's b.s. He's not going to do it. No way he's going to retire."

Lou Johnson walked around the team hotel, unable to speak. "I felt empty. Sandy showed me a kindness that really helped to change my life. Hearing he was gone hurt in every way. The only thing that made it okay was that I thought I got to spend time with somebody who was one of my heroes. But I had problems that day just thinking about it. Like, what do we do now? Let's face it: it was the first thing that dismantled our dynasty, come on now. You knew it that day."

At the age of thirty years and eleven months, a point in life when many players are reaching their peak, Koufax wanted out of the game before it was too late. Seldom has a retiring athlete ever sounded less tortured over his decision. He shed no tears. His voice never quavered. At the Beverly Wilshire Hotel, he spoke matter-of-factly. He told the press he had received "cortisone shots with regularity," adding that to end his career was the only sensible path. "I just feel like I don't want to take a chance on completely disabling myself. . . . I've got a lot of years to live after baseball, and I'd like to live them with the complete use of my body."

An incredulous Tracewski called Koufax: "Are you kiddin', roomie?"

"My arm is still hurting," the voice on the other end said softly. He opened himself more to Tracewski than he had to the reporters. He ran through his options with Tracewski, saying he could continue to "dope up," which meant taking the same anti-inflammatories and pain pills that had left him sometimes feeling half high on the field during the past two seasons—or be rational and quit. "I can't keep using the cortisone," he added, as Tracewski recalls. "I just don't want to do that anymore. The doctors told me the cortisone will probably harm my kidneys and liver if I keep taking it. Lots of bad things could happen. I just gotta retire."

And he was finished talking about it.

In Los Angeles, the news had just begun reaching people, where it sounded like a death of sorts to many, including Zev Yaroslavsky. "It was like I had lost a member of my family," he remembered. "I thought, Oh, shit, I never get to see Koufax again. It was the saddest sports day of my life."

Fifteen-year-old Marti Allen heard about it on a radio while sitting in an orthodontist's chair, being fitted for braces. She held back her emotion until she could find a quiet place to cry. "He was so beautiful and perfect in everything he did," she reflected. "Then he was just gone."

The only serene figure was Koufax. Before telling the world, he had given Bavasi the shortest of warnings. Bavasi responded by asking him to wait on making the announcement until O'Malley arrived home from Japan. Koufax casually declined, not needing O'Malley's presence, the cold reality of this unspoken rejection eventually triggering a public expression of disappointment from Bavasi. Something had been lost for good between the three men amid the resentments of their two long contractual duels.

No one who knew Koufax well was surprised by either the secrecy before his announcement or the way he handled his final moments as a Dodger at the Beverly Wilshire. At home, Wills thought, Good for Sandy—he's done it his way; gone out the way he wanted; stood up for what he wanted. Wills didn't call him. He thought that Sandy, being Sandy, would want to have his privacy. Television could not stop talking about the shock. But his friend's career ended just as Wills always suspected it would: one day Sandy would just pick up and leave. No farewell tour. No need for 55,000 cheers. He would be here one afternoon and gone the next, like an apparition. And the Dodgers would never be the same.

Koufax's retirement had implications for the entire roster. Without him, no longer did O'Malley and Bavasi have any realistic chance of winning a third straight National League pennant. Even an effective Drysdale, Wills, and Tommy Davis, combined with meaningful contributions from the rest of the roster, couldn't make up for the loss of Koufax's twenty-seven victories. The real possibility existed that, with Koufax gone, the Dodgers might sink toward the National League cellar. To lose another star or two would make no meaningful difference.

With that recognition, many players became expendable, especially the one who had fled Japan. The Associated Press found Wills in Los Angeles, where he said his right knee was improving, projecting a confident air. "My only concern now is getting in shape . . . so I can play the kind of ball I know I can play," he said.

Yet, in an ominous sign, he acknowledged he hadn't heard from O'Malley, Bavasi, or anyone else in the team's organization since arriving home. "The Japanese tour was important to Mr. O'Malley, and I suppose he's rather bitter about me leaving," Wills said to the reporter, though he refused to back down, repeating that he might have ruined his career had he continued playing on the bad knee.

O'Malley ordered that Wills be traded, Bavasi would later say, the general manager sympathetic with the owner's conviction that Wills's defiance in Japan amounted to an insult of everyone who was a part of the tour. But in truth the only seriously wounded party was O'Malley. If a player objected to an order from the owner, he better do it in the style of Parker, discreetly and behind the scenes, to signal respect. Wills had publicly spurned an O'Malley dictate, leaving the potentate upstaged at the very moment when he was on an around-the-clock charm offensive with his Japanese hosts. From that instant, it was only a question of when O'Malley would deliver his punishment.

In doing so, he would reveal more than ever about the unchecked power of a major-league owner in the 1960s—and in turn help to stoke the kind of backlash that advanced Marvin Miller and the players' union. "What O'Malley did with Maury was the kind of thing that bred somebody like Marvin," Ferrara said. Most of O'Malley's players struggled to grasp why the Japan tour meant so much to him that he would drag along reluctant players and, in the case of Wills, permit the tour to tear his team apart. But to understand O'Malley, it would always be critical to grasp his restless appetite for growth and expansion. Nothing so absorbed him as the future and what he would do next. The Dodgers' first trip to Japan, in 1956, had cast O'Malley as a goodwill ambassador and a baseball visionary, whose ideas by the end of 1966 included one that he hadn't publicly discussed at length—the possibility of bringing major-league baseball someday to Japan. "After the 1966 tour, [the thought of expansion] occurred to my father," Peter O'Malley said. "An All-Star Japanese team could've competed. The future of baseball in Japan was very good."

To Japanese audiences, O'Malley emphasized his commitment as an American to bring their two nations closer. Nothing about his goal or efforts could fairly be characterized as trivial. It had been only twenty-one years since the end of World War II, twenty-one years since atomic bombs had destroyed the cities of Hiroshima and Nagasaki. When the Japanese honored O'Malley that year in the prime minister's office, noting his role in "fostering the United States–Japan friendship through professional baseball" since his first tour there in 1956, the moment spoke to his contribution in furthering a cultural bond.

The chief problem with O'Malley's quests is that they seldom took into account the desires or needs of his players. One of sports' last emperors, he gave orders to his players that he expected to be obeyed unconditionally even after their regular season contractual obligations to him ended. When they clashed with him, it was rarely for long—their needs swiftly yielded to his own, if for no other reason than that their Dodger careers might depend on it.

Without exception, the defiant player suffered, as Wills would soon find out. O'Malley now moved toward exacting his revenge.

History would never have known O'Malley's precise words at the moment he made his decision about Wills were it not for Bavasi, who in his garrulousness would always be the gift that kept giving to journalists and historians. Less than six months after the episode, Bavasi would write, in *Sports Illustrated*, that what O'Malley said to him during a trans-Pacific phone call was this: "Buzzie, it looks as though the boy's asking for it, and I think we'll have to give it to him."

Koufax's departure had freed O'Malley and Bavasi to cut Wills or anybody else loose. On the morning of November 30, 1966, Tommy Davis was out playing a round of golf with Willie Davis when a TV crew rushed up to him on the course with the news that he had been traded to the Mets. Shocked, Davis needed time to process what he was hearing. He thought he had done everything right. At O'Malley's request, he'd even gone to Japan, where he hit .462. But, in a reflection of his entire '66 season, he played sparingly, with only thirteen at-bats. He still hadn't fully recovered from his injury, and now realized that the Dodgers didn't feel like carrying a question mark for another season. "The doctors told Buzzie: 'Give him two years to re-prove himself. He'll need to rehab,'" Davis recalls. "But they traded me."

By then, whispers of Wills's imminent banishment had reached him in Spokane, where he was spending time with his family. A reporter telephoned to pass along the serious rumor of a trade in the works. More nervous than ever, Wills told the reporter to please pass along word that "I'm praying not to be traded, because I've played my whole career for the Dodgers. The Dodgers are my life. Please tell everybody that."

On December 1, about twenty-four hours after the Davis trade, and just thirteen days after Koufax's retirement, Wills was at a Spokane sports luncheon when reporters rushed up to inform him that he had been traded to Pittsburgh. He tried, unsuccessfully, to stop himself from choking up and crying, and soon escaped to drive himself home. Dodger officials later reached him with the official word: he was on his way to the Pirates, in exchange for third baseman Bob Bailey and shortstop Gene Michael. He hung up and sobbed. He replayed over and over the sequence of events that had led to all this. "Mr. O'Malley felt like I had turned my back on him," he would later say. "If you look at it that way, you can say I had it coming. O'Malley thought he had to teach me and everybody else a lesson and traded me. But other people didn't go to Japan. My knee was hurt. I was in agony playing on it. What did I really do that was wrong?"

On that first day, he would think about it for a while, then start crying again. Something else occurred to him. *Pittsburgh*. He had to go to *Pittsburgh*. He didn't even like their uniforms, all that Pirate black. Nothing was as beautiful as all the blue he'd worn: *that* was his jersey. He thought he was losing his mind. He tried telling himself it would be okay. He tried contemplating his conditioning program, all that he had to do to get back in good shape and have his knee ready. He tried focusing, tried telling himself he had to bounce back from all this. His silent concentration steadied him for a while before he completely lost it again. This was a nightmare. He sobbed for days. *What the hell has happened to me?*

D odger players were largely scornful of the trade. In a reflection of most Dodger attitudes, Parker privately viewed Wills's exile as "an overreaction." Resting at home in Los Angeles as the drama of Wills's revolt played out in Japan and Hawaii and finally back in Southern California, Parker was of two minds about the saga. He regarded O'Malley's anger over Wills's escape to Honolulu as justified. But the trade had badly hurt the team, thought Parker, who identified with Wills's frustrations and anxiety in Japan. "His leg was hurting," Parker said. "He didn't want to be in Japan in the first place. He was exhausted. [O'Malley's] personal feelings overruled what was good for the club, so the trade was a bad overreaction. Maury was our leader. Maury set the table for us. We missed him immediately."

The players' reactions often reflected their own mistreatment by baseball executives. Nothing that happened in baseball any longer surprised Johnson. "I was hurt by Maury's trade," he said. "But I wasn't surprised by it. That was the time when, if a player stood up for himself, he usually got punished. But the trade made it harder for us on the field. We didn't have home run hitters. Maury made us go. That fighter in him wasn't going to be with us."

No one was more upset or blunt than Ferrara, who, a half century later, expressed the raw feelings that even Wills's strongest supporters at the time kept to themselves. "Let's face it: players' rights weren't at all respected then," Ferrara said. "Maury had every right to do what he did in Japan and get the hell out of there. He was hurting. But the attitude of everybody in management was, How dare you? You didn't do something like that then. People didn't have the balls. But Maury had the balls. That trade was made to show everybody on the Dodgers who was boss. It was vengeance. Everybody in the organization knew it. Getting rid of Maury destroyed us the next season."

But Ferrara didn't call Wills to check on him or extend his sympathies. He was not alone in this. Not one of his old teammates contacted Wills, who completely understood why. "What was anybody going to say to me anyway?" he pointed out. "I didn't call players either when they were traded. One day players are just gone. You don't allow yourself to feel too sad. If you do, you can't think about the game. You'll lose your focus."

The sport hardened you, he thought. Else you couldn't get through its jarring moments. "The game conditions you to the point where it's a little bit every man for himself," he said. "You don't have long goodbyes in baseball. Maybe you see them when they're playing for a new team; maybe you don't. You care about them, but everybody moves on. You couldn't get through this if you didn't think that way. After I was traded, I knew I had to rely on myself."

He had spent a whole career trying to make himself stoic in the face of disappointments. But nothing had prepared him for this. His whole identity had been wrapped around being a Dodger. Being cut loose felt like an annihilation. He had his phone close to him in the first days afterward. Desolate, he never picked it up. "I didn't call Sandy or anybody else. I suffered on my own. I was crying a lot. It felt like the end."

His own end was actually far off. But the moment represented the finish of a team's greatness and glory. The Dodger dynasty of the 1960s, which had taken years to build, oddly had required only thirteen days to be dismantled. "Things were ruined in a hurry—Maury was the last straw," Ferrara remembered. "You didn't forget the way they treated him after Japan. We were never going to be the same team after that."

By then, the players' innocence had given way to the kinds of unleashed resentments manifest in Wills's revolt. The era's dynamism had emboldened restless young performers throughout baseball at the very moment that the owners' excesses galvanized them to turn to Marvin Miller. O'Malley showed no signs at that moment of recognizing the revolution coming, let alone of making peace with it. Now, with the emperor's club in tatters, a malaise had settled over his organization. "The guys in charge just refused to accept that the world wasn't going to stay the same," Ferrara said.

As the 1960s rolled along, the Dodger players' indignation over their front office's dictates and missteps not only presaged a discontent that would roil their game but perfectly reflected young Americans' growing distrust of the establishment everywhere. For a twenty-seven-year-old Dodger like Ferrara, increasingly worried during that winter about the fate of his military brother, Frank—who was serving in Vietnam—as well as his own future in baseball, Wills simply had become another example of all that was wrong with entrusting your life, your sport, your city, and your country to current management.

"When people saw Maury that next spring in a Pirates uniform, it reminded everybody just how screwed up everything had gotten," Ferrara reflected. "How did it come to this? How could O'Malley get rid of him like that and ruin our team? It was like everything else going on that year in the country. People were being shipped places they didn't want to go. Things just felt screwed up everywhere, like it was all coming apart."

Chapter 8

Baseball Takes a Backseat to the World

T he winning was over.

There would be no more championships in the 1960s for the Dodgers. Indeed, aside from reliever Bob Miller, there would be no more World Series titles for any member of the 1966 National League champions during the remainder of their playing careers. For a while, even respectability on the field would be elusive for the Dodgers. In 1967 the team sunk to eighth place, finishing with 73 victories and 89 defeats, its worst record since arriving in Los Angeles. A group of heralded new Dodgers, those obtained in trades, had underperformed, while Wills batted an exceptional .302 for the Pirates, and Tommy Davis, playing regularly again, hit .302 for the Mets. The Dodgers' reversal of fortune impacted the entire organization, including the coffers of Walter O'Malley. The on-field woes had an especially startling effect on the team's home attendance, with 952,000 fewer fans coming to the ballpark during 1967 than a year earlier.

While 1,664,352 spectators still made their way through Dodger Stadium's turnstiles that year—an enviable figure for the vast majority of clubs—the falling number reflected diminished fan interest, corresponding with the start of a lengthy stretch of mediocrity for the

Dodgers, who hadn't fared so poorly at the gate since leaving Brooklyn. For the first time in nine years the team failed to top the league in attendance, finishing a distant second in gate receipts to the Cardinals, the year's World Champions. The Dodgers' business numbers would have been far worse had Los Angeles fans, always a finicky lot, caught on sooner to the profound weaknesses of the club. After the casual rooters awakened late in the year to the new reality, the team often played in a ballpark three-quarters empty. In a new Dodger Stadium low, during the team's final ten home games of 1967, average attendance plummeted below 13,000. Amorous couples had entire rows to themselves.

For the first time since the team's arrival in Los Angeles, a professional football game there carried far more importance than any Dodger game. The inaugural Super Bowl had taken place earlier that year in the Los Angeles Memorial Coliseum, and though the great stadium was only about two-thirds full, the game between the NFL's Green Bay Packers and the AFL's Kansas City Chiefs riveted fans across the country in the way the Dodgers no longer did.

At the end of the disappointing season, the Dodgers traded away Roseboro, along with Ron Perranoski and Bob Miller, to the Twins, in exchange for Mudcat Grant and Zoilo Versalles.

Soon to be gone as well was Lou Johnson, who had little reason for happiness that year. Injured in May while sliding into home, he had been out of action for a couple of months, reduced to playing only ninety-one games in the outfield, though still managing to hit .270. In late November, Bavasi let him know he was no longer a Dodger: "You're going to Chicago."

Some players regarded any move to the Cubs as a professional death sentence, but Johnson wasn't one of them. The Cubs had been one of his stops, years earlier. He liked Chicago, he told Bavasi, before thanking him for the opportunity to play with the Dodgers. "Best thing that ever happened to me in my career was being with the Dodgers. When I had to leave I just thought, Man, was I lucky I was ever there. Then I got out to Chicago for the new season, and I had good friends out there already, so I knew I was going to be okay there, too. Ali was there; he was living there."

Muhammad Ali, a fellow Kentuckian, had become a good friend. Raised in Louisville—which had spawned his nickname, the Louisville Lip—Ali had moved to Chicago, where he was now closer to the headquarters and leadership of the Nation of Islam. Nineteen sixty-seven had been rough for him. Convicted of draft evasion and sentenced to five years in a federal penitentiary after refusing induction into the US Army, Ali was out on appeal, though with no chance to make a living in his profession. Several state boxing boards had denied him a license to fight. Boxing's sanctioning bodies had stripped him of his title as heavyweight champion. The possibility loomed that his appeal would be rejected and that Ali would soon be incarcerated. Sometimes Johnson took long walks with Ali, impressed at how cool his friend remained in the face of his struggles.

His attorneys argued that Ali was a conscientious objector; that, among other things, his religion forbade his presence in any country's armed conflict. Ali didn't use any of those terms. He fumed with a rawness that reflected the otherwise muted but growing abhorrence for the war among American athletes, including several Dodgers. Not backing down or asking for a negotiated solution to his own dilemma, the defrocked champion instead delivered a response all his own: "Why should they ask me to put on a uniform and go ten thousand miles from home and drop bombs and bullets on people in Vietnam while the so-called Negro people in Louisville are treated like dogs and denied simple human rights? . . . I have nothing to lose by standing up for my beliefs. So I'll go to jail, so what. We've been in jail for four hundred years."

Johnson listened to his friend with amazement. Having felt transformed by his friendships with Koufax, Roseboro, Wills, Parker, and others, Johnson thought he was learning something new about strength and resolve. "What Ali was doing: that was courage," he said, remembering the early months of 1968. "Because that was the law comin' down on Ali. The law was comin' down fast on people, comin' down *hard*, come on now. They weren't messin' around with that Vietnam stuff."

The only Dodger who would ever serve in Vietnam was already there and fighting.

Roy Gleason—the former bonus baby signed out of Garden Grove High School, seven years earlier; the prodigy personally wooed before that by Ted Williams on behalf of the unsuccessful Red Sox; the talented prospect who had stood in Dodger Stadium during 1963 and doubled in his only major-league at-bat; the one who had experienced frustration in the minors for the next three years; the handsome, strapping six-foot-five, 220-pounder who remembered doing guest spots on two TV series; the twenty-five-year-old who, a year earlier, while eagerly awaiting his chance to impress the big club in spring training, had received an unexpected draft notice from the army—was now in the bush. He was a sergeant whose combat awards would include the Bronze Star and the Purple Heart. But he was a reluctant warrior whose eight-month tour of duty would end as painfully as his military service had begun.

He had fought fiercely not to be there. For years he had believed that, as the sole means of support for his mother and younger sisters, he would be exempt from the draft. His draft board and the army thought otherwise. At his scheduled induction, on April 10, 1967, he initially resisted being sworn into service, declining to raise his hand. "They told me if I didn't take the oath I was going to the brig," he recalls.

He raised his hand and took the oath. He was soon an infantryman in Vietnam. "Out in the bush, we got snipered all the time," he recounts. "I won my Bronze Star for pulling out two guys during a fight. We were kind of guinea pigs. Any enemy movement that happened usually meant that we had to do a sweep—we were the ones exposed. I was a sergeant, so I was the one in charge."

On April 4, 1968, Gleason found himself at a school in Vietnam for noncommissioned officers when he heard, over Armed Forces Radio, that Martin Luther King Jr. had been assassinated in Memphis. "That shook up people," he remembered. "Guys were in an uproar, especially the black guys. You wondered what was going on back in The World, because we were so far away from it."

The World: that's what Gleason and his buddies called virtually any place outside of Vietnam. The World represented everything beyond the hellscape in which they found themselves.

More young conscripts were arriving all the time in Vietnam. Their number had soared above 500,000 by 1968, a year during which more than 16,000 American servicemen there would lose their lives, the most of any year of the conflict. The year had just begun when a surprise enemy assault during a Vietnamese holiday dramatically eroded public support for the war. The massive Tet Offensive, launched jointly in late January of 1968 by the Vietcong and the North Vietnamese Army, ultimately failed, but not before insurgents temporarily seized several major cities in South Vietnam. The many attacks belied the assurances of Lyndon Johnson and his generals that America and its allies had gained the upper hand in the conflict.

Then, on February 27, Walter Cronkite, the Koufax of television news—the model of sublime preparation and composure under pressure—appeared on CBS to deliver a clinical assessment of the war that was made all the more damning by his dispassionate delivery. Cronkite's report, along with an abundance of similarly ominous stories from other American journalists, would have a profound effect on the attitudes of several young Dodgers. In a moment that served as a cold and sobering shower, Cronkite told his viewers: "We have been too often disappointed by the optimism of the American leaders . . . to have faith any longer in the silver linings they find in the darkest clouds." Concluding with an air of inevitability, he observed that the war could be brought to a finish only through a negotiated settlement.

Cronkite's words at once hastened and reflected mainstream America's disillusionment. At that very moment, President Johnson was swiftly becoming a pariah within his own party. In early March he faced a challenge in the 1968 New Hampshire Democratic primary from an antiwar leader, Minnesota senator Eugene McCarthy, who in running close to LBJ in this first contest of the political season had rendered the incumbent president more vulnerable than ever. Soon Robert Kennedy joined the fray, declaring in his candidacy announcement that the country was on "a perilous course" in Vietnam. As March was ending, a sinking Johnson, yielding to political realities, told the nation he would not be a candidate for reelection. His vice president, Hubert Humphrey, swiftly launched a presidential campaign of his own, with the war to be the paramount issue.

Back in Los Angeles, Dodger players watched and read reports that placed American military deaths at several hundred a week. Parker had taken to watching television newscasts and network news specials, which were full of reports about the mess Vietnam had become.

One night Parker heard that twelve ambushed American soldiers had been killed in the Mekong Delta. The specificity of that number, *twelve*, made it worse somehow for him, more grisly; he'd never be able to forget that number. His mind couldn't conjure images of *hundreds* of dead soldiers. But he could imagine twelve young men with a frightening clarity.

Parker was a Republican who loathed the war as ferociously as any Yippie. Aside from the dead, he felt worst of all for the young men who'd come back from Vietnam shattered. When Dodger executive Red Patterson asked him in the late 1960s if he would be willing to visit wounded American soldiers at a Veterans Administration hospital in West Los Angeles, Parker immediately agreed. He showed up a couple of times with a teammate or two. A public relations person would take him into a room and introduce him to servicemen often younger than himself.

Strong, fit guys, he immediately thought.

Except some of them would be without legs. Others would be missing an arm.

Parker would already be thinking, *This is not right, this is not right.*

"Let me introduce Wes Parker, first baseman of the Los Angeles Dodgers," the PR representative would say.

Parker saw no reaction from the men. Nothing hostile. Nothing contemptuous. Just nothing.

"It was like, Nice of you to come, but what can you do about my legs?" he remembered.

He'd speak to them for a while about baseball, ready to discuss anything they might want to ask or share with him, only to see their eyes glaze over, some of their stares fixed on something very far off.

The visits only reminded him just how much this war had ruined men. It was a mark of how much the war seared him that he thought about it late some nights now, the horror momentarily piercing the shell he erected during baseball seasons. Still, by the afternoons, when it was time to go to the ballpark, he was ready. "I had a responsibility to the team then," he said. "You bring no distractions into the clubhouse."

In 1968, although the Dodgers were struggling again, on their way to another losing season and a seventh-place finish, Parker and his teammates found one thing to cheer them. Drysdale was having the greatest run of his pitching career. In addition to pitching a major-league record six consecutive shutouts, he would also toss fifty-eight and two-thirds consecutive innings of scoreless ball, breaking a fifty-five-year-old record established by the immortal Washington Senators' right-hander Walter Johnson.

As Drysdale marched closer to the record books, the legion of his fascinated onlookers included Robert Kennedy, who wanted to meet the pitcher while he was campaigning in California, prior to his pivotal contest against Eugene McCarthy, in the state's Democratic presidential primary on June 8.

Thanks to Drysdale, many home fans whose passion for the team had temporarily dimmed now were returning to the stadium, hoping to see him make history. On Friday night, May 31, as Drysdale sought his fifth straight shutout, with the despised Giants as his foe, the 46,067 spectators included UCLA student Zev Yaroslavsky and an Israeli acquaintance who was seeing his first baseball game. "My interest in baseball had slackened," recalled Yaroslavsky. "Koufax was gone, the Dodgers weren't winning, and I had things going on. But I wanted to see Drysdale. And I thought this Israeli friend might find it interesting. It was a wild game, like a lot of Dodger-Giant games."

Drysdale entered the ninth inning with a three-run lead and a five-hit shutout before running into serious trouble. McCovey walked and gave way to a pinch runner. Jim Ray Hart followed with a single to right, and right fielder Dave Marshall walked, to load the bases with nobody out. The streak seemed likely to end. Torborg, who would play in only thirty-seven games that year and had earned a rare start, walked to the mound to check on Drysdale. "We were hoping for a strikeout or a ground ball and force out at the plate," he remembered. "We wanted to keep Don's streak going if we could. He'd been such a good teammate to everybody all those years."

The Giants' right-handed-hitting catcher Dick Dietz stepped to the plate. On a 2–2 pitch, Drysdale threw what many observers remember as a slider. It hit a motionless Dietz in the elbow, apparently forcing in a run and ending Drysdale's streak at 44 innings. Giants fans roared with glee. But home-plate umpire Harry Wendelstedt declared that Dietz hadn't attempted to get out of the way of the pitch, refusing to award him first base and thereby nullifying the Giants' run. As the Giants looked on in disbelief, Wendelstedt ruled that the pitch would be nothing more than a ball, making the count three balls and two strikes.

Dietz and the Giants' bench erupted. Stupefied Giants manager Herman Franks charged toward Wendelstedt, soon to be ejected from the game. Yaroslavsky's Israeli friend was puzzled. What was happening? Why were the men yelling? Why were there so many on the field kicking dirt, jumping around, acting crazy? "The shit had hit the fan out there," Yaroslavsky remembered, "and I was trying to explain to this friend what was happening and why. I had to try to explain several things at once—the Dodger-Giant rivalry, how it dated back to New York and Brooklyn; the reversal of the umpire's call and why; the importance of Drysdale's shutout-inning streak; the hatred of some of the Dodgers and Giants; the definition of bases loaded and what a player hit by a pitch gets to do. I was thinking, This is hard to explain."

It was too bad the scene eluded explanation, he thought, because the moment was as mad as the era; it was in some ways a perfect representation of the 1960s. "I could just see this Israeli guy wasn't getting it," Yaroslavsky remembered. "As much as I tried, it was too hard to explain. So I just stopped. We got something to eat."

By then Dietz had stepped back into the batter's box, with a full count, and hit a shallow fly to left field for an out. A pinch hitter, the left-handed-hitting Ty Cline, next hit a bouncer to Parker, who threw to home plate; he'd later describe what he did as a routine play. It was routine only because Parker was the one making it. "Under that kind of pressure, all kinds of mistakes can happen for an infielder, especially throwing from first base," Torborg said. "But Wes was so smooth; he made everything look easy. He made the throw, we got the force out at the plate, and we had two outs."

Finally, with the bases still jammed, pinch hitter Jack Hiatt hit a high pop-up that Parker caught for the third out. Drysdale had his fifth consecutive shutout, his scoreless inning streak had reached 45, and reporters and celebrities alike sought to get time with the pitcher.

During the last weekend before the California primary, Kennedy took a brief break from campaigning to come to Dodger Stadium before a game. Accompanied by a few aides, he walked into the Dodger dugout and said hello to Mudcat Grant, congratulating him on his success, before heading into the clubhouse, where he and Drysdale began chatting. Standing nearby was Torborg. "Don told Bobby I was a player and introduced me, and there I was shaking hands with Bobby and he said, 'Nice to meet you,'" Torborg remembered. "I wouldn't say I was in awe. There were always celebrities around. But, you know, this was Bobby. It was special. And I was kind of surprised a little when I met him. He was not the same type of personality as his brother, and he didn't look the same. Bobby was not big. And he didn't have a big voice. I just kind of listened to him and Don. They were just two men talking to each other, enjoying spending some time together. And then everybody was gone and we played a game."

On Tuesday, June 4, at Dodger Stadium, on the brink of a major-league record, Drysdale sought his sixth consecutive shutout. The Pirates were the foe. Only 30,422 attended the game, in part because it was primary night in California. The drama and tension in the ballpark were amplified by the stiff challenge presented by a Pirates lineup that included Clemente, Stargell, Mazeroski, left fielder Manny Mota, and, most deliciously, Maury Wills, who batted second in the order behind Matty Alou. At thirty-five, Wills was running like someone ten years younger, on his way to stealing fifty-two bases on the season and hit .278. "I just saw that game as a great challenge," he remembered. "Don had a chance to set a record, and as much as I admired him, we had a chance to stop it."

Drysdale pitched magnificently, saving his best game for his season's most memorable moment. He threw a three-hitter, walking no one and fanning eight. In the ninth running, with a 5–0 lead, he quickly struck out pinch hitter Manny Jiminez and got Alou to groundout. Wills came to the plate, in no mood to be somebody's final foil in a historic baseball moment. He singled to center, leaving Stargell to hit a grounder for the last out of consecutive shutout number six. At 10:20 p.m. Pacific Daylight Time, Don Drysdale entered the record books.

In the clubhouse, amid the press mob and hoopla for Drysdale, a few reporters mentioned that Kennedy was beating McCarthy, according to early election returns, apparently on his way to a decisive victory. After congratulating Drysdale, Mudcat Grant decided to head with a friend to the Ambassador Hotel, in Los Angeles's Mid-Wilshire district, to be with Kennedy supporters and watch the senator's victory speech. From Dodger Stadium, if traffic wasn't bad, Grant figured he could probably make it to the Ambassador in about a half hour, maybe sooner if he caught a break.

Torborg had decided to get home to watch television's coverage of the returns. He and his wife were renting a home from Joe Moeller, in Manhattan Beach. Suzie Torborg awakened when her husband stepped through the front door. Together, in bed, they watched Kennedy's speech a little after midnight, with Torborg thinking how incredible it was that, just a few days earlier, he had shaken this man's hand, hung out with him, listened to him chat with Drysdale, the two stars on top of the world now. Life was good, Torborg thought. Then his night got even better. Bobby Kennedy was suddenly talking about *Drysdale*. Incredible. He hoped Drysdale was watching this. Bobby congratulating Don. Amazing.

Kennedy was saying this:

"I first want to express my high regard for Don Drysdale, who pitched his sixth straight shutout tonight, and I hope that we have as good fortune in our campaign."

Meanwhile Mudcat Grant was stuck in traffic, still a good distance from the Ambassador. Too bad, he thought. Well, he wasn't going to make it for the speech, but there was still time to get there, say hi to a few people, congratulate them, and enjoy himself.

Torborg and his wife were listening to the entire speech. He still couldn't get over the reference to Drysdale. So great, he thought. A jovial Kennedy informed the audience that the Kennedys' dog, Freckles, had gone to bed ("He thought very early that we were going to win, so he retired"), and next expressed gratitude to his smiling wife, Ethel ("I'm not doing this in the order of importance") and thanked a retired All-Pro defensive tackle who had traveled with him on many campaign stops and was a popular figure in Los Angeles ("And to Rosie Grier, who said he'd take care of anybody who didn't vote for me—in a kind way").

Toward his speech's end, Kennedy made an appeal: "I would hope now . . . that we can concentrate on having a dialogue or a debate between the Vice President and, perhaps, myself, on what direction we want to go in the United States. . . . Whether we're going to continue the policies which have been so unsuccessful in Vietnam. . . . I think we should move in a different direction."

Kennedy concluded by exhorting the crowd: "So my thanks to all of you and now it's on to Chicago and let's win there." Slowly, escorted by aides and buffeted by supporters, he began making his way toward the side of the stage, looking for an exit.

Torborg had thoroughly enjoyed the speech, still flush with all the night's excitement. As he would later remember, the television station he was watching broke away for a couple of minutes from the Ambassador Hotel to show a commercial or two.

It was during the break that Suzie Torborg suddenly sat straight up in their bed and said in alarm, "He's been shot."

Torborg recalls that he immediately tried to reassure her: "No, no, it's a commercial. They're just doing a commercial. They'll be back after the commercial."

"No, he's been shot," a scared Suzie Torborg said.

Torborg, a man on his way to managing five major-league teams and highly respected for his good judgment, was married to a woman with the same kind of reputation. No one will ever know with certainty what made Suzie Torborg say what she did. Perhaps it was nothing more than a terrifying vision sparked by the times, a fear born of an era when a political assassination had ceased to be a surprise, when madness seemed to have temporarily become the natural order of things. Or perhaps, as Jeff and Suzie Torborg would later believe, she had experienced a genuine premonition. It would not be the first or last time in her life, Torborg would explain, that his wife had such feelings.

But, in that first moment, sitting in bed, a shaken Torborg didn't know what to think. The election telecast then returned from its commercial break. "And we heard he'd been shot," Torborg said. "We were stunned. I'd just seen him. And soon everybody was in mourning again, just like with his brother."

An injured Ferrara, forced to spend virtually the entire season rehabbing a broken ankle, was in a bar called the Tail o' the Cock out in the San Fernando Valley, on Ventura Boulevard. He had spent much of 1968 cheering on any candidate who might bring the war to a swift end. His brother Frank would fortunately leave Vietnam alive, but Ferrara sympathized with the many military families grieving over their losses. He was having a drink when he heard over the television that Kennedy had been shot. There were no other details. "I was shocked; I was crazy," he remembered.

At about the same time, a happy Grant was getting closer to the Ambassador. Reports about election figures suddenly gave way to an incomprehensible commotion on the radio. "You couldn't understand anything," he said. "Then they said Senator Kennedy had been shot. It was just bedlam on the radio. We turned around and drove back to the Stadium. We just sat in the empty Stadium parking lot listening to the radio." For an instant he flashed on November 1963 and saw himself sitting in his car after his father-in-law told him what had happened to John Kennedy. "I wondered if it was ever going to end, the killings, the craziness. There were days then when I thought it might never stop."

The formerly impassioned Dodger fan Zev Yaroslavsky was reeling, too. Having become a supporter of Eugene McCarthy, he had attended what the faithful hoped would be a McCarthy victory party at the Beverly Hilton Hotel.

Soon Yaroslavsky and hundreds of others descended on Good Samaritan Hospital, where, after surgery, Kennedy lay in critical condition and a vigil had begun. He would die the following day, Thursday, June 6. "I thought, What's happening to us?" Yaroslavsky said.

It was much the same thing that a numb Wills—who had sat out the final game of the Pirates-Dodgers series as Kennedy clung to life—was asking himself: "How could this happen again? We'd just gone through this a couple of months earlier."

After Martin Luther King's assassination, Pirates players and others from around the game had wanted the major leagues to postpone the opening day of the season, scheduled for April 8, until after King's funeral and burial. In what Clemente, Wills, and other Pittsburgh players regarded as an insensitive compromise, Commissioner William Eckert, once an air force lieutenant general, declared that major-league teams could decide for themselves whether to play on opening day. When the Houston Astros, the Pirates' host to start the season, announced they would begin their season as scheduled on April 8, Pirates players said they wouldn't take the field either that day or the next in Houston, forcing a postponement of both games. With other players around baseball rebelling, Eckert relented. He announced that the season wouldn't begin for any team until April 10, the day following King's funeral.

Now Wills, a Kennedy supporter, and many other players from both leagues wanted baseball to accord the same respect to Robert Kennedy. Few sports observers had forgotten the NFL's callousness in November 1963, when it had gone ahead with its games just two days after President Kennedy's assassination. Eckert, already acquiring a reputation as waffling and feckless, refused to postpone any games on Saturday, June 8—the day of Kennedy's funeral and burial—other than those scheduled to take place in Washington, DC, and the state of New York, which Kennedy had represented in the Senate. All other games, he said, could proceed, with teams merely instructed to start their contests after the conclusion of Kennedy's burial in Arlington National Cemetery. Everything about how to observe Kennedy's death would be left to the teams' discretion.

Some baseball people were going to take matters in their own hands, no matter what the commissioner said. Finding themselves with a scheduled game in San Francisco, the New York Mets as a team and organization told the Giants they wouldn't play on the day of Kennedy's funeral, period, willing to accept a forfeit if it came to that.

The Mets, true to their word, did not play, leaving the Giants no choice but to reschedule the game.

Down in Houston, the Pirates did play that Saturday night, with Wills in the lineup. On their own, the Pirates players had already decided to sit out the game the following day, which Lyndon Johnson had designated a national day of mourning. But on that Sunday, June 9, after Pirates officials privately spoke to Clemente and several other Pirates, all but one of the players agreed to play. Wills refused to budge. Behind closed doors in Houston, he made it clear to the Pirates brass that while he wasn't interested in provoking a public controversy, he wanted to be quietly excused from the game because he couldn't, *wouldn't* play on the national day of mourning. At thirty-five, he was an altogether different man from the scared young player Bavasi had pushed around. He doubted that anyone could intimidate him any longer. "The Pirates could have threatened me all they wanted," he remembers. "I'd decided what I was going to do."

The Pirates tested him. His manager, Larry Shepard, placed him in the lineup, forcing Wills to refuse to play, which enabled the team to characterize his stance as an act of insubordination and fine him. News of the disciplinary move quickly reached the press. Yet defiance that day in Houston already had spread. Astros first baseman Rusty Staub and third baseman Bob Aspromonte declared they weren't playing either, and would soon be fined themselves. In Cincinnati, pitcher Milt Pappas protested as well.

Reports about the rebellion of the four players, as well as the Mets' collective action in San Francisco, reached the chief aides of Robert Kennedy. Soon Wills received a telegram from Frank Mankiewicz, Kennedy's press secretary, which began, "Please accept my personal admiration for your actions." Mankiewicz passed along similar tributes in telegrams to Staub, Aspromonte, Pappas, and Mets manager Gil Hodges.

In time Ethel Kennedy, learning of what Wills had done, invited him to her home on Hickory Hill, in McLean, Virginia, after the 1968 season ended. He found himself sitting down for a meal with a group that included Robert McNamara and Pierre Salinger. Enthralled by Ethel Kennedy's home and her guests, he turned to his companion and said with soft awe, "You know, we're not in Pittsburgh."

In Los Angeles, the Dodgers organization had declined to set aside an official day for mourning by postponing or canceling a home game. But as Drysdale and his teammates ran out on the field on the night Kennedy was laid to rest, they donned black armbands, which they wore through the remainder of their home stand. Drysdale captured the major-league record for consecutive scoreless innings within the next hour. Some baseball men speculated that the new record would never be broken.

But even extraordinary records are usually fleeting: future Dodger pitcher Orel Hershiser would break this one, twenty years later. What endured instead for Drysdale was the memory of that previous Tuesday night and a special bit of praise from a new acquaintance. When Drysdale was found dead of a heart attack at fifty-six in a Montreal hotel room in July 1993—there as part of the Dodgers' broadcasting crew—attendants discovered a cassette tape among his belongings. It was one of his prized possessions, an item he took with him wherever he traveled. On the tape, Robert Kennedy, delivering the last speech of his life, was praising the friend he'd made in the Dodgers' clubhouse.

R oy Gleason was still in the bush as June gave way to July of 1968. Sometimes he received mail from The World. The letters meant everything to him. One of the people who wrote to him regularly for months was Buzzie Bavasi. The notes came from the good Bavasi, the one so kind and interested in so many Dodger players off the field and away from contract negotiations. Bavasi wrote weekly notes to the twenty-four-year-old Gleason, in addition to sending along regular updates about the entire Dodgers organization, everything from news of Drysdale's streak to the latest on the minor leaguers.

"Everything Buzzie sent me reminded me I had a future," Gleason remembers. "I thought, This will be a springboard for me—because I was in good shape over in Vietnam. As soon as I get home, I'll be ready to play. Just Buzzie taking the time to send things to me cheered me up."

Gleason wrote letters, too, along the way reconnecting with someone to whom he hadn't spoken for years. He dashed off a note to Ted Williams, inspired by a magazine article written by the legend about the art of hitting. He wondered if Williams would even recall who he was or that they'd had a barbecue together when the Red Sox tried to sign him. "You might not remember me," began Gleason, who told Williams about what he was doing in Vietnam and shared some of his own thoughts about hitting. He mailed the letter, uncertain he'd ever hear a word back.

But Williams responded with a detailed letter. He said he certainly remembered Gleason and was happy to hear from him. He expounded on his philosophy about hitting. Then Williams, who had served as a combat aviator during the Korean War, wished Gleason the best in his precarious position. "I hope you get out of that rat trap," Williams wrote, as Gleason remembers. "Keep your ass down."

The delivery of Williams's note would be delayed. Mail from The World generally arrived a good week late to the troops under the best of circumstances. In the case of Williams's letter, there was an additional complication, an unforeseen development that meant that Gleason wouldn't get the missive for many weeks.

The complication was an ambush. On July 24, 1968, while Gleason was in the bush with his unit, an enemy shell exploded, killing three of his friends. Shrapnel from the blast, which sent Gleason flying into a moat, ripped open his left calf, put a hole in his left wrist, and damaged his right arm. He was in army hospitals for the next six months, first in Osaka, Japan, where a shaken Lefebvre called him, and later in San Francisco, where he received the letter from Williams.

For the first five months of his recovery, Gleason was usually flat on his back. His rehabilitation would never be altogether successful—he would carry around the shrapnel in his left leg for the rest of his life. And he would never be the same as a ballplayer. Once among the fastest players in the Dodgers organization, he discovered that his calf wound had robbed him of virtually all his speed. The wrist wound had the effect of leaving his left index finger numb; he no longer could grip a bat quite right. He would try out for the Dodgers and Angels in 1969 and 1970, "but, physically, I just didn't have it anymore," he said. He didn't give up on the game right away, even going down to Mexico for a while in a desperate attempt to resurrect his career. Nothing worked.

In another blow, his 1963 World Series ring, which he had stored in his army foot locker, was gone when his possessions were returned to him. Decades later, in a moment that stands out as among the best of his difficult life, the Dodgers would give him a replica of the ring. "Meant so much," he said. Friends have tried to help along the way. In the first years after his baseball dream died, he bartended at a restaurant Drysdale owned before going back into the army for a while. Later, he sold cars. "My spirits are better today," he said in 2014, having retired. "I just wish I'd had a real chance at baseball. Being drafted killed my career. Nothing was going to be the same after that. But the draft and Vietnam did things like that to all kinds of people. That year I got hurt was a bad time for a lot of guys."

"That year" seemed like it was never going to end, Ferrara thought, shaken by the assassinations and the other horrors of the spring and summer. If anything, 1968 continued getting worse. Zev Yaroslavsky had little time for games. In late August, during the 1968 Democratic National Convention, he and other American television viewers would witness baton-wielding Chicago policemen beating antiwar demonstrators on the city's streets. "Vietnam, the Tet Offensive, Martin Luther King's assassination, Bobby's assassination, the vitriol, the tensions, the worry about what was going to happen next: I just remember sighing with relief when 1968 finally was over," Yaroslavsky said. "I wasn't thinking a lot about baseball in 1968."

The upheaval reached the Dodgers. After thirty years with the organization, Bavasi left in the summer of 1968, with Fresco Thompson to serve briefly as the team's new general manager before being diagnosed with cancer and dying before the year's end. Soon, O'Malley had tapped Al Campanis to be the new enforcer.

Bavasi had become the president of the National League's San Diego Padres, an expansion club that would begin play in 1969. He was proud to be a part owner of his new team, a position his former boss had never offered him. In his post-Dodger years, Bavasi's cracks about Walter O'Malley's stinginess would reach the ears of an offended Peter O'Malley, who attributed the barbs to Bavasi's professional disappointments. "A lot of bitterness emerged," the younger O'Malley said. "He was quoted as saying a lot of outrageous things."

Bavasi would be with the Padres for nine years, going on to serve seven more seasons as executive vice president and general manager of the California Angels before retiring. His detractors would never be able to overlook—or in some cases forgive—his deceit and threats during players' salary negotiations. But his friends—and he had many, including some of those he had deceived or threatened—largely saw his excesses as part of a Jekyll and Hyde professional complex. Those like Ferrara, even after being browbeaten in negotiations, loved remembering how Bavasi had interceded on their behalf in personal matters. "Buzzie did it like I was his son," Ferrara said.

In the end, Bavasi's lasting mark was in being neither Jekyll nor Hyde. Rather it was that the furor sparked by Dodgers management and other teams' executives inflamed players' passions and helped to launch a labor revolution. In this respect, despite their later tensions, Bavasi and Walter O'Malley were conjoined twins.

Chapter 9

A Star Comes Home and Others Say Good-bye

The summer of 1969 would be best known in Los Angeles history not for games but for a spree of grisly killings ordered by Charles Manson, whose name became synonymous with madness. The murders unnerved the community and obscured the sudden retirement of Don Drysdale. Plagued by a sore shoulder that had suffered rotator cuff damage, Drysdale pitched his last game on August 5, retiring at a press conference six days later. The Dodgers staged an appreciation day for him at the stadium, where, in a relatively subdued affair, he received gifts that included some animals for his ranch. Then he was gone, just as quietly as Koufax, in a scene altogether overshadowed by the continuing reports about the savage murders whose many victims included actress Sharon Tate, the pregnant wife of director Roman Polanski. It was the summer when the wondrous competed with the numbing for America's attention. It was the summer when Neil Armstrong and Buzz Aldrin walked on the moon. It was the summer when Ted Kennedy drove off a bridge at Chappaquiddick and a young companion named Mary Jo Kopechne lost her life. It was the summer when charges were leveled against an

American soldier for the massacre of unarmed civilians in the South Vietnamese hamlet of My Lai. It was the summer and year when a city and nation basically lost their capacity for surprise.

In the summer of '69, it was entirely possible for a sixteen-year-old from the San Fernando Valley to be offered free Dodger tickets and drugs on the same day. It was entirely possible to be at a party listening to "Foxy Lady" and simultaneously to have a quite sensible discussion with someone claiming to be tripping on a hallucinogen about whether the Dodgers needed to get a couple of new players. It was entirely possible to see Claude Osteen win a game at Dodger Stadium and, on another day, to watch chain-wielding members of a motorcycle gang operate as self-appointed security guards at a rock festival featuring Jimi Hendrix, among others, in a Valley field once better known for its swap meets. It was entirely possible there to become unnerved by the sight of a catatonic man barking like a crazed dog. It was entirely possible to find yourself running, running like the scared kid you were.

The real world never intruded that year at Dodger Stadium. Everything there was as it always had been. You looked out at the hills and the same purple sunset. The organist played the same show tunes. It was its own kind of opiate, a fantasyland. This was baseball's chief appeal that summer. It gave you yesteryear. It was the perfect sedative in 1969.

Maury Wills came home that summer.

Al Campanis, in his first season as general manager, wanted Wills back in a Dodger uniform. Having hated the trade that sent Wills away in the first place, he tried to persuade O'Malley to permit Wills's return. Wills himself would need no persuasion. He had wanted to be back in Los Angeles from the day he left. But never had he felt as miserable as in early '69. The Pirates had left him unprotected in the National League's latest expansion draft, and he had been picked up by the new Montreal Expos, a predictably dreadful team in a cold weather city.

O'Malley had already rejected the idea of bringing him back, according to Wills: "Al said to me, 'I still have hope, so keep staying in shape.' O'Malley was still angry at me for defying him. But Al kept going to O'Malley about it. He didn't give up."

On June 11, while in San Diego with the Expos, Wills learned he had been traded to the Dodgers.

By the afternoon, he was in Los Angeles. By that evening he was standing at shortstop in Dodger Stadium and batting leadoff against the Phillies.

Stepping back into the Dodger clubhouse for the first time since his exile, he encountered a surprise. A small note card hung over his locker, with a handwritten greeting and peace offering:

Welcome home, Maury.
Walter O'Malley

It wasn't the same team Wills had left. Several players with whom he'd never shared a field were now regulars, and others whom he'd mentored had grown from callow youngsters into respected veterans in their late twenties. Parker's self-image, role, and expectations had especially changed. On the one hand, he was enormously happy that Wills was back, although a bit surprised because he never thought that O'Malley and the Dodger front office would allow it to happen. But he also felt the need to tell his old close friend that their relationship would need to change. He had grown as a ballplayer since Wills had left. He no longer needed the same scrutiny or guidance. "You don't have to worry about me now like you did before," he told Wills. "I can stand on my own now."

"I know you can, Wes," Wills said.

Wills was so happy just to be back. He had arrived in Los Angeles batting only .222. For the remainder of the year, he would hit .297

for the Dodgers and run the bases well enough to have 40 stolen bases by the season's end. Willie Davis would hit .311, in a season that saw him produce a 31-game hitting streak. But the team was on its way to finishing a distant fourth, and Wills realized that something had changed with the Dodgers. It wasn't that they couldn't win. It's just that so many of the players to whom he'd been close were gone. "It wasn't the same team," he said. "I had to accept that I hadn't come back to *that* team."

He had always viewed the 1960s as the Dodgers' decade. Only the '60s were ending, he realized.

Lou Johnson's major-league career wrapped up in 1969. A year earlier the Cubs had dealt him to Cleveland, and just before the start of the '69 season, the Indians traded him to the California Angels, which meant playing near Disneyland, in the city of Anaheim, deep in what was then and for many years to come the overwhelmingly white and very conservative bastion of Orange County. The area had acquired a reputation as being less than welcoming to racial minorities. "It wasn't as friendly as the parts of Los Angeles where I lived," Johnson remembered.

He had taken to wearing dashikis. "I got some strange looks," he said. "I'd come out of the ballpark driving a Corvette Stingray. The cops used to stop me once in a while. Just made me appreciate playing in Dodger Stadium even more."

In his worst year ever, he hit .203 for the Angels in 1969, without a single homer, playing in only sixty-seven games, the season ending two weeks after his thirty-fifth birthday. Soon he was done.

"The hardest thing in life is when you got to take off that uniform for good," he said. "You aren't going to be able to do it again ever. Where do you go? What are you ever gonna do that makes you feel that good?"

He had no idea, which terrified him. For a while he got lost, running into a drug and alcohol problem, his life unraveling. But he rebounded, his successful rehabilitation leading him to a steady job with the Dodgers. His recovery was no more remarkable, he thought, than his earlier transformation after joining the team. "The friendship and love those guys made me feel—Sandy, Roseboro, Maury, Wes, Gilliam, Crawford, all of them—that changed me," he said. "That took the pain and hate away. That was more important than even winning the Series."

Oddly, the player whose major injury and diminished mobility were supposed to have quickly driven him out of baseball stayed in the game longer than nearly anyone else from the 1965 squad. Tommy Davis would play for ten more seasons after leaving the Dodgers, the end to his eighteen-year career not coming until the finish of the 1976 season, by which time, at thirty-seven, he had played for ten major-league clubs, his last four seasons spent almost exclusively as a designated hitter. At thirty-five, he hit .306 as the Orioles' designated hitter, on his way to a lifetime average of .294.

But when his ankle broke on the base paths in 1965, his career's trajectory had changed forever. His speed would never come back. "He would have been in the Hall of Fame if he hadn't been injured," Koufax said. "He could do anything with a bat. He could run the bases. The injury changed a lot for Tommy."

Davis didn't dwell on the misfortune. He would have put up with whatever headaches might have awaited to hang around a little longer. Whenever his career ended, it was going to be too soon. "Baseball was the nucleus of my life," he said. "It was hard to leave. It took me a lot of time to get over it."

Chapter 10

The Final Years

As the sun fell on the 1960s, most members of the 1965 championship squad—those not already retired or released by teams—had entered the twilight of their careers. Yet Parker remained desperate to get better. His career-long struggles with the bat preyed on his self-esteem more than ever. "When the student is ready, the teacher will appear," he observed. "And I was ready for someone to help me at that point."

Parker's transformation as a hitter in 1969 and 1970, driven by his absolute compulsion to make it happen, was the most stunning of all Dodger turnarounds late in the decade. Aside from the moment when he sat in the Paris hotel room and decided to become a ballplayer, no goal in his life ever appeared more improbable. At the end of 1968, by then five years into his major-league career, he had never hit higher in a season than a paltry .257. His 1968 season was especially abysmal: in hitting .239, he had looked totally lost in stretches. His close friends at least had helped him laugh about his especially awful at-bats. "You're swinging like horseshit," Lefebvre said to him after a particularly weak pop-out in '68, in response to which, as Lefebvre remembered, Parker loudly laughed and said, "That's the best thing I've ever heard; that loosened me up—at least you're telling me the truth."

By then, however, his image as a weak hitter had solidified around baseball. Even as a Gold Glover, he couldn't reasonably expect to hold on to his first-base job for many years longer without swinging a more effective bat. "I was sick of reading I couldn't hit," he remembered. "I had to prove myself. It became another threat to my self-image."

Privately, Campanis doubted he could do it. Behind closed doors, during spring training in 1969, he bluntly told a minor-league manager in the organization that the problem could hardly have been more basic: Parker just couldn't hit.

Campanis's confidant, the new forty-one-year-old manager of the Dodgers' Triple-A farm club in Spokane, a former pitcher in the organization named Tommy Lasorda, forcefully disagreed. "He *can* hit," said Lasorda, who, despite the many naysayers around him, liked what he had seen of parts of Parker's hitting stance and swing. He thought Parker possessed terrific reflexes and great vision. Above all else, Lasorda believed, Parker had discipline; he was the kind of player who thought nothing of fielding hundreds of ground balls, an athlete who kept in shape and was determined to get better. Why the hell shouldn't this guy be able to hit? Lasorda said to people.

"He can't hit, Tommy," Campanis insisted.

The two men argued. During his long playing career in the minors, punctuated by his brief, unsuccessful stints in the majors, Lasorda had always displayed more pugnacity than talent. Yet his drive and fire, never enough to compensate for his lack of elite skills on the mound, made him ideally suited for exhorting greenhorn players as a coach and manager in the minors. He had proven to be a winner, having led a Dodger farm club in Ogden, Utah, to three championships. His elevation to the Spokane team would be just one more step in his long march toward becoming the Dodger manager in the next decade.

An exasperated Campanis barked, "Okay, wise guy, fine. Let's see what you can do with him."

A potential hurdle was that Lasorda and Parker hardly knew each other. And you couldn't find a more unlikely pairing than the alternately backslapping, wisecracking, profane, tempestuous Lasorda and the subdued, mannerly, diffident Parker. Lasorda approached him in the Dodgertown cafeteria, sat down, and had some meals with him. "Then I started really laying the bricks to the guy," Lasorda recalls.

He began insulting Parker, challenging his pride. If Lasorda had a gift in such moments, it was that his barbs could be as funny as a comic's. Nonetheless, they penetrated. "If I'd gotten to pitch to guys like you when I was in the majors, I'd have been a star," he told Parker. "I would send a limousine to pick up guys like you just to make sure you made it to the ballpark. You know, I could get you out right now."

Lasorda remembers that one day, after a few more insults along this line, Parker, rising to the challenge, shot back: "You think so?"

"Yeah," Lasorda said. "Let's go out there and see."

"When?"

"Right now."

That's how it began, recalled Lasorda, who pitched extra batting practice to Parker before and after spring training games, making a habit of mercilessly ridiculing the quiet player. "He had these weird expressions when he was insulting me," Parker said. "He'd say, 'You couldn't hit me as long as you have a hole in your ass.'"

What Lasorda couldn't possibly have known in their first days together was the depth of his pupil's self-doubt. Long before, Parker had silently cataloged his own physical shortcomings, everything from his lack of great bat speed to his puny wrists and forearms. He waited for Lasorda to impart some advice he could actually use: "He just tore me up for a while when he was pitching to me. Then he started building me back up. When I got a good hit off him, he'd sometimes say, 'How did you hit that pitch? *Nobody* hits my curveball.'"

Still, Lasorda didn't like Parker's demeanor or body language in the batting cage. It didn't take him long to recognize what some Dodger officials had overlooked: Parker's hitting woes began with a startling lack of confidence. One day after another batting session, he motioned Parker to sit down, then hit him with a question. "If it's the bottom of the ninth inning in Cincinnati, the Reds are up, the bases are loaded, there are two outs, and we have a one-run lead, what guy out there do you want the Reds to hit the ball to?"

"Me," Parker answered.

"Okay. Now if we're up at bat in the ninth inning, we're losing by a run, the bases are loaded, and there are two outs, who do you want to have batting for us?"

"Who's pitching?" Parker asked.

"Wes, that's not the answer I expected to hear. That's not the answer I want to hear. The answer I should hear from you is, *Me, me.* Your answer to that question should be as strong as your answer to that other question. Son, you gotta believe. That's what you gotta do."

Parker listened silently.

"Wes worked hard," Lasorda said. "But first he had to believe the ability was there."

Lasorda pitched a nine-inning game against Parker one afternoon, simultaneously serving as the umpire. Parker hit reasonably well.

Afterward, Lasorda sat him down again. "You know, you *can* hit. You have all the ability in the world. If you keep workin' at this, you could hit as good as Pete Rose. You're already the best-fielding first baseman who's ever lived. You could be the best hitter. Why *can't* you be the best hitter? I know you can do it because I'm seeing it here."

In the years ahead, opinion among players in the Dodgers organization about Lasorda would always be divided. Some players worshipped him; others would say bluntly, though only with anonymity, that he was a gabby, rah-rah presence in the dugout who could grate on players, the utter antithesis of the typically impassive Alston. But Parker would never feel anything but immense gratitude for his instructor, who, against the conventional wisdom, had succeeded in jump-starting him at the advanced baseball age of twenty-nine. "I think a lot of people doubted whether I'd ever be able to hit," he reflects. "But Lasorda was good to me. When he said things like, 'You could be the best hitter,' he made me believe. He changed my mental state."

In 1969 Parker was a different hitter. By the All-Star break, he was batting .296, with 51 RBIs and 13 homers. An emergency appendectomy sidelined him for three weeks, leaving him weakened for the season's remainder. Still, he hit .278, the highest average of his career, excited for the first time about getting into the batter's box during the following season. "Tommy gave me the first half of what I needed," Parker observed.

Most of the other half came from Dodgers hitting coach Dixie Walker, who had spotted fundamental flaws in his swing. "You're uppercutting," Walker said at the beginning of their work together, having detected that Parker, whether batting right- or left-handed, routinely dropped his back shoulder before swinging. The habit left Parker prone to hitting under the ball and making feeble contact. "Dixie got my back shoulder up and my hands higher," Parker recounts, next offering an explanation that to the unaware sounds counterintuitive. "With my back shoulder up, I was able to start swinging *down*—Dixie drummed in the importance of hitting down on the ball, your hands above the ball, in order to get a flat swing on a level plane."

Walker and Lasorda accounted for roughly 90 percent of his transformation, Parker believed. The final 10 percent came from his own savvy in selecting a new bat for himself, a unique model that no other Dodger used. Until the spring of 1969, he generally swung thin-handled, smaller, lighter bats—typically 34 inches long and weighing 33 or 34 ounces. He liked the feel of the bats. He liked the sense that he could whip the smaller bats around faster than a bigger, heavier bat. But soon he discovered that there was no margin of error with the smaller bats. If he didn't hit the ball absolutely squarely, nothing good happened.

The Dodgers had a big bin of bats. Parker looked down at them, plucked one out, and swung it a little. It was an odd-looking bat. It had no knob on its bottom. For many seeing it the first time, it looked unfinished, as if someone had gotten bored right in the middle of making it and just walked away. "It was a gigantic bat," Parker remembered. The knobless bat, made by the venerable Hillerich & Bradsby Company and called the U1, was 36 inches long and weighed 36 ounces. Parker swung it around some more and liked it, deciding to try it out in batting practice and some spring games.

The heavier, longer bat meant less bat speed. But Parker immediately saw benefits to it: "You could have a bad hitch in your swing with a lighter bat. But you couldn't have a hitch or false start with the U1 and still get around on a pitch—there just wasn't time for that because of the bat's added weight. The U1 helped to purify my swing." Parker's experiment was a success. The U1 became his bat for good. He'd happily discovered another advantage: "The added plate coverage [with the new bat] was important. Pitches on the outside: the U1 helped you reach those because it was two inches longer. It worked for me. And I wasn't the only one."

He had discovered that Roberto Clemente—his favorite player in baseball ("Charisma oozed out of his body; he was the best all-around player of the era")—used the U1 too. When the Dodgers traveled to Pittsburgh, Parker fell into a conversation with the superstar, the two swapping enthusiastic stories about the bat, which had enabled Clemente to stand farther back from the plate and dive into pitches wherever they were thrown. No pitch was too far away for Clemente to reach with the U1. "Knowing that he used it just made me feel better about my decision," Parker remembers. "But I went to the U1 on my own. That made me feel good, too. I was so locked in that season. I did everything right. I committed and sacrificed to be a success."

Parker adopted a new regimen before the start of the 1970 season. He rigorously lifted weights, in an era when few players did. He decided to forgo any real social life, vowing to himself that he would think of nothing but baseball from early March to the season's October end.

By early May of 1970, he was batting better than ever. During a Dodgers' extra-inning victory in Shea Stadium, on a night when he already had doubled, homered, and singled, he delivered a two-run triple in the tenth inning that served as both the game-winning blow over the Mets and the climax to a head-turning performance in which he hit for the cycle for the first time in his major-league career.

The next night, in Philadelphia, the former .239 hitter found himself in a role that, two years earlier, would have been unthinkable. He became his team's cleanup hitter. He drove in two runs in a Dodger win and doubled twice, during a season in which his forty-seven doubles led the National League. Although the Dodgers finished fourteen and a half games out of first place, Parker placed fifth in the MVP balloting. He ended the year with 196 hits and a .319 average, the fifth highest in the league, along with 111 runs batted in, an unusually high number for someone with only ten homers, a testament to the power of all those doubles and base hits. No Dodger since Tommy Davis had driven in as many runs. "I felt fulfilled and vindicated," he said.

Still, the pressure to live up to his own and others' expectations had chipped away at him. He was unsuited for all the stresses heaped on him by success. "I don't need another season like that," he confided to Lefebvre, who, having expected to hear of Parker's excitement, would best remember his expression of weariness. "Frenchy, that was so hard," Parker went on, adressing Lefebvre by his nickname. "These people who have to compete every year for batting average titles have so much pressure. I'd rather just be a good, ordinary player."

Parker thought that, if anything, the season had increased his isolation. "I was a virtual recluse from the winter before the 1970 season until its end," he remembers. "It was the most unenjoyable year I ever had. I was just too intense, too lonely. I never wanted to go through anything like that again. But I needed to prove the naysayers wrong."

In early 1971 came a head-spinning honor. In the midst of spring training, he landed on the cover of *Sports Illustrated*, his face and tousled hair alongside a headline reading BASEBALL'S SUDDEN STAR. He learned from a staffer at *Sports Illustrated* that the other major candidate for the magazine's cover had been the famed University of Indiana swim team, led by the soon-to-be Olympic legend Mark Spitz. But in the end the editors had chosen Parker, with all the Los Angeles cool and glamour that his grinning visage embodied. Parker was euphoric. He rushed to a newsstand in Vero Beach and bought every copy of the magazine.

"Being on that cover was something beyond pride for me," he recalls. "It was a deep affirmation of my worth as a human being. I thought, I'm not crap. I'm not worthless. I have value to people. That's what my childhood did to me; when you're constantly embattled, you need those reminders that you're not crap."

His reaction, including how he expressed it, was virtually identical to what he had felt during past moments of high praise and achievement. Now, as then, his joy slowly faded as the months passed. Nothing would ever be quite enough—no magazine cover, no dose of the fans' idolatry, no awed look from a female admirer. The mocking voices of his youth blunted all of it if he thought about the voices too long. In moments it helped to put on street clothes and hit fly balls to kids, in the Dodger Stadium parking lot, after Sunday afternoon games; helped to imagine that he was bringing a little happiness to children with their own problems perhaps. On other days he tried to spend less time dwelling on his victimizers and more in recognizing that he hadn't permitted his past to ruin him, that his own dogged accomplishments had lifted him out of the pit. "Some of us win the parental lottery," he reflected, "and some of us just don't. My parents had good qualities. They just didn't know how to be good parents. . . . I tried everything possible to save myself. I did the best I could."

Before the start of spring training in 1970, Torborg, who had succeeded Fairly as the Dodgers' player representative, did something bold. He refused to sign the contract for the new season that Campanis had given him, which offered a puny raise. "I thought it was time for something better," Torborg remembered. Torborg had never made even $20,000 during a season, and now he wanted to earn as much as $25,000.

Campanis said he wouldn't increase the offer. Torborg began a holdout, which was all the more daring because the twenty-eight-year-old catcher appeared to have little, if any, negotiating leverage. He was coming off a season in which he'd batted a mere .185. A year earlier, he'd hit a dreadful .161. Holdouts were generally associated with stars whose teams couldn't possibly do without their services, a category that Torborg would never fall into. Indeed, it was a struggle to remember any other reserve in major-league history who had launched such a quixotic holdout.

Nonetheless, Marvin Miller saw a possibility for Torborg to make history, if he were willing to buck Campanis and O'Malley and possibly serve as a test case in a challenge of baseball's labor rules. "If you don't sign and you go through the whole season without a contract, I think you'd be a free agent," speculated Miller, who at that moment envisioned a possible legal challenge that might lead at last to a toppling of the owners' oligarchical control, with Torborg as the symbolic spearhead.

Torborg understood what Miller was driving at. He just wasn't interested in professional martyrdom. Besides, he thought, he was all wrong for the role Miller had in mind. "I'm not a big player, Marvin," he remembers saying to the union chief. "I'm barely a marginal player. You need a big player for that."

That ended all talk of a dramatic challenge to management's dictate. When Campanis finally called, it was only to warn Torborg that, unless he signed, he wouldn't play. "You must sign," Campanis declared.

Torborg gave in. Later, he wouldn't be able to remember how much he signed for, only that it was less than $20,000.

He then had a season that resembled most of his Dodger years, one characterized by his subpar hitting and his quiet excellence in steadying pitchers in stressful moments. On July 20, in a lightly attended weekday game against the Phillies that began in Dodger Stadium at the odd hour of four o'clock, he was again a part of history, as twenty-six-year-old right-hander Bill Singer threw a no-hitter.

Torborg's playing days in Los Angeles and his short tenure as the team's player representative ended during the next off-season, when he was unceremoniously sold to the Angels. During his three seasons with the Angels, he remained as close as ever to Miller and the union. On the field, while generally a reserve, he continued to display a special talent during pitchers' big games. In 1973, his final major-league season, he was the catcher when Nolan Ryan threw the first of his seven no-hitters, with Torborg to go down as one of only three players in history to have caught a no-hitter in each league.

The feat would be his last noteworthy one as a player. The bonus baby had never looked remotely like a star during his ten-year career. But few players had ever prepared themselves so ably for leadership, or looked so comfortable guiding peers at such a young age. At thirty-five, only four years after his final game as a player, he would become the Cleveland Indians' manager, the first of his five jobs as a major-league skipper. "You knew all along that Jeff was a leader," his friend and former roommate Joe Moeller said. "He wasn't a great hitter, but he had command and respect. It turned out he was going a lot further than most people."

Dick Tracewski remained close to Koufax, who, six weeks after retiring from baseball, signed a ten-year, $1 million contract to be part of a baseball broadcasting crew for NBC. He swiftly became unhappy in his new job.

Television was not baseball. Television brought all the minuses of fame for Koufax, and none of the competitive benefits that he had thrived on. The most stubborn of misconceptions about Koufax—that he was less than a lover of the game—would be increasingly exposed as a canard. Jim Kaat saw Koufax at an event long after a

Dodger team doctor, orthopedic surgeon Frank Jobe, successfully performed an ulnar collateral ligament reconstruction on the elbow of the pitcher for whom the surgery would come to be known, Dodger left-hander Tommy John. After his 1974 operation and a year's rehabilitation, John became a better pitcher than ever, enjoying three twenty-win campaigns. His twenty-six-year career wouldn't end until the conclusion of the 1989 season, by which time the forty-six-year-old John had amassed 288 career victories.

The surgery that saved John's career had become commonplace. A curious Kaat had a question for Koufax: If the surgery had been available during your career (with an adjustment made for an arthritic elbow), do you think you could have pitched longer?

Definitely, a wistful Koufax answered.

But the arrival of the surgical procedure wouldn't come until eight years after he left the game. Without baseball and a steady income, he had plodded along in his NBC job for the remainder of the 1960s and into the '70s. It hadn't taken long for Koufax and television critics to discover that he was astoundingly ill suited for broadcasting. "Sandy hated it," Tracewski recalled.

By contrast, as the 1970s began, Tracewski could hardly have been happier. He'd had a wonderful four years as a utility player for the Tigers. In 1968 the Tigers defeated the Cardinals in a thrilling seven-game Series. "I'd decided by then that when the Dodgers traded me away, it was the best thing that ever happened to me," he says.

His playing days with the Tigers ended following the 1969 season, after which he managed a minor-league team in the Tigers organization for two seasons before becoming a coach for the big club in 1972. He had found what he wanted to do for the remainder of his professional life. That year, with a Tigers road trip having taken him to Boston for a few days, Tracewski sat down away from the ballpark for a long private conversation with Koufax, who wanted nothing more than to end his broadcasting relationship with NBC. "He said to me, 'I can't do it anymore,'" Tracewski remembers. "We spent the whole night, into the morning, talking about it. He said, 'I don't want to do it. I'm not good at it.' He tried. All that attention: it was just too hard for him."

Tracewski, perhaps as contented as any former Dodger, wouldn't leave his Tigers coaching position for twenty-four seasons, finally retiring in 1995. Koufax would be gone from his television job by early 1973, with four years still left on his NBC contract. He focused on other interests. He golfed. He fished. He ran. He remained involved—usually from afar—in the lives of former teammates, especially in the aftermath of friends' personal setbacks. When Wills—long after his playing days, an unsuccessful managerial stint with the Seattle Mariners, and a bout with drugs—landed an instructional position with the Mets, a team principally owned by Koufax's friend and high school teammate Fred Wilpon, Koufax carefully monitored his old Dodger friend's well-being. Torborg, who had been fired as Mets manager and was mulling over a possible opportunity with another team, told Koufax that he might call Wills and ask him to join any new staff he assembled.

Koufax responded with an objection that sounded brotherly in its intensity. "Leave him alone," Koufax told Torborg. "He's happy where he is."

Torborg never made the call. "Sandy is that way with friendship—there's no b.s. to him, but he always lets you know in his own way that he cares about you and the other guys," he said. When popping into somebody's town, Koufax frequently calls, if for no other reason than to say hello and quickly catch up.

His conversations have natural limits that are understood by now. "I don't know" is a common and truthful answer when friends are asked what he is doing.

The Maury Wills who had returned to the Dodgers didn't hesitate challenging Dodger management if it said no to a request he thought was perfectly reasonable. When Muhammad Ali, who had become a friend, told him he was coming to see a game, Wills requested that the Dodgers' public relations department put the fighter's name on the scoreboard, something the Dodgers frequently did for celebrities in attendance. The Dodgers resisted. "Red Patterson tried to talk me out of it," Wills remembered. "He said that half the people there might boo Ali."

Wills didn't care. "He's my guest and he's my friend, Red—I'd like his name on the board."

Between innings, the Dodgers' staff put Ali's name on the big scoreboard, informing fans the fighter was in the crowd.

Here came the roars. A fascinated Wills listened to the simultaneous expressions of joy and rage, a reflection of America's divide: "Red was right: 25,000 cheered and 25,000 booed—which was what you expected then with Ali."

In 1971, the same year that Ali saw his draft conviction reversed by the Supreme Court, the thirty-eight-year-old Wills had his last great season. He led the Dodgers to within a game of the National League West title, hitting .281 and finishing sixth in the MVP balloting. He ran sparingly now, stealing only fifteen bases. But he could bunt, chop the ball, and hit line drives as well as ever. He reacquired much of the influence that he had possessed as captain before the Dodgers sent him into his temporary exile. Al Downing, the former Yankees pitcher who had joined the Dodgers that year, remembers Wills coming to the mound with a criticism and an order after Downing had spent too much time nibbling at the corners: "You're being too careful with this guy. *Challenge him.*"

"So I did," Downing said.

Downing—whom Wills affectionately called "Ace," as the newcomer was on his way to winning twenty games that season—appreciated his new captain's strong hand during games. "He acted like a manager on the field," Downing remembered. "He'd say something to you like, 'This is a bunt play coming up.' He was invaluable in that respect. He demanded people pay attention."

The team went north for a series against the Giants. There, Downing learned about the aging captain's uncompromising standards. "It was really cold up in San Francisco one day, like frigid," he recalls, "and somebody asked Maury if he knew whether we were practicing the next morning at Candlestick before a game, because it was going to be *really cold*. And Maury said, 'Yeah, batting practice at 10:30 a.m.' Like, *Of course we're having batting practice, we always practice—no question about it, why would you ask me a question like that?* He'd tell people to work on their bunting. He got the most out of people and got more out of himself than anybody. He was the one responsible for keeping us in that race. I just wish I could have played with him a lot longer."

Two days after the 1971 season ended, Wills turned thirty-nine. A few weeks later he sat down with Al Campanis, ready to discuss his contract for 1972. He was excited, believing his outstanding year and the club's close finish in the divisional race would earn him a nice boost over his previous year's salary of $92,000. The prospect of a $100,000 contract had never seemed more realistic. It could only help that he'd always enjoyed a good relationship with Campanis.

Campanis warmly shook his hand and offered $97,000.

Wills sat silently for a moment, thinking Campanis's figure was close, a good start. Then he told Campanis that he really wanted $100,000.

Campanis revealed that he had talked to Walter O'Malley about that possibility, and that O'Malley had said no.

Wills didn't really care about the additional $3,000. Such a sum was insignificant to him. But reaching the $100,000 mark would be a milestone. He yearned for the additional respect that would come with belonging to the $100,000 club, whose roster of stars had kept growing over the years. Before it was too late, he wanted to join them. And he wanted the world to know about it. He didn't think it was too much to ask the Dodgers to give him an additional $3,000 after all the good and great years he had delivered, all his fighting, clawing, winning. He wanted $100,000, and that's all there was to it.

He turned to his best argument. Al, it's only a three-thousand-dollar difference.

Campanis said the offer was final.

Wills tried to persuade Campanis that his many years of success and devotion should count for something. He could see he was getting nowhere.

In his desperation, he began pleading: Al, it would mean so much to me.

No, Maury, Campanis said.

"Al, if a difference of three thousand dollars means that much to everybody, I'll pay the Dodgers the three thousand dollars." Wills had tears in his eyes by then. "If you give me a hundred thousand dollar contract, I'll immediately give you three thousand back. Please, Al."

Campanis said the offer was $97,000. "Take it or go home."

Wills excused himself to step into the hallway of the Dodgers executive offices. He was crying. He had stood up to the executives so resolutely in recent years that it was strange being back in this place where he had capitulated so often as a younger man.

Now, as then, he decided he had no choice.

"I'll sign it," he said to Campanis.

Marvin Miller led a strike of major-league players in early April 1972. It lasted thirteen days, during which all teams were affected. Games were canceled and never replayed. In the end, the owners yielded to the demand that salary arbitration be included at last in the collective bargaining agreement, and the two sides agreed to add $500,000 to the players' pension fund. "Marvin knew what he was doing," remembered Cardinals player representative Tim McCarver.

It would be a year of monumental baseball labor decisions. In

June the Supreme Court would uphold the reserve clause, in a case involving star outfielder Curt Flood, who—after refusing to accept a trade in which the Cardinals had sent him to the Phillies—filed suit in 1970 against Major League Baseball and commissioner Bowie Kuhn, charging that the reserve clause violated American antitrust laws. Flood's loss before the high court would be the players' last major defeat. In 1975 a federal arbitrator would essentially kill the reserve clause by declaring that players competing for one year without a contract became free agents. During the following year, the owners would surrender to reality, haggling for a deal, eventually agreeing to allow players with six years in the majors to become unfettered free agents. The titans' oligarchy would soon be dead.

When player representatives later reflected on the history of the union, and its key moments, many cited the 1972 strike as the moment when they believed they gained the upper hand. Long before the strike began, the Dodger players had selected Parker during a clubhouse meeting to be their player representative, for reasons that would always be murky. Parker thought that the vote was probably nothing more than an indication that they viewed him as a likable veteran and guessed he could probably do the job. Fairly, long gone from the team, thought it wasn't even that complicated: Parker just looked the part. "He was bright, personable, and he was the only guy who had an attaché case," Fairly remembered.

Yet no one on the team could have been a poorer fit for the job of player representative than Maurice Wesley Parker III, of the Bel Air Town and Country School, the Harvard School, and the Los Angeles Country Club. It was akin to giving a devoted descendant of Henry Ford a seat on the board of the United Auto Workers and asking him to lead the union's picketing.

Parker had grown up hearing from successful men about not labor's woes but management's burdens. He didn't think the issue of pension funding was worth striking over.

No other player alive could have been less aggrieved with baseball management, or more grateful to an organization and owner for giving him a chance to play ball. "I owed everything to the Dodgers organization," he recalls. "That's why I didn't want to strike, because I knew how close I'd come to dying from the fear and discouragement I suffered in my home life. It was a miracle to me that I was even playing in the majors. Why would I strike against the team that gave me an opportunity to save my life? Mr. O'Malley and the organization had given me my chance. That literally saved me."

He would be the only player representative in the major leagues to oppose the strike.

Some of his teammates were outraged, especially when Parker publicly defended his position. The Dodgers' assistant player representative, Jim Brewer, angrily told him to stop talking. "He was ready to punch my lights out," Parker remembers. "I thought there might be a fight. Finally, someone asked me to step down as player rep. I agreed. I understood. I never really had wanted to do it."

It wasn't long before Parker quietly reassumed his place as the genial, soft-spoken teammate liked by all. His on-field reliability made it easier for strike activists to forgive him. Even so, a hint of change for the team came on opening day of the 1972 season in Cincinnati. With Parker in need of a few days of conditioning at the strike's end, Alston started twenty-two-year-old Bill Buckner at first base. Several years earlier, at the prodding of Lasorda, Buckner, then a minor leaguer, had sent Parker a letter in which he said he was coming to Los Angeles to take away his job. Parker was both unruffled and unamused. "Lasorda had all his minor leaguers do that to different Dodgers," Parker recalls. "I don't think Buckner even wanted to send it. It was all Lasorda."

Yet a youth movement was quietly under way. Other infielders who would be team regulars within a couple of years—Steve Garvey and Ron Cey among them—had arrived. Although Parker would be back at first base within two days, on his way to hitting a solid .279 for the season, the emergence of Buckner and other promising young players portended a club overhaul, if not quickly, then not terribly far down the road.

By nature, Wills didn't permit himself to think about the end. Less than a year from his fortieth birthday, he believed he could defy time; he wanted to prove he could play shortstop as well as he did ten years earlier. He aimed for another great season or two, another Dodger championship if it were in the cards, and a $100,000 contract.

But his own conditioning concerned him a little. He'd arrived late to spring training, and then the players' strike made it difficult to work out. The season began, and he got off to the worst start of his career, going 0-for-18. He picked up a hit in Atlanta, and then his slump immediately resumed. Late in the month, the truth became apparent to observers: his gifts had left him.

On Thursday, April 27, at home against the Expos, Wills went hitless in three more at-bats, his average sinking to .106. In the bottom of the seventh inning, Alston approached and patted him on the shoulder. The manager loved no player more than Wills, and he couldn't have handled the next moment more compassionately. He motioned toward the tunnel and the clubhouse: "Why don't you go in, get a whirlpool, and let the kid pick you up."

Twenty-three-year-old Bill Russell, a year removed from the minors, stepped to the plate in place of Wills and singled to right field, the first of his two hits in the game. The next night Russell started at shortstop and went 1-for-2 against the Mets, batting in the eighth position, with Parker shifting to become the temporary leadoff hitter. Then, in Game 14 of the season, at home on Saturday night, April 29, in an 11–1 victory over the Mets, Russell went 2-for-3 and drove in a run. No one would yet officially say it, but Russell had become the new starting shortstop of the Los Angeles Dodgers.

Reduced to being a utility infielder, Wills would play in the field during only fifty-seven games that year, hitting .129, with one stolen base. "Bill became our leading hitter for a stretch," Wills remembers. "And then he just kind of took over the position and I was out. It happened quietly. But it was a lot easier for me to take my shortstop position from Don Zimmer in 1959 than to give up my own. I tried to do my best with the whole thing. I didn't want to do to Bill what some of the Brooklyn guys did to me when I took over. I tried to give Bill what help I could. But it was hard. No matter what anyone else tells you, that's the way it is for players. That whole year hurt like hell."

Parker had no need to cope with such agonies. He would go on to win his sixth consecutive Gold Glove that season. Just as during 1966, when he had risen to the challenge from Dick Stuart, he played with such command in his 120 games at first base that Buckner, who hit .319 that season and would eventually become a National League batting champion, was utilized mostly in the outfield. First base belonged to Parker for the indefinite future.

Parker's seamless run of excellence at the position had made him a fixture. He had committed so few errors over the years that he could remember most of them, including his single error in the 1968 season, a disputed error at that, a bad-hop shot off his shoulder.

In 2007, more than forty years after he became a regular, the Rawlings Sporting Goods Company would announce its all-time defensive team, which covered a half century beginning with the introduction of the Gold Glove award in 1957. Featuring a pitcher, a catcher, a single player at each infield position, along with three outfielders, the team consisted almost entirely of immortal figures—Willie Mays, Roberto Clemente, Ken Griffey Jr., Brooks Robinson, Ozzie Smith, Joe Morgan, Johnny Bench, and Greg Maddux. Its first baseman was Wes Parker.

Among the nine players chosen in the fans' balloting, the only one never to make it into the Hall of Fame would be Parker, who perfectly understood he had no place being in the Hall, given the limits of his offense. That he would never be mistaken for a superstar only made his selection to the mythical team more moving for him. From the beginning, he had hoped his career, if nothing else, would help to illuminate the athletic and aesthetic possibilities for the first-base position, which, he said upon receiving the honor, "has been slighted over the years by players thinking they have only to catch throws and dig balls from the dirt to play it well. Nothing could be further from the truth. Dedicated first basemen take risks, go after everything. And in doing all this they expand the position from one of passivity and conservatism to one of action, excitement, daring, beauty and grace."

Increasingly, in 1972, Parker felt content about his achievements. At thirty-two, he had no worries. Yet neither did he have reason for exhilaration that season: the Dodgers were en route to finishing a distant second behind the Reds. Motivation and hunger had suddenly become issues for him. Something startling happened next, a sensation he kept to himself: there were occasional nights in Dodger Stadium when he simply did not wish to be there. "Just a nice sunset could do it to me," he said.

He would try imagining what it would be like to see the sunset from another part of Los Angeles—say, the beach. If the game became lopsided, he sometimes had a powerful desire to flee and experience life. "It'd be the seventh inning at home and we're losing, ten to two, and fans are leaving," he remembers. "And I'd think, I wish I could go with them."

He had come to realize something else: "I'd needed professional baseball, but I didn't love it. Well, I loved it in the beginning. But then I got burned out. Pete Rose and I had conversations when we were playing. Pete loved and needed baseball. I'd grabbed for it because I'd needed to be saved. I needed baseball more than I loved it. If not for my parents, I'd never have been a ballplayer. I had to get away from them, and baseball was the only way I could do it. That I became a warrior in baseball felt like it was almost forced on me. But it saved my life. I was so fortunate I had baseball. But I was getting more interested at that point in broadening my interests, meeting people, having a life."

Parker began thinking more seriously about the possibility of retirement, an idea he had first privately considered during the previous off-season. Making an exception to his rule against receiving therapy during a season, he met with a psychologist to discuss the pros and cons of saying good-bye. "I thought I needed to get away from the game and finally face up to my past, my childhood," he recalls. "The war inside me was becoming too great. It was getting overwhelming. Everything in me was saying, 'Get out, get out.' Do I get out? Is that the smart thing to do? Or would it be a mistake to walk away? I wanted to connect with life in a way I hadn't; I wanted to make a human connection that I'd been avoiding because of my fragility—I'd shut down my whole emotional side because of the abuse I'd suffered as a kid. But I was also wrestling with my feelings and questions about baseball: whether I'd reached my goals; whether I'd be quitting too soon. As a player, I could also see a positive to leaving: I would be remembered as retiring at my peak. I didn't want to go through a horrible decline like many players—I didn't want that embarrassment."

His final week of the season would be remarkable for how little emotion he felt while approaching the biggest decision of his professional life. In Cincinnati, on Sunday afternoon, October 1, he pinch-hit in the eighth inning for a Dodger newcomer, twenty-three-year-old catcher Steve Yeager. Gripping his knobless bat, staring at Reds left-hander Don Gullett, Parker tapped a ground ball to shortstop Dave Concepcion, who turned it into a double play in what would be Parker's final at-bat of the season and, as it turned out, his major-league career. "It was like my ghost at the plate; it wasn't really me," he remembers. Three nights later, when the season ended with a Dodger victory in Atlanta and Parker shed his uniform, he experienced none of the sadness familiar to players pondering retirement. "I'd heard about guys fighting their emotions when they were leaving the clubhouse for maybe the final time, but I was at peace," he recalls. "If this was it, I felt relieved my long war was over. I had no regrets."

On the same night Wills, two days past his fortieth birthday, entered the game in the ninth inning as a pinch runner, soon to score the 1,067th run of his career. It would be his last. On October 24, in a quiet office at Dodger Stadium, team officials thanked him for his many years of wonderful play and told him they would not be re-signing him. They shook his hand and wished him well.

Nothing they said was a shock to him, but this made it no less numbing. When the meeting ended, he left the office, stood alone in an aisle down the third-base line on the Club Level, and gazed out at the empty stands and field.

My career is over.

I'm finished.

What am I going to do at forty? I didn't go to college. What am I prepared to do?

He was fortunate for a while, doing well in sports broadcasting. But the 1980s would be rough. After a short-lived failed managerial stint with the Seattle Mariners, he went into a spiral that included a long bout with alcohol and drugs. "I'd lost everything," he remembers. "I was humiliated over what had happened in Seattle. My drinking had started, it was pretty bad. And when that wasn't enough, I did other things. My relationships with my children were harmed. I hurt myself and the people close to me. I'd lost my self-worth, my self-respect."

Fred Claire, who would be best known in baseball as the Dodgers general manager for eleven years into the late '90s, heard a rumor that Wills had suddenly died. Claire grabbed Don Newcombe and said, "We're going to Maury's house right now." They arrived at Wills's Marina del Rey home, only to find it boarded up. "We all cared about Maury," Claire recalled. "We weren't leaving. He wasn't dead; he was lost; he was suffering from cocaine addiction. There was no time to waste. I thought, I need to make this happen right now." Claire got Wills to come outside and wasted no time in checking him into a rehab center in Orange County.

The Dodgers helped to pay for Wills's recovery treatment, and in turn he has since talked about his past struggles unflinchingly, hoping this will aid others. At eighty-three, he has been sober and clean for decades, having spent much time as a roving instructor for the Dodgers. Over the years, after working with players before games in Dodger Stadium, he has regularly changed out of his baseball uniform into a suit and headed toward a stadium dining room frequented by season ticket holders. He is that rare octogenarian who bears a striking resemblance to his thirtysomething self. He still has the lean face of his playing days, his toothy smile, and his hair. Balding, paunchy middle-aged fans who cheered him during their youth shyly approach with baseballs to be autographed, and he obliges.

Now and then, someone will ask him to sign "Maury Wills, Hall of Fame." He says he can't do that. He offers instead to sign his name and jot the number of lifetime bases, 586, that he stole. He chats about baseball and passes along advice to children, still sounding like the captain, part of the reason why the Dodgers, even in the team's post-O'Malley era, have turned to him at different points with community relations tasks. "I've always tried to be there for the Dodgers, because they provided me with support when I most needed it," he says one afternoon in the stadium. "I have a lot of good memories with the club, and I had a few tough days with them, too. That's just what life is like with people who are close to you. Things happen, good and bad. Baseball is like family in that way. But I'm always a Dodger." He gestures at third base and smiles. "That's where it happened in '62; that's where I stole the hundred and fourth base—I slid in right there against the Giants. When I'm in the ballpark, I still see all that stuff from the sixties. Good things, bad things. It was intense. You couldn't forget those times even if you wanted to."

The '60s lived on into 1972, when the era quietly died in its sleep. The fascination with Flower Power had waned. Within the previous two years Jimi Hendrix, Janis Joplin, and Jim Morrison had all died. Love beads were out.

The autumn of 1972 garroted the last of the '60s zeitgeist. In the presidential election, in an outcome as lopsided as any of the Cubs' worst seasons, liberal icon George McGovern—fresh off toppling the Democratic Party establishment during primary season—was defeated in a landslide by Richard Nixon, whose Oval Office secret taping system, abuses of power, and cover-up of colossal wrongdoing that year in the Watergate affair would eventually cost him his presidency. Everywhere the '60s seemed to be saying good-bye. Old legends were yielding to the inevitable. It was as good a time as any for Wills to move on, and for Parker to ponder it.

A few weeks after the season's finish, Parker sat down with Peter O'Malley and told him he was thinking of retiring. O'Malley, who had assumed the presidency of the club and would become its owner after his father died in 1979, expressed surprise: "You have five more years left."

"It's time," Parker said.

O'Malley urged him not to make an immediate decision. "Will you at least take a few more days to think it over?"

Parker took a couple of days.

He asked himself a question: Is there anything I haven't done in baseball that I want to do?

He couldn't think of anything. He had his six Gold Gloves. He had his memories of the 1965 World Championship and of playing in two World Series. Two years earlier, in a powerful rebuttal of his skeptics, he had made himself into one of the league's best hitters during the most surprising season of his career. In the ten years since embarking on his dream, he had risen from the kid signed for a bonus of zero to become the greatest fielding first baseman of his generation. He decided he had fulfilled his athletic goals, exceeded them even.

The case for retiring seemed stronger than ever. The life of an established ballplayer, with all its heady adulation and comforting insulation, had come to feel like a crutch, something he was leaning upon to avoid having to stand on his own and confront his past. He couldn't go on this way. Besides, there was no longer a need for the crutch. He was no emotional invalid. He wouldn't go so far in that moment as to say he felt emotionally strong. But he believed he was *stronger* than at any other time in his life, strong enough that he could confront whatever challenges an everyday existence without baseball might bring.

"I thought, I can do this," he recalls. "I was a different person. I had a ways to go, but I had more self-confidence and self-esteem than ever before. My teammates, the fans: they'd had such an effect on me. The distance between where I started and where I'd reached was gargantuan, and all that was ten times more important and remarkable than having become a big-league player. All the pressure I'd faced before games, and the way I finally responded to it, made me see I possessed an inner core of strength. I'd hated myself growing up, but I liked myself as a player and person now. Baseball had given me all that."

He saw another benefit to leaving. He could go on his own terms, without Dodger brass calling him into an office one day and issuing him the kind of unconditional release they'd given to Wills. Whether he was stronger or not, he had doubts that he could weather a blow that big. "It might have broken me if I ever got hit by something like Maury did. I was still so fragile in a way. I don't think I could have withstood that kind of rejection."

He sat down again with Peter O'Malley and other Dodger officials and told them his decision was final.

"I want no press conference," he said; a short statement from the team would suffice. "I just want to privately retire."

O'Malley repeated that he didn't want him to leave; that he would always be welcome with the Dodgers.

But it was over. Parker drove out of the stadium as a retired player.

He had given up playing, but he couldn't altogether go cold turkey on the game. When the Reds called and asked him if he might serve as a broadcaster for their games during the following season, he said yes. "It dropped in my lap. I wasn't sure what I was going to do anyway, so it seemed a good transition."

After a year, he said good-bye to the Reds. Another opportunity had come his way. He played ball during the 1974 season in Japan for the Nankai Hawks, for whom he hit .301 while predictably winning the Pacific League's Diamond Glove Award for his defensive play. "It was a chance to spend time in Japan, see the country and pay off the mortgage on my home," he remembers. "It was only a hundred-and-thirty-game season over there. I had a good time."

He'd had his fill of baseball and Japan by then. At season's end, he returned to Los Angeles in time to see a September game with a date at Dodger Stadium, as his old team closed in on their first pennant since 1966. Al Campanis spotted him, walking over with a colleague and smilingly handing Parker a mock contract. After the laughter faded, Campanis turned serious. He had a proposition: he wanted Parker, still only thirty-four, to consider returning to the Dodgers as a backup center fielder the following year. The Dodgers' power-hitting center fielder Jimmy Wynn was experiencing arm problems that hampered his throws, explained Campanis, who viewed Parker as the best kind of insurance.

Parker was flattered, if nothing else.

The general manager kept pressing: "Wes, I really want you to think about it."

Parker had begun to say he would give Campanis a call when he decided it was pointless to keep the executive in suspense. Nothing ever was easier for him than what he said next: "Look, Al, I'm not playing anymore."

He knew at that moment he had moved on.

Over the next four decades, Parker's professional journey included stops in broadcasting and small roles over the years as a television actor. Investments and his family's wealth helped him to lead what, in another era, would have been called a gentleman's life: he regularly golfed at the Los Angeles Country Club; he traveled; and he set aside time for films and cultural outings that included the Los Angeles Philharmonic. Yet he worked hardest at trying to find what has proven to be an elusive peace. In 2014, after years of therapy and reflection, he remarked, "I can't say I'm beyond all the emotional damage of my past. But I'm much better. I'm probably 75 to 80 percent recovered. I still have things to work out. But I've never been better than today. And any chance I ever had started with baseball."

Never had he stopped viewing the game as the purest thing ever to touch his life. Into the twenty-first century, it still enthralled him, still triggered something boyish in him, still evoked memories of childhood afternoons spent fielding hard ground balls on his front lawn hit to him by his brother, the first clues to his gift, the gift that made baseball men take notice, the gift that offered the boy a way out, that gave him a sense of worth in a house where he was otherwise made to feel worthless. The gift freed him.

It still does. When handling a piece of his old baseball equipment, he beams. During a warm autumn afternoon, a month shy of his seventy-fifth birthday, he walked around in his Los Angeles home wearing a first baseman's glove from his playing days. Having brought it out to demonstrate his famously improbable play against Tim McCarver in 1966, he dropped to the floor without warning. Rolling around in khakis, astonishingly limber, he stretched out his gloved right hand just as he had on that day when he stabbed at a gray blur and backhanded it. Splayed, he reached with his free hand into the glove for a baseball resting there deep in the pocket. He grinned. "And then I did this," he said, plucking the ball from the glove, rolling onto his side, slightly lifting his legs, and describing the play in the manner of an announcer. "And Koufax is running toward the bag to take the throw ahead of McCarver. It's a close play. I flip it like this." He tossed the ball gently, effortlessly.

That afternoon he had several pictures in his mind's eye. The ones he could see best all had something to do with baseball. But his favorite was of a day and place thousands of miles from Los Angeles and any American baseball diamond. He saw himself at twenty-two, fleeing a hotel and dashing in the rain toward a TWA ticket office, saw a young man propelled by a sudden vision as hallucinatory as any acid trip: he would make a phone call and launch a professional baseball career. The kid showed no signs of understanding that he might as well have leaped off his hotel's roof into nothingness. The kid was a goner. It didn't matter. In the instant he did it, he thrilled to the sensation of at last feeling bold, rash, utterly alive. *I can do this, I can do this.* In his mad innocence, as the Parisian rain pelted him, he believed. His deliverance could have come no other way.

Acknowledgments

During 2009, after a long stretch of writing for the *Washington Post* largely about politicians, I wanted nothing more than to do a story about baseball. I sought an interview with a Dodger legend I hadn't seen in person since my youth in Los Angeles, Maury Wills, who, in 1962, had broken Ty Cobb's legendary single-season stolen-base record and whose absence from the Hall of Fame had long struck me as a historical oversight. I flew to Los Angeles, where I sat in an empty and very hot Dodger Stadium with the then-seventy-six-year-old Wills, hoping for an hour of his time. He talked for the hour and then the next three. He was indefatigable. He recounted his chase of Cobb before moving on to discuss the Dodgers' pennants and World Series titles during his playing days, his famous teammates, his childhood in segregated Washington, DC, his career's great highs and lows, the 1960s, Jim Crow, the civil rights movement, his struggles to get paid fairly during the height of his stardom, his post-playing life, his successful rehabilitation from drugs, and his work with the Dodgers in the decades since.

By the end of that month, after the publication of my story in the *Post*, another discussion with Wills, and interviews with many of his former teammates about their own experiences, I decided there was a book to be written about this group of Dodgers and their odyssey during the turbulent 1960s. No one had a larger role in enabling me to see the literary possibilities than Wills and Wes Parker. Like Wills, Parker candidly spoke about his difficult past as well as his triumphs, proving to be deeply insightful about both the game and larger social forces at work in the 1960s. The two men were expansive, eloquent, and blessed with encyclopedic minds. For the next few years, both Parker and Wills participated in a series of long in-person interviews. In addition, they made themselves available for telephone discussions when I was at home in the Washington area. (I'd conservatively estimate that, in Wills's case, our interviews lasted more than twenty-five hours; in the case of Parker, it was more than forty.) They were as giving and passionate as subjects can be.

Next was Dick Tracewski, who graciously spoke for several hours over the course of four phone interviews and later sat down with me for yet another long and illuminating discussion. Tommy Davis made himself available for two lengthy and revealing interviews in Alta Loma, California. Jeff Torborg, speaking from Florida, sat for several hours of phone interviews, patiently taking me through everything from his horror upon learning of the assassinations of John and Robert Kennedy to his exquisite tension in catching Koufax's perfect game. Lou Johnson, who first did a phone interview during my *Post* story on Wills, later sat for a three-and-a-half-hour interview in a quiet Dodger Stadium, keeping me riveted with tales of his improbable climb from the minors to World Series stardom. In 2009, Sandy Koufax consented to a brief but revealing telephone interview about Wills and their friendship for the *Post* story. Indeed, it was to Koufax that I first indicated my burgeoning interest in the possibility of a longer story or a book about the Dodgers, in response to which he politely made clear that his only interest was in speaking about his old friend. I am grateful for the time he gave me on that single day.

Among the other Dodgers, no one was more hilarious, conversant about the 1960s, or knowledgeable about the Dodgers' mercurial general manager, Buzzie Bavasi, than Al Ferrara. As much as any other interview subject, Ferrara revealed for me over the course of several discussions the many sides of Bavasi. He also colorfully depicted the arrival on the scene of Marvin Miller, as the players moved toward establishing their union. Joe Moeller was particularly insightful in depicting the resentments borne by some illustrious but underpaid veterans for young so-called bonus babies, a tension that was entirely a function of the miserly ways of baseball management. Jim "Mudcat" Grant provided a compelling account of his early baseball years, his World Series battles against the Dodgers, and his stint with the team in 1968. Then there were the many Dodgers who played important roles in illuminating key episodes from the era: Ron Fairly, Claude Osteen, Jim Lefebvre, Doug Camilli, John Kennedy, Norm Sherry, Wally Moon, Nate Oliver, John Werhas, Larry Burright, Roy Gleason, Jimmy Campanis, and Billy Grabarkewitz.

I am also appreciative of the prestigious Dodger rivals who kindly made themselves available for interviews: Jim Kaat, Tim McCarver, Bill White, Dick Groat, Joe Morgan, Brooks Robinson, Chris Krug, Phil Linz, Jim Bouton, Andy Etchebarren, and Joe Nossek—along with two others who, like Mudcat Grant, would become Dodgers late in their careers: Al Downing and Len Gabrielson. In addition, Bob Locker's perspective on Marvin Miller and baseball labor issues was highly enlightening.

My thanks to Peter O'Malley for his candor about an array of subjects during our interview in Los Angeles, and to two of his key associates, Brent Shyer and Robert Schweppe, whose development of a captivating website for readers about the career of Walter O'Malley was a great aid in my research. I am also grateful to Fred Claire and Tommy Lasorda for their many insights during our interviews.

My book benefited from the intimate recollections of family members and friends of key Dodgers. In that regard, I wish to thank Don Wills, Nancy Fieux, Mike Ley, Ann Meyers Drysdale, Celia Joslyn, Biff Naylor, and Bill Arce.

Three figures added immeasurably to my understanding of the traumas of the 1960s and the role sports sometimes played in easing anxieties: Zev Yaroslavsky, Mel Levine, and Robert Oswald.

I salute the *Los Angeles Times'* talented sports staff of the 1960s for the quality of the newspaper's Dodgers coverage. I am thankful for the superb *Baseball Reference* website and for *The Baseball Encyclopedia*, which proved to be valuable research tools. And I greatly appreciate the efforts of the Dodgers media relations department, in helping me to make contact with some of the players involved.

My thanks to my editor, David Hirshey, for his enormous support throughout the writing of the book and for his skillful editing. My agent, David Black, provided me with sterling editorial advice and abundant encouragement. I benefited from copy editor Miranda Ottewell's keen eye and deft edits, and I can't thank Kate Lyons enough for all her efforts, including expertly guiding me through the many stages of production. Thanks also to production editor David Koral for his skill and meticulous care, and to William Ruoto for the book's outstanding design. And I'm grateful to the *Washington Post* sports editor Matt Vita, for shepherding my original newspaper story about Wills.

My passion for this subject was ignited long before I even had a driver's license. My thanks to the many people who took me during my youth to Dodger Stadium, including my father, John V. Leahy. A special note of appreciation goes to my old childhood friends Kevin Allen and Marti Allen (today Marti Squyres); their late father, Fred; and late mother, Mary. The Allens regularly brought me to Dodger games, including Koufax's perfect game and the August 1966 contest in which Parker made his epic grab of Tim McCarver's smash. It is difficult to imagine how I could have written those two scenes if the Allens hadn't been so kind as to invite me along.

And I'm forever thankful for the many mentors, colleagues, and friends who over the years have provided support, counsel, and laughs: my late father-in-law, Dr. Russell P. Sherwin; Steve Gelman;

David Sendler; Edward Sierra; Craig Smith and Diann Sutherlin Smith; Ron Rogers and Lisa Specht; Marcia Burnam; Norman Burnam; Bruce Burnam; Barbara and Gordon Hughes; Griffin Smith Jr.; David Rowell; Tom Jackman; and Steve, Pam, and Austin Mount, with whom, in need of a vital sounding board during one of our many dinners together in Santa Monica, I discussed my hopes for the book.

No acknowledgments would be complete without noting the valuable advice, perspective, and encouragement my son, Cameron, provided for passages about the music and culture of the 1960s.

Finally, this book doesn't happen without my wife, Jane Leahy. I mean that. It doesn't happen. Every fifty-year-old newspaper and magazine clipping from around the country that I needed to see (and had no clue how to put my hands on) she found. And every line of the book reflects her toil and wisdom. When I wrote until three in the morning, she was up until three in the morning, reading, prodding, listening. She is at once an enormously supportive and demanding editor. Her talents, insights, and advice have elevated the book. I am the lucky one.

—*Michael Leahy, January 2016*

Appendix

THE PRINCIPALS

Maury Wills (Dodgers shortstop, 1959–1966 and 1969–1972)
Wes Parker (Dodgers first baseman, 1964–1972)
Sandy Koufax (Dodgers pitcher, 1955–1966)
Tommy Davis (Dodgers outfielder and third baseman, 1959–1966)
Jeff Torborg (Dodgers catcher, 1964–1970)
Dick Tracewski (Dodgers infielder, 1962–1965)
Lou Johnson (Dodgers outfielder, 1965–1967)

INTERVIEWS CONDUCTED WITH OTHER DODGERS PLAYERS, RIVAL PLAYERS, BASEBALL OFFICIALS, FAMILY MEMBERS OF THE PLAYERS, PROMINENT OBSERVERS, AND FANS

Kevin Allen (attorney)
Bill Arce (Wes Parker's coach at Claremont)
Jim Bouton (Yankees pitcher in the 1963 World Series)
Larry Burright (Dodgers infielder, 1962)
Doug Camilli (Dodgers catcher, 1960–1964)
Jimmy Campanis (Dodgers catcher, 1966–1968)
Fred Claire (Dodgers general manager, 1987–1998)
Al Downing (Yankees pitcher in the 1963 World Series; Dodgers pitcher, 1971–1977)

Ann Meyers Drysdale (widow of Don Drysdale)

Andy Etchebarren (Orioles catcher in the 1966 World Series)

Ron Fairly (Dodgers right fielder and first baseman, 1958–1969)

Al Ferrara (Dodgers outfielder, 1963–1968)

Nancy Fieux (sister of Don Drysdale)

Len Gabrielson (Dodgers outfielder, 1967–1970)

Roy Gleason (Dodgers pinch hitter and pinch runner, 1963)

Billy Grabarkewitz (Dodgers infielder, 1969–1972)

Jim "Mudcat" Grant (pitcher for the Twins in the 1965 World Series; Dodgers pitcher, 1968)

Dick Groat (Pirates, Cardinals, Phillies, and Giants shortstop)

Celia Joslyn (Wes Parker's sister)

Jim Kaat (pitcher for the Twins in the 1965 World Series)

John Kennedy (Dodgers infielder, 1965–1966)

Chris Krug (Cubs catcher, 1965–1966; Padres catcher, 1967)

Tommy Lasorda (Dodgers manager, 1976–1996)

Jim Lefebvre (Dodgers second baseman and third baseman, 1965–1972)

Mel Levine (former United States congressman; attorney)

Mike Ley (cousin of Don Drysdale)

Phil Linz (Yankees pinch hitter in the 1963 World Series)

Bob Locker (White Sox, Pilots, Brewers, Athletics, and Cubs pitcher)

Tim McCarver (Cardinals, Phillies, Expos, and Red Sox catcher)

Joe Moeller (Dodgers pitcher, 1962, 1964, and 1966–1971)

Wally Moon (Dodgers outfielder, 1959–1965)

Joe Morgan (Astros, Reds, Giants, Phillies, and Athletics second baseman)

Biff Naylor (Wes Parker's high school teammate)

Joe Nossek (center fielder for the Twins in the 1965 World Series)

Nate Oliver (Dodgers second baseman, 1963–1967)

Peter O'Malley (Dodgers president, 1970–1998; Dodgers owner, 1979–1998)

Claude Osteen (Dodgers pitcher, 1965–1973)

Robert Oswald (retired businessman)

Brooks Robinson (Orioles third baseman in the 1966 World Series)

Robert Schweppe (an associate of Peter O'Malley)

Norm Sherry (Dodgers catcher, 1959–1962)

Brent Shyer (an associate of Peter O'Malley)

Marti Squyres (television costume designer)

John Werhas (Dodgers third baseman, 1964–1965 and 1967)
Bill White (Giants, Cardinals, and Phillies first baseman)
Don Wills (brother of Maury Wills)
Zev Yaroslavsky (former Los Angeles city councilman and LA county
    supervisor)

Sources

The foundation of this book was shaped by the recollections and insights of the principal subjects and other players during our interviews. In addition to the attributed quotes from the players (Dodgers and rivals) and other individuals (former baseball officials, prominent Los Angeles figures, and fans of the team during the 1960s), the book also relies on information gathered during my research of historical sources. This material includes newspapers and magazines from the 1950s, '60s, and '70s; books from the same period; film footage of key moments in the 1963 World Series; the original NBC telecast of Game 7 of the 1965 World Series; television documentaries; Dodgers broadcaster Vin Scully's original play-by-play call of the ninth inning of Koufax's perfect game; and my own personal recollections and impressions from the 1960s and early 1970s. Unless otherwise specified, all quotations from Dodger officials in the 1960s were found in the *Los Angeles Times*. The notes and bibliography are intended to present the sources for information not already indicated by quotes from the players, club officials, newspaper reporters of the era, and other figures in the book. The notes also reflect an effort to expound on some of the book's points and provide the reader with additional research sources.

GENESIS

The book's opening anecdote about the murder in New York City of a Yankees fan (who was also a city police detective) by a Dodger supporter during the 1956 World Series was the subject of an Associated Press article published on October 8, 1956, in the *Miami News*. "Killed in Row over Series," said the headline, which was a lurid match for the subhead: "Bums Fan Ambushes N.Y. Cop."

Theodore H. White's quote about the effect of the World Series on the era's major campaigns, including presidential contests, can be found on page 294 of his landmark book *The Making of the President 1960*.

The reference to the Dodgers' 1962 domination of the Los Angeles Rams at the box office is supported by the *Los Angeles Times*' October 1, 1962, article about the Rams' woes on the last day of September, when the losing team drew only 26,907 spectators. That same day, the Dodgers drew 15,000-plus more fans.

Mario Cuomo's brief professional baseball career is noted in a *New York Times* story about his life, written by Adam Nagourney and published shortly after Governor Cuomo's death on January 1, 2015.

The passage about Franklin Delano Roosevelt's 1944 campaign appearance at Ebbets Field was inspired by riveting film footage from *The Roosevelts: An Intimate History*, a 2014 PBS documentary by Ken Burns.

The two lengthy passages that appear in "Genesis" and chapter 5 about Bob Oswald derive from a telephone interview I conducted with Oswald on August 14, 2014, and from my two in-person interviews with him in October and November of 1997 for an article I wrote about his life in the years since the Kennedy assassination for the *Arkansas Democrat-Gazette*, which published the story on November 16, 1997.

CHAPTER 1: SURVIVING THE SIXTIES

The passage involving Wills and Koufax at the beginning of the chapter is the result of my interviews with the two men. The scenes and biographical material involving Wills in the chapter—including his recollections of the 1962 All-Star Game in Washington—stem from my interviews with him. My passage about his MVP performance in the All-Star Game was buttressed by information gathered from film footage of the game, posted on YouTube.

The athletic gifts and rising stature within the Dodger organization of minor-league infielder Mike Korcheck, who tragically lost his life in an automobile accident, were ably detailed by Dick Tracewski, among other players.

Wills's younger brother Don Wills added to my understanding of what Maury's childhood was like in the Washington, DC, community of Parkside during the 1940s.

The passages about Wes Parker in the sections entitled "The Rich Boy" and "Weekends in the Nobody League" derive from my interviews with him. My interview with Mudcat Grant was the basis for the section "A Man Named Mudcat."

The racial harassment that Nat King Cole faced in Hancock Park has been well chronicled over the years, in publications that include the *Hollywood Reporter* and the *Los Angeles Times*.

Eventually, in 1975, Doris Day would deny in her autobiography that she ever had an affair with Wills. But in late 1962, the growing whispers had spurred a small group of journalists, including several from respected African American publications such as the *Los Angeles Sentinel*, to press Wills for a statement. In the wake of his tense meeting with Bavasi, he did his best for a long while to avoid any reporter wishing to discuss the subject. But the pressure wore on Wills. Finally, he tersely denied the rumored affair to the *Sentinel*, which would run a story with his denial on January 3, 1963. He managed to avoid the subject with other journalists, including a persistent reporter from the *Baltimore Afro-American* newspaper. On January 8, 1963, the reporter expressed his frustration in print over his inability to reach Wills via telegram or telephone. He began his story this way: "Maury Wills, star shortstop of the Los Angeles Dodgers, maintained a discreet silence as rumors of a romance with film beauty Doris Day circulated about the heads of both through the holiday period." The accompanying headline of the *Baltimore Afro-American* story posed a question: "WILLS, DORIS DAY ROMANTIC?" A subhead added: "MAURY'S STAYING MUM." The subject was not going away. But in largely ignoring it, Wills and Day successfully defused it over time. Although the rumors remained alive in Los Angeles, Bavasi would never raise the issue with Wills again.

During one of our interviews, Tommy Davis recalled that Buzzie Bavasi left a fake contract with Wills's name on it within his sight during a contract negotiation. He also recounted the incident in "Tommy Davis's Tales from the Dodger Dugout," which he wrote with Paul Gutierrez.

Bavasi's tale about how he had outwitted Tommy Davis during contract negotiations before the 1963 season appeared in the *Los Angeles Times* on January 17, 1964.

CHAPTER 2: THE FRENZY OF 1963

Players recounted what they had heard of the near riot around the Dodgers ticket booth before the start of the 1963 World Series. But the most detailed and accurate information came from the angry Series ticket buyers who spoke about the subject during the first week of October 1963 to several *Los Angeles Times* reporters, whose vivid accounts that week served both as the basis for my passage about the episode and as reminders of the intimacy of newspapers' local coverage during the 1960s. The *Times* stories on October 1, October 3, and October 5, 1963, were especially illuminating.

Yankees manager Ralph Houk's syndicated newspaper column predicting victory in the 1963 World Series ran in the *Los Angeles Times* on October 2, 1963. In addition, during our interviews, Dick Tracewski (later a coach under Houk) detailed Houk's thoughts and recollections in the aftermath of the Series.

The projections of TV viewership for the 1963 World Series came from NBC, the network televising the event, with the *Los Angeles Times* reporting the forecasted figures on October 2, 1963.

Recollections of the Dodgers' scouting report about the Yankees' strengths and vulnerabilities were provided by Tracewski and Wills.

The passage about the integration of the Dodgers' spring training ballpark, Holman Stadium, come from the accounts of Tommy Davis and Peter O'Malley during our interviews.

Koufax's discussion with reporters after his September 1963 shutout victory on the road against the Cardinals and Stan Musial's reaction to Koufax's performance were chronicled in a September 18, 1963, *Los Angeles Times* postgame story.

Alston's concern that World Series umpires might not call balks on Yankee pitchers, thereby frustrating Dodger base stealers, was the subject of an October 2, 1963, *Los Angeles Times* story (a confident Houk had no concerns about anything).

Yankees scout Mayo Smith's assessment of Koufax as "simply the best" in a scouting report sent to Houk and expressed during a meeting with Yankee players was related to me by a source who insisted the disclosure not be attributed to him. Puzzled, I asked why (it seemed a rather benign piece of information). The source responded that he would never want to say anything that "hurt Whitey," a reference to Whitey Ford. The remark reflects just how beloved Ford (who has frequently voiced his admiration of Koufax) remains more than a half century after that milestone Series. Indeed, the legendary Yankees ace is nearly as revered among fierce Yankee partisans and baseball friends as Koufax is in Los Angeles. Yet the source wasn't the only person with knowledge of the Yankees' scouting report.

Renowned *Washington Post* sportswriter Shirley Povich, learning of Mayo Smith's view of Koufax, provided his readers with the information the day after Game 1.

CHAPTER 3: THE DODGERS' VICTORY, A PRESIDENT'S ASSASSINATION, AND THE FIRST SEEDS OF A PLAYERS' REBELLION

A *Los Angeles Times* story on October 3, 1963, detailed Southern Californians playing hooky from jobs to watch Game 1 of the World Series.

Wills spoke to me about nervously having a belt of the brandy in the clubhouse before Game 1 of the 1963 Series. (In his autobiography, the late John Roseboro provided his own recollection about the brandy.)

After Game 1, in a moment reported by the *Los Angeles Times* on October 3, 1963, Koufax spoke to reporters about his fatigue at some points during the game, later expanding on this point in his autobiography, *Koufax*.

After the Yankees' losses in the Series' first two games, the unshaken confidence of Whitey Ford and the serenity of Ralph Houk were the subjects of a story that ran in the *Los Angeles Times* on October 4, 1963.

The account of an irritable Mantle's behavior at the Los Angeles International Airport, prior to Game 3 of the Series, was described in a *Los Angeles Times* story on October 4, 1963.

Jim Bouton and Phil Linz provided accounts of their off-the-field activities in Los Angeles, before Game 3, during my separate interviews with each man.

The mood and antics of Dodger fans during Game 4 of the Series were captured in a *Los Angeles Times* story that appeared on October 7, 1963. The subdued postgame celebration of the Dodger Stadium crowd was the subject of a separate story running in the newspaper on the same day.

Bob Hope's shrewdness in having Koufax, Drysdale, and Tommy Davis agree to a deal before the 1963 World Series (after which their appeal, value, and fee would have undoubtedly increased) to appear on one of his TV specials was the subject of a Hedda Hopper column that appeared in the *Los Angeles Times* on October 22, 1963.

The birth of Sandy Warshauer, born four minutes after the Dodgers' 1963 Series victory and named after Koufax by her parents, was reported by the *Los Angeles Times* in an October 8, 1963, story.

The tragic story of Bruce Gardner was first related to me by a sympathetic player, who didn't want the horrific account attributed to him. The player had learned about the depth of Gardner's struggles from coverage in the *Los Angeles Times*.

The acclaimed historian William Manchester—who, in 1967, wrote *The Death of a President*, the definitive narrative of JFK's assassination and of the few days immediately preceding and following the horror for Kennedy intimates especially—reported on White House Associate Press Secretary Andy Hatcher's absence from the Texas trip. Wrote Manchester, a tad obliquely: "[Press Secretary] Pierre [Salinger] told [President Kennedy] that Mac Kilduff would act as his press secretary in Texas. Normally the No. 2 man in the press office was Andy Hatcher, but Hatcher, a Negro, would stay in Washington." The unseemliness of such divisions did not affect everyone connected with the Kennedy group. An African American agent was part of the Secret Service detail on the Texas trip. But such an obscure member of the president's protective force wouldn't be in the public eye; he wouldn't possess anywhere near the same stature as the president's official press spokesperson in Texas. Hatcher's absence said everything about the worry over southern racial resentments at that point in history. Like so many other uncomfortable matters involving race in 1963, there is no record in the Manchester book of a discussion about the matter.

CHAPTER 4: AN UPHEAVAL BEGINS

The Dodger seemingly most excited about music from the 1960s was Al Ferrara, who in time would become a huge fan of The Doors. Most of his teammates, who had come of age in the 1950s, didn't share his passion for the era's rock. Yet what fascinated many of them, even if they were not big fans of groups such as the Rolling Stones or the Beatles, was the daringness of such bands, in their lyrics especially. It was one more factor in making them believe that a social revolution had arrived, with promising implications for ballplayers. The Stones' genius, which included a penchant for lyrics that bled with the epoch's spirit of rebellion, estrangement, and a frankness that lurched into contempt for the established forces, had not escaped players' attention. Later in the decade, having heard that the Stones were singing about everything from the assassinations of the Kennedys to how "all the sinners [are] saints" in their classic "Sympathy for the Devil," Ferrara wouldn't be able to recall the title of the song, only that the Stones and the band's music were more proof that the old rules were finished for good.

The biographical material about Roseboro comes both from Torborg's recollections during our interviews and from Roseboro's autobiography, *Glory Days with the Dodgers and Other Days with Others*, written with Bill Libby.

The tensions between Koufax and the Dodgers organization (especially Bavasi) became more public than ever after the protracted salary negotiation ended and he signed his contract for the 1964 season. The *Los Angeles Times* printed new expressions of resentment from Koufax. The stories ran on March 1 and March 3, 1964. In the March 3 story, Koufax provided details of his contentious salary discussions with Bavasi. The story of a dismissive Bavasi declaring he didn't have anything in particular to say to Koufax was published on March 6, to be followed by a story about a brief Koufax-Bavasi meeting in Vero Beach on March 7.

The passage about the Koufax-O'Malley meeting in Vero Beach stems from accounts in the *Los Angeles Times* and Koufax's autobiography.

Much of the introductory biographical material about Buzzie Bavasi is informed by Bavasi's 1987 autobiography, *Off the Record*, written with John Strege.

All quotes from Peter Bavasi were in the form of written answers to my questions.

The passages about the relationship between Bavasi and Dodger player Al Ferrara derive from Ferrara's recollections during our interviews.

The passage regarding Bavasi's boast about successfully deceiving a young player (an unidentified Ron Fairly) during a contract negotiation can be found in *Sports Illustrated*'s May 22, 1967, issue.

Bavasi's declaration that the player budget would be cut for the 1962 season because of some underperforming players appeared in the *Los Angeles Times* on January 4, 1962.

The *Los Angeles Times*' Frank Finch's flattering assessment of Bavasi's negotiating style appeared in the newspaper on February 8, 1962.

The tensions between Duke Snider and Joe Moeller in 1962 were described at length by Moeller during our interviews. A Dodger teammate, speaking with anonymity as he didn't wish to offend any Snider admirers on the team, confirmed Moeller's characterization of the tensions with Snider as well as Snider's effort to make certain that Moeller did not receive a player's full share of a prospective World Series bonus that season. An October 26, 1962, story in the *Los Angeles Times* confirmed that Moeller was voted only a half share.

Bavasi's observation about Walter O'Malley's tightfistedness appeared in the *San Diego Union-Tribune* on May 11, 2005.

During one of our interviews, Wills recollected that O'Malley paid him for playing his banjo at the St. Patrick's Day party.

In 1962, demographers in the California Department of Finance forecast that the state would exceed New York in population on December 21, 1962. The *Los Angeles Times'* story about the subject ran on June 10, 1962.

The website *Baseball Reference* lists Parker as the 9,830th player to make his major league debut.

The San Fernando Valley Fair Housing Council's report about housing segregation in the Valley was the subject of the council's presentation to a California Senate committee, according to a *Los Angeles Times* story that appeared on January 18, 1964.

Cardinals team physician Dr. I. C. Middleman's description of Koufax's elbow injury appeared in a *Los Angeles Times* story that ran on April 23, 1964. Dr. Robert Kerlan spoke about the injury to the *Times* on April 24, 1964, in the same article that described Koufax's mood in Kerlan's office.

In the context of Koufax's image in the middle 1960s, several stories about him are worth studying: the October 22, 1965, story in *Time* magazine; a story in the July 11–July 21, 1962, issue of the *Saturday Evening Post*; and an October 3, 1963, article in the *Chicago Tribune* in which he is reflexively described as "calculating." To get a different perspective, it is worth reading an insightful and sympathetic story, written by Jack Olsen for *Sports Illustrated* in 1963, that debunks the perception of Koufax as the calculating egghead. But sometimes even his admirers missed. Jim Murray's column describing Koufax as "a captive" of the sport appeared in the *Los Angeles Times* on September 19, 1963.

Political columnist Morrie Ryskind's expression of admiration for Koufax appeared in the *Los Angeles Times* on July 29, 1964.

The Associated Press reported on Koufax's thoughts after his 1964 no-hitter against the Phillies, with the story appearing on June 5, 1964, in the *Los Angeles Times*.

Immediate southern reaction to the enactment of the 1964 Civil Rights Act, including the heated resistance of future Georgia governor Lester Maddox, was the subject of an Associated Press story that appeared in the *Los Angeles Times* on July 4, 1964. Another Associated Press story, published by the *Times* on July 24, 1964, shed further light on efforts to enforce the new law in the face of stiff opposition from segregationists. The Supreme Court's decision to uphold the Civil Rights Act was the subject of a story from United Press International that ran in newspapers around the country in December 1964.

Yankee shortstop Tony Kubek raised the "pay TV" issue in a story that appeared in the *Los Angeles Times* on April 14, 1964.

A civil rights demonstration in Los Angeles against a white segregationist group and its political agenda was the subject of a *Los Angeles Times* story on August 4, 1964.

Koufax's painful late-August throwing session in St. Louis, which effectively ended his season, was the subject of a *Los Angeles Times* story on August 29, 1964.

CHAPTER 5: THE RIOTOUS SEASON

Buzzie Bavasi talked to reporters about Tommy Davis's "bad year" and possible trades before the 1964 season had even ended. An article about the subject appeared in the *Los Angeles Times* on September 15, 1964.

In Los Angeles, NAACP executive director Roy Wilkins expressed his concerns about the Los Angeles Police Department during an appearance on KNXT television. The *Los Angeles Times* wrote of Wilkins's statement on December 10, 1964.

The biographical material about Lou Johnson derives from my Dodger Stadium interview with him.

Jim Murray's column about Vero Beach appeared in the *Los Angeles Times* on April 9, 1965.

In the aftermath of the Watts riots, Roseboro discussed his four-month role as a community-relations specialist for the LAPD in both a February 25, 1966, *Los Angeles Times* article and his autobiography.

Vin Scully's play-by-call of the ninth inning of Koufax's perfect game is available online for those interested.

In the immediate aftermath of his perfect game, Koufax spoke about his performance. The *Los Angeles Times* reported on his comments in a story published on September 10, 1965.

The passage about Robert Oswald in this chapter stems from my interviews with him.

The passage about the NBC telecast of Game 7 of the 1965 World Series was made possible thanks to the game's availability on YouTube.

CHAPTER 6: BASEBALL'S WATERSHED

In our interview, Peter O'Malley offered his recollections of Buzzie Bavasi's behavior during the Koufax-Drysdale holdout.

Bavasi's recollection about the sarcastic note that Walter O'Malley sent him at the end of the Koufax-Drysdale holdout was part of an article in the *San*

Diego Union-Tribune on May 11, 2005.

In our interviews, Al Ferrara and John Kennedy provided detailed accounts of the Dodger players' first meeting with Marvin Miller.

CHAPTER 7: THE LAST MARCH

In gathering Dodger players' individual accounts of the 1966 World Series, one invariably hears about the team's preoccupation with the upcoming Japan trip. As Parker indicates, the idea of additional baseball games made many Dodgers miserable.

Torborg recalls that, after the Dodgers went on a losing streak in Japan, they jokingly feared they might need to return their $250 bonuses to O'Malley.

CHAPTER 8: BASEBALL TAKES A BACKSEAT TO THE WORLD

The two passages about Roy Gleason's military service derive from my interview with him. Gleason also described his wartime experiences in his book, *Lost in the Sun*, written with Wallace Wasinack and Mark Langill.

Amid the social unrest in America and the war in Vietnam, Yaroslavsky struggled to get excited about the losing Dodgers. Across the country, in an indication that winning counts for something, Harvard Law School student Mel Levine, having temporarily fallen hard for the talented Boston Red Sox, was engaging in acts of baseball infidelity, going so far as to occupy a seat on many nights in Fenway Park.

CHAPTER 9: A STAR COMES HOME AND OTHERS SAY GOOD-BYE

The rock festival that I reference in the chapter's opening section was called Newport '69. The festival helped to mark the 1960s' symbolic arrival in the ordinarily placid Valley suburb of Northridge, where I grew up and where Ron Fairly and his family had settled years earlier. On a weekend in late June, during which the Dodgers were out of town, 200,000 mostly young spectators descended on Northridge's Devonshire Downs to be a part of the three-day extravaganza, which included performances by the Jimi Hendrix Experience, Ike and Tina Turner, Joe Cocker, Taj Mahal, Creedence Clearwater Revival, Jethro Tull, Booker T. & the M.G.'s, Marvin Gaye, Buddy Miles (whose performance included a jam with Hendrix), the Byrds, and Three Dog

Night. To the horror of home owners in proximity of the Downs, many visitors bedded down on people's front lawns. The LAPD was called out. Predictable battles and arrests ensued. It was the year of festivals: Woodstock, in August, was apparently muddier and happier; Altamont, in December, was colder and infinitely darker.

CHAPTER 10: THE FINAL YEARS

During our interviews, Wills spoke at length about his salary discussion with Dodgers general manager Al Campanis, in the aftermath of his outstanding 1971 season. Some reference sites, relying on uncorroborated information from the seventies, have reported over the years that Wills earned roughly $100,000 for the 1972 season. Certainly, no player during the sixties and seventies could have possibly wanted to earn $100,000 more than Wills, who yearned to reap the additional stature that would have accompanied being a part of the small group of baseball stars earning six-figure incomes at the time. No player would have been prouder to say that he had signed a contract for the magical figure. Yet it never happened. His pained account during our interviews of his failed negotiation with Campanis, during which a surrendering Wills finally agreed to play the 1972 season for a salary of $97,000, is convincing, particularly as it is supported by two Dodger employees from the period who, as admirers of Walter O'Malley, spoke with anonymity about their knowledge of the Wills-Campanis meeting.

Tommy Lasorda observes that his role in helping to spur Parker's transformation as a hitter was one of his happiest achievements, suspecting that it had the added benefit at the time of reminding club officials like Campanis that he could get the job done in pushing players to succeed.

About the Author

Michael Leahy is the author of *Hard Lessons* and *When Nothing Else Matters: Michael Jordan's Last Comeback*, which *GQ* magazine called "the best sports book of the year . . . easily the most fully formed portrait of Jordan ever written and one of the best sports books in recent memory." His award-winning career has included thirteen years as a writer for the *Washington Post* and the *Washington Post Magazine*. Leahy's 2005 *Washington Post Magazine* story about a California sperm donor won the Society of Professional Journalists' Sigma Delta Chi Award for best magazine story of the year. His stories have been selected four times for the annual Best American Sports Writing anthologies. He lives outside Washington, DC.